Joining a Community of Readers

P9-BYS-699

Joining a Community of Readers

A Thematic Approach to Reading

Sixth Edition

Roberta Alexander
San Diego City College

with

Jan Jarrell
San Diego City College

WADSWORTH
CENGAGE Learning·

Australia • Brazil • Japan • Korea • Mexico • Singapore • Spain • United Kingdom • United States

**Joining a Community of Readers:
A Thematic Approach to Reading,
Sixth Edition**
Roberta Alexander *with* Jan Jarrell

Editor-in-Chief: Lyn Uhl

Director, Developmental Studies: Annie Todd

Executive Editor: Shani Fisher

Development Editor: Terri Wise

Editorial Assistant: Erin Nixon

Media Editor: Christian Biagetti

Brand Manager: Lydia LeStar

Market Development Manager: Erin Parkins

Senior Marketing Communications Manager:
Linda Yip

Rights Acquisitions Specialist: Alexandra
Ricciardi

Manufacturing Planner: Betsy Donaghey

Art and Design Direction, Production
Management, and Composition:
PreMediaGlobal

Cover Image: © iStockphoto/Thinkstock

© 2014, 2011, 2008 Wadsworth, Cengage Learning

ALL RIGHTS RESERVED. No part of this work covered by the copyright herein may be reproduced, transmitted, stored, or used in any form or by any means graphic, electronic, or mechanical, including but not limited to photocopying, recording, scanning, digitizing, taping, Web distribution, information networks, or information storage and retrieval systems, except as permitted under Section 107 or 108 of the 1976 United States Copyright Act, without the prior written permission of the publisher.

For product information and technology assistance, contact us at
Cengage Learning Customer & Sales Support, 1-800-354-9706.

For permission to use material from this text or product,
submit all requests online at **www.cengage.com/permissions.**
Further permissions questions can be e-mailed to
permissionrequest@cengage.com.

Library of Congress Control Number: 2012950563

Student Edition:

ISBN-13: 978-1-133-58682-1

ISBN-10: 1-133-58682-1

Wadsworth
20 Channel Center Street
BOSTON, MA 02210
USA

Cengage Learning is a leading provider of customized learning solutions with office locations around the globe, including Singapore, the United Kingdom, Australia, Mexico, Brazil, and Japan. Locate your local office at **international.cengage.com/region**

Cengage Learning products are represented in Canada by Nelson Education, Ltd.

For your course and learning solutions, visit **www.cengage.com.** Purchase any of our products at your local college store or at our preferred online store **www.cengagebrain.com.**

Instructors: Please visit **login.cengage.com** and log in to access instructor-specific resources.

Printed in the United States of America
1 2 3 4 5 6 7 16 15 14 13 12

For Abdullah and Hassan,
May they inherit a more just, peaceful, and healthy planet.

To contribute to the health of the planet and to preserve garden biodiversity, the authors are contributing five percent of their royalties to support the work of Seed Savers Exchange.

© 2014 Wadsworth, Cengage Learning

Brief Contents

© 2014 Wadsworth, Cengage Learning

Detailed Contents

© 2014 Wadsworth, Cengage Learning

Chapter 2   Working with Words: Technology and You   58

© 2014 Wadsworth, Cengage Learning

© 2014 Wadsworth, Cengage Learning

Chapter 4 Unstated Main Ideas: Challenges in Education 162

© 2014 Wadsworth, Cengage Learning

Chapter 5   Main Ideas and Supporting Details: Popular Culture   200

© 2014 Wadsworth, Cengage Learning

© 2014 Wadsworth, Cengage Learning

© 2014 Wadsworth, Cengage Learning

© 2014 Wadsworth, Cengage Learning

© 2014 Wadsworth, Cengage Learning

© 2014 Wadsworth, Cengage Learning

To the Instructor

The sixth edition of *Joining a Community of Readers* weaves compelling content with important reading skills to strengthen the integration of reading, writing, and critical thinking. The completely revised Chapter 6 brings a current and complex issue—*drugs*—to the fore. Students consider the impact of alcohol, prescription drugs, and recovery on individuals and communities as they develop their summary writing skills. Other chapters offer engaging new material as well. In Chapter 1, there's a new reading about a true survivor, college student Joanie Lopez. In Chapter 2, we read about how natural disasters can spark imagination and invention. In Chapter 4, students reflect on how fear may affect their success in school. Students will be eager to discuss and write about these varied and intriguing topics. Instructors and students alike will find this edition of *Joining a Community of Readers* to be a textbook they look forward to exploring and sharing.

Joining a Community of Readers, Sixth Edition, provides guided instruction in the reading and learning process and abundant practice in reading and study skills. As the first-level college reading text in a two-book series, *Joining a Community of Readers* follows the same integrated, holistic approach as its successful companion text, *A Community of Readers*. However, *Joining a Community of Readers* focuses more intensively on fundamental reading skills, such as finding the main idea, identifying supporting details, and writing summaries. At the same time, it provides greater accessibility for students from various language and academic backgrounds.

The first chapter of *Joining a Community of Readers* focuses on strategies for becoming a successful student, including the *PRO* reading process for becoming an active reader. Each of the following chapters presents a contemporary theme—technology, how we look, education, popular culture, drugs in our society, families, coming of age, social connectedness and community—and challenges students to employ their reading and related skills, both individually and collaboratively. As students progress through the chapters, they learn, practice, and revisit the reading and learning skills they need to succeed in their college courses. Because each unit of the text builds on a single theme, students have the time to develop schema and exchange knowledge on a particular topic.

Hallmark Features

This sixth edition of *Joining a Community of Readers* continues to offer innovative features that enhance the student's learning experience and facilitate instruction for experienced and novice instructors alike:

- **Teaching Tips.** Integrated throughout the Annotated Instructor's Edition of the text, these teaching tips provide fresh pedagogical suggestions as well as reminders for sound instructional practices.

© 2014 Wadsworth, Cengage Learning

- **Holistic approach to reading.** Reading skills are presented in the context of real-life issues to help students adapt reading and study strategies to all their academic courses, as well as to work situations.
- **Thematic organization.** Each chapter focuses on one theme so students can work with the ideas long enough to begin to understand and use the material in its complexity. The explanations of the readings and examples used for skills are connected and related to the chapter theme, so the skills themselves are more accessible.
- **Focus on the reading process.** The essential steps to reading— *prereading activities, active reading*, and *postreading tasks*—are built into each chapter. Students apply the new skills learned within the context of the reading process.
- **"Make Connections and Write."** This recurring exercise emphasizes the reading-writing connection: It encourages students to work collaboratively and to relate reading content to their own experience and previous knowledge.
- **Interactive opening pages.** Chapter openers provide a valuable introduction to the chapter themes and skills. Illustrations, epigraphs, and questions are designed to motivate students and promote a thought-provoking and lively discussion that prepares students for the chapter.
- **Abundant examples and practice.** Each skill is introduced with clear explanations and examples. The theme-based content of the practice exercises within the chapters progresses from sentences and paragraphs to longer passages, with exercises tailored to reinforce skills through longer readings. The application of skills, especially vocabulary and finding the main ideas and support, is emphasized throughout the text.
- **Vocabulary skills.** In addition to a chapter on vocabulary skills, exercises reinforcing vocabulary skills are integrated throughout the text.
- **Critical thinking skills.** By focusing on one theme at a time, students have the opportunity to understand the topic and its context in more depth. This greater depth allows students to apply critical thinking skills more effectively in class discussions, assigned writings, and collaborative activities. Exercises throughout the text ask students to apply their background knowledge to evaluate issues and make connections among various points of view. For example, the important and complex reading skill of making inferences is the sole focus of Chapter 8. The theme of this chapter is "Coming of Age," a subject that promotes deep reflection for students as individuals and members of families, communities, and society. Chapter 9, on critical reading, provides instruction on distinguishing fact and opinion, recognizing the author's worldview, point of view, and purpose, and drawing conclusions. Readings on the theme of social connectedness and community engage students and challenge them to think critically about their communities and the world around them.
- **Collaborative work.** Exercises throughout the text encourage students to collaborate with their peers and to be active learners. Collaborative skills reviews and problem-solving tasks help students in their academic work as well as in their careers.

© 2014 Wadsworth, Cengage Learning

- **Organize to Learn.** Learning strategies (including outlining, summarizing, mapping, and listing) are introduced (with ample practice material) throughout the text and highlighted in features labeled "Organize to Learn."
- **Language Tips.** To provide nonnative speakers of English and other beginning college students with strategies to better understand their reading materials, this feature provides instructional sections and exercises on language issues such as word forms, complete sentences, and paraphrasing.
- **Put It Together.** These summary charts provide chapter reviews to facilitate student learning and retention.
- **Chapter Reviews.** Each chapter concludes not only with a "Put It Together" summary chart of core skills and concepts, but also with a series of activities that helps students review and apply the skills they have learned in their own writing and in collaborating with others. Assignments get them outside the framework of the classroom and into their college and neighborhood communities. The interactive assignment, "Work the Web," directs students to apply their skills in reading and critical thinking while doing interesting and relevant work on the Web.
- **Mastery Tests.** Each chapter concludes with two Mastery Tests that present a reading selection followed by vocabulary, comprehension, and thought-provoking "making connections" questions. In addition, two **Cumulative Mastery Tests** at the back of the book assess all the core skills covered in *Joining a Community of Readers*. They can be used as pretest and posttest instruments to measure student progress or for student practice at the end of the term.
- **Additional Readings and Exercises.** These readings are carefully chosen for their accessibility and appeal, and to provide additional perspectives and information related to chapter themes as well as additional skills-based practices.
- **Instruction on reading visual aids.** In the text, Chapters 4 and 8 help students learn to read graphs and visual clues in photographs and cartoons.

New to the Sixth Edition

- *NEW!* **Chapter 6 Drugs and Our Society.** Chapter 6 has a new theme, "Drugs and Our Society," which has been designed to strengthen students' summary writing skills. The six new readings include readings on both legal and illegal drugs, prescription and over the counter drugs, the traditional ritual uses of peyote, as well as prevention and policy approaches to drug abuse. New pedagogy on writing a summary of an autobiography or memoir addresses an important and common writing need.
- *NEW!* **Fourteen new readings.** Two new textbook readings come from important sociology college textbooks. Two new personal narratives address overcoming challenges and adjusting to college life. Three readings are adaptations of important and recent *New York Times* articles. Three readings about drugs and our society were written expressly for the sixth edition of *Joining a Community of Readers*. A new cumulative test is a college

© 2014 Wadsworth, Cengage Learning

textbook reading about how the inequities of wealth distribution affect our lives.

- *NEW!* **Thematic updates,** Chapter themes on technology, education, and popular culture have been updated to reflect recent developments.

Chapter Organization

Each chapter in *Joining a Community of Readers* is designed to teach specific reading and learning skills within a thematic context. Students encounter the theme, are encouraged to reflect on that theme, and then prompted to generate responses to the theme. To accomplish this progression, each chapter contains the following features:

- **An opening illustration and quotation** introduce the chapter theme and provide prereading questions that ask students to explore their background knowledge and opinions on the topic.
- **Skills instruction** is carefully interwoven with thematic readings within the chapter. Examples are taken predominantly from content-related material.
- **Chapter Reviews** provide an innovative format for students to collaboratively or individually organize and review the skills introduced in the chapter. Postreading extension activities allow for collaborative group work, and writing assignments are based on the chapter content. Work the Web exercises provide original and meaningful Web-based activities.
- **Mastery Tests.** Two Mastery Tests at the end of each chapter give students further opportunities to master the skills learned in each chapter and provide a regular format for evaluation.

The Ancillary Package

APLIA FOR *JOINING A COMMUNITY OF READERS*

- Enhance your course with Aplia's engaging content and intuitive navigation that will motivate students to become stronger readers! Through diagnostic tests, succinct instruction, and engaging assignments, Aplia's online reading and learning solution reinforces key concepts and provides students with the practice they need to build stronger reading skills. The new Aplia for *Joining a Community of Readers* starts students off with a theme-based question related to the sixth edition. For more information and a complete demo, visit http://www.aplia.com/developmentalenglish.

COMPANION WEB SITE

- The **Instructor Companion Web site** features a variety of teaching tools, including the Instructor's Manual and Test Bank, and PowerPoint slides for each chapter in the text. Faculty can access the Instructor Companion Web site at http://login.cengage.com.

© 2014 Wadsworth, Cengage Learning

INSTRUCTOR'S MANUAL AND TEST BANK

The Instructor's Manual and Test Bank offers: teaching tips, including suggestions for integrating critical thinking and group activities into class; a section on helping ESL students succeed with this text; a sample course syllabus; sample "answers" to exercises that require more extensive responses (maps, outlines, summaries); and a robust test bank featuring two exams for each chapter.

© 2014 Wadsworth, Cengage Learning

Acknowledgments

I am grateful to my family—Marley for his help, and Elena, Paul, and Aasiya for their patience and moral support. I would also like to thank all of my reading students and colleagues for their help and positive support over the years, especially Anna Rogers, Nadia Mandilawi, Christy Ball, Ella de Castro Baron, Enrique Dávalos, María Figueroa, Barry Hicks, Kelly Mayhew, Trissy McGhee, Jim Miller, Elva Salinas, and Ross Warfel. Jan Lombardi gets the credit for getting me started on this project in the first place and for coauthoring the early editions of this text.

A special thank you to Shani Fisher, Executive Editor for Developmental Reading and College Success at Cengage Learning, for her support and encouragement, and to Kayti Purkiss, Assistant Editor, for helping with my questions and requests. Thank you to Terri Wise, my development editor, who helped me to revise the text so successfully. Finally, I would like to extend my sincere appreciation to Gunjan Chandola who helped us finish the production process with her professionalism, calm, grace, and a good eye to detail.

Thank you to the reviewers across the country:

Susan Dalton, Alamance Community College
Elizabeth Holmes, Harford Community College
Judith Johnson, John Tyler Community College
Candace Komlodi, GateWay Community College
Susan Larson, Portland Community College
Deborah Paul Fuller, Bunker Hill Community College
Jackie Roberts, Richland Community College
Natalie Russell, Truckee Meadows Community College
Danhua Wang, Indiana University of Pennsylvania
Jacquelyn Warmsley, Tarrant County College Southeast Campus

ROBERTA ALEXANDER

© 2014 Wadsworth, Cengage Learning

Features of *Joining a Community of Readers*, Sixth Edition

Reading Skill	Theme	Vocabulary	Organize to Learn	Language Tips
Chapter 1: The Reading Process				
PRO: • **P**repare to Read • **R**ead actively • **O**rganize to learn	Becoming a Successful Student		Setting goals; managing your time; previewing a textbook	Reader's questions and active reading
Chapter 2: Working with Words				
	Technology and You	Textbook aids; context clues; word parts; dictionary skills; choosing the right definition	Personal vocabulary plan	Word forms
Chapter 3: Main Ideas				
Topics; stated main ideas; thesis statement	How We Look	Practice and review	Marking texts	Following directions
Chapter 4: Unstated Main Ideas				
Unstated main ideas; writing main idea sentences	Challenges in Education	Practice and review	Working in Groups	Writing Complete Sentences
Chapter 5: Main Ideas and Supporting Details				
Recognizing supporting details; separating general from specific details; using supporting details to find unstated main ideas	Popular Culture	Practice and review	Outlining	Facts

© 2014 Wadsworth, Cengage Learning

Reading Skill	Theme	Vocabulary	Organize to Learn	Language Tips
Chapter 6: Writing Summaries				
Distinguishing between levels of supporting details; writing a summary	Drugs in Our Society	Practice and review	Mapping	Paraphrasing and Plagiarizing
Chapter 7: Patterns of Organization				
Examples; listing; chronological order; definition; classification; comparison and contrast; cause and effect	Families	Practice and review	Time lines; circle diagrams; concept maps	Transitions
Chapter 8: Inferences				
Recognizing inferences;	Coming of age	Practice and review	Separating Personal opinion from Reasonable Inferences	Language of imagery and Connotation
Chapter 9: Critical Reading				
Recognizing facts and Opinions; recognizing author's worldview, point of view, and purpose; drawing conclusions	Social Connectedness and Community	Practice and review	Listing	Word clues for Recognizing Opinions

© 2014 Wadsworth, Cengage Learning

To the Student

WELCOME TO *JOINING A COMMUNITY OF READERS*.

You have probably bought this book because you need to strengthen your reading skills and strategies to be ready for the demands of college reading. If you are prepared to take responsibility for your own learning, and if you are prepared to commit yourself to the work involved, you will learn the strategies and skills you will need to become an effective, thoughtful reader. Reading skills are necessary not only to pass this course, but for success in college in general, and, even more importantly, for success in the workplace of the twenty-first century.

WHY IS READING SO IMPORTANT?

Read any newspaper today, talk to any employer or human resource manager, and you will realize that the demands of today's society—not only of college study—require you always to be able to learn new skills and even take on whole new jobs or professions. During your lifetime, you will probably be faced with the need to change jobs or professions three, four, or more times. And even if you are one of the few who stays in one position or who is successful at creating your own business, you will constantly face the need to upgrade your skills. Professionals of any kind must stay up to date in their field. This is true of office professionals, medical professionals, teachers, engineers, auto mechanics, managers, computer programmers, and industrial workers.

Learning cannot stop when you get your certificate or degree—learning is a lifelong process. For this reason, the one ability that will not become outdated and that can serve you for the rest of your life is the ability to *know how to learn and grow*. In writing this text we have addressed the basics that will help you become a strong reader and therefore a successful student. The skills you acquire now in school will prepare you for the challenges of lifelong learning for the workplace and equip you to be effective, fulfilled adults and citizens of the modern world.

A recent survey of major businesses and industrial firms concluded that the workplace basics to learn in school are:

1. *Learning to learn*. This text, *Joining a Community of Readers*, will show you how to become active in your own reading and learning process (Chapter 1). You will learn how you study best and how to put your study time to good use.
2. *Listening and oral communications*. As a college reader, you will learn that reading is reinforced and made more meaningful when you listen to other people's ideas about a subject and you express your ideas to your classmates (all chapters).
3. *Competence in reading and writing*. As you work through this course, your reading competence will constantly improve. You will learn, review, and practice all the basic skills necessary to be a strong reader: the reading process (Chapter 1); vocabulary (Chapter 2); identifying main ideas (Chapter 3 and 4); understanding details (Chapter 5) writing summaries (Chapter 6); identifying patterns of organization (Chapter 7); recognizing inferences

© 2014 Wadsworth, Cengage Learning

(Chapter 8); recognizing facts versus opinions and author's point of view (Chapter 9); and organizing what you read so that you can retain information and understanding for tests and future needs (all chapters).

4. *Adaptability based on creative thinking and problem solving.* As a member of your classroom and a community of readers, you will be involved in bringing what you already know and what you learn through reading and discussion to a variety of issues, and you will practice thinking creatively and problem solving (all chapters), making inferences (Chapter 8), and recognizing facts versus opinions (Chapter 9).

5. *Group effectiveness characterized by interpersonal skills, negotiation skills, and teamwork.* You will learn to work with your classmates, sharing your strengths and learning from each other (all chapters).

6. *Organizational effectiveness and leadership.* You will develop your organizational and leadership skills in the process of working with your classmates toward a common goal.

ARE YOU READY?

If you are ready to tackle the material of this course, you will be taking a big step toward a successful college career. Can you answer "yes" to the following key questions?

- Is learning and practicing college reading skills a priority for you at this time?
- Are you willing to make the effort to be *actively* involved in your learning?
- Have you decided that you can and will succeed, one small step at a time?
- Do you have the time to commit to being a student? Remember that as a student, you have a job. The payoff is not only passing grades and a degree, but more importantly, the development of reading and learning skills that you will use for the rest of your life.
- Are you willing to share ideas and to work together with other students to reach your goals?
- Are you willing to learn new reading strategies and apply them, not just to pass this class but to any new challenges that come your way?
- Are you willing to open your mind to new ideas and ways of thinking?
- Are you willing to think about ideas and arguments and form opinions for yourself and with others?

Did you answer "yes" to all or most of these questions? If so, we will help you reach your goals by assisting you to become a lifelong reader and learner. Welcome to *Joining a Community of Readers*!

© 2014 Wadsworth, Cengage Learning

Joining a Community of Readers

1 The Reading Process

BECOMING A SUCCESSFUL STUDENT

Christopher Futcher/istockphoto

Step by step, I can't see any other way of accomplishing anything.
—*MICHAEL JORDAN*

- What are your goals for the next two or three years?

- What steps do you need to take to prepare yourself to accomplish your goals?

- Your level of self-confidence influences your ability to meet your goals. Why do you think this is true? How can you increase your self-confidence?

- What do you picture yourself doing after graduating or after completing your current educational goals?

Getting Ready to Read

What does it take to be a successful student? One way to answer that question would be: "It takes a combination of skill and attitude." But what do we mean by "skill" and "attitude"? The skills that are probably most important are (1) setting your goals, (2) organizing your time accordingly, and (3) applying the reading process to succeed in your studies. The attitudes that may be most important are (1) recognizing that you have what it takes to be successful, (2) focusing on constructive choices, and (3) recognizing that having good relationships with other people can help you meet your goals and enjoy the process.

In this chapter, you will read and use information about achieving success in college and in life. As you do, you will improve your organizational and reading skills by learning how to:

- Set short- and long-range goals
- Manage your time effectively
- Use PRO, a reading system to help you become a stronger reader in college

© 2014 Wadsworth, Cengage Learning

Reading 1

Be Here Now

— DAVE ELLIS

TEXT BOOK **Dave Ellis is the author of a popular college success textbook, *Becoming a Master Student*. In this reading, Ellis has a simple, yet profound, message about how to be successful as a student and in life. As you read, think about how his message applies to you and people you know.**

1   Being right here, right now is such a simple idea. It seems obvious. Where else can you be but where you are? When else can you be there but when you are there? The answer is that you can be somewhere else at any time—in your head. It's common for our thoughts to distract us from where we've chosen to be. When we let this happen, we lose the benefits of focusing our attention on what's important to us in the present moment.

2   To "be here now" means to do what you're doing when you're doing it. It means to be where you are when you're there. Students consistently report that focusing attention on the here and now is a powerful tool for success.

3   We all have a voice in our head that hardly ever shuts up. If you don't believe it, conduct this experiment: Close your eyes for ten seconds, and pay attention to what is going on in your head. Please do this right now. Notice something? Perhaps a voice in your head was saying, "Forget it. I'm in a hurry." Another might have said, "I wonder when ten seconds is up?" Another could have been saying, "What little voice? I don't hear any little voice."

4   That's the voice.

5   This voice can take you anywhere at any time—especially when you are studying. When the voice takes you away, you might appear to be studying, but your brain is somewhere else. All of us have experienced this voice, as well as the absence of it. When our inner voices are silent, time no longer seems to exist. We forget worries, aches, pains, reasons, excuses, and justifications. We fully experience the here and now. Life is magic.

6   Do not expect to be rid of the voice entirely. That is neither possible nor desirable. Inner voices serve a purpose. They enable us to analyze, predict, classify, and understand events out there in the "real" world. The trick is to consciously choose when to be with your inner voice and when to let it go. Instead of trying to force a stray thought out of your head, simply notice it. Accept it. Tell yourself, "There's that thought again." Then gently return your attention to the task at hand. That thought, or another, will come back. Your mind will drift. Simply notice again where your thoughts take you, and gently bring yourself back to the here and now. Goals are tools that we create to guide our action in the present.

7   Time management techniques—calendars, lists, and all the rest—have only one purpose. They reveal what's most important for you to focus on right *now*. The idea behind this process is simple. When you listen to a lecture, listen to a lecture. When you read this book, read this book. And when you choose to daydream, daydream. Do what you're doing when you're doing it. Be where you are when you're there. Be here now . . . and now . . . and now.

8   Time is an equal opportunity resource. No matter how famous we are, no matter how rich or poor, we get 168 hours to spend each week—no more, no less. It cannot be

© 2014 Wadsworth, Cengage Learning

saved. It can't be seen, heard, touched, tasted, or smelled. If you're out of wood, you can chop some more. If you're out of money, you can earn a little extra. If you're out of love, there is still hope. If you're out of health, it can often be restored. But when you're out of time, that's it. When this minute is gone, it's gone.

Exercise 1

Recall and Discuss

Answer these questions about Reading 1, and prepare to discuss them in class.

1. What is a powerful tool for success according to Ellis?

   focusing attention on the Here and Now is a powerful tool for success

2. What is the "voice in our head" and why is it important for students to understand it?

   Inner voices searve a purpose, the voice in our head is a guide. It takes us to different thoughts then it pulls us back to the task at hand.

3. Is it easy or difficult for you to be in the here and now? Why is this idea important for you as a college student? Explain.

   Sometimes difficult, other times easy. As a collage student you have an ammount of time to complete assignments. When that time runs out, you will fail and can't go back.

Setting Goals and Achieving Them

© 2014 Wadsworth, Cengage Learning

setting goals deciding what you want to accomplish

Setting goals is not an easy job. It involves deciding what is important to you and what you want to accomplish. The many decisions you make every day influence your life in both small and large ways. It's important that decisions move you toward, not away from, your goals. To become a successful student, set your goals at the beginning of your college years.

Goals can be broken into different categories based on when and how easily they can be achieved. There is an old Chinese saying: "The longest journey begins with a single step." This certainly is true when we think of our life's goals. When you write your own goals, you need to think about both short- and long-term goals.

© 2014 Wadsworth, Cengage Learning

short-term
applying to the
day, the week,
the month, or the
semester

*I always wanted
to be somebody,
but now I realize I
should have been
more specific.*

— COMEDIAN LILY
TOMLIN

long-term
applying to the years
from now, or even
your lifetime

Short-term goals can be accomplished in a limited period of time, such as goals for a day, a week, a month, or a semester. State your goals very specifically, so you can determine whether you achieve them or not. For example, one of your goals for next week might be to complete a complicated biology lab assignment on time and earn a grade of C or better on it. To reach this goal, you can make steps for yourself that are very clear and direct. You can say: (1) I will attend the biology lab; (2) I will make sure I understand the assignment by asking the instructor for clarification; (3) I will spend two hours working on this assignment on Monday, on Tuesday, and on Wednesday; and (4) I will look at my work again before I turn it in to be sure that it is complete. Once you receive your grade, it will be easy to tell whether you achieved your goal and to analyze why you did or did not.

Another fairly short-term goal might be to improve your English skills and to get a B or better in this class. To accomplish this goal, again, you will want to decide on the steps you will take. It's probably not too helpful to decide simply "I will study harder this semester," because that goal is too vague. It's better to decide something specific like "I will study at least six hours a week for this class this semester."

Long-term goals take more time to achieve because they include goals for the distant future. For example, your long-term goal might be to become a research biologist with three children and a house on the beach. In this case, a successful biology lab assignment goal would be one small step toward accomplishing the larger goal. Although our life goals cover all categories—personal, social, economic, and academic—our focus in this chapter is on the goals related to this course and to your future as a student.

Exercise 2

Set Short-Term Goals

Write at least three goals that you plan to achieve this semester, and write the steps that you will take to accomplish those goals. Be specific in your wording so that you can tell at the end of the semester whether you have achieved your goals.

Specific Semester Goals

1. Improve reading skills. Get a B
   in this class.
   _____

2. _____
   _____
   _____

3. _____
   _____
   _____

Steps to Accomplish Them

a. Study and review six hours per week.

b. Attend every class meeting.

c. Be on time for class every day.

a. _____

b. _____

c. _____

a. _____

b. _____

c. _____

MANAGING YOUR TIME

One important way to achieve your goals is to be aware of how you spend your time. Being a full-time student is a full-time job. You must learn how to find the time to be a student—to attend classes regularly and to study—as well as to do everything else that you need to do in your life. Once you have found the time for your classes and your study, you must use that time effectively.

time management
a system for using
your time wisely

✳**Time management** will help you accomplish everything you want to do in the time you have available. It involves four essential steps:

1. Assess your commitments.
2. Assess your use of time.
3. Get organized.
4. Check your progress.

Time is the coin of your life. It is the only coin you have, and only you can determine how it will be spent.

— POET CARL SANDBURG

Assess Your Commitments Figure out what your commitments are now and how much time you have for your studies. Decide what is most important for you at this time of your life. You may have to make decisions about what you can and cannot do. To help you assess your commitments, fill in the blanks in the following section about how you use your time.

Student Responsibilities If you are to be successful, you will need to plan to spend a certain amount of time on school responsibilities each week. Calculate the amount of time you need to be a student by adding up the number of hours you are in class per week and then adding to that two study hours for every hour in class. For example, if you are taking two three-unit classes (that meet for three hours per week), you need to plan on spending nine hours per week for each class, which means 18 hours per week for both classes. If you are taking 12 units, you should plan on 36 hours of class attendance and study time. Based on this formula, how many hours per week do you need to dedicate to school?_____

Extracurricular Responsibilities Are you involved in some school activities? Are you a member of an organization? How many hours per week do you spend on these activities?_____

Work Responsibilities How many hours per week do you work?_____

Family and Community Responsibilities Are you responsible for other people? Are you married? Do you have children or brothers and sisters to take care of? Do you attend church or do any volunteer work in your community? How many hours per week do you need to spend on these responsibilities?_____

Personal Responsibilities Remember, you cannot take care of all the people in your life or meet all your goals if you do not take care of yourself. Be sure to schedule some time for yourself, for socializing (_____), exercising (_____), and relaxation (_____). Don't forget sleeping. You need 8 hours of sleep per night (_____). Now total up the hours you wrote down in parentheses to determine the number of hours per week you need to take care of yourself. _____

Miscellaneous Time Don't forget that you need to set your time allotments realistically. How about little things like shopping, cooking, and doing household chores? Also, transportation to and from the places you have to go takes time. Estimate how many hours per week you need for miscellaneous things. _____

© 2014 Wadsworth, Cengage Learning

Total Time   Now total up all your time entries. _____ There are 168 hours in a week. If you are like many students, your total time entries add up to more than 168 hours!

Exercise 3

Schedule Your Time

Now check the accuracy of your estimates, and get a more graphic picture of where your time goes. Look at the sample Weekly Schedule shown on page 9, and fill in the blank schedule on page 10 with your own information. Be realistic with your time allotments, and do not underestimate the time it takes to do things. Fill in your class hours, your extracurricular hours, your work hours, your family- and community-responsibility hours, your personal hours, and your miscellaneous time requirements. Then mark off the hours that are open for study.

Assess Your Use of Time   When you totaled your time estimates, was your total less than 168 hours? _____ If not, you will need to make some changes. One way is to analyze how you use your time.

Study Time   Take a careful look at the times you have identified for studying on your Weekly Schedule chart. Have you scheduled time so you can prepare for each class meeting? Have you scheduled time to review regularly, so that you don't have to waste time relearning information? Also, remember that sometimes small amounts of time can pay off in a big way. One such example is reviewing your notes from the last class session and looking over the reading right before you attend a class. Such a review, either the night before or the day of the class—or even five minutes before class begins—will help you be more alert and involved during the class. You will remember where the lesson left off; and if there is a quiz, you will be much more likely to know the answers. If you have some questions about the reading or the lesson, plan to ask the instructor.

Energy Level   Look again at the boxes that you highlighted in your chart for hours devoted to your studies. Think about your own habits: Are you a morning or a night person? When are your study times scheduled? If you are a morning person and your study hours are blocked off at 3 P.M., you may have designated poor hours to devote to school. You might be more ready to take a nap at this time than to "crack the books." As you look over your chart, adjust your schedule so that you can study during your peak hours. Other chores or responsibilities that may not require the intense focus that studying does—such as shopping, cleaning the house, cooking—can be scheduled for those hours when your ability to think clearly is not at its peak.

concentration
giving close attention to what you are doing, focusing on your reading

Concentration   Once you designate the times of the day when you are full of energy for your studies, consider whether you will be able to concentrate to your fullest during those times. **Concentration**—giving close attention to what you are doing, focusing on your reading—is important. If you are distracted, you will not be able to use your study time well. There are two basic kinds of distractions: environmental and mental.

© 2014 Wadsworth, Cengage Learning

Sample Weekly Schedule

	Sunday	Monday	Tuesday	Wednesday	Thursday	Friday	Saturday
6:00 A.M.							
7:00 A.M.							
8:00 A.M.		Exercise		Exercise		Exercise	Study
9:00 A.M.	Church	Biology	P.E.	Biology	P.E.	Biology	↓
10:00 A.M.	↓	Reading	Bio Lab	Reading	Bio Lab	Reading	↓
11:00 A.M.		Study	→	→	→	→	
12:00 P.M.	Relax-movie	Lunch	Lunch	Lunch	Lunch	Lunch	
1:00 P.M.		Speech	Study	Speech	Study	Speech	Volunteer
2:00 P.M.		Study	Math	Study	Math		
3:00 P.M.	↓	↓	↓	↓	↓		↓
4:00 P.M.	Open						Grocery Shopping Laundry
5:00 P.M.		Work		Work		Dinner w/ Friends	
6:00 P.M.							
7:00 P.M.		↓		↓	Choir Practice	↓	↓
8:00 P.M.					↓		Relax
9:00 P.M.		Study	Study	Study	Study	Study	
10:00 P.M.	↓	↓	↓	↓	↓	↓	↓
11:00 P.M.							

© 2014 Wadsworth, Cengage Learning

Weekly Schedule

	Sunday	Monday	Tuesday	Wednesday	Thursday	Friday	Saturday
6:00 A.M.							
7:00 A.M.							
8:00 A.M.							
9:00 A.M.							
10:00 A.M.							
11:00 A.M.							
12:00 P.M.							
1:00 P.M.							
2:00 P.M.							
3:00 P.M.							
4:00 P.M.							
5:00 P.M.							
6:00 P.M.							
7:00 P.M.							
8:00 P.M.							
9:00 P.M.							
10:00 P.M.							
11:00 P.M.							

© 2014 Wadsworth, Cengage Learning

environmental distractions things that are happening around you that may prevent you from concentrating on your work

mental distractions things you may be thinking about that prevent you from concentrating on your work

Environmental distractions <u>are things that are happening around you that may prevent you from concentrating on your work</u>, such as children playing, a television program in the background, or the telephone ringing. Set up your study time and location when and where you won't have to struggle against environmental distractions. Perhaps there is a quiet room in your house, or maybe you could study in the library.

Mental distractions <u>are all the things you may be thinking about that will prevent you from concentrating on your work</u>, such as the bills you need to pay, the argument you had with your spouse or friend, or your social plans. To help yourself overcome these distractions, take care of these concerns as best you can before you sit down to study. Sometimes it helps if you put these concerns and their possible solutions on a "to do" list so you know you will not forget to follow up on them. Then you can stop worrying about them and get back to studying.

Priorities As you think about your use of time, also think about what is important at this point in your life. Deciding the order of importance of different goals or parts of your life is called **setting priorities**. For example, if you are a full-time student, doing well in school may be your highest priority. If you are a parent, taking care of your children may take priority and being a good student might have to take second place.

setting priorities deciding the order of importance of your goals and activities

Be creative in your thinking. Maybe you will have to reduce or cut out the time that you spend hanging out in the cafeteria or the student union. Maybe you can decrease the number of hours you work, or perhaps you can find an on-campus job that could save you commuting time. Possibly you should consider dropping a class or reducing the number of other commitments that you have.

Exercise 4

Plan Your Time

Write out your plan to focus on what is important to you now and to reduce your commitments to activities or things that are not your current priorities.

1. I will focus on _____

   _____

   _____

2. I will cut back on _____

   _____

   _____

3. To give my studies the attention they deserve, I will _____

   _____

   _____

© 2014 Wadsworth, Cengage Learning

Organize Your Time You need to think about two basic levels of organization in planning the best use of your time. Both are short-term in the sense that they relate to the next few months, but the first is more long-range than the second.

Monthly Calendar First, establish a calendar for yourself in which you record all your long-range assignments. When your instructors pass out the course syllabi and announce assignments, such as the dates of final exams and papers, write down this important information on your calendar. When you make other appointments for yourself or if you have school activities or community meetings, be sure to write them down on the *same* calendar. Use the sample Semester Calendar on page 13 as a guide.

"To Do" List Second, at the end or beginning of each day, make yourself a "to do" list like the one shown below. Write down your specific jobs for the day and exactly what you plan to do with your time. Be sure to check your monthly calendar so that you don't forget the upcoming big assignments, tests, or appointments. It is very important to check your "to do" list during the day to be sure that you are not forgetting something. At the end of the day, cross or check off the things that you did. Write anything you weren't able to do on the following day's list.

To Do List		
	Date _____	
	Priority (a, b, or c)	Completed
1. Prepare for tomorrow's biology test	(a)	✓
2. Do the laundry	(b)	✓
3. Call parents	(b)	✓
4. Plan Johnny's birthday party	(a)	✓
5. Begin notes for English 101 paper	(a)	✓
6.		

It's a good idea to prioritize your "to do" lists. You might not get around to something and decide that postponing it is okay. Try to do those things that are most important to you first. For example, if you have an exam in biology, be sure to give yourself the time to review your biology notes, even if it means putting off that trip to the laundromat for a day. (Maybe you could remember to take your biology book and notes to the laundromat and do both tasks at the same time!)

Check Your Progress It takes approximately three weeks to establish a new habit. Commit yourself to working on your time management every single day for the next several weeks. Hopefully, you will establish a habit that will serve you well not only throughout school, but also for the rest of your life.

© 2014 Wadsworth, Cengage Learning

Semester Calendar _Fall,_

Month _September_

Sunday	Monday	Tuesday	Wednesday	Thursday	Friday	Saturday
				1	2	3
4 Church	5 Labor Day	6 Classes begin	7	8 Choir	9	10 Volunteer
11 Church	12	13 Campus newspaper	14	15	16	17
18 Church	19	20	21	22 Choir	23	24 Volunteer
25 Church	26	27 Campus newspaper	28	29 Bio Lab Math Test	30 Rdg Test	1 October

Month _October_

Sunday	Monday	Tuesday	Wednesday	Thursday	Friday	Saturday
2 Church	3	4	5	6 Choir	7	8
9 Church	10	11 Campus newspaper	12	13 Bio report	14 Rdg test	15 Volunteer
16 Church	17	18 Short speech 5 min	19	20 Math test Choir	21	22
23 Church	24	25 Campus newspaper	26	27	28 Bio test	29 Volunteer
30 Church picnic	31					

Month _November_

Sunday	Monday	Tuesday	Wednesday	Thursday	Friday	Saturday
	1		2	3	4 Bio test	5 Jogathon Balboa Park
6 Church	7	8 Campus newspaper	9	10 Choir	11	12 Volunteer
13 Church	14	15	16	17 Math Test Choir	18 Rdg Test	19 Scholarship applic due
20 Church	21	22 Short speech 5 min newspaper	23	24 Thanksgiving	25 No school	26
27 Church	28	29	30			

Month _December_

Sunday	Monday	Tuesday	Wednesday	Thursday	Friday	Saturday
				1 Choir	2	3 Mom's birthday
4 Church	5 Campus newspaper	6	7 Speech due (10 min)	8 Math test	9	10 Volunteer
11 Church	12 9:00–11:00 Bio Final	13 12–2 Math Final	14 10:00–12:00 RDG Final 1–3:00 Speech Final	15 Choir	16	17
18 Church	19 Newspaper party!	20	21	22	23	24 Christmas Eve
25 Christmas Church	26	27	28	29	30	31 New Year's Eve

© 2014 Wadsworth, Cengage Learning

After you work with your monthly calendar and "to do" lists for a week or so, take some time to make sure they are working for you. Are you able to keep up with all the activities that you schedule? Are you making sure that nothing is falling through the cracks by writing down everything you need to do in the appropriate places? Are you alert and able to concentrate during the times you have set aside for your studies? Most important of all, does your allocation of time correspond to your priorities?

Managing your time means making decisions. Let's begin this decision-making process with a short exercise.

Exercise 5

Make Decisions

List all the "roles" you have right now as an individual. Who are you, as defined by the different roles, responsibilities, or jobs you fill? Each role you list must be a noun or a name of a role or job in your life. For example, are you a father? An employee of Target? A tennis player? A television viewer?

1. List as many roles as you can identify. (You don't have to limit yourself to six.)

   a. _____

   b. _____

   c. _____

   d. _____

   e. _____

   f. _____

2. Next, write these roles again in the order of their *importance* to you. Letter "a" should be the most important role or responsibility in your life, "b" the next most important, and so on.

   a. _____

   b. _____

   c. _____

   d. _____

   e. _____

   f. _____

3. Last, because you're more conscious of how you spend your time now, it should be easy to list the roles you fill in the order of the *amount of time* you

© 2014 Wadsworth, Cengage Learning

spend on each. Letter "a" should be the role in which you spend the most time on the average. Letter "b" should be the role in which you spend the next greatest number of hours. Caution: Answer this with the *actual* way you spend your time, not how you think you should spend it.

a. _____

b. _____

c. _____

d. _____

e. _____

f. _____

4. As you completed this exercise, did you discover any conflicts between where you spend your time and what you think are your most important roles, your priorities, in life? Describe any conflicts in the space provided here. Most of us will notice numerous conflicts when we complete an exercise like this, so don't be surprised by what you discover.

_____

_____

_____

_____

Exercise 6

Make Connections and Write

Write short answers to the following questions based on your answers in Exercise 5.

1. Do you need to make changes in your priorities? Explain.

_____

_____

2. Do you need to make changes in your current use of time? Explain.

_____

_____

© 2014 Wadsworth, Cengage Learning

3. How possible is it for you to make the changes, if any, that you've indicated in answers 1 and 2? Explain.

_____

_____

MEETING OTHERS, JOINING AN ACADEMIC COMMUNITY

Becoming a successful student involves managing your time in a new way that helps you fulfill the new responsibilities and new challenges you've assumed. One of the major challenges facing you as a new college student is that of entering a new community—an *academic community*—with ease.

Making Friends The first step you need to take to feel comfortable in your new college environment is to *get to know your fellow students*. The most successful college students are those who know their classmates and who actively build with them a vital and supportive *community of learners*. If you get to know other students in your classes, you can help each other by working together: sharing notes, phoning, texting, or e-mailing for information if you are absent, and preparing for exams together. Plan on making new friends. Choose people who are also serious about school.

Exercise 7

Introduce Yourself: Collaborative Activity

Think about your answers to the following questions and make some notes on the following lines. When you finish, introduce yourself to your class group by discussing your answers. Be prepared to introduce the members of your group to the whole class.

1. What is your name, and can you give us some ways to remember it? (Does your name have a special meaning? Does it sound like a word that could be used to describe you?)

_____

_____

_____

2. Why are you going to college? What is your major? What is your career goal?

_____

_____

_____

© 2014 Wadsworth, Cengage Learning

3. What is one of the special accomplishments you have achieved in your life so far? (Be specific. Select something that you do, or have done, especially well.)

_____

_____

_____

© 2014 Wadsworth, Cengage Learning

Reading 2

I'm a Survivor

— JUANITA (JOANIE) LÓPEZ

In the following reading, community college student Joanie López describes the enormous obstacles she has had to overcome. Even though most students don't experience the exact challenges she faces, we all encounter barriers to reaching our goals. Joanie López's attitude toward life and her strategies for success in school could help us all.

1 When I was nine, my third grade teacher asked me what I wanted to be when I grew up, and I responded, "I want to become a teacher just like you." A few weeks later she asked me to speak at her graduation from her credentialing program. I remember as if it were yesterday how I took the microphone and said, "I look up to you. You have inspired me to teach people someday." I had already made the first big decision of my life, and I announced it into a microphone! Little did I know that my life would soon completely shift direction. In the future, I would have to make a lot more choices, and the options were not always rosy or clear.

CATASTROPHE

2 Less than a year after my teacher's graduation, everything changed. My father took my brother and me to my cousin's quinceañera celebration in Tijuana. At the party my dad had a few beers; and then he spotted the hard liquor. I am not quite sure how much alcohol he consumed that night, but it would be his last night of binge drinking. We were supposed to sleep at my grandmother's house, but my drunken father decided to drive us back to San Diego. He grabbed the keys and took off with us in his small Hyundai that had only lap belts.

quinceañera
special Latin American birthday coming-of-age celebration for girls turning 15

Tijuana
the Mexican city that borders San Diego

3 I will never know everything that happened on the night of November 6, 1999. However, I do know that my father died that night, and my life changed forever. According to the official report, my 48-year-old dad slammed our car into a parked California highway patrol vehicle on the freeway. My dad was killed instantly. My seven-year-old brother woke up screaming in pain and could see me lying there, unconscious, in a pool of blood.

aorta
the main artery in the human body that pumps blood from the lungs to the heart

4 I had lost so much blood, I was expected to die within 72 hours, but somehow I survived. I had a ruptured aorta, a broken spine, and damaged intestines. I was put in a room with my brother so that my mom could be with both of us. The doctors placed

"I'm a Survivor", by Juanita López. Reprinted by permission.

me on turning tables because I couldn't even move an inch of my body. They sedated me so I was unable to speak. When I asked for something to drink because my mouth was painfully dry, they told me they couldn't give it to me.

5   A month later, a nurse told me I had been in a car accident and the doctors weren't able to save my dad. I heard my brother's sobs next to me. As I glimpsed over, I saw him with a blanket over his face; we were both aching with physical and emotional pain. Then the doctors told me I wouldn't be able to use my legs. They explained that I would undergo therapy to strengthen my arms so that I could maneuver around on my own in a wheelchair. The simple things that we all take for granted now became complicated, time-consuming, and difficult for me.

6   Going back to fourth grade was tough. A week before I entered school, one of my nurses visited my classmates to tell them I would be returning in a wheelchair. Although I only lived five minutes away, I had to use school transportation. An assistant helped me during that first year after the accident as I learned how to be independent. At first, when kids at school would ask what had happened, I was hesitant to answer their questions because I was still learning to adapt to my new life. After being asked many times, I became used to their questions and started to give brief answers. Luckily, most of my classmates wanted to help me by pushing me around in my wheelchair.

CHOICES

7   More than 12 years have passed since I returned to the fourth grade. Although I didn't think about it at the time, I made the choice after the accident to move forward with my life. Even though it was painful, I learned how to talk to people about what had happened. I learned how to stay physically strong so I could push my wheelchair. I learned how to schedule my time so that even though everything took me longer than other people, I could still keep up. And I learned to ask for help when I needed it. I think that these strengths have helped me get where I am today, and I'm not sure I would have developed these traits if my life had been "normal."

8   Today I hold my head up high as a successful San Diego City College student. I am proud to say that I am in the Honors Program at my college. I have become an active leader in our campus M.E.Ch.A[1] club, and I've made a point of getting to know my professors and my classmates. I have found a supportive community on campus, and I feel at home.

9   It's been a long journey to get here, and most of my friends didn't make it this far. My parents only attended school up to the sixth grade back in Mexico, and they worked hard their whole lives. They raised my brother and me to appreciate what they were able to give us. Although she had very little education, my mother's words of wisdom and unceasing support have constantly motivated me. A lot of the people in my neighborhood are like my parents, and we are proud of our heritage, our rich culture, and the struggles we've endured. We treasure our musicians, poets, and unbelievably beautiful urban murals.

10   But that's not the whole story. Of the many people I knew in elementary and middle school, only two of us graduated from high school. I saw my closest friends throw away their dreams because of drug addiction; they were doing everything—crystal meth, marijuana, and crushed prescription drugs. I tried to help, but sometimes my help wasn't enough. Some friends were murdered by rival gangs or ended up in youth authority detention centers or prison. Others joined the military with high hopes, but after they served time in Iraq, many returned with post traumatic stress disorder. Many girlfriends became teenage mothers. I even have friends who were deported to Mexico because they could not provide proof that they were U.S. citizens when immigration

© 2014 Wadsworth, Cengage Learning

authorities stopped them on the trolley or on their way to school! Gradually I saw my friends lose their possibilities in life because they chose the wrong ways to deal with the daily pressures of unemployment, poverty, violence, and low expectations. I became even more determined to get my diploma and be the first in my family to go to college. I decided to make new friends who had similar goals.

11   I now realize that at some point I decided how I was going to react to life situations, especially at school. I've met barriers, but by knocking them down I've grown to understand that there are times when it is okay to get angry. Sometimes I am late to class since the elevators are often out of order, and I'm forced to take the longer—and more tiring—route. It's very frustrating. I don't know if anyone ever stops to think about the difficulties a disabled person may go through in an environment that is not wheelchair friendly, but let me be the one to tell you it is not a simple task. My college consists of steep hills and ramps that I can't wheel alone. Fortunately I have friends, and I am not afraid to ask them for help.

SURVIVOR WITH SOME HURDLES

12   Though I have achieved a lot, I am facing some huge academic challenges as well. I've received good grades in English, Philosophy, and History classes, but I failed developmental math. I was afraid to ask questions in that class because I didn't want my classmates to think I wasn't smart. When I got bad test scores, I would just stuff the results in my bag and try to forget about them. In order to succeed, I needed new strategies. After failing twice, I finally decided to ask my math professor for help with the material I didn't comprehend. Next, I read a book about math study skills, and I have started putting into practice the techniques it recommends: reviewing my notes; doing the odd-number problems (even when they aren't assigned); checking my answers; figuring out where I make my mistakes; and finally, doing the problems again until I get them right. At the end of last semester I passed the course, but I still need to complete three more levels of math.

13   I'm a survivor, and giving up is not an option. No, I cannot use my legs to walk, but I can use the strengths I possess to help me take small steps toward achieving my goals. I sometimes wake up and have frustrations like everyone else, but I try not to waste my energy being angry about things I can't change. Yes, I have trouble in math, but I have to stick to my system so I can pass the course and move on to my next goal. I continue to make connections with my professors and fellow students. I hope to impact people with my story. Disabled or not, we are all entitled to pursue our dreams in life. I have the option to choose what is best for my future, and I've set my mind to do so.

aspiration
hopes for achieving something

aspire
to hope to achieve something

Note

1. MEChA stands for Movimiento Estudiantil Chicano de Aztlán. It is a club for students of Latino descent who are interested in supporting one another and their communities.

Exercise 8

Check Your Understanding

Write brief answers to the following questions about Reading 2.

1. Make a list of the barriers that Joanie faced to graduate from high school and to attend community college.

   _____

   _____

© 2014 Wadsworth, Cengage Learning

2. What were the reasons that Joanie's classmates did not graduate high school and go to college? How did Joanie respond?

_____

_____

_____

_____

3. What are Joanie's short- and long-term goals?

_____

_____

4. What ideas does Joanie emphasize repeatedly?

_____

_____

5. How would you describe Joanie's attitude?

_____

6. What are Joanie's strategies for being successful in school?

_____

_____

_____

Exercise 9

Make Connections and Write

Write answers to the following questions based on Reading 2, your experience, and your observations. Then discuss your answers with your class group. Working together, prepare a report for your class as a whole or a written summary for your instructor.

1. Which barriers do you think are more difficult for people to overcome to go to college? Their background and the neighborhood they grew up in? Or physical limitations? Explain your answer.

_____

_____

_____

© 2014 Wadsworth, Cengage Learning

2. What barriers did you have to cross to get to college? What obstacles do you have to overcome to be successful?

_____

_____

_____

3. What have you learned in this reading that might help you overcome the obstacles you face?

_____

_____

_____

The Importance of Reading Reading is a conversation, a way of communicating with others and learning about yourself. Through reading you can think about and learn from the ideas of people you have never met, who may live in other countries or have lived in other times. You also learn from your classmates by reading with them and sharing ideas about what you have read. Reading is communication.

Reading also makes it possible for you to understand ideas you've never encountered before, to master skills and concepts you may have thought were beyond your grasp, and to reinforce understandings you have gained in your own life experience. Reading helps you know yourself.

Reading makes an academic community work. By reading better, you become a stronger part of this community.

Becoming an Active Reader: The *PRO* System

Joining an *academic community* means learning to take charge of your future by setting your goals and managing your time so success is possible. It also means that you will change your learning habits. The word "learning" itself implies "a change in behavior." In college you will discover ways to use all your learning skills—reading, writing, listening, speaking, computing, and thinking—to become a successful student and to be competent in the career of your choice.

By choosing to enter college, you have joined a community of learners, which includes fellow students, teachers, counselors, librarians, other staff, and administrators. Your learning skills, especially reading and listening, make communication in this community work for you. They will help you to know yourself and others.

The communication involved in reading is easier to understand if you view reading as a *process*. That is, the understandings you acquire by reading don't just happen automatically by looking at a page, or a computer screen, full of print. There are three basic steps that can help you succeed in reading and studying.

© 2014 Wadsworth, Cengage Learning

All good readers follow these steps even though they may not be aware that they are doing so. First, they *prepare* to read, then they *read actively*, and then they *organize to learn*. You can remember this process by using the initial letters to form **PRO**.

PRO The process or system you should use to succeed in reading and studying. It stands for *preparing to read*, *reading actively*, and *organizing what you read*

1. P = *P*repare to read
2. R = *R*ead actively
3. O = *O*rganize to learn

When you've mastered this system, you will be a reading "pro"!

1. PREPARE TO READ

The first step in the reading process is preparing to read. When you prepare to read, you carry out various activities consciously or unconsciously that help get your brain ready to receive information actively, in a way that makes it easier to understand and think about what you have read, and consequently easier to remember the reading.

Concentrating The first consideration in preparing to read is a very practical one. Begin by choosing a time when you won't be disturbed and a place where you can concentrate. By establishing regular times and places to study, you can form a habit of reading effectively. Plan to avoid environmental distractions and mental distractions.

Previewing Once you have chosen an appropriate atmosphere for reading you are ready to begin the process itself. The first step is to **preview**, or to look quickly at, what you are going to read before you read it. For studying purposes, it's best to preview only a section (no more than three or four pages) at a time. The preview of a short piece should not take more than a couple of minutes. In your preview, look for the "framework" of the reading. The framework is the basic structure, like the skeleton of a house that is being built. In your preview, look over the following things:

preview a quick look at what you are going to read before you read it

- Titles and subtitles
- First paragraph
- Headings and subheadings
- Pictures, charts, tables, and other illustrations or graphics, with their captions
- Special print: words that appear in **boldface**, *italics*, or are <u>underlined</u>
- Summary or conclusion

Exercise 10

Prepare to Read

Now you can practice preparing to read with Reading 3, titled "Your Psychosocial Health," on the next page. Before you read, preview the entire reading. Quickly read the special introduction to the reading, which appears in italics under the title. Look over the title and headings and the first paragraph. Study the italicized words and phrases, which are defined in the margins, and the illustration with its caption. Notice how much information you learn from this quick preview. After your preview, write brief answers to the following questions about Reading 3.

© 2014 Wadsworth, Cengage Learning

1. What is the reading about? (*See title, introduction, and first paragraph.*)

_____

_____

2. What is "psychosocial health"? (*See paragraph 1, the illustration, and the definition in the margin.*)

_____

_____

3. What does "social health" mean? (*See the heading and italicized term in paragraph 7.*)

_____

_____

4. List two traits that indicate good social health.

a. _____

b. _____

Reading 3   ## Your Psychosocial Health

— [ADAPTED FROM] REBECCA J. DONATELLE

TEXT BOOK   **In this reading, from a college health text, Rebecca Donatelle explains an aspect of health and wellness that has been ignored in the past: psychological, social, spiritual, and emotional well-being, which she calls our "psychosocial health."**

1   For a very long time we have thought of health in terms of our physical health. Increasingly, health professionals recognize that there's more to it than that. Psychosocial health may be just as important as our physical health in influencing our quality of life and even how long we live. The concept of psychosocial health includes the mental, emotional, social, and spiritual dimensions of health (see illustration on the next page).

2   Psychosocially healthy people are mentally, emotionally, socially, and spiritually resilient—that is, they can bounce back after disappointments—and they are able to draw on their wisdom in times of crisis. They have experienced pain and pleasure, and they have learned from these experiences and grown as individuals. They know when to call on friends for help, when to give help to others, and when it is okay to just

psychosocial health
the concept of health that includes mental, emotional, social, and spiritual health

© 2014 Wadsworth, Cengage Learning

Donatelle, Rebecca J.; Davis, Lorraine G., *Access to Health*, 7e, ©2002. Reprinted and Electronically reproduced by permission of Pearson Education, Inc., Upper Saddle River, New Jersey.

be alone. They respond to challenges, disappointments, joys, frustrations, and pain in appropriate ways most of the time, despite occasional slips.

MENTAL HEALTH

mental health
the "thinking" park of psychosocial health

3   The term *mental health* is often used to describe the "thinking" part of psychosocial health. As a thinking being, you have the ability to reason, interpret, and remember events from a unique perspective; to figure out and evaluate what is happening; and to solve problems. In short, you are intellectually able to sort through the clutter of events, mixed messages, and uncertain ties to come to an understanding of them.

4   A mentally healthy person is likely to respond in a positive way even when things do not go as expected. For example, a mentally healthy student who receives a *D* on an exam may be very disappointed, but she will try to assess why she did poorly. Did she study enough? Did she attend class and ask questions about the things she didn't understand? Even though the test result may be very important to her, she will find a constructive way to deal with her frustration. She may talk to the instructor, plan to devote more time to studying before the next exam, and even talk to or form a study group with students who did well. In contrast, a mentally unhealthy person may take a distorted view and respond in an irrational manner. She may believe that her instructor is out to get her or that other students cheated on the exam. She may allow her low grade to provoke a major crisis in her life. She may spend the next 24 hours getting wasted, decide to quit school, try to get back at her instructor, or even blame the people she lives with for preventing her from studying.

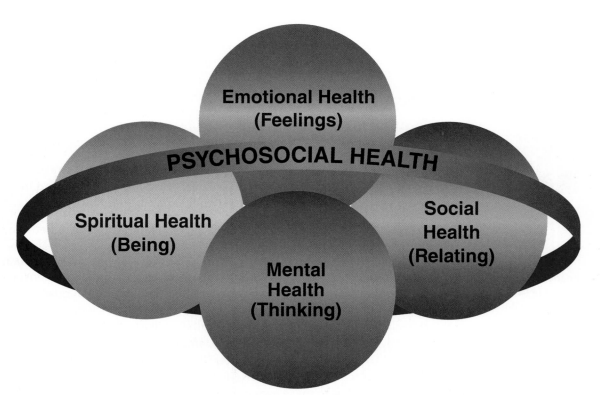

Psychosocial health is a complex interaction of mental, emotional, social, and spiritual health.

© 2014 Wadsworth, Cengage Learning

EMOTIONAL HEALTH

emotional health
the "feeling," or
subjective, side of
psychosocial health

5   The term *emotional health* is often used interchangeably with mental health. Although emotional health and mental health are closely intertwined, emotional health more accurately refers to the "feeling," or subjective, side of psychosocial health. Emotions are intensified feelings that we experience on a minute-by-minute, day-to-day basis. Love, caring, hate, hurt, despair, release, joy, anxiety, fear, frustration, and intense anger are some of the many emotions we experience. As thoughtful people, it is our responsibility to evaluate our individual emotional responses, the environment that is causing these responses, and the appropriateness of our actions.

6   Emotionally healthy people are usually able to respond in an appropriate manner to upsetting events. When they feel threatened, they are not likely to react in an extreme way or by making an attack. Even when their feelings are trampled upon or they suffer agonizing pain because of a lost love, they keep their emotions in check.

SOCIAL HEALTH

social health
interaction with
others and the ability
to adapt to social
situations

7   *Social health* deals with interaction with others and the ability to adapt to social situations. Socially healthy individuals have a wide range of social interactions with family, friends, acquaintances, and individuals with whom they may only occasionally come into contact. They are able to listen, to express themselves, and to form healthy relationships.

8   Many studies have documented the importance of social life in achieving and maintaining health, and two aspects of social health have proven to be particularly important.[1]

interpersonal
between and among
people

nurturance
affectionate care and
attention

- Presence of strong social bonds. Social bonds, or social connections, reflect the general character of our interpersonal contacts and interactions. Social bonds generally have six major roles: (1) providing intimacy, (2) providing feelings of belonging to or integration with a group, (3) providing opportunities for giving or receiving nurturance, (4) providing reassurance of one's worth, (5) providing assistance and guidance, and (6) providing advice. In general, people who are more "connected" to others manage stress more effectively and are much more resilient when they need to deal with crises.

- Presence of key social supports. Social supports refer to relationships that bring positive benefits to the individual. Social supports can be either expressive (emotional support, encouragement) or structural (housing, money). At college, as well as within families, students can find both expressive and structural support. You can find support from other students who are focused on doing well in school; from your professors, especially if you make an attempt to get to know them better by asking questions and going to their offices; and from tutorial and counseling services. You can find structural support from the campus health services and, if you are eligible, from financial aid or book grants. Psychosocially healthy people create a network of friends and family with whom they can give and receive support.

manifestations
forms

overt
open

9   Social health also reflects the way we react to others. In its most extreme forms, a lack of social health may be represented by aggressive acts of prejudice and bias toward other individuals or groups. Prejudice is a negative evaluation of an entire group of people that is typically based on unfavorable (and often wrong) ideas about the group. In its most obvious manifestations, prejudice is reflected in acts of discrimination against others, in overt acts of hate, and in purposefully harming individuals or groups.

© 2014 Wadsworth, Cengage Learning

10   A stable, loving support network of family and friends is key to psychosocial health. Social supports and the social bonds that come from close relationships help us get through even the most difficult times. Having people with whom we can talk, share thoughts, and not fear losing their affection or love is an essential part of growth.

SPIRITUAL HEALTH

spiritual health
a belief in some unifying force that gives purpose or meaning to life

11   *Spiritual health* refers to a belief in some unifying force that gives purpose or meaning to life. For some, this force is nature; for others, it is a feeling of connection to other people; for still others, the unifying force is a god or some other spiritual symbol. Spiritual health means your possessions don't give meaning to your life. You don't need to worry so much about the car you drive, the house you live in, or the clothes and shoes you wear. Rather, you develop a connectedness within yourself, and to others, to nature, and to a larger meaning or purpose.

TRAITS OF PSYCHOSOCIALLY HEALTHY PEOPLE

traits
characteristics or qualities

12   We have the power to understand our behavior and even to change it—thus shaping our own personalities. People who have the following traits appear to have what it takes to be psychosocially healthy:[2]

- Extraversion. The ability to adapt to a social situation and demonstrate assertiveness as well as power or interpersonal involvement.
- Agreeableness. The ability to conform, be likable, and demonstrate friendly compliance as well as love.

compliance
going along with what others want

- Openness to experience. The ability to demonstrate curiosity and independence.
- Emotional stability. The ability to control emotions in appropriate ways.
- Conscientiousness. The ability to demonstrate self-control and dependability as well as a need to achieve.

Notes

1. C. Ritter, "Social Supports, Social Networks, and Health Behaviors," in *Health Behavior: Emerging Research Perspectives,* ed. D. Gochman (New York: Plenum, 1998).
2. P. Zimbardo, A. Weber, and R. Johnson. *Psychology* (Boston: Allyn and Bacon, 2000), 403.

Exercise 11

Check Your Understanding

Choose the best answers to the following multiple-choice questions based on Reading 3.

1. Until recently, we thought about health as
   a. physical well-being.
   b. physical and psychosocial well-being.
   c. having a spiritual component.

2. Psychosocially healthy people
   a. have had lonely childhoods, so they need to learn good adaptation skills.
   b. have not had to deal with a great deal of pain or grief.
   c. are resilient.

3. A mentally healthy person reacts to getting a *D* on an exam by
   a. pointing out that the teacher is not very good.
   b. figuring out why she did poorly.
   c. proving that other students cheated on the exam.

© 2014 Wadsworth, Cengage Learning

4. Emotional health can also be referred to as
   a. spiritual health.
   b. mental health.
   c. the "feeling" part of psychosocial health.

5. Emotionally healthy people
   a. react in an extreme way when they feel threatened.
   b. respond appropriately to upsetting events.
   c. feel emotional pain less than other people.

6. "Social bonds" refer to
   a. social connections and contacts with other people.
   b. the ability to be satisfied spending time alone or with other people.
   c. the ability to manage stress.

7. Spiritually healthy people
   a. never worry about their possessions.
   b. believe that life has purpose and meaning.
   c. don't need to spend time in nature.

8. The author believes that
   a. we have the power to change our behavior and to improve our psychosocial health.
   b. we are influenced by our experiences, and psychosocial health can be attained only by people with a positive family background.
   c. it is possible to be healthy even if your psychosocial health is poor.

9. Someone who is able to be curious demonstrates
   a. extraversion.
   b. agreeableness.
   c. openness to experience.

10. Someone who is dependable and has a need to achieve is
    a. emotionally stable.
    b. conscientious.
    c. agreeable.

Exercise 12

Make Connections and Write

Write answers to the following questions based on Reading 3, your experience, and your observations. Then discuss your answers with your class group. Working together, prepare a report for your class as a whole or a written summary for your instructor.

1. What can you do to promote your social health as a student?

   _____

   _____

   _____

   _____

© 2014 Wadsworth, Cengage Learning

2. How do you respond to disappointments? Do your reactions to disappointments show that you are an emotionally healthy person?

_____

_____

_____

_____

3. Everyone can improve his or her emotional or spiritual health. What are some things you or your classmates can do to accomplish this goal? Explain your ideas. (Focus your answer on either emotional or spiritual health, not both.)

_____

_____

_____

_____

Using Previous Knowledge After your preview, think about what you already know about a topic. In your preview you will often recognize information about which you have **previous knowledge**—from your experience and prior learning. For example, in previewing Reading 3, "Your Psychosocial Health" you may have considered what you already know about mental health. If you are reading a chapter in a health text about nutrition, you probably already know many things, like fresh vegetables and fruit are healthy parts of a diet and french fries and candy are not. Recognizing what you already know will make it easier to understand the new material and to see how it relates to the skills and information you already have. When you preview, always consider how this new material fits in with what you already know.

previous knowledge what you already know about a topic from your experience and prior learning

Asking Preparing-to-Read Questions and Predicting The last thing you need to do to prepare to read is to ask yourself questions about what you are going to read, questions you think the reading will answer. In this part of the reading process you are **predicting** what you will learn. By predicting, you are preparing to be actively involved as you read.

predict to express what you think you will learn in the reading

Use the framework you look at in your preview—titles, headings, *italics*, **boldface print**, etc.—to predict what you will learn in the reading. Turn these predictions into questions. Then answer the questions as you read. Answering these **preparing-to-read questions** will make sure you are actively engaged when you read.

preparing-to-read questions questions you ask to prepare yourself to read

© 2014 Wadsworth, Cengage Learning

For example, as you previewed Reading 3, "Your Psychosocial Health," the first thing you saw was the title. From the title you might form the question: What is psychosocial health? From the illustration on page 24, you might form the questions: What do each of the parts of psychosocial health mean? How are the parts of psychosocial health related to one another? From the heading "Social Health," you could ask: Why is social health important? From the heading "Traits of Psychosocially Healthy People" and the bulleted list at the end of the reading, you could ask: What are the traits of a psychosocially healthy person?

Notice how many of these questions begin with "who," "what," "when," "where," "why," or "how." These are the **journalist's questions.** They are the key questions a reporter needs to answer to write a story. They will help you form your preparing-to-read questions, too.

To practice asking preparing-to-read questions, preview the following excerpt. Read the first sentence or two and the *italicized* words. Then write three questions you predict the excerpt will answer.

journalist's questions
questions that begin with
• "who,"
• "what,"
• "when,"
• "where,"
• "why,"
• "how"

1. _____

2. _____

3. _____

Since reading of any sort is an activity, all reading must to some degree be *active*. Completely passive reading is impossible; we cannot read with our eyes immobilized and our minds asleep. Hence, when we contrast active with passive reading, our purpose is, first, to call attention to the fact that reading can be *more* or *less* active, and second, to point out that the *more active* the reading the *better*. One reader is better than another in proportion as he is capable of a greater range of activity in reading and exerts more effort. He is better if he demands more of himself and of the text before him. (Adler and Van Doren, *How to Read a Book*)

You may have written questions similar to these:

1. What is active reading?

2. How can reading be more or less active?

3. Why is more active reading better?

Among the possible sources for your questions are the following:

• **Preview**—When you do your quick preview of a passage, you will find that you might want to formulate questions based on the titles or the words that are highlighted in some way. (In the preceding excerpt, important words are italicized.)

• **Your experience and previous knowledge**—Think about your own experience and what you already know about the topics to form questions about what you read.

© 2014 Wadsworth, Cengage Learning

- **Instructor's directions**—Listen carefully. Very often the instructor will make suggestions for reader's questions.
- **Reading introductions**—Many textbooks, including *Joining a Community of Readers,* provide readings from a variety of sources, and introductions to these readings can help you get started thinking about the content of a reading before you begin. This is an excellent place to think about reader's questions.
- **Course objectives**—Keep in mind your purpose in studying for this course. Reread your syllabus from time to time to be sure you're focusing on the right things.
- **Study guides**—Often your instructor or the text itself will provide study guides for the material. Keep these in mind when you form your reader's questions.
- **Questions in the book**—Some textbooks provide reader's questions or discussion questions at the beginning of a section. They often include questions at the end of a section as well. You can use these questions as your reader's questions.

Raising questions as you prepare to read is an important habit to acquire in mastering the reading process. At first you will need to actually write out questions. Eventually, you will be in the habit of forming questions in your mind every time you begin to read something new, and you may not need to write them out.

Exercise 13

Preview a Reading

Preview Reading 4, "Some Reflections on Reading" by Daniel R. Walther (on pages 31–33). List the information you noticed in your preview:

Title: _____

Subject announced in the first paragraph: _____

_____

Heading: _____

Subheadings

1. _____

2. _____

3. _____

4. _____

Italicized quotation in the margin:

_____

_____

© 2014 Wadsworth, Cengage Learning

© 2014 Wadsworth, Cengage Learning

Exercise 14

Ask Preparing-to-Read Questions

What questions can you ask about the information you recorded in Exercise 13 from your preview of Reading 4? Ask one or more questions for each of the items identified in your preview. The first two have been done for you.

Item from Preview	Preparing-to-Read Question
Title	What are reflections? What are the author's ideas about reading?
Subject announced in the first paragraph	What does the author mean by "reading process"?
Heading	
Subheadings	
Italicized quotation in the Margin	

Reading 4

Some Reflections on Reading

— DANIEL R. WALTHER

TEXT BOOK **The following reading is from *Toolkit for College Success,* Walther's widely recognized text written to help students develop the skills and habits they need to be successful in college. While you read, think about the questions you asked in Exercise 14.**

From Walther, *Toolkit for College Success*, 1e. © 1994 Cengage Learning.

1   This chapter does not presume to teach you how to read. You already know how to do that. But most students have never approached the process of reading from the perspective of understanding what happens when reading takes place and what practices might be useful to make reading textbook assignments an easier and more fruitful activity. That's what this chapter is all about.

2   In this theory section, our concern is to develop a better grasp of the process of reading. We can begin by focusing on some new perspectives on the reading process.

READING PRINCIPLES

We Become Better Readers by Reading

3   Many people are under the impression that reading improvement comes from learning "tricks" or mastering some mechanical gimmicks that will magically improve reading speed and comprehension. However, most reading professionals agree that we learn to read better simply as a result of reading widely. So much of reading depends on our "prior knowledge"—that information that we carry inside our head when we open the page and begin reading. Many learning theorists maintain that we remember new information only if we relate it to knowledge we already hold. There is no greater guarantee of a person's reading efficiency than extensive experience with words on the printed page. You can make slow but steady progress as a reader simply by reading more extensively to increase your base of knowledge.

extensive
a lot

MORE THAN ANYTHING ELSE, READING IS A PROCESS OF PREDICTING

4   If you were to pick up a book, turn to the first page, and read the line, "Once upon a time, in a magical land and a magical time . . ." your mind automatically begins to make predictions: "This is a fairy tale or fable of some kind . . . some of the characters will be 'bad' and others will be 'good.' There will probably be a happy ending, and the story will teach a simple little lesson . . ." and so on. As we actively read, our mind is always racing ahead of where our eyes are on the page, wondering, speculating, predicting, and then eventually either confirming those predictions or correcting those predictions that were not accurate. (In understanding that reading is largely a process of predicting, you are well under way to learning how to improve your comprehension and reading rate in text reading assignments. . . .)

confirming
agreeing with

READING IS AN INTERACTIVE PROCESS, NOT A PASSIVE ONE

5   Many students are under the impression that reading is a "laid-back" activity—that the mind is some sort of sponge that soaks up meaning as the eyes move across the page. Effective readers are mentally involved—questioning, probing, analyzing, disagreeing, doubting, criticizing, or in some other way *reacting* to the words on the page.

interactive
involving two-way
communication

6   Because textbook reading is an interactive process, we must treat it differently from the reading we do for leisure or entertainment. You may be able to take a spellbinding novel to your bed, tuck a comfortable pillow under your head, and spend an hour or more reading. You may even have a radio going in the background and still stay focused on your book. Using the same strategy with your chemistry textbook, however, can lead to disaster. You may find that you can read your textbooks much more successfully if you put yourself in a different environment. Go to the library, the kitchen table,

© 2014 Wadsworth, Cengage Learning

Reading is a means of thinking with another person's mind: it forces you to stretch your own.

—CHARLES SCRIBNER JR.

or your desk. Read sitting straight up and in a well-lighted area. Choose an environment with a minimum of distractions. You may see a marked improvement in your reading efficiency if you treat reading as the challenging mental activity it is and put yourself in an environment and a posture that will better support it.

COMPREHENSION IMPROVES AT A RATE SLIGHTLY ABOVE OUR HABITUAL, COMFORTABLE RATE

7   As we fail to do with so many other mental activities, we typically do not work up to our mental potential when we read. More often than not, we lapse into a nice comfortable rate—one that barely keeps the mind busy and that allows us to be distracted by our surroundings or other pressing thoughts unrelated to the task of reading. Many students have been led to believe that they will read better if they just slow down, but that advice is as valid as saying that they will "drive better" if they slow down to 45 miles per hour on an interstate highway. The slow driver is prone to being distracted by the scenery, may become drowsy from the slower pace, or perhaps will attend to other, more interesting, pursuits, such as adjusting the graphics equalizer on the car stereo system. Driving thus becomes only one of the activities competing for the driver's attention.

8   You will probably do a better job of reading if you press yourself to read 10 percent or so above your typical rate, just enough to require your mind to stay alert and focused. (You are probably capable of reading 30 or 40 percent faster with some effort, but the point is not to make reading a frenzied activity—just a focused one.)

Exercise 15

Check your Understanding

Choose the best answers to the following multiple-choice questions based on Reading 4.

1. Which of the following will help people improve their reading?
   a. learning tricks
   b. mastering mechanical gimmicks
   c. reading a lot

2. What is "prior knowledge"?
   a. Information that we carry inside our heads
   b. information that has priority
   c. knowledge in general

3. How can more reading make us better readers?
   a. More reading means we do not need to improve our reading skills.
   b. More reading makes reading more interesting.
   c. More reading gives us more experience with words and increases our base of knowledge.

4. Reading is primarily a process of "actively"
   a. predicting.
   b. focusing.
   c. remembering.

5. What is meant when the author says that reading is an "interactive process"?
   a. Information is gained in reading by means of a one-way process.
   b. Reading involves a reaction from the reader.
   c. Readers passively receive information from the writer.

© 2014 Wadsworth, Cengage Learning

6. You may see a great deal of improvement in your reading efficiency if you
   a. put yourself in an environment where you can be alert.
   b. read while relaxing in bed.
   c. have the radio playing in the background.

7. Reading slowly
   a. helps you understand better.
   b. is likely to allow you to be distracted.
   c. will make you a more active reader.

8. You will probably do a better job of reading if you
   a. read more slowly.
   b. eat while you read.
   c. try to press yourself to read a little faster.

Exercise 16

Check your Preparing-to-Read Questions

Write brief answers to the following questions about the process you followed in Reading 4.

1. Did answering your own questions help you answer the questions in Exercise 10, on pages 22 and 23? Why or why not?

2. How much of the content of the reading did you "predict" with your questions? Which of your questions were answered? Which were not?

3. How did your focus on preview items help you understand the framework of the reading?

Exercise 17

Work with Preparing-to-Read Questions: Collaborative Activity

Compare your preparing-to-read questions with those of other members of your class group. Of all the questions, pick the ones that you think were the best predictors of what Reading 4 covered. Then answer the questions that your group chose.

Choosing a Reading Strategy Once you have previewed and asked reader's questions, you are ready to choose a strategy for reading. This is the final step before actually reading.

© 2014 Wadsworth, Cengage Learning

purpose your reason for reading (for fun, to study for a test, to use the information at work)

Purpose Ask yourself, what is your **purpose** in reading this material? Do you just need a general understanding of the information? You might read the morning newspaper or a magazine article for a general understanding of current events; however, for college course work your purpose is often much more demanding. For example, if you are assigned a chapter in a health text, you may need to be prepared for a quiz on the content at the next class meeting. Or perhaps you are planning to use this information for a job in the future, such as working as a personal trainer in a gym. In both cases, your purpose for reading is much more serious than when you are reading for general understanding, and your reading strategy should reflect this. Plan to devote plenty of time to the reading assignment, and be sure you can concentrate on completing the task.

Difficulty Level A second consideration in determining your reading strategy is to ask yourself: What is the level of difficulty? Will the material take a lot of time and effort to understand? Plan for more time than you think you will need. How much do you already know about this topic? If the material is familiar to you or looks fairly easy, you can plan to read it faster and a little less carefully. The amount of time it takes you to complete a reading task will vary from assignment to assignment, and it certainly varies from student to student. Schedule your time carefully. Monitor the time it takes to complete assignments. As your reading and study skills improve, your use of time should become more efficient.

© 2014 Wadsworth, Cengage Learning

Organize to Learn: Preview a Textbook

As you begin the semester, it's helpful to preview your textbooks. Most college textbooks are divided into a number of parts, or sections. Each of these sections has its own title, and you can expect to find certain information in it. Here is a chart of these divisions, their usual location, and their use to you as a student.

Part of a Book	The Information It Gives	Where to Find It
Title page	Title of the book, name of the author(s), place of publication	The first page of the book
Copyright page	Number of editions, date of publication, ordering information	On the back of the title page
Table of contents	A list of the book's major topics and subtopics in the order they will be presented, organized in chapters, sections, or units with page numbers	After the copyright page
Preface	Information about the book's purpose, special features, student aids	Before the first chapter

Appendix (appendices)	Additional useful information such as maps, lists (e.g., of presidents), charts, and tables	At the back of the book
Glossary	A dictionary of important terms for the text	At the back of the book, after appendices
Index	Usually an *alphabetical* list of all important topics, terms, and names found in the text, with page numbers for each	At the back of the book, after appendices and glossary
Bibliography	A list of sources for additional information on a topic, including books, journals, audiovisual materials, and Web sites	At the end of a chapter or in a special section at the end of the book
Answer keys	Answers to exercises so students can check their work	At the back of the book or in an appendix

Exercise 18 Preview the Parts of a Textbook

Preview this text, *Joining a Community of Readers*, and answer the following questions about it.

1. Who is the author of this book?

   _____

2. When was the sixth edition of this book published?

   _____

3. In which chapters do you learn how to identify main ideas?

   _____

4. Where do you find out what you will be working on in each chapter?

   _____

5. In which chapter will you be reading about video games?

   _____

6. Where will you find instructions on how to write a summary?

   _____

7. Where in this book can you find exercises on vocabulary?

   _____

© 2014 Wadsworth, Cengage Learning

8. Which chapter looks most interesting to you?

_____

9. How many additional readings are in the back of the book?

_____

2. READ ACTIVELY

Active reading is involved reading. As you've already learned in doing the readings and exercises in this chapter, to succeed as a reader you must be alert and actively involved in every part of the reading process. You must:

1. Prepare to read.
2. Check as you read to be sure you understand everything.
3. Make connections to what you already know.
4. Think about what you know and what new information you are getting from the reading.

As Charles Scribner Jr. says, "Reading is a means of thinking with another person's mind: it forces you to stretch your own." This openness to new ideas, "stretching your mind," is part of what makes active reading happen.

critical reader a reader who makes connections and questions whether or not to agree with the reading

connect put together what you know with what the writer is saying

Making Connections Reading is a way to receive the ideas of others, to learn what other people want us to learn. But you must also be a **critical reader**. Think about what you read, and **connect** it to what you already know. The new information you are acquiring may or may not fit with information you have learned or experiences you have had in the past. Making connections, using all the information available to you, is part of the process of being a critical reader.

Thinking Critically As you think about new information in light of what you know, *question* whether you will accept all of what you are reading. In other words, ask yourself if you agree with everything the writer says. Do you agree with part of what she says? Do you think the opposite is true? Do you question her facts? Are some facts missing? Are her points reasonable?

   For example, if you are reading an article in which a smoker argues that he smokes because he enjoys it and he doesn't care about the future consequences, you already know what the consequences of smoking are (lung cancer, emphysema, constant cough, etc.). As an active reader, you make connections between what the writer is saying and what you know. You think about what you read and come to your own conclusions about the topic.

© 2014 Wadsworth, Cengage Learning

Language Tip:
Reader's Questions and Active Reading

Questions are a critical part of the reading process. Active readers ask themselves questions as they read and answer their questions continuously. Here is a list of types of questions, with examples, to ask yourself during the reading process.

Preparing-to-read questions:
- What do I think this passage will be about?
- What do I already know about this topic?
- What questions do I hope or expect will be answered?

Checking-comprehension questions:
- Do I understand?
- Were my reader's questions answered?

Making-connections questions:
- How does this fit in with what I already know?
- What do I know that I could add this information to?

Critical-thinking questions:
- Do I agree with everything I'm reading? If not, what part do I agree with?
- What part don't I agree with?

Exercise 19   Create Reader's Questions for Active Reading

Choose one reading from the Additional Readings and Exercises at the back of the book, pages 463–481. Prepare to read it, and fill in the first set of blanks for Question 1 that follows. Then read it, and fill in the additional blanks for Questions 2–5.

1. Preparing-to-read questions:

   a. _____

   b. _____

   c. _____

2. Checking-comprehension questions:

   a. _____

   b. _____

   c. _____

© 2014 Wadsworth, Cengage Learning

3. Making-connections questions:

a. _____

b. _____

c. _____

4. Critical-thinking questions:

a. _____

b. _____

c. _____

5. In what way did asking questions improve your understanding and enjoyment of the reading? Did active reading help you? Explain how.

a. _____

b. _____

c. _____

© 2014 Wadsworth, Cengage Learning

Exercise 20

Make Connections

Read the following excerpt about active reading, and answer the questions that follow.

Reading and listening are thought of as receiving communication from someone who is actively engaged in giving or sending it. The mistake here is to suppose that receiving communication is like receiving a blow or a legacy or a judgment from the court. On the contrary, the reader or listener is much more like the catcher in a game of baseball.

Catching the ball is just as much an activity as pitching or hitting it. The pitcher or batter is the sender in the sense that his activity initiates the motion of the ball. The catcher or fielder is the receiver in the sense that his activity terminates it. Both are active, though the activities are different. If anything is passive, it is the ball. It is the inert thing that is put in motion or stopped, whereas the players are active, moving to pitch, hit, or catch. . . . The art of catching is the skill of catching every kind of pitch—fastballs and curves, changeups and knucklers. Similarly, the art of reading is the skill of catching every sort of communication as well as possible. (Adler and Van Doren, *How to Read a Book*)

1. Have you ever played catcher on a baseball team? Or simply played catch? What do you have to do to be good at catching a ball?

_____

_____

2. When you read, do you feel that you are actively receiving the message that the writer is sending? Explain.

_____

_____

3. Do you agree with the writer that reading is very much like catching a ball? Why or why not?

_____

_____

4. To what other activities do you think active reading could be compared?

_____

_____

3. ORGANIZE TO LEARN

After you have completed the first two steps in the *PRO* reading process—preparing to read and reading actively—you are ready to organize what you've read in order to learn it. Organizing what you've read accomplishes two things:

- It helps you to understand better what you've read.
- It helps you to remember what you've read for future tests or job requirements.

There are a number of ways to select and use—that is, to organize—reading material. They include asking and answering questions, marking the text, charting, outlining, mapping, summarizing, and others. (You will learn more about these strategies in later chapters.) Then, recite or test yourself on what you have learned. Review periodically to make sure you are prepared for the test.

In organizing to learn, consider which ways you learn best. What is your preferred learning style? Do you learn best when you hear information? You might try recording the key points you need to memorize and listening to them. Are you a very social person? Take time to learn and review in study groups. Are you primarily a visual learner? Making a chart, map, or some kind of visual aid may be very useful to you. Does motion help your learning process? Try reviewing math formulas as you jog around the track.

© 2014 Wadsworth, Cengage Learning

Exercise 21

Organize to Learn

How do you learn best? By hearing? By reading? By working with other people? By looking at something? Or by something else? Explain your answer. Then list three concrete ways you can study that will help you learn.

_____

_____

a. _____

b. _____

c. _____

Chapter Review

To aid your review of the reading skills in Chapter 1, study the Put It Together chart.

Put It Together: The Reading Process	
Skills and Concepts	Explanation
PRO Reading Process	The *PRO* reading process includes the three basic steps that can help you succeed in reading and studying. They include *prepare to read, read actively,* and *organize what you've read.*
P = Prepare to Read (see pages 22, and 28–30)	Prepare to read, the first step in the *PRO* reading process, includes the following activities: 1. Concentrate. 2. Preview. 3. Use previous knowledge. 4. Ask preparing-to-read questions and predict. 5. Choose a strategy.
R = Read Actively (see pages 37–38)	Read actively, the second step in the *PRO* reading process, includes the following activities: 1. Check on your preparing-to-read questions. 2. Check your understanding. 3. Make connections to what you already know. 4. Think critically about the new information.

© 2014 Wadsworth, Cengage Learning

Put It Together: The Reading Process	
Skills and Concepts	**Explanation**
O = Organize What You've Read (see page 40)	Organize what you've read, the third step in the *PRO* reading process, includes the following activities: 1. Ask and answer questions. 2. Mark the text. 3. Make charts. 4. Outline. 5. Map. 6. Summarize. 7. Test yourself.
Preview a Textbook (see pages 35–36)	Previewing a textbook—looking it over and understanding its features—is an important activity to do at the very beginning of the semester. When you preview a textbook, you look at the title page, copyright page, table of contents, preface, appendices, glossary, index, bibliography, and answer keys.
Reader's Questions (see page 38)	Actively asking questions is an important part of the reading process. There are four types of reader's questions. 1. Preparing-to-read questions 2. Checking-comprehension questions 3. Making-connections questions 4. Critical-thinking questions

To reinforce your learning before taking the Mastery Tests (beginning on page 45), complete as many of the following activities as your instructor assigns.

REVIEW SKILLS

Answer the following skills review questions individually or in a group.

1. In the Put It Together chart, circle all the steps in the reading process that you already use. Which steps do you need to add to improve your reading process? Explain briefly how you will use the steps of the reading process to complete your reading assignments.

   _____

   _____

   _____

   _____

© 2014 Wadsworth, Cengage Learning

2. Are there additional steps you recommend for any part of the process? Explain.

_____

_____

_____

_____

3. Write an example of each type of reader's question.

a. _____

b. _____

c. _____

d. _____

Write

Choose one of the following topics to write about. Your instructor will tell you how much to write and how to organize your writing.

1. Using the goals you have identified in Exercise 2, on page 6, write a paragraph or a short essay explaining your goals and how, step-by-step, you plan to accomplish them.

2. Describe yourself 10 years from now. What goals have you accomplished? Explain in a paragraph or short essay what steps you took to achieve your goals.

COLLABORATE

Share with your class group your goals for this semester. Discuss in a group what steps each of you can take to achieve your goals. How can you support each other in meeting your goals for this class?

EXTEND YOUR THINKING

1. Choose a textbook from any of your other college courses and preview it. Identify the various features of the book. Does it have any unique parts? What parts, as a student, will you find most helpful?

_____

_____

© 2014 Wadsworth, Cengage Learning

2. List some of the campus resources available to you, such as the library, tutorial center, counseling office, etc. Investigate two of them and report back to the class. Include in your report the following:

Name of campus resource: _____

Hours of operation: _____

Location: _____

Services offered: _____

WORK THE WEB

To learn more about study skills that can help students succeed, use a search engine such as Google to go to the Web site of the Worcester Polytechnic Institute Academic Resources Center. Look at the list of "Tips for Academic Success." Find a topic that interests you. There are many to choose from, such as "Set Your Goals, Achieve Total Success," "Motivation," "Learning a Subject," and "Test-Taking Skills." Click on the topic that interests you, read it, and then answer the following questions.

1. What topic did you pick? _____

_____

2. List four tips that you found for mastering the skill covered in your topic.

_____

_____

_____

_____

3. Do you recommend that other students go to this topic? Explain your answer.

_____

_____

_____

_____

© 2014 Wadsworth, Cengage Learning

© 2014 Wadsworth, Cengage Learning

Name _____ Date _____

Preparing to Read "Thriving in a Diverse World"

Write short answers to the following questions.

1. The reading is titled "Thriving in a Diverse World." List some ways people can be "diverse".

_____

_____

_____

_____

_____

2. From your preview of the reading, write two preparing-to-read questions that you think will be answered.

_____

a. _____

_____

b. _____

Thriving in a Diverse World

— OSCAR VELÁSQUEZ

thriving
being successful,
flourishing

TEXT BOOK **In this reading from a college success textbook, Oscar Velásquez advises students on how to be successful in dealing with the many forms of diversity that we can encounter in college and in life. He points out that diversity includes many kinds of differences—in age, ethnicity, religion, sexual orientation, marital status, and even political viewpoints. As you read, think about your own background and life experiences. What experiences do you have with people who are different from you? Also, carefully consider the suggestions in this reading for how to get along with and learn from people of different backgrounds.**

1 Higher education could bring you into the most diverse environment of your life. Your fellow students could come from many different ethnic groups, cultures, and countries. Consider the larger community involved with your school—faculty members, staff

From Ellis. *Becoming a Master Student,* 12e. © 2009 Wadsworth, a part of Cengage Learning, Inc.
Reproduced by permission. www.cengage.com/permissions.

members, alumni, donors, and their families. This community can include anyone from an instructor's newborn infant (age 0) to a retired instructor (age 80). Think of all the possible differences in their family backgrounds, education, and political viewpoints. Few institutions in our society can match the level of diversity found on some campuses.

2   To get the most from your education, use this environment to your advantage. Through your encounters with many types of people, gain new perspectives and new friends. Acquire skills for living in multicultural neighborhoods and working in a global economy.

3   You can cultivate friends from other cultures. Do this through volunteering, serving on committees, or any other activity in which people from other cultures are also involved. Then your understanding of other people unfolds in a natural, spontaneous way. Also experiment with the following strategies.

perspectives
ways of understanding the world

SWITCH CULTURAL LENSES

4   Diversity skills begin with learning about yourself and understanding the lenses through which you see the world. One way to do this is to intentionally switch lenses—that is, to consciously perceive familiar events in a new way. For example, think of a situation in your life that involved an emotionally charged conflict among several people. Now mentally put yourself inside the skin of another person in that conflict. Ask yourself. "How would I view this situation if I were that person? Or if I were a person of the opposite gender?Or if I were a member of a different racial or ethnic group? Or if I were older or younger?"

5   Do this consistently and you'll discover that we live in a world of multiple realities. There are many different ways to interpret any event—and just as many ways to respond, given our individual differences.

perceive
experience, think about

REFLECT ON EXPERIENCES OF PRIVILEGE AND PREJUDICE

6   Someone might tell you that he's more likely to be promoted at work because he's white and male—and that he's been called "white trash" because he lives in a trailer park. See if you can recall incidents such as these from your own life. Think of times when you were favored due to your gender, race, or age. Also think of times when you were excluded or ridiculed based on one of those same characteristics. In doing this, you'll discover ways to identify with a wider range of people.

7   To complete this process, turn your self-discoveries into possibilities for new behaviors. For example, if you're a younger student, you might usually join study groups with people who are about the same age as you. Make it your intention to invite an older learner to your group's next meeting. When choosing whether to join a campus organization, take into account the diversity of its membership. And before you make a statement about anyone who differs significantly from you, ask yourself: "Is what I'm about to say accurate, or is it based on a belief that I've held for years but never examined?"

examined
thought about carefully

LOOK FOR COMMON GROUND

8   Students in higher education often find that they worry about many of the same things—including tuition bills, the quality of dormitory food, and the shortage of on-campus parking spaces. More important, our fundamental goals as human beings—such as health, physical safety, and economic security—are desires that cross culture lines.

© 2014 Wadsworth, Cengage Learning

9   The key is to honor the differences among people while remembering what we have in common. Diversity is not just about our differences—it's about our similarities. On a biological level, less than 1 percent of the human genome accounts for visible characteristics such as skin color. In terms of our genetic blueprint, we are more than 99 percent the same.[1]

LOOK FOR INDIVIDUALS, NOT GROUP REPRESENTATIVES

skewing
making something
uneven, distorting

10   Sometimes the way we speak glosses over differences among individuals and reinforces stereotypes. For example, a student worried about her grade in math expresses concern over "all those Asian students who are skewing the class curve." Or a white music major assumes that her African American classmate knows a lot about jazz or hip hop music. We can avoid such errors by seeing people as individuals—not spokespersons for an entire group.

BE WILLING TO ACCEPT FEEDBACK

11   Members of another culture might let you know that some of your words or actions had a meaning other than what you intended. Perhaps a comment that seems harmless to you is offensive to them. And they may tell you directly about it. Avoid responding to such feedback with comments such as "Don't get me wrong," "You're taking this way too seriously," or "You're too sensitive."

12   Instead, listen without resistance. Open yourself to what others have to say. Remember to distinguish between the *intention* of your behavior from its actual *impact* on other people. Then take the feedback you receive and ask how you can use it to communicate more effectively in the future. If you are new at responding to diversity, then expect to make some mistakes along the way. As long as you approach people in a spirit of tolerance, your words and actions can always be changed.

SPEAK UP AGAINST DISCRIMINATION

homophobic
fearful of or insulting
to homosexuals

13   You might find yourself in the presence of someone who tells a racist joke, makes a homophobic comment, or utters an ethnic slur. When this happens you have a right to state what you observe, share what you think, and communicate how you feel.

14   Depending on the circumstance, you might say:

- "That's a stereotype and we don't have to fall for it."
- "Other people are going to take offense at that. Let's tell jokes that don't put people down."
- "I realize that you don't mean to offend anybody, but I feel hurt and angry by what you just said."
- "As members of the majority culture around here, we can easily forget how comments like that affect other people."
- "I know that an African American person told you that story, but I still think it's racist and creates an atmosphere that I don't want to be in."

biased
having an unfair
preference or dislike
of something

candid
honest and direct

integrity
strong moral values,
honesty

15   This kind of speaking may be the most difficult communicating you ever do. And if you *don't* do it, you give the impression that you agree with biased speech. In response to your candid comments, many people will apologize and express their willingness to change. Even if they don't, you can still know that you practiced integrity by aligning your words with your values.

© 2014 Wadsworth, Cengage Learning

SPEAK AND LISTEN WITH CULTURAL SENSITIVITY

16   After first speaking to someone from another culture, don't assume that you've been understood or that you fully understand the other person. The same action can have different meanings at different times, even for members of the same culture. Check it out. Verify what you think you have heard. Listen to see if what you spoke is what the other person received. If you're unsure about how well you're communicating, ask questions: "I don't know how to make this idea clear for you. How might I communicate better?" "When you look away from me during our conversation, I feel uneasy. Is there something else we need to talk about?" "When you don't ask questions, I wonder if I am being clear. Do you want any more explanation?" Questions such as these can get culture differences out in the open in a constructive way.

REMEMBER DIVERSITY WHEN MANAGING CONFLICT

17   While in school or on the job, you might come into conflict with a person from another culture. Conflict is challenging enough to manage when it occurs between members of the same culture. When conflict gets enmeshed with cultural differences, the situation can become even more difficult.

18   Keep the following suggestions in mind when managing conflict:

- *Keep your temper in check.* People from other cultures might shrink from displays of sudden, negative emotion—for example, shouting or pointing.
- *Deliver your criticisms in private.* People in many Asian and Middle Eastern cultures place value on "saving face" in public.
- *Give the other person space.* Here the word *space* has two definitions. The first is physical space, meaning that standing close to people can be seen as a gesture of intimidation. The second is conversation space. Give people time to express their point of view. Allowing periods of silence might help.
- *Address people as equals.* For example, don't offer the other person a chair so that she can sit while you stand and talk. Conduct your conversation at eye level rather than from a position of superiority. Also refer to people by their first names only if they use *your* first name.
- *Stick to the point.* When feeling angry or afraid, you might talk more than usual. A person from another culture—especially one who's learning your language—might find it hard to take in everything you're saying. Pause from time to time so that others can ask clarifying questions.
- *Focus on actions, not personalities.* People are less likely to feel personally attacked when you request specific changes in behavior. "Please show up for work right at 9 A.M." is often more effective than "You're irresponsible."

Note

Maia Szalavitz, "Race and the Genome: The Howard University Human Genome Center," National Human Genome Center, 2001, http://www.genomecenter.howard.edu/article .htm (accessed April 26, 2008).

© 2014 Wadsworth, Cengage Learning

Write brief answers to the following questions about the reading.

3. Did you think about the ways that people can be diverse as you read "Thriving in a Diverse World"? Look back at your list on page 45. What additional ways can you add now?

_____

_____

_____

4. Were your preparing-to-read questions answered? Explain.

_____

_____

_____

Choose the best answer to the following multiple-choice questions about the reading.

5. With which of the following statements does Velásquez, the author of the reading, agree?
   a. Diversity is a problem that you need to learn to handle.
   b. Diversity is unavoidable.
   c. Diversity can and should work to our advantage.

6. The author states that diversity skills begin by understanding the "lenses" through which you see the world by consciously "switching lenses." By this he means that
   a. our understanding of the world is a result of our education.
   b. we live in a world of multiple realities.
   c. our understanding of the world is fundamentally unchanging.

7. Why does the author tell you to think about how you would react to situations if you were younger or older, of a different racial or ethnic group, or of the opposite gender?
   a. He wants you to understand that people experience the same event in different ways.
   b. He wants to clarify that diversity can mean many things.
   c. He believes that you should live your life as if you were a person of a different background.

8. What does Velásquez say you should consider when joining groups on campus?
   a. He suggests that you join groups with people who have the same interests as you.
   b. He suggests that you join groups that are diverse.
   c. He suggests that you join groups that have interests different from your own.

© 2014 Wadsworth, Cengage Learning

9. When the author says to "listen without resistance," he means we should
   a. be thinking of our responses as we listen so we can keep the conversation interesting.
   b. remain open-minded so that we can understand what someone else has to say.
   c. just be quiet if people take what we say the wrong way.

10. When someone "utters an ethnic slur" it probably means that person is
    a. making an insulting remark about people of a certain ethnicity.
    b. listening without resistance.
    c. carefully considering the effect the remark will have on people of a certain ethnicity.

11. According to this reading, one of the most difficult kinds of communicating that you ever do is when you
    a. have to give a speech in front of class.
    b. are honest in responding to people who make inappropriate remarks about others.
    c. need to consider how your facial expressions will be interpreted.

12. When you "practice integrity," you follow
    a. along with other people.
    b. diverse values.
    c. your moral values.

13. According to this reading, not being publicly embarrassed is more important
    a. in some cultures than in others.
    b. in the United States.
    c. for most men.

Write short answers to the following questions based on your reading, your experiences, and your observations.

14. Have you ever heard offensive remarks made about a group of people? What was said? Who said it? How did you respond?

    _____

    _____

    _____

    _____

15. What kind of diversity have you lived with in your life? Give examples.

    _____

    _____

    _____

    _____

© 2014 Wadsworth, Cengage Learning

16. How has your life been enriched by the diversity you have experienced?

_____

_____

_____

_____

17. What challenges have you faced in interacting with people who are different from you? Explain.

_____

_____

_____

_____

18. What incidents can you think of when something good has happened to you because of your racial, ethnic, gender, religious, or age group? Why do you think you were favored in this situation? Explain your answer.

_____

_____

_____

_____

19. When were you excluded or ridiculed or insulted because of a group that you are a part of? Explain what happened.

_____

_____

_____

_____

© 2014 Wadsworth, Cengage Learning

20. What, in your opinion, are the most important tips the author provides in this reading for "thriving in a diverse world"?

_____

_____

_____

_____

© 2014 Wadsworth, Cengage Learning

Preparing to Read "Choose Your Conversations"

Write short answers to the following questions.

1. The reading is titled "Choose Your Conversations." What do you think the author is suggesting to you based on this title?

   _____

   _____

   _____

2. From your preview of the reading, write two reader's questions that you think will be answered.

   _____

   _____

   _____

"Choose Your Conversations"

—DAVE ELLIS

TEXT BOOK **In the following reading, adapted from the college success textbook** *Becoming a Master Student*, **Dave Ellis expands the idea of conversation to include the thoughts that we say to ourselves, outside sources of information that constantly speak to us (such as television, radio, and movies) as well as the conversations we have with other people. He explains why it is important to think about the conversations that we have, because they can change the way we behave and even the way we live our lives.**

1   Conversations can exist in many forms. One involves people talking out loud to each other. At other times, the conversation takes place inside our own heads, and we call it thinking. We are even having a conversation when we read a magazine or a book, watch television or a movie, or write a letter or a report. These observations have three implications that wind their way through every aspect of our lives.

implications
consequences

CONVERSATIONS SHAPE OUR LIVES

2   First of all, conversations exercise incredible power over what we think, feel, and do. We become our conversations. They shape our attitudes, our decisions, our opinions, our emotions, and our actions. Each of these is primarily the result of what we say over and over again, to ourselves and to others. If you want clues as to what a person will be like tomorrow, listen to what she's talking about today.

From Ellis, *Becoming a Master Student*, 13e. © 2011 Cengage Learning.

© 2014 Wadsworth, Cengage Learning

CONVERSATION IS CONSTANT

3 This leads to a second discovery. Given that conversations are so powerful, it´s amazing that few people act on this fact. Most of us swim in a constant sea of conversations, almost none of which we carefully and thoughtfully choose.

4 Consider how this works. It begins when we pick up the morning paper. The articles on the front page invite us to a conversation about current events. Often the headlines speak of war, famine, unemployment figures, and other species of disaster. The advertisements start up a conversation about fantastic products for us to buy. They talk about hundreds of ways for us to part with our money.

part with
spend

5 That's not all. If we flip on the radio or television, or if we surf the Web, millions of other conversations await us. Thanks to modern digital technology, many of these conversations take place in CD-quality sound, high-resolution images, and living color 24 hours each day.

We are what we imagine ourselves to be.
— Author Kurt Vonnegut Jr.

6 Something happens when we tune in to conversation in any of its forms. We give someone else permission to dramatically influence our thoughts—the conversation in our heads. When we watch a movie, scenes from that movie become the images in our minds. When we read a book, passages from that book become the voice in our heads. It's possible to let this happen dozens of times each day without realizing it.

YOU HAVE A CHOICE

7 The real power of this process lies in a third discovery: We can choose our conversations. Certain conversations create real value for us. They give us fuel for reaching our goals. Others distract us from what we want. They might even create lasting unhappiness and frustration. We can choose more of the conversations that exhilarate and sustain us. Sometimes we can´t control the outward circumstances of our lives. Yet no matter what happens, we can retain the right to choose our conversations.

exhilarate
make happy, thrill
retain
keep

8 Suppose that you meet with an instructor to ask about some guidelines for writing a term paper. She launches into a tirade about your writing skills and lack of preparation for higher education. This presents you with several options. One is to talk about what a jerk th instructor is and give up on the idea of learning to write well. Another option is to refocus the conversation on what you can do to improve your writing skills, such as working with a writing tutor or taking a basic composition class. These two sets of conversations will have vastly different consequences for your success in school.

tirade
sharp, negative criticism

9 The conversations you have are dramatically influenced by the people you associate with. If you want to change your attitudes about almost anything—prejudice, politics, religion, humor—choose your conversations by choosing your community. Spend time with people who speak about and live consistently with the attitudes you value. Use conversations to change habits. Use conversations to create new options in your life.

10 A big part of this process is choosing *not* to participate in certain conversations. Sometimes we find ourselves in conversations that are not empowering—gripe sessions, gossip, and the like. That´s a time for us to switch the conversation channel. It can be as simple as changing the topic, politely offering a new point of view, or excusing ourselves and walking away.

© 2014 Wadsworth, Cengage Learning

antagonism
hostility

11   Some conversations are about antagonism. Instead of resolving conflict, they fan the flames of prejudice, half-truths, and misunderstanding. We can begin taking charge of these conversations by noticing where they start and choosing ways to change them.

GO FOR BALANCE

12   One immediate way to take charge of any conversation is to notice its *time frame*—whether the conversation dwells on the past, the present, or the future.

13   Conversations about the past can be fun and valuable. When we focus exclusively on the past, however, we can end up rehashing the same incidents over and over again. Our future could become little more than a minor variation of what has already occurred in our lives.

scenario
possible sequence
of events

14   Conversations with a focus on the future can also be empowering. A problem arises if these conversations focus on worst-case scenarios about what could go wrong next week, next month, or next year. Having too many of these conversations can add a baseline of worry and fear to our lives.

15   As an alternative, we can choose to have constructive conversations about the present as well as the past and future. Conversations about the past can dwell on what we learn from our experiences. Conversations about the present can focus on what we currently love about our lives and on ways to solve problems. Instead of worrying about the future, we can use our planning skills to set goals that we feel passionately about and consider ways to prevent potential problems.

16   In looking for ways to balance our conversations, we can also select among four categories of *topics*: things, other people, ourselves, and relationships. Most conversations fall into one of these categories.

17   Many people talk about things (cars, houses, trips, football games, weather) or gossip about others (politicians, actors, neighbors, kids, coworkers) far more than they talk about anything else. To create more balance in your conversations, remember the other two categories of topics. Talk about yourself—you heartfelt desires, fears, and joys—and about ways to create more loving relationships as well.

CONVERSATIONS PROMOTE SUCCESS

18   Excelling in higher education means allowing plenty of time for conversations that start in class and continue in your reading and your notes. Extend those conversations by visiting with your instructors during their office hours, talking to classmates, and forming study groups.

19   When we choose our conversations, we discover a tool of unsurpassed power. This tool has the capacity to remake our thoughts—and thus our lives. It's as simple as choosing the next article you read or the next topic you discuss with a friend.

20   Start choosing your conversations and watch what happens.

© 2014 Wadsworth, Cengage Learning

3. Was your answer to the question on page 53 about the meaning of the title of the reading correct or partially correct? Explain your answer.

_____

4. Were your reader's questions answered in the reading? Explain your answer.

_____

What are the three basic types of "conversations" that Ellis refers to in the first paragraph of this reading? (List them below for numbers 5-7.)

5. _____

6. _____

7. _____

_____

What are the three implications, or consequences, of our conversations? (List them below for numbers 8–10.)

8. _____

9. _____

10. _____

_____

Choose the best answers to the following multiple-choice questions about the reading.

11. The author writes "Most of us swim in a constant sea of conversations" because he
    a. thinks we're drowning in all the conversations.
    b. wants to emphasize how many conversations we are exposed to all the time.
    c. believes that we are involved in too many negative conversations.

12. The author is worried about the conversations that we are exposed to because he believes that
    a. without realizing it, we give someone else the power to influence how we think.
    b. conversations in the media are exaggerated and not good for the health of our mental processes.
    c. it is actually easy to filter the conversations you are exposed to.

13. What conversations does the author say we should try to change or to avoid?
    a. conversations on the Internet
    b. conversations outside of classes
    c. conversations that bring us down

© 2014 Wadsworth, Cengage Learning

14. If you have a negative experience with an instructor who puts you down, and tells you that you can't write well enough to be in college, how does the author suggest that you respond?

    a. Drop the class because instructors like that are bad for your self esteem.
    b. Change the focus of the conversation to what you can do to improve your writing skills.
    c. Tell your friends not to take a class with that instructor.

15. Which of the following conversations should you avoid?

    a. conversations that focus on all the bad things that may happen in the future
    b. conversations that help you learn from your past mistakes
    c. conversations about what is important to you and how to create more loving relationships

16. Which of the following types of conversations should you choose to be involved with?

    a. conversations about antagonism and conflict
    b. conversations to keep up with the most recent gossip
    c. conversations that will help you be successful

Write answers to the following questions based on the reading, your experience, and your observations.

17. How do you think the Internet has affected the conversations we are involved in? What have been some of the good effects? What have been some of the negative effects?

    _____

    _____

18. Why do you think the author includes the quotation, "We are what we imagine ourselves to be"? (page 54)

    _____

    _____

19. What kinds of conversations do you avoid? Explain why you think you avoid them.

    _____

    _____

20. What kinds of conversations do you think will help you to be successful in college and to be successful in you courses? Explain your answer.

    _____

    _____

© 2014 Wadsworth, Cengage Learning

2 Working with Words

TECHNOLOGY AND YOU

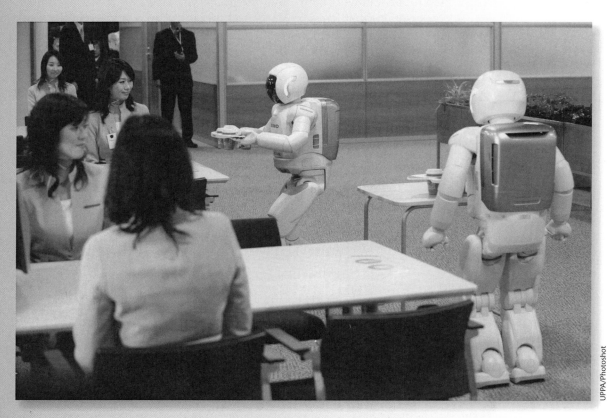

UPPA/Photoshot

Maybe technology gives us too many things, some of which are not always desirable, but without science and technology we would have very few things at all.
—JOHN LANGONE

- Describe the technology you see in the photo.

- Do you think this technology will change our lives? If so, when and how?

- What recent technological advances can you think of that have changed your life?

- What do you think of John Langone's view?

Getting Ready to Read

Technology has always affected the way people live—where we work, where we live, and how much time we spend with our families or with other people. Human life has constantly changed as we have learned to control the world around us. Now, we are on the edge of rapidly accelerating advances in technology, unlike anything our parents or generations before them experienced. How will these changes affect our lives?

In this chapter, you will read and think about how technology has changed lives and social relations in the past and how new developments might affect your life now and in the future. As you do this, you will increase your reading and communication skills by learning how to improve your vocabulary through:

- Textbook vocabulary aids
- Context clues
- Word parts
- Dictionary skills
- Personal vocabulary systems

© 2014 Wadsworth, Cengage Learning

Reading 1

From One Tragedy, Tools to Fight the Next

— [ADAPTED FROM] NICOLE LAPORTE

Earthquakes and tsunamis—giant waves caused by earthquakes under the ocean floor—have created some of the worst natural disasters in recent history. In December 2004, an earthquake and tsunami starting in the Indian Ocean devastated Indonesia and Thailand, as well as other countries. It claimed the lives of over 200,000 people. In March 2011, a powerful earthquake hit Japan. The earthquake caused a 23-foot high tsunami, which swept away houses, cars, buildings, and boats. It also caused an explosion and radioactive leak in a nuclear power plant. Over 15,000 people were killed in that disaster. This article, adapted from the *New York Times*, shows how two men responded to these tragedies with inventions that could help save lives in a future disaster.

---

1   When the devastating earthquake and tsunami struck northern Japan in March 2011, Shoji Tanaka's home did not suffer any major damage. But he worked as a volunteer in the disaster zone, supplying clothing and helping with clean-up, and said he was shocked "by the horrifying damage." The experience motivated Mr. Tanaka, who is an inventor and president of Cosmo Power, a Japanese engineering company: It "spurred me to work hard to complete Noah," he says.

spurred
pushed

2   "Noah" is Mr. Tanaka's version of a modern-day ark, and his answer to the possibility of another deadly tsunami. It is a bright yellow globe, four feet in diameter—picture a giant tennis ball. Noah is made of fiber-reinforced plastic that can withstand blows from a sledgehammer. Up to four people can fit inside the pod, which automatically rights itself in water and can survive a drop of 33 feet.

withstand
handle

Oh Hyun/Reuters Staff/Reuters

© 2014 Wadsworth, Cengage Learning

LaPorte, "From One Tragedy, Tools to Fight the Next." From *The New York Times*, January 21, 2012. © 2012 *The New York Times*. All rights reserved. Used by permission and protected by the Copyright Laws of the United States. The printing, copying, redistribution, or retransmission of this Content without express written permission is prohibited.

3   Mr. Tanaka designed his pod as a "temporary refuge" (shelter). The idea is that in a tsunami people can get inside and be carried along by the water for one or two hours, until help arrives. Small air ducts, or passages, make it possible to breathe, and there is a small window to see outside. The product is already on the market and costs about $3,800. Mr. Tanaka says he has orders from Japanese customers for more than 1,000 pods, some of which have already been delivered.

4   As the saying goes, necessity is the mother of invention. But so, apparently, is anticipation of possible necessity. The tragedy in Japan and limitations in the country's disaster preparedness system spurred some of Japan's greatest minds to come up with innovations to deal with future natural catastrophes.

innovations
new ideas; inventions

5   Some of these inventions weren't created from scratch. They were designed from products that already existed, so the process was much quicker and cheaper. The inspiration for Noah came from a product Mr. Tanaka developed three years ago to protect people if their house collapsed in an earthquake. But that unit was a different shape, and it wasn't intended to be submerged in water. "So I redid it as a complete sphere," he said. He also "strengthened the water tightness and made Noah able to withstand a tsunami." He hopes that Noah will become a standard safety item in Japanese households near the ocean. "It is simple for anyone to have a Noah," he says, "and I want as many people as possible to have one."

submerged in
put under

6   The Japanese tsunami is not the only recent disaster to inspire technological thinking. After witnessing the effects of the earthquake and tsunami on Thailand in late 2004, Hidei Kimura was disturbed by the communications breakdown in the area. "Due to heavy traffic, mobile phones were no use," he says. "There was no way to access emergency information."

7   As chief executive of Burton Inc., a Japanese company that specializes in 3-D displays, Mr. Kimura had an idea. He believed that if information could be written in mid-air, without the need for a screen, "far more people could see it and have access to valuable information." Mr. Kimura says that the concept was based on common sense, but that "no such device existed" at the time. So it became his mission to create a large-scale, 3-D display that could be used to broadcast messages in the air during a disaster.

luminous
bright

8   The result is Aerial 3D, which uses laser beams to create text out of tiny, luminous dots. The technology is now available to rent through Burton, though it is still being improved. At this point, the projected images can be no more than 16 feet high and 16 feet wide, but by the end of 2012 those dimensions should double. As for the advantage of 3-D, "a lot of people can actually see it," Mr. Kimura says. "If it's only 2-D, you can only see it from one direction." Practical use aside, he says, people are intrigued by his creation on a less serious level: "They say it's just like 'Star Wars.'"

intrigued
curious

© 2014 Wadsworth, Cengage Learning

Exercise 1

Recall and Discuss

Answer these questions about Reading 1, and prepare to discuss them in class.

1. What does the expression "necessity is the mother of invention" mean? How does it relate to the reading?

   _____

   _____

_____

_____

_____

2. Why did Shoji Tanaka name his invention "Noah?"

_____

_____

_____

3. What shape is Noah? What words are used to describe it?

_____

_____

_____

4. Why does Tanaka call Noah a "temporary refuge?" What do you think "refuge" means?

_____

_____

_____

5. What does Aerial 3-D do? Why did Hidei Kimuri invent it?

_____

_____

_____

_____

6. Why do people like the idea of Aerial 3-D?

_____

_____

_____

© 2014 Wadsworth, Cengage Learning

7. What other inventions can you think of that were developed because of trag-edies or natural disasters?

_____

_____

_____

8. Have you ever been in a natural disaster or emergency situation? What tech-nology might have helped?

_____

_____

_____

Working with Words

With every advance in technology, many new words are introduced into our language. Words that are familiar to you now, such as *download, software,* and *e-mail,* simply did not exist 50 years ago. To keep up with developments in technology, you have to keep up with the language of technology, and new words are emerging every day.

Every field of study has its own specialized language; therefore, as a student, you will encounter many new words in your college courses. In fact, anyone who reads a lot will come across new words all the time. Each new word you learn to recognize and use expands your ability to understand others and express your-self. In this chapter, you will learn some of the most basic ways of building your vocabulary and of dealing with unfamiliar words.

READING AND VOCABULARY

Probably the one activity that will most improve your vocabulary is reading, whether you are reading a printed book or an electronic device. The more you read, the more words you will learn. It's as simple as that. The more words you know, the easier it is for you to read, and the more you will enjoy reading for its own sake. So, maybe instead of watching a rerun of a television program or play-ing a video game, try to set aside about half an hour a day to read for fun. Pick anything that you enjoy reading—sports magazines, women's magazines, mystery novels, graphic novels, the newspaper, blogs. It doesn't matter what you read at first, as long as you get into the habit. Then, gradually try to push yourself to read material that is a little more challenging and that expands the type of reading you do. Still, you want to enjoy this reading, so pick things that interest you. You will find that developing the lifelong habit of reading a lot will help you continue to build your general vocabulary. Having a large vocabulary helps you in many ways:

© 2014 Wadsworth, Cengage Learning

in school, at work, and whenever you want to communicate. A strong vocabulary is a powerful tool that you can put to work for you.

TEXTBOOK VOCABULARY AIDS

specialized vocabulary terms unique to a particular field of study

Most college courses have a **specialized vocabulary**, and you need to learn that new, unique vocabulary in order to succeed in the course. When you take a course in math, sociology, psychology, biology, business, computer science, or other subjects, your instructor may explain new terms the first time they are introduced. In class lectures, if your instructor thinks a word is important enough to write on the board, you should write it down, make sure you understand it, highlight it in your notes, and study it.

Your textbook will also provide many valuable aids to help you understand the new terms and essential concepts.

vocabulary textbook aids all the features that textbooks provide to assist students in understanding new vocabulary

Some of the most common **vocabulary textbook aids** for learning specialized vocabulary are:

- The use of **boldface** or *italics* to emphasize the word when it first appears
- Definitions in the margins of the reading itself
- Key words and concepts sections at the end of the chapter
- Vocabulary questions in the chapter reviews
- **Glossaries** at the end of the chapter or book

glossary a dictionary of words, frequently found in the back of a college textbook

When you practiced previewing textbooks in Chapter 1, you were introduced to many of the vocabulary aids textbooks provide.

When you encounter a term in your reading that is crucial for understanding a chapter or a reading assignment, be sure to look first at the textbook itself for the author's definition or explanation. Do not go to a separate dictionary until you have checked all the sources in the textbook. The author's definitions will be more precise and appropriate for the specialized field you are studying.

Exercise 2

Use Textbook Vocabulary Aids

Examine two textbooks that you are using this semester. One can be this text, *Joining a Community of Readers*. Write the name of the text on the left, and then list the kinds of vocabulary aids the book has on the right.

Textbook Title	**Vocabulary Aids**
1. _____	_____
_____	_____
_____	_____
2. _____	*use of boldface for key terms*
_____	*definitions in the margins, vocabulary*
_____	*exercises*

© 2014 Wadsworth, Cengage Learning

CONTEXT CLUES

Not every book you read in college will have vocabulary aids. Most books, in fact, do not offer this kind of help. One important skill you need to develop is figuring out the meaning of words you do not know from the *context* in which they appear. **Context** is the surrounding words and phrases. It may include the entire sentence or even a paragraph or more. Often you can make a very good guess about what a word means by understanding the surrounding words.

context the sentence or paragraph in which a word occurs

For practice in understanding the clues context gives you, read the following sentences, which have some words that you don't know but you will probably understand from the context.

> Last night, my wife and I went to a *baccalunga* to buy some *wylieny* for my car. It was running rather *prohamply* yesterday, and I saw a *seminque* that I thought would help.

Of course, the italicized words in the preceding passage are not really words, but they could be. From the context, you know that *baccalunga* is probably a store, *wylieny* is something for the car, and *prohamply* describes how the car was running. *Seminque* appears to be something else that would make a car run better. Why were you able to understand something about these "words"? Because you understood the meaning of the rest of the sentence and paragraph. You understood the *context* in which the words appeared. Although you do not know precisely what each word means, you have an idea of what it refers to.

Four kinds of context clues can help you in understanding a word:

- Definition and synonym clues
- Example clues
- Comparison and contrast clues
- General information clues

Definition and Synonym Clues   Sometimes the context gives you the actual **definition** of a word. A definition answers the question "What does it mean?" Look at the following sentences on postindustrialism.

definition answers the question "what does it mean?"

> In 1973, sociologist Daniel Bell created the term *postindustrialism* to refer to technology that supports an information-based economy. In industrial societies, production centers on factories and machinery to manufacture things. Postindustrial economies, on the other hand, are based on computers that create, process, store, retrieve, and analyze information.

In this excerpt, the context tells you directly what *postindustrialism* is. (It even gives the name of the person who first used the word.) It means "technology that supports an information-based economy." The next three sentences explain further how postindustrialism is different from industrialism by expanding on the differences between them.

When a new term is defined directly, the definition is usually given close to where the word is introduced. As in the postindustrialism example, the meaning often follows the word itself, which may be boldfaced or italicized for emphasis. The definition may also appear:

- After the words *is, means, called, refers to, defines*
- Between commas
- In parentheses
- Between dashes

© 2014 Wadsworth, Cengage Learning

synonym a word
that has the same or
similar meaning

A definition may also use synonyms to help explain the meaning. A **synonym** is a word that has the same or a very similar meaning as the new word. For example, notice how a synonym for *query* in the following sentence is introduced by the word *or*:

A computer *query,* or search, on a popular topic may produce hundreds of links.

The word *search* is a synonym for *query* in this sentence. This one-word synonym helps you to understand what a query is.

Exercise 3

Use Definition and Synonym Clues

Read the following sentences from or related to the readings in this chapter, and write in the definition or synonym for the italicized word or words, using the meanings provided in the sentences themselves.

1. All of these examples demonstrate how *technology*—the many ways we extend our human abilities—changes our lives.

   technology _____

   _____

2. Mr. Tanaka designed his pod as a "temporary *refuge*" (shelter).

   refuge _____

   _____

3. Small air *ducts*, or passages, make it possible to breathe, and there is a small window to see outside.

   ducts _____

   _____

4. Yoshiyuki Sankai, an engineering professor at University of Tsukuba near Tokyo, was similarly inspired to update one of his inventions after the tsunami. In his case, he transformed his *Hybrid Assistive Limb, or HAL*—a lower-body, robotic skeleton on the outside of the body—so it could assist people working at radiation sites. (LaPorte, "From One Tragedy, Tools to Fight the Next")

   Hybrid Assistive Limb, or HAL _____

   _____

5. *Artificial intelligence*, the field of computer science that seeks to make computers behave in human-like ways, explores the question of whether machines can "think."

   artificial intelligence _____

   _____

© 2014 Wadsworth, Cengage Learning

6. Though most young people readily embrace all forms of technology, many older people experience *technophobia*—the fear of technology.

technophobia _____

_____

Example Clues Sometimes you can figure out the meaning of a word because you understand the examples provided in the context. Examples are introduced with clue words such as

- *for example*
- *for instance*
- *such as*
- *including*

Read the following sentence, and see if you can understand the meaning of *polyglot*. Notice the clue words.

> The young man is a true *polyglot*, speaking English and other languages such as Arabic, French, and Spanish.

In this sentence the examples are the four languages—English, Arabic, French, and Spanish. Taken together, you can understand that a *polyglot* is someone who speaks several languages.

Exercise 4

Use Example Clues

Read the following sentences, and write in the definition or synonym for the italicized word or words, using the clues provided by examples. Then write the clue words that signaled the use of an example.

1. Facebook provides people with a form of communication that can address a variety of *subgroups* in our society including anorexics, recovering alcoholics, rap fans, or country music fans.

subgroups _____

_____

clue words _____

2. E-mail is a *versatile* medium; it allows you to do many different things, such as explain a work assignment, send a note to a friend in another country, or share a recipe with a family member.

versatile _____

clue words _____

© 2014 Wadsworth, Cengage Learning

3. Because we have electricity, homes now are filled with technological *accoutrements* people once considered luxuries. Such things include furnaces, fans, air conditioners, refrigerators, stoves, light bulbs, washing machines, and various digital items; few of us would function well without them (Langone, *How Things Work*).

accoutrements _____

clue words _____

4. Personalized computer files, such as *signature files*, save people from the tedium of typing the same thing repeatedly in their e-mail.

signature files _____

clue words _____

5. The *graphic component* of the new book on how technology works is impressive; for example, there are more than 300 full-color photographs, technical drawings, and diagrams.

graphic component _____

_____

clue words _____

Compare and Contrast Clues Sometimes you can figure out the meaning of a word by understanding what it is similar to, or what it is different from. An author may **compare** two terms by explaining how they are alike or similar. The following clue words signal that a comparison is being used:

compare show how items are alike or similar

- *like*
- *alike*
- *similarly*
- *in comparison*
- *as . . . as*
- *same, same as*

contrast show how items are different

An author may also **contrast** two words by explaining how they are different from or even the opposite of each other. Following are some clue words that indicate a contrast is being used:

- *but*
- *on the other hand*
- *in contrast to*
- *however*
- *although*
- or
- *unlike*

© 2014 Wadsworth, Cengage Learning

Consider the following sentence about technology and sports achievement.

There is a lot of disagreement in the sports community about whether an athlete with a *prosthesis* has a similar challenge to the athlete who runs on his own two legs.

Here you know that a *prosthesis* has to mean an artificial leg because the writer is arguing that an athlete who has a prosthesis is similar to an athlete who does not. The similarity clue is *similar to*.

Now in the following sentence, notice the contrast clues.

Unlike the old analog TVs that do not work without a special converter box since the switch to digital in 2009, digital televisions are not yet *obsolete*.

In this sentence, we know that *obsolete* means no longer useable because analog televisions (which don't work by themselves anymore) are contrasted with digital televisions, which have continued to work after 2009.

Use Comparison and Contrast Clues

Read the following sentences, and write in the definition or synonym for the italicized word or words using the clues provided by comparisons and contrasts. Check whether the meaning is clear from comparison or contrast. Then write the transition that signaled the use of a comparison or contrast.

1. Although many jewelry-making techniques are now done *mechanically*, some of the work must still be done by hand.

   mechanically _____

   _____ Comparison _____ Contrast

   transition: _____

2. Many people don't object to the *cloning* of pigs, but they draw the line at making copies of people.

   cloning _____

   _____ Comparison _____ Contrast

   transition: _____

3. An Internet connection with a lot of *bandwidth* is one that allows you to move a lot of files around as fast as possible. . . . Bandwidth is like a pipeline: the bigger the pipe, the faster the throughput. (Lehnert, *Light on the Internet*)

   bandwidth _____

   _____ Comparison _____ Contrast

   transition: _____

© 2014 Wadsworth, Cengage Learning

4. In fact, *browsing* [the Web] is a lot like daydreaming: You simply go where your interests lead you. (Lehnert, *Light on the Internet*)

browsing _____

_____ Comparison   _____ Contrast

transition: _____

5. You can browse Web pages *casually* for entertainment, or you can browse with a serious goal in mind. (Lehnert, *Light on the Internet*)

casually _____

_____ Comparison   _____ Contrast

transition: _____

General Information Clues Sometimes you can understand an unfamiliar word because you understand, in general, the rest of the information in the surrounding sentence or group of sentences. It was from this type of context clue that you were able to understand the example using the "words" *baccalunga* and *seminque* on page 65. The context for the words that follow is a little more complicated, but you will probably be successful in figuring out the meanings of the italicized words because you will understand the context. Often, in the context of technology, explanations of what something does are clues that help you understand the meaning of the new term. Consider the term *universal design* in the following excerpt:

> Good customer service means providing a welcoming environment, respectful treatment and needed information. *Universal Design* provides an important toolset for companies seeking to provide these advantages for their customers and for their employees, who also want to feel welcome and respected, and who require adequate and timely information to do their jobs. Universal Design (UD) is a strategy for making products, environments, operational systems and services welcoming and usable to the most diverse range of people possible. Its key principles are simplicity, flexibility and efficiency. Originally developed in response to the needs of the aging population and people with disabilities, UD has much broader applicability. UD increases ease of access to products, places and services for multiple, diverse populations. Using UD means that facilities, programs, and services take into account the broad range of abilities, ages, reading levels, learning styles, languages, and cultures in their diverse workforce and customer base. (Button, "Universal Design," United States Department of Labor Web site)

In this excerpt, the author begins his description of universal design by including it as part of a description of good customer service. We learn that a goal of universal design is to be "welcoming" and "usable." We further understand that although UD was first developed to address the needs of the elderly and disabled, it

© 2014 Wadsworth, Cengage Learning

now applies to many different groups and needs. Adding up these various general information clues, the reader understands that *universal design* must mean designing products and services that work for everyone.

Exercise 6

Understand Words in Context

Read the following excerpt from *Time* magazine about the increase of women using the Internet and guess the meaning of the italicized words by using context clues. Write your definition on the line. Then, in the multiple-choice question, pick the clue—*definition, example, comparison and contrast,* or *general information*—that helped you determine the meaning. Be sure your definition fits the context.

More women are *logging on* (1), or signing on, to the computer than men. While the percentage of teen girls is increasing the fastest, women 55 and older are a close second. What's the *lure (2)?* Many attractive Web sites entice girl and women *surfers* (3) to the net. Teenage girls chat on sites like teen.com and cosmogirl.com, while working moms save time shopping at sites like babygear.com and walgreens.com. Older women frequent health and family *sites* (4), such as merck.medco.com and familyhistory.com. . . .

A retired teacher, Nancy Close, 70, first went online six months ago at her daughter's urging. Now the Columbus, Ohio, widow spends three hours a day auctioning paper dolls on eBay, researching health facts for her Chihuahua, and sending e-mail. Why didn't she make the leap sooner? "It was *intimidating* (5)," she says because, at first, it seemed so difficult. "But now I'm trying to get all my senior friends online." (Adapted from Hamilton, "Meet the New Surfer Girls")

1. *logging on* _____

   Which clue helped you identify the meaning?
   a. definition
   b. comparison and contrast
   c. general information

2. *lure* _____

   Which clue helped you identify the meaning?
   a. definition
   b. comparison and contrast
   c. general information

3. *surfers* _____

   Which clue helped you identify the meaning?
   a. definition
   b. general information
   c. example

4. *sites* _____

   Which clue helped you identify the meaning?
   a. definition
   b. example
   c. comparison and contrast

© 2014 Wadsworth, Cengage Learning

5. *intimidating* _____

Which clue helped you identify the meaning?
a. synonym
b. general information
c. comparison and contrast

Reading 2

Technology: What Is It and How It Changes Our Lives

— [ADAPTED FROM] JAMES M. HENSLIN

TEXT BOOK **In the following reading, adapted from a sociology textbook, the author carefully defines "technology" and discusses how it reshapes our society, including our relationships to people in our lives and our values.**

1   *Technology* has a double meaning. It refers to both the *tools,* the items used to accomplish tasks, and the skills or procedures needed to make and use those tools. Technology refers to tools as simple as a comb and as complicated as a computer. Technology's second meaning—skills or procedures needed to make and use tools—refers in this case not only to the procedures used to manufacture combs and computers, but also to those required to "produce" an acceptable hairdo or to gain access to the Internet. Another way to think about technology is to define it as the *artificial means of extending human abilities.*

2   All human groups make and use technology, but today, our postindustrial society (also called postmodern society) is defined by our technology, which greatly extends our abilities to analyze information, communicate, and travel. These new technologies allow us to do what had never been done before in history: to probe space, to communicate almost instantaneously anywhere on the globe; to travel greater distances faster; and to store, retrieve (get back), and analyze vast amounts of information.

probe
search into, explore

3   Change is rapid. Desktop computers are giving way to laptops—and some laptops are being replaced by handheld devices that contain keyboards and cameras. This is just the beginning. We may even "wear" computers, storing data on holograms located in our own proteins. With the many twists and turns yet to come on our journey to the future, no one knows what our life will be like, but it is challenging and enjoyable to imagine the possibilities.

TECHNOLOGY CHANGES OUR LIVES

4   The field of sociology studies how technology changes our way of life. When a technology is introduced into a society, it forces other parts of society to change. In fact, *new technology can reshape society.* Let's look at some ways it can do that.

Henslin, *Sociology: Down to Earth Approach,* 7e © 2005. Reproduced by permission of Pearson Education, Inc.

© 2014 Wadsworth, Cengage Learning

Changes in Social Organization

5 Technology changes how people organize themselves. Before machine technology, most workers worked alongside their families at home, but new power-driven machinery required them to leave their families and go to factories. In the first factories, each worker still made an entire item. Then it was discovered that workers could produce more if each person did a specialized task. One worker would hammer or bolt on a single part, someone else would take the item and do some other repetitive task before the third person took over, and so on. Henry Ford built on this innovation by developing the assembly line: Instead of workers moving to the parts, machines (conveyor belts) moved the parts to the workers.

Changes in How We Think about the World

6 Technology also changes our ideas about the world. Karl Marx noted that when workers did repetitive tasks on just a small part of a product, they did not feel connected to the finished product. They didn't feel as though the product was "theirs." Workers had become *alienated*—or separated from the product of their labor. Marx stressed how *alienation* led to dissatisfaction.

7 Marx also noted that the factory owners, or capitalists, treated workers like machines—just another replaceable part. According to Marx, capitalists squeezed every ounce of sweat and blood they could out of the workers. If the workers quit, others would take their place. Marx believed that this exploitation, taking advantage of workers, would lead to a workers' revolution. The capitalists believed that maximizing their profits—making as much money as possible even if it meant paying their workers a poverty wage—was a moral goal. They believed their work benefited society and pleased God as well.

alienated
feeling separated from the product of one's work

Changes in Values

8 Our values are also influenced by technology. Today's technology produces an abundance of things we can buy. Americans are proud of our electronic devices, basketball shoes, cars, boats, and vacations, and many of us make certain that our jeans and pullovers have trendy labels prominently displayed. Today's technology has made us desire to have more things, and this desire to have more material goods has made us become more materialistic.

Changes in Relationships

9 Technology also changes how people relate to one another. When men left home to work in factories, they grew isolated from many of the day-to-day affairs of the family. One consequence of becoming relative strangers to their wives and children was more divorce. Later changes in technology drew more women away from the home to offices and factories. This change has had similar consequences—greater isolation from husbands and children and increasingly fragile marriages.

Exercise 7   Use Context Clues

For the italicized words in the sentences below, write the definitions on the lines provided. Then write the context clue or clues you used to find the meaning: *definition and synonym, example, comparison and contrast, general information*. You will notice that *technology* appears two times because it has more than one definition.

© 2014 Wadsworth, Cengage Learning

1. *Technology* has a double meaning. It refers to both the tools—the items used to accomplish tasks, and the skills or procedures needed to make and use those tools. (par. 1)

   technology _____

   clues _____

2. Another way to think about *technology* is to define it as the artificial means of extending human abilities. (par. 1)

   technology _____

   clues _____

3. All human groups make and use technology, but today, our postindustrial society (also called *postmodern society*) is defined by our technology, which greatly extends our abilities to analyze information, communicate, and travel. (par. 2)

   postmodern society _____

   _____

   clues _____

4. Then it was discovered that workers could produce more if each person did a specialized task. One worker would hammer or bolt on a single part, someone else would take the item and do some other repetitive task before the third person took over, and so on. Henry Ford built on this *innovation* by developing the assembly line: Instead of workers moving to the parts, machines (*conveyor belts*) moved the parts to the workers. (par. 5)

   innovation _____

   clues _____

5. *conveyor belts* _____

   clues _____

6. Workers had become *alienated*—or separated from the product of their labor. (par. 6)

   alienated _____

   clues _____

© 2014 Wadsworth, Cengage Learning

7. Marx believed that this *exploitation*, taking advantage of workers, would lead to a workers' revolution. (par. 7)

exploitation _____

clues _____

8. Americans are proud of our electronic devices, basketball shoes, cars, boats, and vacations, and many of us make certain that our jeans and pullovers have trendy labels prominently displayed. Today's technology has made us desire to have more things, and this desire to have more material goods has made us become more *materialistic*. (par. 8)

materialistic _____

clues _____

Exercise 8

Check Your Understanding

Circle the best answers to the following multiple-choice questions about Reading 2.

1. Two examples that the author gives for technology are
   a. brooms and vacuum cleaners.
   b. stoves and microwaves.
   c. combs and computers.

2. Which of the following technologies are products of postindustrial society?
   a. Printing press and duplicating machines
   b. Communications, information analysis, and space probes
   c. Power-driven machinery and automobiles

3. According to the author, sociology studies
   a. scientific advances for medical purposes.
   b. how technology changes our way of life.
   c. why technological advances are sometimes not profitable.

4. Before machine technology most families
   a. worked together at home.
   b. did not have enough food to eat.
   c. left the children at home during the day.

5. Henry Ford
   a. invented machine technology.
   b. developed the assembly line.
   c. developed the first factories.

6. Karl Marx believed that workers were dissatisfied at work because
   a. they were basically lazy.
   b. they missed their families.
   c. they were alienated from the product of their work.

© 2014 Wadsworth, Cengage Learning

7. A synonym for capitalist is
   a. farmer.
   b factory owner.
   c. worker.

8. The author believes that machine technology changed the way people related to each other because
   a fathers and sometimes mothers working away from home led to weaker marriages.
   b. parents working away from home led to stronger marriages because people appreciated the time they had together more.
   c. people working away from home made them more materialistic.

Exercise 9

Make Connections and Write

Write short answers to the following questions based on Reading 2, your experience, and your observations. Then discuss your answers with your class group. Working together, prepare a report for your class as a whole or a written summary for your instructor.

1. What kind of work do you do or have you done? Do or did you feel a sense of accomplishment with your work (at home or for an employer)? Do you feel "exploited"? Explain your answer.

   _____

   _____

   _____

2. Henslin states that we have become materialistic, that is, we want to have more stuff. What types of material goods are important to you? Explain why these things are important to you.

   _____

   _____

   _____

3. Is materialism a good or bad thing? Explain your answer.

   _____

   _____

   _____

© 2014 Wadsworth, Cengage Learning

WORD PARTS

word parts words or elements of words joined together to make new words

root core part of a word to which prefixes and suffixes are added

prefix an addition at the beginning of a word that changes its meaning

suffix ending of a word, often indicating the part of speech

One way to multiply the number of words in your vocabulary quickly is to become aware of how words in English are made. Often two words are simply put together to create a new word. Consider the word *weekend*. If you know what a *week* is and what *end* means, you have an excellent chance of understanding *weekend*. Many new terms related to technology are created in the same way. Think about the computer terms *download* and *online*. If you recognize the meaning of the parts of these words, you know what these new terms mean, too.

Word parts are the words or elements of words joined together to make new words. Not all of these words can stand on their own, however. The core part of a word, which can often stand on its own, is called the **root**. Elements of words that are added before the root are called **prefixes**; these often change the word's meaning. Elements of words that are added after the root are called **suffixes**; these often indicate the word's part of speech, or function in a sentence. Consider the word *imagine*. If we add the suffix *able* to the root word, we have *imaginable,* a new word that means "able to be imagined." Then, if we add the prefix *un* to this new word, we have yet another new word—*unimaginable*—a word which means "not able to be imagined."

Remember:

- Roots can be at the beginning, middle, or end of a word.
- Prefixes appear at the beginning of the word and change its meaning.
- Suffixes appear at the end of a word and indicate its function in a sentence.

Knowing the meaning of many common word parts can greatly increase your vocabulary. For example, if you know that *media* is a root that means "ways of conveying or expressing," you can understand many words relating to media. For example, *multimedia* begins with the common prefix "multi," which means "many," so a multimedia presentation is one that uses many different media, or ways, to communicate its message.

Roots The root is the core part of the word. It usually provides the basic meaning of a word. Roots may occur at the beginning, middle, or end of a word and may be combined with prefixes and suffixes to form a different word. Following is a list of some important roots along with their meanings and an example of each in a word. As you go through this list, add another example for each root in the space provided. If you can't think of another example, use the dictionary to find one.

Root	Meaning	Example	Your Examples
aqua, aque	water	aquarium	_____
auto	self	automatic	_____
bio	life	biology	_____
cept	receive	reception	_____
chron	time	chronology	_____
cogi	think, know	recognize	_____
duct	lead	aqueduct	_____

continued

© 2014 Wadsworth, Cengage Learning

gamy	marriage	polygamy	_____
logy	study	sociology	_____
mini	small	minimum	_____
mit, miss	send	emit	_____
nov, novi	new	renovate	_____
patr, patri	father	patriarch	_____
ped	foot	pedestrian	_____
port	carry	transport	_____
vers	turn	versatile	_____
vid, vis	see	vision	_____
vit, vivi	life	vitality	_____

Prefixes On pages 78–80 are four lists of common prefixes along with their meanings and an example of each in a word. The prefixes in the first group identify a number. Those in the next group mean "no" or "not." Those in the third group identify a time. Those in the fourth group identify a place or position. As you go through each list, add your own examples in the spaces provided. If you can't think of other examples, use the dictionary.

Number A prefix indicating number can completely change the meaning of a word. For example, *tri*angle is a three-sided figure; a *quad*rilateral has four sides, and a *penta*gon has five sides. Similarly, a *bi*llion dollars ($1,000,000,000) is a lot of money, but a *tri*llion ($1,000,000,000,000) is more and a *quad*rillion ($1,000,000,000,000,000) is much more money.

Prefix	Meaning	Example	Your Examples
mono	one	monogamy	_____
uni	one	uniform	_____
bi	two	bigamy	_____
tri	three	tricycle	_____
quad	four	quadruplet	_____
multi	many	multitalented	_____
poly	many	polygamy	_____
semi	half, part	semiconscious	_____
dec	ten	decimal	_____
cent	hundred	centimeter	_____

© 2014 Wadsworth, Cengage Learning

Negative Negative prefixes can reverse the meaning of a word. For example, if you add *il* to *legal*, you change something lawful to unlawful or *illegal*. Notice that several other prefixes mean "not" as well.

Prefix	Meaning	Example	Your Examples
anti	against	antiabortion	_____
de	down, away, off	deflate	_____
dys	ill, difficult	dysfunctional	_____
il	not	illegible	_____
im	not	immature	_____
in	not	inaccurate	_____
ir	not	irresponsible	_____
mal	bad, abnormal	malfunction	_____
un	not	unmarked	_____

Time Some prefixes indicate the time that something occurs. For example, the prefix *pre* means "before," so we know that *pregame* activities happen before the game. However, we expect *post*game activities to take place after the game.

Prefix	Meaning	Example	Your Examples
ante	before	anteroom	_____
post	after, behind	postindustrial	_____
pre	before	prebirth	_____
proto	first	prototype	_____
re	again	return	_____

Place or Position Other prefixes show position or location. For example, *appear* means "to show up." When we add the prefix *dis*, we get the word *disappear*, which means "to go away" or "to become invisible." Notice how each of the following prefixes affects location.

Prefix	Meaning	Example	Your Examples
circum	around	circumcise	_____
co	with, together	cooperate	_____
com, con	with, together	communicate	_____

© 2014 Wadsworth, Cengage Learning

dis	apart, away	disappear	_____
en	in, into	entrap	_____
ex	out of, from	exhale	_____
inter	between, among	international	_____
para	beside, related to	parachute	_____
sub	under, below	submarine	_____
sur	over, above, on top of	surcharge	_____
tele	far off, distant	telephoto	_____
trans	across	translate	_____

Exercise 10

Build Your Vocabulary Using Prefixes: Collaborative Activity

In your class group, compare your examples of words with prefixes. Then make a class master list. If the list is less than 100 words, brainstorm additional prefixes and words with prefixes until you have 100. Use the dictionary to help you. Each group can share its list with the class to make a master list of 200 to 300 words. Discuss which of the words would be most important to learn, then make a master list to photocopy so each person in the class has a personal list for vocabulary building.

Exercise 11

Use Roots and Prefixes

Read the following excerpt from an article about biometrics and the new technology of voice security. Then use the lists of prefixes and roots, as well as context, to explain the meaning of the italicized words. Identify the prefix or root that helped you and its meaning. The first one has been done for you.

> *Biometrics* (1) is a science that makes use of an individual's *unique* (2) identifiers, easily reading them by *automated* (3) processes. The clues to individual identity that biometrics uses include fingerprinting, analyzing hand shape, eye scans, signature verification, and facial and voice recognition. Voice identification uses *multiple* (4) speakers, a set of speakers who have provided samples of their speech. In the cellular phone industry, using voice security can make a stolen or fraudulently obtained unit *inoperable* (5) and dramatically reduce fraud. (Adapted from "Voice Security," *PC Tips*)

1. *biometrics* Science that measures some aspects of human life for purposes of identification

   prefix or root: "bio"—life and "metric"—measure

2. *unique* _____

   prefix or root: _____

3. *automated* _____

   prefix or root: _____

4. *multiple* _____

   prefix or root: _____

5. *inoperable* _____

   prefix or root: _____

Language Tip: Word Forms

Becoming familiar with various word forms can increase your comprehension of what you read, and it can also improve your editing. Word forms are the shapes and spellings that English words assume as they change functions in a sentence. These functions include nouns, verbs, adjectives, and adverbs.

- Noun: name of a person, place, thing, or idea—for example, woman, city, house, communication
- Verb: a word that shows action (go, buy) or a state of being (be, is, are, seem).
- Adjective: a word that describes a noun—for example, *beautiful* picture, *sad* face
- Adverb: a word that describes a verb or an adjective—for example, plays *carelessly*, is *very* careless

Notice how the meaning and form of the word success change in each of the following sentences.

1. The new computer game was a big *success.* (noun)
2. The computer game was the most *successful* new product this year. (adjective—it describes the game)
3. Mari *successfully* loaded the game on her home computer. (adverb—it describes how well she loaded the game)
4. She *succeeded* in mastering all the levels of the game. (verb, in the past tense)

As you see, the word success has a noun form as well as verb, adverb, and adjective forms. Many words go through spelling changes like this as they change function. Recognizing these changes allows you to understand a word that at first looks unfamiliar. If you know the meaning of the root word, you'll have no trouble understanding its forms.

© 2014 Wadsworth, Cengage Learning

Exercise 12   Use Word Forms

In the chart below, list the other forms of the word that is given. The first one has been done for you. Use your dictionary if you need help. Not all words have every form.

Noun	Verb	Adjective	Adverb
1. explosion	explode	explosive	explosively
2. _____	_____	_____	creatively
3. _____	trick	_____	_____
4. _____	inform	_____	_____
5. _____	_____	supportive	_____
6. _____	_____	_____	cautiously
7. sympathy	_____	_____	_____
8. _____	_____	correct	_____
9. imagination	_____	_____	_____
10. _____	_____	_____	radiantly

Suffixes   Suffixes are the endings of many words. They frequently tell us what **part of speech** the word is; that is, whether it is a noun, adjective, or adverb. Parts of speech tell you what function a word has within a sentence. Dictionaries also identify the parts of speech for a word and its various forms.

Look carefully at the following list of common suffixes. As you go through the list, write your own examples in the spaces provided. If you can't think of other examples, browse through the dictionary to find some.

part of speech classification of a word according to its function in a sentence, such as noun, verb, adjective, adverb

Nouns   Nouns are the names of persons, places, things, ideas, or qualities. Following are some noun suffixes.

Suffix	Meaning	Example	Your Examples
-or, -er, -ist	a person	communicator,	_____
-ee, -ian		teacher, futur-ist, referee, physician	_____ _____
-acy, -archy	an act, form of government	democracy, oligarchy	_____ _____
-ence, -ance	an act	attendance,	_____

© 2014 Wadsworth, Cengage Learning

-ation, -tion	a state	communication, retention	_____ _____
-sion, -ment	a condition	restriction, tension, resentment	_____ _____
-ism	a belief, form of government	socialism	_____ _____
-ship, -hood -ness	having to do with, referring to	relationship, neighborhood, friendliness	_____ _____ _____
-logy	the science or study of	biology	_____
-ability, -ibility	a quality	responsibility, dependability	_____

Adjectives Adjectives modify (add to, describe in more detail) the meaning of nouns and pronouns. Following are some adjective suffixes.

Suffix	Meaning	Example	Your Examples
-able, -ible	able to be	reliable, responsible	_____
-al, -ic, -ing	having a char-	practical, toxic,	_____
-ive, -ous	acteristic, related to	insulting, communicative, serious	_____ _____
-ful	full of	plentiful	_____ _____

Adverbs Adverbs explain how or when an action occurs. Following are some applications of the adverb suffix *ly*.

Suffix	Meaning	Example	Your Examples
-ly	describes *how* something is done (sometimes they are added to the endings of adjectives)	effectively, responsibly, insultingly, quickly	_____ _____ _____

© 2014 Wadsworth, Cengage Learning

Exercise 13

Use Suffixes (Part 1)

Add suffixes to each of the following words to change its function.

	Noun	Adjective	Adverb
1. help	_____	_____	_____
	_____	_____	_____
2. play	_____	_____	_____
3. tolerate	_____	_____	_____
4. mess	_____	_____	_____
5. tempt	_____	_____	_____

Exercise 14

Use Suffixes (Part 2)

Read the following excerpt from an article about distance education. Circle the words with suffixes that you recognize. Then list five of these words in the space provided, and identify each word's part of speech.

> With online courses, schools can draw students from just about anywhere. That's especially appealing to what educators call "nontraditional" students, who may be trying to fit in school with responsibilities at work and home. This group is one of the fastest-growing in the education world, and it's a main reason that the number of distance-learning programs in colleges and universities has skyrocketed in the last few years. More than 1.5 million students signed up for courses. (Kantrowitz, "Finding a Niche in Education")

	Word	Part of speech
1.	_____	_____
2.	_____	_____
3.	_____	_____
4.	_____	_____
5.	_____	_____

© 2014 Wadsworth, Cengage Learning

Reading 3

A Little Help from Our (Robot) Friends

— Guaya B. López

The following reading discusses the possibility of personal service robots becoming a part of our lives. As you read, consider the likelihood that you or someone you know or know about will have one of these robots in your lifetime. Also, watch for the meaning of words in context and the use of word parts.

1   Too busy to wash the clothes or do the dishes? Is the house a mess? Are the kids making you crazy? Is Grandma lonely for company? What you need is a personal robot. He or she or it can take your worries away!

2   For decades, people have speculated about or considered the possibilities of helpful personal robots—machines that could live with us, work for us, entertain us, and even be our companions. Movies and TV shows like *The Jetsons* and *Futurama* have depicted, or shown, robot characters living alongside humans performing a variety of roles. While

fictional
imaginary

these fictional robots might seem far-fetched to most people today, many industry specialists say that soon robots will be serving us coffee, dancing with us, taking care of our grandparents, and fetching us beers from the refrigerator.[1] Robotics is a competitive and fast-growing industry, and the demand for these smart machines in our increasingly digital and busy society is also growing fast. Soon, many people's dreams of robot servants, secretaries, and friends will become reality.

3   Already robots—in many forms and for varied purposes—are increasingly common. The world's total robot population has already passed 4.49 million, and in a 2006 study the International Federation of Robotics predicted that the world robot population will grow to 18.3 million in the next five years. More than half of the world's robots are service robots. While some of these are used in military and security applications, most are personal service robots.[2]

4   The personal service category includes a wide range of robots, from furry robot pets, robot vacuum cleaners, and lawnmowers, to humanoid robots that look and "act" like people. They can carry trays, hold your hand, guard your house, and sing you songs. This category of robots is the one that will have the most noticeable impact on our lives in the future, and it is the one that has most fascinated the popular imagination. The innovations, or new developments, in industrial robots that work in factories, milk cows, and defuse bombs will have only an indirect effect on our lives.

5   When they think of a "robot," many people immediately imagine upright robots with a head, a face, two arms, and two legs. However, many of today's personal robots are not human-like at all. Some are like animals. Giga Pets and Tamagotchi toy robots were popular with kids after their release in 1996 and 1997. The keychain-sized computers with a tiny screen depicted a virtual animal that required feeding, cleaning, and attention from its owner. Today's robot pets are advanced versions of Giga Pets or Tamagotchis that can walk around, play games, make noises, and enjoy being petted. These robot pets are not just toys for kids; some are promoted as helpful therapy tools for hospital patients, the mentally ill, and the elderly. One such therapy pet is a fluffy seal called Paro, built by Japan's National Institute of Advanced Industrial Science and Technology. An engineer from the institute explains that nursing home residents' stress levels go down after interacting with Paro. "We know that pet therapy helps physically,

Guaya B. López. Written for *Joining a Community of Readers*. Used by permission.

© 2014 Wadsworth, Cengage Learning

psychologically and socially, and Paro does the same thing for people who are unable to care for a live pet," he claims.[3] Such robots are especially useful companions for elderly and sick people who do not receive much human attention. This type of robot is important in the industrialized countries where lower birth rates mean that there are fewer young people to take care of the elderly.

6   One of the most well-known pet robots and the world's first mass-marketed robot was Sony's dog called AIBO.[4] AIBOs are similar to real dogs in many ways but can be kept in any apartment, don't need food, and don't need to go to the bathroom. They can learn to recognize the faces of three people as well as up to 100 words and commands. They are also programmed to develop individual personalities based on how they are raised by their owners. Because of AIBO's friendly character, it established a customer base of many happy owners.

7   Of all the types of personal service robots, the humanoid ones are the most exciting and have the most potential. Some corporations, stores, and museums already use them as receptionists, guides, and assistants. Some of these robots have starred in music videos, toured the world, and been featured on TV shows. Honda Motor Company is the maker of today's most advanced bipedal, or two-legged humanoid robot. The robot is called ASIMO, a name that stands for Advanced Step in Innovative Mobility, and was created with the intention of helping people in need.[5] ASIMO is designed to function alongside people in a human environment. This robot is just tall enough to reach door handles, counters, tables, and computers with its hands while also able to look at seated adults in the eyes for natural conversation. ASIMO is also able to walk up stairs and move at 3.7 mph, the speed necessary for it to do the things that people need. It is programmed to listen to human voices and respond to simple verbal commands. These abilities allow ASIMO to be useful in many places doing many jobs. It would be the perfect assistant for a disabled or elderly person who needed help around the house.

8   Another humanoid service robot is Wakamaru, made by Mitsubishi. This robot is meant to fit in as a member of the family. It can carry out household tasks but is also a skilled communicator, recognizing ten faces and engaging people in conversations.[6] This cute-looking robot can memorize your schedule and remind you of appointments as well as send emails for you and take telephone messages when you are out of the house. While you are away from home, Wakamaru can maintain video surveillance of your house and contact you if anything unusual occurs. Wakamaru is a good example of the type of robot that may soon be operating in many people's homes.

9   It won't be long before ASIMO, Wakamaru, and the other humanoid service robots can be programmed to do important tasks just as well as or better than humans. Their work will free up time for humans and make our lives better and easier. Elderly people, children, and disabled people will especially benefit. But, because we're human, do you think we'll begin worrying about our robots? Will we wonder if they are happy, or too tired to wash the clothes or do the dishes? Because they are so helpful, we might begin to think that they are human, too!

Notes

1. "'Bot Battle between Sony, Honda," at www.wired.com/gadgets/miscellaneous/news/2002/03/51161 (accessed 2/12/09).

2. Erico Guizzo, "10 Stats You Should Know about Robots," at http://blogs. spectrum. ieee.org/automaton/2008/03/21/10_stats_you_should_know_ about_robots.html (accessed 2/12/09).

© 2014 Wadsworth, Cengage Learning

3. Marsha Walton, "Meet Paro, the Therapeutic Robot Seal," at www.cnn. com/2003/ TECH/ptech/11/20/comdex.bestof/ (accessed 2/12/09).

4. Yuri Kageyama, "Sony Scraps Four-legged Robot Pet Aibo," at www.usatoday.com/ tech/news/robotics/2006-02-01-goodbye-aibo_x.htm (accessed 2/12/09).

5. "ASIMO News Archive," at http://asimo.honda.com/News.aspx (accessed 2/12/09).

6. Wakamaru Communication Robot, http://www.mhi.co.jp/en/products/detail/ wakamaru.html (accessed 6/1/12).

Exercise 15

Work with Words

Read the following sentences from Reading 3. Based on the context and word-part clues, write brief definitions of each italicized word.

1. For decades, people have *speculated about* or considered the possibilities of helpful personal robots—machines that could live with us, work for us, entertain us, and even be our companions. (par. 2)

   speculated about _____

2. Movies and TV shows like The *Jetsons* and *Futurama* have depicted, or shown, robot characters living alongside humans performing a variety of roles. (par. 2)

   depicted _____

3. The personal service category includes a wide range of robots, from furry robot pets, robot vacuum cleaners, and lawnmowers, to *humanoid* robots that look and "act" like people. (par. 4)

   humanoid _____

4. The *innovations*, or new developments, in industrial robots that work in factories, milk cows, and defuse bombs will have only an indirect effect on our lives. (par. 4)

   innovations _____

5. Some of these robots have starred in music videos, toured the world, and been featured on TV shows. Honda Motor Company is the maker of today's most advanced *bipedal*, or two-legged humanoid robot. (par. 7)

   bipedal _____

6. It is programmed to listen to human voices and *respond* to simple *verbal* commands. (par. 7)

   respond _____

© 2014 Wadsworth, Cengage Learning

7. *verbal* _____

8. While you are away from home, Wakamaru can maintain video *surveillance* of your house and contact you if anything unusual occurs. (par. 8)

   surveillance _____

Exercise 16

Check Your Understanding

Choose the best answers to the following multiple-choice questions about Reading 3.

1. The personal service category of robots includes
   a. robots used in the auto manufacture industry.
   b. military and dairy robots.
   c. humanoid as well as vacuum and lawn mowing robots.

2. An example of a humanoid personal robot is the
   a. Tamagotchi robot.
   b. the ASIMO.
   c. the AIBO

3. Which of the following tasks *can't* the ASIMO do?
   a. walk up stairs.
   b. star in music videos.
   c. cry when its feelings are hurt.

4. The Wakamaru robot is designed to
   a. fit in as a member of the family.
   b. greet people in offices.
   c. assist in surgical rooms.

5. Which of the following statements best describes how the author feels about robots?
   a. Robots will make people lazy.
   b. Robots will make our lives better.
   c. Robots are great, but are too expensive for most people to benefit from them.

Exercise 17

Make Connections and Write

Write answers to the following questions based on Reading 3, your experience, and your observations. Then discuss your answers with your class group. Working together, prepare a report for your class as a whole or a written summary for your instructor.

© 2014 Wadsworth, Cengage Learning

1. Do you think it's a good idea to have a robot that takes care of children and old people? Explain your answer.

   _____

   _____

   _____

2. What can you think of that might limit our access to personal robots? Explain your answer.

   _____

   _____

   _____

3. If you could have a personal robot, what kinds of things would you like it to do? Why?

   _____

   _____

   _____

4. Do you think that people will begin to think of the robots with which they live as having feelings? Explain your answer.

   _____

   _____

   _____

5. What are some of the things people do that a robot will never be able to do? Explain your answer.

   _____

   _____

   _____

© 2014 Wadsworth, Cengage Learning

DICTIONARY SKILLS

The ultimate resource for understanding new words is the dictionary. When you read for college classes, it's important to have a dictionary handy. But do not look up a new word in the dictionary as soon as you see it. Doing so will distract you from your reading. If you look up five words on a page (which is really not all that many), by the time you get to the end of the page you will not remember what you have read.

Instead of going straight to the dictionary, put a *small check in pencil* by the word. When you finish the page or the section of the text, go back to it. Maybe you have already been able to figure it out from context or word parts. If not, look for it in the textbook aids. If you don't find it there, then go to the dictionary.

The dictionary is the last resort. Before you look up new words in the dictionary, ask yourself these questions:

- Do I need to know the exact meaning of the word to understand the reading?
- Is the word important? Will it be necessary to remember that word because it is key to understanding the subject?
- Have I tried to figure out the meaning of the word from the context but still feel unsure about the meaning?

If you answered yes to these questions, go to the dictionary or glossary. If the word you need to look up is in the glossary of your textbook, that will be the best definition for the context.

Parts of a Dictionary Entry   If you decide to go to the dictionary, you will have a number of choices. There are many different types of dictionaries, including books, Web applications, and CD-ROMs. Dictionaries do not all provide the exact same definitions. Some dictionaries will be easier to understand and may include features such as sample sentences. Some also have an audio portion to help you with the pronunciation of a word. However, all dictionary entries share certain characteristics. You will want to be aware of the different kinds of information every dictionary entry provides. For example, if, in a recent computer magazine about new technology in music, you read, "Online radio allows free access to a dizzying array of programming," you might want to check the meaning of the word *array* in the dictionary.

You would find an entry something like this:

> **ar·ray** (ə-rā′) *tr.v.* **ar·rayed, ar·raying, ar·rays. 1.** To set out for display or use; place in an orderly arrangement: *arrayed the whole regiment on the parade ground.* **2.** To dress in finery; adorn. **-ar·ray** *n.* **1.** An orderly, often imposing arrangement: *an array of royal jewels.* **2.** An impressively large number, as of persons or objects: *an array of heavily armed troops; an array of spare parts.*

(American Heritage Dictionary)

Notice that the dictionary entry gives you a great deal of specific information. With some variations, most dictionaries list the following information.

- *Pronunciation* (in parentheses after the word). A phonetic key at the beginning of the dictionary, or sometimes at the bottom of every page, will help you figure out how to pronounce the word.

© 2014 Wadsworth, Cengage Learning

- *Part of speech* (after each form given for the word). The dictionary has, usually in the beginning, a list of abbreviations that includes those for the parts of speech. The entry for *array* has the abbreviation *tr.v.*, which means transitive verb. Transitive verbs must be followed by another word called an object. *Arrayed, arraying,* and *arrays* are other spellings of the verb *array* used to express tense. After the entry for *array* as a verb, there is another entry for the same word as a noun, and in this case, the abbreviation *n.* follows the word. In the sentence "Online radio allows free access to a dizzying array of programming," *array* is used as a noun. (The abbreviation *n.* means noun, *v.* means verb, *intr.v* means intransitive verb, *adv.* means adverb, and *adj.* means adjective.)
- *Definition(s)*—usually numbered. Often there is more than one meaning for a word. The dictionary shows various meanings by listing additional definitions using both letters and numbers. Notice that *array* has two definitions as a verb and two definitions as a noun listed here.
- *Other forms of the word.* The word *array* has two forms—noun and verb. Some words, as we have seen, have adjective and adverb forms as well.
- *Examples of how the word is used.* Phrases in italics show how the word is used. Some dictionaries give a quotation in which the word has been used by a famous author.
- *Other information.* Some dictionary entries also give *synonyms; idioms,* or special uses; slang or informal usages; and the origins of words.

Exercise 18

Use a Dictionary

The sentence we examined—"Online radio allows free access to a dizzying array of programming"—has other words we might look up in the dictionary. Examine the following dictionary entry for *dizzying,* and answer the questions that follow. (Notice that *dizzying* is not the main entry because it is just one of the forms of the word *dizzy.*)

diz·zy (dĭz′ē) *adj.* **diz·zi·er, diz·zi·est. 1.** Having a whirling sensation and a tendency to fall. See Synonyms at **giddy. 2.** Bewildered or confused. **3.a.** Producing or tending to produce giddiness: *a dizzy height.* **b.** Caused by giddiness; reeling. **4.** Characterized by impulsive haste; very rapid: *"The American language had begun its dizzy onward march before the Revolution"* (H.L. Mencken). **5.** *Slang.* Scatterbrained or silly. **–diz·zy** *tr.v.* **diz·zied, diz·zy·ing, diz·zies. 1.** To make dizzy. **2.** To confuse or bewilder. **–diz′zi·ly** *adv.* **– diz′zi·ness** *n.* **–diz′zy·ing·ly** *adv.*

(American Heritage Dictionary)

1. What are the adjective forms of *dizzy?*

   _____

2. How many noun forms of *dizzy* are in this dictionary entry? Name one.

   _____

© 2014 Wadsworth, Cengage Learning

3. Which of the definitions best fits the meaning of *dizzying* in the context of the sentence?

_____

4. Although the word *dizzying* is used as an adjective in the sentence, what word form is it listed under in this dictionary entry?

_____

Choosing the Right Definition As you've now seen from entries for *array* and *dizzy,* dictionary entries can present several different definitions of a single word. You must choose the correct definition for the word you want to understand. In addition, sometimes it may be important to consult more than one source in order to find the best definition for the context, or the definition that helps you to understand most clearly. Though the meaning should be similar, print dictionaries, online dictionaries, and textbooks all use different words in their definitions.

For example, if you read this sentence, "YouTube streams more than four billion videos a day," you might want a more exact definition of *stream*. If you decide to look it up in the dictionary, you will find at least five different definitions of *stream* as a noun and four different definitions as a verb. Common definitions for the noun form include "flowing water, like a narrow river," "a continuous current," and "a series of events or ideas that follow one another." As a verb, *stream* can mean to "move or flow in a specific direction," "give off an ongoing beam of light," or "transmit audio or video material over the Internet." Only the final definition fits the context of your original sentence. However, if you were to find the definition in a computer science textbook, it would probably give more information than the standard dictionary definition. The text would likely explain that to stream audio or video is to play files that have not been completely downloaded from the Internet or to play these files while they are in the process of being downloaded. The text would also clarify that streaming large audio or video files requires a fast Internet connection in order to avoid interruptions or breaks.

Exercise 19

Use a Dictionary

Read the following excerpt from an article on a Web game from *Computer Graphics World*, paying close attention to the *italicized* words. Then find the correct definition for each italicized word using a dictionary. Write the definition and the part of speech (noun, verb, adjective, adverb) on the lines provided. Some of these words will be familiar to you, but your job here is to find them in a dictionary entry and choose the correct definition for this context.

© 2014 Wadsworth, Cengage Learning

Have you ever wondered what it's like to get behind the wheel of an Indy car, *zoom* around the *track* at the Indianapolis 500, and get the wave of the checkered flag? Now, racing fans can trade in their backseat-driver title and compete against the actual performances of Buddy Lazier and other Indy Racing League (IRL) champions in a new online racing game.

Developed by AniVision of Huntsville, Alabama, the Net Race Live game places Internet players in the driver's seat of a *virtual* Indy car, which is inserted into data captured from actual Indy events. Within 20 minutes of an Indy race's completion, all the track data from the event–including each pit stop, caution flag, and crash—is *streamed* to the company's Web site where a player can participate in a re-created *simulation* of the event. (Moltenbrey, "Real-Time Racing")

Definition	Part of Speech
1. *zoom*	
2. *track*	
3. *virtual*	
4. *streamed*	
5. *simulation*	

© 2014 Wadsworth, Cengage Learning

Organize to Learn:
Your Personal Vocabulary Plan

Having a good vocabulary is one of the most important factors in becoming a strong reader. Probably the best way to improve your vocabulary is to develop your own system, or vocabulary plan. This system should include general vocabulary as well as the specialized vocabulary you need for your college courses and career plans.

To develop your personal vocabulary start by listing words you need to learn. Choose them carefully. They should be words that you have encountered more than once, that are important and useful, and that are fairly common in the English language generally or in your field of study specifically.

Enter each word in a notebook, in separate computer documents, or on a three-by-five card. Be sure to keep your notebook, documents, or cards in a place where it will be easy for you to check them periodically for a quick review. Using textbook vocabulary aids or a college-level dictionary, write the appropriate definition and part of speech for each word. Next, copy the sentence in which you first saw the word used, followed by a sentence of your own in which you use it. Finally, write the other forms of the word listed in the glossary or dictionary and the part of speech of each.

If you use three-by-five cards, they might look like this:

Word: SIMULATION

Appropriate definition: Imitation or representation of a real situation or experiment

Sentence from reading. "Within 20 minutes of an Indy race's completion, all the track data from the event – including each pit stop, caution flag, and crash – is streamed to the company's Web site, where a player can participate in a recreated simulation of the event."

My sentence using the word: I wonder if playing with the basketball game simulation at Children's Museum will help my brother's game.

Other forms of the word:

    Simulate, simulated, and simulating - verbs

    Simulator - noun

    Simulated and simulative - adjectivesv

Exercise 20   Start Your Personal Vocabulary System

Select five words that you would like to learn from the readings in this chapter or from any other college reading you're currently doing. Record them and practice using them in a notebook, in a computer document, or on three-by-five cards. When you have used your new words successfully a number of times, they will have become permanent parts of your personal vocabulary.

© 2014 Wadsworth, Cengage Learning

| Reading 4 | # Orwell's Future Has Arrived |

— Myesha Ward

In the following reading, Myesha Ward reports on surveillance or spying technologies that exist and are being developed. She is concerned about our gradual loss of privacy, as well as our loss of constitutional rights, because these new computer-driven devices can discover and report the most intimate details of our lives. Although she emphasizes the dangers of these developments, think about the benefits as well as the risks of surveillance technology and watch for new words you may want to add to your vocabulary.

1   In 1949, George Orwell published a novel titled *Nineteen Eighty-Four*. In it, he created a dark vision of a future society in which people's actions and minds are effectively monitored with "telescreens" in every room and controlled by Big Brother. His book was classified as science fiction, that is, a work of literature based on the imagination, dealing with the consequences of science and technology—real or imagined—on society and individuals. Unfortunately, at the beginning of the twenty-first century, more than a half century after Orwell's novel was published, the key element—all-pervasive spying on the citizens—has left the realm of imagination and become our reality. Today the technology exists for corporations and the government to know everything about you. You might wonder what this means, and why you should worry about it.

2   Here are some possible scenarios we could see in the near future: [1]

affluent
wealthy

- An African American man from an inner-city neighborhood visits an affluent area of town to attend the barbeque of a coworker. A crime takes place that same night, and the police review all of the surveillance camera images to identify the man. The next day they interrogate him at his home because he was in a part of the city where he "didn't belong." This makes him a suspect in a crime.
- A tourist happens to stop and glance at the display window of a sex shop. The store has a customer identification system which gets information about her from her driver's license. A week later, she gets an advertisement in the mail mentioning her "visit" to the shop, embarrassing her in front of her family.

These are only a few of the scenarios that are possible in the very near future. What are these scenarios based upon, and why are people worried?

3   One of the scariest and most widely criticized governmental projects was the Total Information Awareness (TIA) system, a project of the Department of Defense. [2] Established in the fall of 2002, its purpose was supposed to be to create a database to prevent terrorism. The system, once put into place, would have put together information about everyone in the United States, including travel and telephone records, credit card use, purchasing habits, driver's license history, and Internet use like e-mail. Although Congress blocked the TIA, many worry about where the invasion of personal privacy could lead us. Indeed, information databases, combined with the availability of tiny sensors, cheap hardware, and wireless networks, lead to some frightening possibilities. According to Declan McCullagh of CNETNews.com, we may eventually "face the emergence of unblinking electronic eyes that record where we are and what we do, whenever we interact." [3]

sensors
devices that can pick up sounds and/or visual images

emergence
introduction and use of something new

© 2014 Wadsworth, Cengage Learning

Myesha Ward. Written for *Joining a Community of Readers*.

Some Scary Technology

iris
colored portion of
the eye

4   A variety of biometric technologies can identify people on the basis of certain attributes such as iris patterns, facial characteristics, and fingerprints. Some people are even proposing that we have national ID cards with our DNA (our unique genetic makeup) encoded into them. Already, fingerprint scanners are used for security or payment mechanisms for office buildings, grocery stores, and even some fast-food restaurants. Many companies are trying to perfect a chip that would hold our DNA and be able to identify individuals instantly.

5   Many of the things you may already own can track your movements and tattle on you.

- *Cell phones.* The government has required that each cell phone be capable of reporting its exact location. Originally this feature was added to aid the caller making a 911 call. But the phones can track location at all times, and it is easy to imagine that one day the government will allow phone companies to give out information about the movements of their customers.
- *Car computers.* All cars manufactured today have computers in them. And these computers could be used to report you to the police. One car rental agency already tried to charge a customer extra because it found out he had exceeded the speed limit.
- *RFID chips.* These devices put out a signal with a unique code. They are now used for toll-booth speed passes. But in the near future, according to the American Civil Liberties Union (ACLU), "They will allow everyday objects to 'talk' to each other— or to anyone else who is listening. For example, they could let market researchers scan the contents of your purse or car from five feet away, or let police officers scan your identification when they pass you on the street." The ACLU explains further, "It is easy to imagine how national IDs could be combined with an RFID chip to allow for convenient, at-a-distance verification of ID. The IDs could then be tied to access control points around our public places, so that the unauthorized could be kept out of office buildings, apartments, public transit, and secure public buildings. Citizens with criminal records . . . or low incomes could be barred from accessing airports, sports arenas, stores, or other facilities. Retailers might add RFID readers to find out exactly who is browsing their aisles, gawking at their window displays from the sidewalk, or passing by without looking. A network of automated RFID listening posts on the sidewalks and roads could even reveal the location of all citizens at all times. Pocket ID readers could be used by FBI agents to sweep up the identities of everyone at a political meeting, protest march, or Islamic prayer service."[4]
- *Implantable GPS chips.* A special computer chip that can record and broadcast its location. The GPS chip could be hidden in a purse or wallet so that a jealous husband or wife could spy on one another. These chips can also be planted under the skin.

unauthorized
not officially approved

What's Happening to the Bill of Rights?

Bill of Rights
the first ten
amendments to the
U.S. Constitution

6   Every schoolchild in this country learns about the U.S. Constitution and the Bill of Rights as establishing our country's basic democratic principles. But even the fundamental rights guaranteed in these documents to every American citizen are being undermined.

7   The First Amendment to the Constitution guarantees the right to freedom of speech. However, people who exercise that right by legally gathering to protest actions of the

© 2014 Wadsworth, Cengage Learning

amendment
an addition (or change) to the U.S. Constitution

government that they oppose are now subjected to camera surveillance. Washington, D.C has special video cameras located in strategic locations around the city that record participants in mass demonstrations. Not so many years ago, we used to think that only totalitarian regimes (such as that of North Korea) would use publicly located cameras to spy on their citizens.

8   The Fourth Amendment to the Constitution guarantees the right of the people to be protected from "unreasonable searches and seizures." Now, the technologies available give the government abilities that are like Superman's X-ray vision. The government is capable of "searches and seizures" of information about us without our knowing it, and without even entering our homes or cars.

9   Although technological snooping like that described in Orwell's science fiction is already here, there are elected officials, rights advocacy groups, and informed citizens all over the country who are actively fighting to protect your privacy rights. To find out more about this issue and about what you can do about it, look up the Web page of the American Civil Liberties Union. Using a search engine, such as Google, type "American Civil Liberties Union privacy" into the search box in order to find this page.

Notes

1. Jay Stanley and Barry Steinhardt, "Bigger Monster, Weaker Chains," *American Civil Liberties Union report,* January 2003, 1.

2. "Total Information Awareness," *Washington Post,* November 16, 2002 , A20.

3. Declan McCullagh, "George Orwell, Here We Come," CNET News.com, January 6, 2003.

4. Stanley and Steinhardt, 7, 13.

Exercise 21

Work with Words

Read the following sentences from Reading 4, and write a brief definition of the italicized word or words using your knowledge of context clues, word parts, and the dictionary.

1. His book was classified as *science fiction*, that is, a work of literature based on the imagination, dealing with the consequences of science and technology—real or imagined—on society and individuals. (par. 1)

   science fiction _____

   _____

2. Unfortunately, at the beginning of the twenty-first century, more than a half century after Orwell's novel was published, the key element— *all-pervasive* spying on the citizens—has left the *realm* of fiction and become our reality. (par. 1)

   all-pervasive _____

3. *realm* _____

   _____

© 2014 Wadsworth, Cengage Learning

4. The next day they *interrogate* him at his home because he was in a part of the city where he "didn't belong." (par. 2)

   interrogate _____

5. A variety of *biometric* technologies can identify people on the basis of certain *attributes* such as iris patterns in the eyes, facial characteristics, and fingerprints. (par. 4)

   biometric _____

   _____

6. *attributes* _____

7. *iris* _____

   _____

8. But even the fundamental rights guaranteed in these documents to every American citizen are being *undermined*. (par. 6)

   undermined _____

9. The First Amendment to the Constitution guarantees the right to freedom of speech. However, people who exercise that right by legally gathering to protest actions of the government that they oppose are now subjected to camera *surveillance*. (par. 7)

   surveillance _____

10. Although technological snooping like that described in Orwell's science fiction is already here, there are elected officials, rights *advocacy* groups, and informed citizens all over the country who are actively fighting to protect your privacy rights. (par. 9)

    advocacy _____

Exercise 22

Check Your Understanding

Choose the best answers to the following multiple-choice questions about Reading 4.

1. George Orwell was a
   a. scientist.
   b. novelist.
   c. technology expert.

© 2014 Wadsworth, Cengage Learning

2. The Total Information Awareness system was a plan to
   a. protect the privacy rights of American citizens.
   b. depend on the expertise of Declan McCullagh.
   c. create a database of information about everyone in the United States.

3. Which of the following is an example of scary technology given by the author?
   a. CNETNews.com
   b. a display window of a sex shop
   c. RFID chips

4. The bulleted list in paragraph 5 is a list of
   a. possessions that can transmit and record your movements.
   b. all aspects of car computer capabilities.
   c. all aspects of implantable GPS chips capabilities.

5. The author emphasizes the ways in which
   a. our consumer rights are threatened by the new technology.
   b. our Bill of Rights is threatened by the new technology.
   c. the new technology is really no threat because it will be closely monitored.

Exercise 23

Make Connections and Write

Write short answers to the following questions based on Reading 4, your experience, and your observations. Then discuss your answers with your class group. Working together, prepare a report for your class as a whole or a written summary for your instructor.

1. Briefly explain our First and Fourth Amendment rights.

   _____

   _____

   _____

   _____

2. Do you think that there are some good reasons why these rights should be taken away? Explain your reasons for your answer.

   _____

   _____

   _____

   _____

© 2014 Wadsworth, Cengage Learning

3. What kinds of laws do you think could be passed to protect citizens' First and Fourth Amendment rights from some of these technological advances?

_____

_____

_____

_____

4. How many times is your picture taken during a regular day? Who takes your picture and for what purposes?

_____

_____

_____

_____

5. Do you think it's appropriate for businesses to use surveillance technology and, if so, under what circumstances? Explain your answer.

_____

_____

_____

_____

6. What, in your opinion, are the most important benefits of the available surveillance technology?

_____

_____

_____

_____

© 2014 Wadsworth, Cengage Learning

Chapter Review

To aid your review of the reading skills in Chapter 2, study the Put It Together chart.

Put It Together: Working with Words	
Skills and Concepts	Explanation
Clues to help you understand the meaning of a word	
Textbook Vocabulary Aids	All of the features that textbooks provide to assist students in understanding new vocabulary
Context (see pages 65–66)	Context is the sentence or paragraph in which a word appears.
Definition (see pages 65–66)	A definition answers the question: "What does it mean?"
Synonym (see pages 65–66)	A synonym is a word that has the same or a similar meaning as another word.
Example (see page 67)	Example clues help you understand the meaning of a word based on examples.
Compare (see pages 68–69)	To compare shows how items are alike or similar.
Contrast (see pages 68–69)	To contrast shows how items are different.
General information (see pages 70–71)	General information clues help you understand the meaning of a word by putting together all the information you have surrounding the word.
Word parts to help you figure out the meaning of a word	
Root (see pages 77–78)	A root is the core part of a word to which prefixes and suffixes are added.
Prefix (see pages 78–80)	A prefix is an addition at the beginning of a word that changes the word's meaning.
Suffix (see pages 82–83)	A suffix is an ending of a word that often indicates the part of speech.
Dictionary skills (see pages 90–91)	Important dictionary skills include knowing when you need to look a word up in the dictionary, picking the appropriate definition of the word, and understanding dictionary entries.

© 2014 Wadsworth, Cengage Learning

To reinforce your learning before taking the Mastery Tests, complete as many of the following activities as your instructor assigns.

REVIEW SKILLS

Collect 20 technology-related terms from this chapter, from magazines, or from other textbooks. Then, on a separate piece of paper, write a definition for each and state where you got the definition—textbook aid, context, word parts, or the dictionary.

COLLABORATE

Work together in a group to answer the following questions:

1. What kinds of communications technology do you now use?
2. How has this technology already been improved since you first started using it?
3. How has this technology changed your way of doing things? How has it changed your way of life?

Enter your group's answers in the following chart.

Technological Devices or Applications	Improvements	Lifestyle Changes
1. _____	_____	_____
2. _____	_____	_____
3. _____	_____	_____
4. _____	_____	_____

Write

Use your imagination, the information you read in this chapter, and the information your group accumulated in the collaborative activity to write a description of the communication patterns and technology that you think will be in place 10 or 20 years from now. Feel free to dream about what you see as ideal or, on the other hand, to warn about problems technology might create in the future.

EXTEND YOUR THINKING

How advanced is your academic community in utilizing technology to enhance communication? Devise a simple survey and conduct it at your college. What communications technology does your institution use? Is the technology used by a select few, or do all students and faculty members have access to it and the skills to use it? What are the college's plans for technology in the future?

© 2014 Wadsworth, Cengage Learning

WORK THE WEB

1. Use a search engine such as Google to go to the Web site of the online version of the technology magazine *Wired*. Your search might be "Wired Magazine on-line." When you find the *Wired* Web site, click on "Magazine." Then select an article that interests you and read it.

2. What is the title of your article?

   _____

3. Write five words that are new to you. Write the word, the sentence in which it appears, and then use context clues and your dictionary skills to write an appropriate definition and part of speech.

   a. _____

   _____

   b. _____

   _____

   c. _____

   _____

   d. _____

   _____

   e. _____

   _____

© 2014 Wadsworth, Cengage Learning

Name _____ Date _____

Small, Smaller, Smallest: Medical Technology of Today and for the Future

— PAUL HURSEL

In the following reading, Paul Hursel explores recent technology for diagnosing and curing disease. The direction toward very small and even microscopic computers has exciting possibilities for the future of medicine. As you read, use your vocabulary skills from Chapter 2 to help you understand unfamiliar words.

1   When my children were young, one of our favorite books to read together was *The Magic School Bus: Inside the Human Body.*[1] In it, a wonderful schoolteacher with red frizzy hair named Ms. Frizzle took students on a field trip through the human body. The children all boarded a school bus that got smaller and smaller as it traveled through the body, first being swallowed, going down the <u>esophagus</u>, through the stomach, then the small intestines, the blood stream, and finally through the muscles, back to the heart and the lungs. At the end, they got sneezed out of the nose. The book had funny illustrations of the bus traveling through the body, and was a fun way to learn human <u>anatomy</u>. Today, medical doctors can take that trip through the human body, but they do it by using a tiny camera that the patient swallows, which then takes pictures as it travels through the digestive system. Afterward, the doctor can see a "movie" of the in-side of a person's body by watching the images on a computer screen. And pretty soon, doctors will be able to do even more fantastic things as their instruments get smaller and smaller and finally <u>microscopic</u>.

illustration
picture

The Pill

2   Elizabeth Mullikan was one of the first people to benefit from taking a tiny pill, an M2A, with a miniature, disposable color video system and a tiny flashlight contrap-tion in it. The purpose of this vitamin-sized pill is to explore the digestive track, record-ing pictures of everything it "sees." In the process, it transmits the video signals to a little device worn by the patient on a belt. After several hours, doctors can examine the video on their computer screens to diagnose the patient's intestinal problems. The process is relatively painless and much more effective than older procedures for exam-ining the small intestine. Mrs. Mullikan had been suffering from painful intestinal prob-lems for years and had gone through a variety of very uncomfortable procedures, but doctors were unable to figure out the problem. Eight hours after swallowing the M2A, however, her doctor pinpointed her problem: a damaged artery. It was later corrected with surgery.[2]

device
electronic invention

3   Other advances in medical technology have allowed doctors to probe into the deepest <u>recesses</u> of the body. Tiny computerized monitors can detect heart rhythm problems and sometimes even correct them. Diabetics have computerized pumps im-planted under their skin that can deliver regular <u>infusions</u> of insulin. Research is going on now to allow doctors to implant drug dispensers under people's skin that would release exact doses of medication on a specific schedule. Surgical implements are

Paul Hursel. Written for *Joining a Community of Readers*.

© 2014 Wadsworth, Cengage Learning

becoming so small, including tiny computerized robots, that surgery can be much less invasive. Someday a miniature telescope could be placed in the eye, connected to computer chips that would restore vision to the blind.

Nanotechnology

4 All these examples and Mrs. Mullikan's little M2A are just a preview of the uses of miniature technology. The future is in <u>nanotechnology</u>. In fact, the introduction of this new technology will most likely make surgery as we know it today <u>obsolete</u>. It will no longer be necessary to get into the messy business of cutting open a patient in order to "fix" or change something. We will begin to see machines that are so small that even a trillion of them would not be seen by the naked eye. Nanotechnology is the term used to describe research about objects that are measured in nanometers (a billionth of a meter or a millionth of a millimeter). This technology will be applied to telephones, computers, airplanes, as well as to medical uses.

5 Kevin Bonsor describes his vision of nanotechnology's future medical <u>applications</u> in his article, "How Nanotechnology Will Work":

> Nanotechnology may have its biggest impact on the medical industry. Patients will drink fluids containing nanorobots programmed to attack and <u>reconstruct</u> the molecular structure of cancer cells and viruses to make them harmless. There's even speculation that nanorobots could slow or reverse the aging process, and life expectancy could increase significantly. They could fix your teeth, strengthen your bones and clean your body. Nanorobots could also be programmed to perform delicate surgeries—such nanosurgeons could work at a level a thousand times more precise than the sharpest scalpel. By working on such a small scale, a nanorobot could operate without leaving the scars that conventional surgery does. Additionally, nanorobots could change your physical appearance. They could be programmed to perform cosmetic surgery, rearranging your atoms to change your ears, nose, eye color or any other physical feature you wish to alter. [3]

6 The U.S. government is so interested in nanotechnology that it has granted hundreds of millions of dollars to university research laboratories through the Department of Defense and the National Science Foundation. The European Union and Japan have also spent hundreds of millions more funding research. In the private sector, major corporations such as Intel, IBM, Sony, Bell, and Compaq see nanotechnology as the wave of the future, and they want to stay ahead of the times so that they won't lose out on the profits it will generate.

Areas of Concern

7 There are some problems with the tiny tools that you should be aware of. First, instruments such as Mrs. Mullikin's pill are very expensive. The pill itself costs about $450, and the computer system used to "read" the information costs about $26,000. But perhaps a more disturbing problem could develop and science fiction writers like Michael Crichton are fascinated by it. [4] Nanorobots will be programmed to <u>replicate</u> themselves. That means they will reproduce, and some well-respected scientists are concerned with the very real possibility of the evolution of intelligent robots we might not even be able to see that could be developed for destructive purposes. [5]

molecular
having to do with one or more atoms forming the smallest unit of an element

speculation
consideration based on careful thought

alter
change

© 2014 Wadsworth, Cengage Learning

Notes

1. Joanna Cole and Bruce Degan (illustrator), *The Magic School Bus: Inside the Human Body* (New York: Scholastic Inc., 1989).

2. Rob Stein, "Take a Camera and See What Develops," *Washington Post National Weekly Edition,* January 6-12, 2003, 31.

3. Kevin Bonsor, "How Nanotechnology Will Work," on Howstuffworks.com, at www .howstuffworks.com/nanotechnology.htm (accessed 1/19/03).

4. Michael Crichton, *Prey* (New York: HarperCollins, 2002).

5. Bill Joy, "Why the Future Doesn't Need Us," *Wired.com,* April 2000.

Read the following sentences from or about the reading. Use the context clues and word-part clues, and, if necessary, your dictionary to choose the best definitions of the italicized words in the following sentences from the reading.

1. The children all boarded a school bus that got smaller and smaller as it traveled through the body first being swallowed, going down the *esophagus,* through the stomach, then the small intestines, the blood stream, and finally through the muscles, back to the heart and the lungs. (par. 1)

   esophagus
   a. a part of the stomach
   b. a tube leading to the stomach
   c. the top of the mouth

2. The book had funny illustrations of the bus traveling through the body, and was a fun way to learn human *anatomy.* (par. 1)

   anatomy
   a. the science of chemical relationships
   b. the science of physics
   c. the science of the structure of animals and plants

3. And pretty soon, doctors will be able to do even more fantastic things as their instruments get smaller and smaller and finally *microscopic.* (par. 1)

   microscopic
   a. invisible without a microscope
   b. too far away to see with the eye alone
   c. essentially disappeared

4. Other advances in medical technology have allowed doctors to probe into the deepest *recesses* of the body. (par. 3)

   recesses
   a. rest periods
   b. inner areas
   c. organs

5. Diabetics have computerized pumps implanted under their skin that can deliver regular *infusions* of insulin. (par. 3)

   infusions
   a. a specially prepared tea
   b. doses
   c. concoctions

© 2014 Wadsworth, Cengage Learning

6. In fact, the introduction of this new technology will most likely make surgery as we know it today *obsolete*. It will no longer be necessary to get into the messy business of cutting open a patient in order to "fix" or change something. (par. 4)

    obsolete
    a. more modern
    b. messy
    c. out of date

7. *Nanotechnology* is the term used to describe research about objects that are measured in nanometers (a billionth of a meter or a millionth of a millimeter). (par. 4)

    Nanotechnology
    a. study of objects measured in nanometers
    b. nanorobotics
    c. study of future technology

8. Kevin Bonsor describes his vision of nanotechnology's future medical *applications* in his article, "How Nanotechnology Will Work." (par. 5)

    applications
    a. forms for applying to work or college
    b. extensions
    c. uses

9. Patients will drink fluids containing nanorobots programmed to attack and *reconstruct* the molecular structure of cancer cells and viruses to make them harmless. (par. 5)

    reconstruct
    a. build again
    b. make harmless
    c. drink again

10. Nanorobots will be programmed to *replicate* themselves. That means they will reproduce, and some well-respected scientists are concerned with the very real possibility of the evolution of intelligent robots we might not even be able to see that could be developed for destructive purposes. (par. 7)

    replicate
    a. reproduce
    b. placate again
    c. reduce

Choose the best answers to the following multiple-choice questions about the reading.

11. Elizabeth Mullikan was
    a. one of the first doctors to work with the M2A.
    b. a nanotechnology researcher.
    c. a patient who swallowed the M2A.

12. Today, doctors can diagnose some diseases with new techniques using
    a. nanotechnology.
    b. tiny wireless video cameras.
    c. intuition.

© 2014 Wadsworth, Cengage Learning

13. The M2A is an
    a. miniature video system, the size of a pill.
    b. a form of medicine, the size of a pill.
    c. an advanced X-ray machine.

14. The M2A is better than other techniques for diagnosing intestinal problems because
    a. it is more comfortable and more effective.
    b. it is not a very expensive procedure.
    c. it allows the doctor to see the video images while they are being taken.

15. Which of the following is *not* one of the possibilities of nanorobots mentioned in the reading?
    a. They can be used for a variety of medical purposes.
    b. They can be used to change a person's appearance.
    c They can help you become a better student.

16. In paragraph 6, the author focuses on
    a. the importance of nanotechnology
    b. the amount of money and energies being put into nanotechnology.
    c. the many possible applications for nanotechnology.

17. The author probably mentions that the United States, the European Union, and Japan are supporting nanotechnology research so that we
    a. will worry about the future of the planet.
    b. understand the military implications of this technology.
    c. recognize that this technology has very important potential.

18. In paragraph 7 the author focuses on
    a. the disadvantages of the M2A.
    b. the expense of the new technologies.
    c. the problems of the new technologies.

Write short answers to the following questions based on your reading, your observations, and your experience.

19. Who do you think will benefit most from nanotechnology? Explain your answer.

    _____

    _____

    _____

    _____

20. What do you think could be some negative uses of nanotechnology?

    _____

    _____

    _____

    _____

© 2014 Wadsworth, Cengage Learning

Name _____ Date _____

The Cutting Edge of Change

— [ADAPTED FROM] JAMES M. HENSLIN

TEXT BOOK **The following reading from a college sociology textbook presents the reality and potential of computer technology in our society. The author specifically mentions the use of computers in education, the workplace, and in war and terrorism. As you read, consider how computers have influenced your school and work life and how effective you think our technology can be in keeping the world safe from terrorism.**

1   Angela looked in her rearview mirror and realized that the flashing lights and screaming siren might be for her. She felt confused. When she pulled over, an angry voice on a loudspeaker ordered her out of the car.

2   "Back up with your hands in the air!" the voice commanded as she got out of the car. <u>Bewildered</u>, Angela stood frozen for a moment. "Put 'em up now! Right now!" She did as she was told.

3   The officer crouched behind his open door, his gun drawn. When Angela reached the police car—still backing up—the officer grabbed her, threw her to the ground, and handcuffed her hands behind her back. She heard words she would never forget. "You are under arrest for murder. You have the right to remain silent. Anything you say can and will be used against you in a court of law. You have the right to an attorney. If you cannot afford one, one will be provided for you."

4   Angela had never even had a traffic ticket, much less been arrested for anything. Angela's nightmare was due to a "computer error." Her car's license number had been mistakenly entered into the police database instead of the number of a woman wanted for a brutal killing earlier that day.

5   We are all affected by computers, but few of us have felt their power as directly and dramatically as Angela did. For most of us, the computer's control lies quietly <u>behind the scenes</u>. Although the computer has <u>intruded</u> into our daily lives, most of us never think about it. Our grades are computerized, and our paychecks probably are as well. When we buy groceries, a computer scans our purchases and presents a printout of the name, price, and quantity of each item.

6   Many people are happy with the computer's <u>capacity</u> to improve the quality of life. Others, however, have serious concerns about our computerized society. They worry about errors that can creep into computerized records. They fear that something similar to Angela's problem could happen to them. For others, identity theft and privacy are the issues. Then there is the matter of political control. With terrorists and other criminals moving freely about our society, there are proposals to <u>inject</u> a chip the size of a grain of rice into our bodies. This chip could store our name, address, age, weight, height, hair and skin color, race-ethnicity, where we went to school, our grades, and our work and medical history. It could also include the names and addresses of our friends and associates and even any acts of suspected disloyalty. The chips would be activated by radio, without our knowing that our activities were under surveillance. These types of computerized techniques could allow the government total control over our lives.

7   Let's consider how the computer is changing education, the workplace, and war and terrorism.

Henslin, *Sociology: Down to Earth Approach*, 7e © 2005. Reproduced by permission of Pearson Education, Inc.

© 2014 Wadsworth, Cengage Learning

Computers in Education

8 Computers have become a standard item in education, including our grade schools. Schools that can afford the latest technology are able to better prepare their students for the future. That advantage, of course, goes to students who attend private schools and live in the richest public school districts. This continuing inequality in technology and education helps to <u>perpetuate</u> the social inequalities between the rich and the poor.

Computers and the Workplace

9 The computer is also <u>transforming</u> the workplace. At the simplest level, it affects how we do our work. For example, we now e-mail documents across long distances, saving time, energy, and money.

10 The computer is also bringing changes on a deeper level because it <u>alters</u> social relationships. This change can be both positive and negative. Several million workers now remain at home while computers and <u>modems</u> connect them with their bosses and fellow workers at locations around the country or the world. Working at home could bring families closer together. At the same time, electronic work and "conversations" could reduce our face-to-face contact with fellow workers.

Changes in War and Terrorism

11 Computers have also altered warfare. For example, high-tech planes such as the <u>unmanned</u> Predator can <u>transmit</u> video back to the base even though it has no pilot or crew. When operators on the base see a target they want to hit, they press a button, and the Predator beams a laser onto the target. Enemy ground troops don't know what hit them. They don't see the Predator; they are unaware of the laser. Perhaps just before they are blown to bits, they hear the sound of an incoming bomb. Even outer space may become "weaponized" in the near future. There are plans to use oxygen suckers, robotic bugs, kinetic energy rods—and whatever else military planners can <u>devise</u>. It is one thing, however, to fight an enemy that uses old, outdated technology. It is a different story to face an enemy that possesses technology similar to ours. If this happens, technology will not make war seem like a bloodless game.

Use context clues, word-part clues, and, if necessary, the dictionary to choose the best definitions of the italicized words in the following sentences from the reading.

1. *Bewildered*, Angela stood frozen for a moment. (par. 2)
   bewildered
   a. confused
   b. satisfied
   c. aware

2. For most of us, the computer's control lies quietly *behind the scenes*. (par. 5)
   behind the scenes
   a. obvious
   b. silent
   c. unnoticed

© 2014 Wadsworth, Cengage Learning

20000Name _____ Date _____

3. Although the computer has *intruded* into our daily lives, most of us never think about it. (par. 5)

   intruded
   a. departed peacefully
   b. moved in forcefully
   c. pleasantly changed

4. Many people are happy with the computer's *capacity* to improve the quality of life. (par. 6)

   capacity
   a. ability
   b. inability
   c. enthusiasm

5. With terrorists and other criminals moving freely about our society, there are proposals to *inject* a chip the size of a grain of rice into our bodies. (par. 6)

   inject
   a. care for
   b. place inside
   c. give a shot

6. This continuing inequality in technology and education helps to *perpetuate* the social inequalities between the rich and the poor. (par. 8)

   perpetuate
   a. continue
   b. create
   c. reduce

7. The computer is also *transforming* the workplace. (par. 9)

   transforming
   a. changing
   b. eliminating
   c. reducing

8. The computer is also bringing changes on a deeper level because it *alters* social relationships. (par. 10)

   alters
   a. eliminates
   b. improves
   c. changes

9. Several million workers now remain at home while computers and *modems* connect them with their bosses and fellow workers at locations around the country or the world. (par. 10)

   modems
   a. devices that connect computers to the Internet
   b. machines that type out messages
   c. small quantities of material

© 2014 Wadsworth, Cengage Learning

10. Computers have also altered warfare. For example, high-tech planes such as the *unmanned* Predator can *transmit* video back to the base even though it has no pilot or crew. (par. 11)

    unmanned
    a. without a pilot
    b. with women pilots
    c. with an all-female crew

11. *transmit*
    a. edit
    b. exercise
    c. send

12. There are plans to use oxygen suckers, robotic bugs, kinetic energy rods—and whatever else military planners can *devise*. (par. 11)

    Devise
    a. cancel
    b. plan
    c. resist

Choose the best answer to the following multiple-choice questions about the reading.

13. Angela's story at the beginning of the reading
    a. criticizes police brutality
    b. proves that computers don't make mistakes.
    c. demonstrates that sometimes the information in computer databases can be wrong.

14. An example the author uses for how computers affect our lives is
    a. our television viewing habits.
    b. our paychecks.
    c. voting.

15. Many people believe that
    a. it's better for people to use pen and paper so we won't have to worry about computer errors.
    b. computer technology can lead to identity theft and serious privacy problems.
    c. computers really can solve most of the problems that we create.

16. Which of the following examples does the author use as a privacy problem?
    a. pilotless aircraft
    b. chips injected in our bodies that store information about us
    c. modems that connect computers to the Internet

17. Which of the following examples does the author use as future technology for warfare?
    a. Predator aircraft
    b. semiautomatic weapons
    c. ground troops

© 2014 Wadsworth, Cengage Learning

18. According to the reading, by changing where and how we work, computers
    a. assist mothers in taking care of their children.
    b. make it easier to earn more money.
    c. change our social relationships.

Write short answers to the following questions based on your reading, your observations, and your experience.

19. What do you use a computer for? Explain the things you do with computers.

    _____

    _____

    _____

    _____

    _____

20. What would your life be like without the computers you use? (Mention school, employment, and entertainment.) Would it be better? Explain.

    _____

    _____

    _____

    _____

    _____

© 2014 Wadsworth, Cengage Learning

3 Main Ideas

HOW WE LOOK

Beauty is only skin deep.

- How do you think the couple in the photo wants people to perceive them?

- In what ways is appearance important to all of us?

- Describe a time when you were judged because of something about your appearance.

- Describe a time when you judged other people based on their appearance.

- What do you think the quotation means?

Getting Ready to Read

All of us are concerned with how we look, and we know that perceptions often depend on our looks. "Am I good-looking?" we ask ourselves. "Can I be better looking?" We spend a lot of time, energy, and money developing and expressing our physical image. We wear certain clothes, fix our hair a certain way, decorate our bodies, and even change our bodies to reach—or try to reach—the look we want.

In this chapter, you will read and think about the search for good looks that all of us undertake in one form or another. As you do, you will improve your reading skills by learning how to:

- Identify topics
- Identify main ideas in paragraphs
- Identify central ideas in longer passages or readings
- Identify thesis statements in persuasive readings

© 2014 Wadsworth, Cengage Learning

Skin Deep Matters

— MARTÍN DE LA CRUZ

The following reading suggests how physical appearance can affect your life. As you read, think about how important someone's physical appearance is to you and how it influences the way you react to that person.

1   We like to think that beauty is only skin deep. We recognize that a person's true character, personality, intelligence, compassion, sense of humor—all the characteristics that are important—cannot be measured or guessed by physical appearance or facial features. The truth is, unfortunately, that physical appearance matters.

magnetic resonance imaging technology
a technique for making a picture showing how the brain reacts to something

2   Some interesting studies have investigated how people react to beauty. Harvard Medical School and Massachusetts Institute of Technology researchers used magnetic resonance imaging (MRI) technology to study men's brains when they saw pictures of beautiful women's faces. The pattern they discovered was that the same part of the brain is stimulated as when a hungry person sees food, a gambler sees money, or an addict sees a fix. Beauty, hunger, and addiction apparently cause similar responses in the same part of the brain.

3   For women and children, a first impression of a man may be influenced mainly by his height. Andrea McGinty, who founded a dating service called It's Just Lunch, reports that women will accept almost any shortcoming in a man, as long as he's not short. In an experiment ABC News set up to test McGinty's assertions, women selected tall men over short men even when they were told that the short men were extremely successful: a doctor, a best-selling author, a champion skier, and a millionaire. In another test, elementary school students were asked to match short, medium, and tall men with a series of words. They linked tall men to words like *handsome, strong,* and *smart.* The shortest man was linked to words like *scared, sad,* and *weak.*

4   As these studies indicate, people's lives can be profoundly affected by their looks. Other studies, reported by *Social Psychology Quarterly,* demonstrate that college students and teachers usually perceive attractive individuals as brighter and more capable than those who are less attractive. Employers tend to favor applicants who are more attractive and hire them over less attractive candidates with the same experience and qualifications. And good-looking people earn, on average, 10 percent more than less attractive people. This bias toward good looks holds true in many occupations in which appearance should not matter at all, such as gardening and computer programming.

5   It's interesting to note, however, that marriage choices are strongly influenced by a tendency to homogamy—choosing someone similar to oneself. We may all have dreams about who our eventual mate will be, but we usually marry someone close to our own level of attractiveness. In casual dating, this tendency is not as strong, but the more committed the relationship, the more likely that each person will be very similar to the other on a scale of attractiveness.

6   Most people, once they get to know someone, are capable of changing their first impression. Teachers, after becoming familiar with a student's work and contribution to class, frequently revise their initial assessments of ability. Friendships last because of trust and shared interests, and marriages last not only because of love, but also because of open communication and a willingness to work through difficult situations together. First impressions are certainly influenced by appearance, but lasting relationships are not sustained by appearance alone. In the end, who we are inside is what counts, and ultimate happiness is not tied to good looks.

Written by Martin de la Cruz. Reprinted by permission of the author.

© 2014 Wadsworth, Cengage Learning

Exercise 1

Recall and Discuss

Answer these questions about Reading 1, and prepare to discuss them in class.

1. What does the research at Harvard Medical School and Massachusetts Institute of Technology say about men's brains and beauty?

   _____

   _____

   _____

2. Describe the results of the experiment on women and elementary school students' opinions of men's height.

   _____

   _____

   _____

3. What are some of the ways that people are prejudged because of their appearance?

   _____

   _____

   _____

4. Considering the information in the reading about how people choose marriage partners, do you think that all women prefer tall men for committed relationships? Explain.

   _____

   _____

   _____

5. Do you agree with the author that ultimate happiness is not tied to good looks? Explain your answer.

   _____

   _____

   _____

© 2014 Wadsworth, Cengage Learning

What is a Paragraph About?

The goal of reading is to understand the information the author is trying to communicate. Recognizing the topics and the main ideas in a paragraph are important skills that assist you in understanding everything you read.

TOPICS

topic a key word or phrase that describes the focus of a reading; it says what the paragraph is about

You should always be able to answer one basic question when you read a paragraph: *What is this paragraph about?* When you answer this question, you are identifying the **topic** of the paragraph. You should be able to name the topic in just a few words. The topic is a key word or short phrase that describes the focus of a paragraph.

MAIN IDEAS

main idea what the paragraph says about the topic

main idea sentence a broad or general statement of the main point of the paragraph

In addition to recognizing the topic of a paragraph, you need to be able to answer another question: *What did the paragraph say about the topic?* When you answer this question, you are identifying the **main idea** of the paragraph. The main idea should be stated as a *complete sentence*. The **main idea sentence** is a broad, or general, statement of the main point of the paragraph.

WORKING WITH TOPICS AND MAIN IDEAS

To understand the difference between topics and main ideas, it's helpful to see how they work in example paragraphs. Remember, the topic is what the paragraph is about, and it can be stated in a few words. The main idea is the overall point the author is making about the topic, and it should be a complete sentence. See if you can tell the difference between the topic and the main idea in the following paragraph from Reading 1.

> For women and children, a first impression of a man may be influenced mainly by his height. Andrea McGinty, who founded a dating service called It's Just Lunch, reports that women will accept almost any shortcoming in a man, as long as he's not short. In an experiment ABC News set up to test McGinty's assertions, women selected tall men over short men even when they were told that the short men were extremely successful: a doctor, a best-selling author, a champion skier, and a millionaire. In another test, elementary school students were asked to match short, medium, and tall men with a series of words. They linked tall men to words like *handsome, strong,* and *smart.* The shortest man was linked to words like *scared, sad,* and *weak.*

What is the topic in this paragraph? The topic is *the importance of men's height*—a very brief answer to the question "What is the paragraph about?" Note that the experiments discussed in this paragraph emphasize how taller men make a more positive first impression.

What is the main idea of the passage? Once you have decided on the topic, you need to answer the question: "What is the author saying about the topic?" So, the main idea statement is: *For women and children, a first impression of a man may be influenced mainly by his height.*

© 2014 Wadsworth, Cengage Learning

Identify Topics and Main Ideas

Exercise 2

Read the following paragraphs from Reading 1 and, in the spaces provided, write "T" for the best topic and "MI" for the best main idea.

1. As these studies indicate, people's lives can be profoundly affected by their looks. Other studies, reported by the *Social Psychology Quarterly,* demonstrate that college students and teachers usually perceive attractive individuals as brighter and more capable than those who are less attractive. Employers tend to favor applicants who are more attractive and hire them over less attractive candidates with the same experience and qualifications. And good-looking people earn, on average, 10 percent more than less attractive people. This bias toward good looks holds true in many occupations in which appearance should not matter at all, such as gardening and computer programming.

    _____ a. Employers tend to favor applicants who are more attractive.

    _____ b. People's lives can be profoundly affected by their looks.

    _____ c. the effect of appearance

2. It's interesting to note, however, that marriage choices are strongly influenced by a tendency to homogamy—choosing someone similar to oneself. We may all have dreams about who our eventual mate will be, but we usually marry someone close to our own level of attractiveness. In casual dating, this tendency is not as strong, but the more committed the relationship, the more likely that each person will be very similar to the other on a scale of attractiveness.

    _____ a. attractiveness and marriage choices

    _____ b. casual dating

    _____ c. We usually marry someone close to our own level of attractiveness.

3. Most people, once they get to know someone, are capable of changing their first impression. Teachers, after becoming familiar with a student's work and contribution to class, frequently revise their initial assessments of ability. Friendships last because of trust and shared interests, and marriages last not only because of love but because of open communication and a willingness to work through difficult situations together. First impressions are certainly influenced by appearance, but lasting relationships are not sustained by appearance alone. In the end, who we are inside is what counts, and ultimate happiness is not tied to good looks.

    _____ a. Most people, once they get to know someone, are capable of changing their first impression.

    _____ b. open communication

    _____ c. changing first impressions

© 2014 Wadsworth, Cengage Learning

Stated Main Ideas

stated main idea the main idea sentence as found directly stated in the reading itself

topic sentence the name used for a main idea sentence in writing classes

Often, you will be able to identify a single sentence in a paragraph that states the main idea. A **stated main idea** is a sentence that sums up the paragraph's overall point. In writing classes, the main idea sentence is called the **topic sentence**. Writers use topic sentences to guide their writing and to make their ideas clear to readers. Not all writers state their main ideas directly, but when they do, they may put a main idea sentence at the beginning, in the middle, or even at the end of a paragraph.

MAIN IDEAS AT THE BEGINNING

The main idea of a paragraph is often stated at the beginning, in the first or second sentence. Writers know that putting main ideas at the beginning makes it easier for readers to understand these ideas. Readers know right away what to expect from the paragraph, and they have a framework for what's to come. Textbook writers often state their topic and main idea at the beginning of a paragraph and then go on to explain the main idea in more detail. Read the following example of a paragraph that has a stated main idea at the beginning.

> The number of new cosmetic products introduced every year seems astronomical. There are special lines (brands) of cosmetics advertised only in infomercials. There are direct marketing lines, such as Mary Kay. There are new department store and drugstore lines. And there are always new products introduced by these brands.

> What is the topic? *increasing numbers of cosmetic products*
> What is the main idea sentence? *The number of new cosmetic products introduced every year seems astronomical.*

The rest of the sentences in the paragraph give examples of cosmetic lines and how they market their products—infomercials, direct marketing lines, new department-store and drugstore lines—and all the new products that each of these brands introduces.

MAIN IDEAS IN THE MIDDLE

Sometimes writers place the main idea statement closer to the middle of a paragraph. For an example, read the following paragraph.

> María Luisa Martínez uses the same routine for her face every day. First, she washes it, then she uses a nonirritating toner, and finally she gently rubs in a light moisturizer. Most important, she recognizes some truths about the skin care industry: Spending more money does not guarantee getting a better product for your skin. So, instead of going out and buying an expensive brand, María Luisa follows the advice of Paula Begoun, a well-recognized skin care expert and author of the book *Don't Go to the Cosmetics Counter Without Me.* María Luisa's use of skin care products proves the point well. She knows that expensive soap by Erno Laszlo is not better for her skin than an inexpensive bar of Dove. And a toner by Neutrogena that doesn't have irritants in it is as good or perhaps better than an expensive toner by Orlane or La Prairie.

© 2014 Wadsworth, Cengage Learning

What is the topic? *skin care products*
What is the main idea sentence? **The main idea is stated in the middle:** *Spending more money does not guarantee getting a better product for your skin.*

The rest of the sentences in the paragraph give examples of less expensive products—soap and toner—that are just as good for your skin as more expensive ones.

MAIN IDEAS AT THE END

Sometimes writers wait until the end of a paragraph to state their main idea. Often they do this when they are trying to argue a point, because you, as reader, may be more likely to be convinced if you hear the facts first and then hear the conclusions or suggestions. For example, read the following paragraph.

> Young men are anxious to have it on their faces. Older men are anxious to have it on their heads. Some men would like to have less on their backs. Other men grow it long for religious reasons. Women usually don't want to have too much on their bodies. But most women want to have lots on their head. Sometimes people want it to be curly. Sometimes people want it to be straight. It's safe to say that most people have concerns about their hair—too much, too little, in the wrong places, or the wrong kind.

What is the topic? *hair or concern about hair*
What is the main idea sentence? **The main idea is stated at the end:** *It's safe to say that most people have concerns about their hair—too much, too little, in the wrong places, or the wrong kind.*

In this case, the writer gives you a series of observations and then leads you to the conclusion, or main idea.

Exercise 3

Identify Topics and Stated Main Ideas

Read each of the following paragraphs, and circle the letter of the topic and the stated main idea for each. Remember that the stated main idea might be at the beginning, in the middle, or at the end of a paragraph.

1. Human obsession with hair removal has been well documented since 4000 B.C. Originally, hair removal was necessary for sanitary purposes, to keep lice and other parasites from infesting the body. Ancient peoples used sharpened rocks and shells to scrape off hair. Sumerians and Romans used crude tweezers to remove the hair from their faces. Ancient Arabians used the threading method, which required the use of a string wound between the fingers and then drawn briskly across the skin to encircle the hair and pull it out by the root. They also developed a taffy-like substance from sugar, lemon, and water to remove unwanted hair from their entire bodies. Shaving instruments have been found in ancient Rome and in Egyptian tombs. (Salinas, "Culture of Hair Removal")

   What is the topic?
   a. tweezers for hair removal
   b. Roman and Egyptian methods of hair removal
   c. ancient history of hair removal

© 2014 Wadsworth, Cengage Learning

What is the stated main idea?
a. Shaving instruments have been found in ancient Rome and in Egyptian tombs.
b. Human obsession with hair removal has been well documented since 4000 B.C.
c. Originally hair removal was necessary for sanitary purposes, to keep lice and other parasites from infesting the body.

2. Waxing, electrolysis, tweezing, and threading are all widely used hair removal procedures that have specific disadvantages. Chemical depilatories and waxes can cause burns and leave scars on the skin. On the other hand, laser treatments and electrolysis are extremely pricey. As a whole, hair removal procedures can be expensive or painful, or both. (Salinas, "Culture of Hair Removal")

What is the topic?
a. waxing, electrolysis, tweezing, and threading
b. disadvantages of hair removal
c. laser treatments for hair removal

What is the stated main idea?
a. As a whole, hair removal procedures can be expensive or painful, or both.
b. Laser treatments and electrolysis are extremely pricey.
c. Chemical depilatories and waxes can cause burns and leave scars on the skin.

3. Indeed, hairy women are considered to be less feminine and less beautiful. In most cultures, vast numbers of women suffer a great deal because they are expected to have smooth, hairless bodies. Unfortunately, this expectation creates enormous anxiety for most women who are born with genes for hairy legs, face, and body and cannot replicate the images of beauty they are bombarded with every day unless they are willing to endure a great deal of pain and pay a lot of money. Many are so embarrassed that they secretly pay to have waxing or other hair removal treatments done without letting their loved ones know. Some will not wear clothing that will bare their legs or arms, lest they expose their superfluous hair. Many avoid the beach or swimming pool because wearing a bathing suit would require them to rid themselves of an enormous amount of hair. (Salinas, "Culture of Hair Removal")

What is the topic?
a. women who avoid the beach and swimming pool
b. women's suffering because of expectations about hair
c. the multibillion-dollar hair removal industry

What is the stated main idea?
a. Many [women] are so embarrassed that they secretly pay to have waxing or other hair removal treatments done without letting their loved ones know.
b. Some will not wear clothing that will bare their legs or arms.
c. In most cultures, vast numbers of women suffer a great deal because they are expected to have smooth, hairless bodies.

© 2014 Wadsworth, Cengage Learning

4. Some women have defied normal fashion about facial hair and set their own image of beauty. But very few women have embraced their hairiness like the feminist icon, Frida Kahlo. In the 1930s, this famous Mexican artist incorporated her facial hair into her self-portraits, exaggerating her thick eyebrows and including a mustache to symbolize her bisexuality. In the 1980s, Brooke Shields, a feminine sex symbol, wore very thick eyebrows brushed in an upward direction to symbolize natural beauty. These eyebrows became quite the rage in the United States and other parts of the world as women let their eyebrows grow out and began brushing them in an upward direction using clear mascara to keep them up. (Salinas, "Culture of Hair Removal")

What is the topic?
a. Brooke Shields's eyebrows
b. Frida Kahlo's facial hair
c. women with different ideas about facial hair

What is the stated main idea?
a. Some women have defied normal fashion about facial hair and set their own image of beauty.
b. In the 1980s, Brooke Shields, a feminine sex symbol, wore very thick eyebrows brushed in an upward direction to symbolize natural beauty.
c. But very few women have embraced their hairiness like the feminist icon, Frida Kahlo.

5. Men have also become important customers for the hair removal business. Some men, especially athletes, will have their backs, legs, and arms waxed. Cyclists and swimmers believe that a hairless body increases performance, while body builders require well-oiled, smooth, hairless skin to show off their developed muscles. Many men have their backs waxed because women find smooth, hairless backs more attractive. Men are now shaping their eyebrows as well, getting rid of the Frida uni-brow effect and removing some of the hair from underneath their eyebrows to create an illusion of larger, sexier eyes. (Salinas, "Culture of Hair Removal")

What is the topic?
a. body builders and hair removal
b. athletes and hair removal
c. men and hair removal

What is the stated main idea?
a. Some men, especially athletes, will have their backs, legs, and arms waxed.
b. Men have also become important customers for the hair removal business.
c. Cyclists and swimmers believe that a hairless body increases performance, while body builders require well-oiled, smooth, hairless skin to show off their developed muscles.

© 2014 Wadsworth, Cengage Learning

Organize to Learn: Mark Main Ideas

In Chapter 1 you learned that effective readers *organize* (O in the PRO system) what they have learned after they read. One popular way students do this is simply to *mark* the important points in the text itself. Now that you know how to identify stated main ideas, you can begin to mark them in the material you read. There are different ways to mark texts; many students use a highlighter, but you may also choose to underline with a pen or pencil. Be careful not to mark too much, because then everything will look important when you come back to review.

Begin by highlighting or underlining the main idea. The act of marking will reinforce the main points you have learned, and the marked text will make it easier for you to review key points when you study for tests. In Chapters 5 and 6 you will learn how to select important supporting details to mark as well.

Read the following paragraph. Notice that the stated main idea has been underlined for you.

> <u>When you shave, your hair does not actually grow back thicker and darker even though it appears to do so.</u> In fact, hair structure is predetermined by genetics and is formed in the hair papilla. When someone shaves, this creates a blunt end on the hair, so when new growth appears this blunt end gives the illusion of coarseness. The new hair is darker, but only because it has not been lightened by the sun, soaps, and cosmetics. (Salinas, "Culture of Hair Removal")

The topic of this paragraph is *hair growth after shaving*. The paragraph provides an explanation of what determines hair structure (genetics) and what happens when hair grows back. The main idea is best stated in the first sentence, which provides an overview of what the more detailed information in the paragraph will explain.

Exercise 4   Mark Stated Main Ideas and Identify Topics

Read each of the following paragraphs, and underline the stated main idea. Then write the topic in your own words. The first one has been done for you.

1. <u>*There are really only two types of hair removal, depilating and epilating.*</u> Depilating removes the hair at the skin surface, while epilating removes the hair root from the hair follicle. Some popular examples of depilating are chemical depilatories and shaving. Although depilating methods are effective, the stubble can be felt in a few days. Examples of epilating are waxing, tweezing, electrolysis, and laser hair removal. Waxing and tweezing provide longer-lasting smoothness of up to eight weeks, while electrolysis and laser treatments can provide permanent results if done professionally and effectively. (Salinas, "Culture of Hair Removal")

   topic: *two types of hair removal*

© 2014 Wadsworth, Cengage Learning

2. In the 1920s it was considered good-looking to shave off the eyebrow and draw a thin straight line across the brow using an eyebrow pencil—the flapper look. This line later changed to the shape of the McDonald's arches, making the wearer look as if she had been shocked or surprised—the Marlene Dietrich look. In the 1940s, many movie stars wore their eyebrows in a thick, clearly defined arch, creating a sophisticated, almost wicked look like that worn by Joan Crawford. It is important to note that styles in eyebrows change constantly. Eyebrow templates were created and sold in drug stores in the 1960s so that women could hold these models over their eyebrows, brush some powder over the mold and have instant Elizabeth Taylor or Marilyn Monroe eyebrows. Many women who have had their eyebrows tattooed on (this process is called "permanent makeup") will find in a few years that the shape is quite outdated. (Salinas, "Culture of Hair Removal")

topic: _____

3. Most men simply shave their beards. Most women opt for shaving, an inexpensive hair removal method that can be done in the privacy of their own home. According to a 1990 survey conducted by Gillette in the United States, 92 percent of women 13 or older shave their legs. Of those women, 66 percent shave the entire leg and 33 percent shave from the knee down. While 98 percent of the women shave their underarms, only 50 percent shave their bikini line. (Salinas, "Culture of Hair Removal")

topic: _____

4. Chemical depilatories are the hair removers of choice in much of the Mediterranean and South America. These chemicals for removing hair have definite disadvantages. Products such as Nair and Neet contain a derivative of lye and work by dissolving the protein in the hair called keratin. Chemical depilatories contain the same active ingredient as Drano, a drain unclogger that also works by dissolving proteins. Depilatories can cause a chemical burn if left on the skin for too long because they will dissolve skin protein as well. These products are least effective on coarse hair since the products are not strong enough to dissolve the hair entirely. (Salinas, "Culture of Hair Removal")

topic: _____

5. The next most popular method of hair removal is waxing. The techniques for waxing have an interesting history, and a variety of applications today. This method was developed in the Middle East by boiling water, sugar, and lemon over a flame until it becomes a sticky taffy-like substance. This taffy is rolled into a ball, spread over the hairy area, and pulled off quickly—taking the trapped hair with it. This technique, spreading and pulling the wax, is still used today in the two types of modern wax: cold wax and hot wax. Hot wax (resin or paraffin) is heated up in the microwave or over a special heater, applied to the area, covered with a fabric strip, and then removed quickly. Cold wax is

© 2014 Wadsworth, Cengage Learning

considered more sanitary to use and does not require heat to trap the hair. All forms of waxing are painful, especially around the mouth, underarms, and bikini line, because of the number of nerve endings in those areas. (Salinas, "Culture of Hair Removal")

topic: _____

6. Many men are more concerned with keeping or growing back hair that they've lost than with getting rid of excess hair. The businesses for curing baldness are numerous. A quick glance at the list of solutions to baldness on the Internet documents the existence of dozens of companies that claim to be able to make a bald man's hair grow once again. Other businesses will sew hair back onto a man's scalp, just a few hairs at a time. Then, of course, there are also the wig manufacturers, whose products include cheap toupees as well as those that are carefully molded to the customer's head and blended with his hair type and color.

topic: _____

Thesis Statements and Central Ideas

central idea the overall general statement or main point the author is making in a reading

thesis statement the main point the author is making in a persuasive essay

Now that you've practiced identifying main ideas in paragraphs, you're ready to tackle longer passages. Short essays are generally organized around a **central idea**—the overall general statement or main point the author is making in a complete reading, or the **thesis statement** of a persuasive essay. You'll usually find the central idea or thesis statement close to the beginning of the essay, but it could be at the end.

Sections of textbooks, too, are often built around a single concept. Each paragraph may not have a separate main idea, but together the paragraphs present the central idea, or thesis statement, often given at the beginning but sometimes the middle, or even the end, of the section.

Exercise 5

Identify Topics and Thesis Statements

Read the following excerpts about people's search for good looks. Notice how in each passage the separate paragraphs are unified by an overall main idea. Write the topic and central idea or thesis statement for each.

1. The male members of many species are adorned in fascinating ways. Male peacocks have larger and far more colorful feathers than the female, the peahen. Male lions have showy manes, but females have no mane at all. Today, in the human species, many males create their public image, not so much by adorning themselves but by adorning the things they own, especially their cars. And this tendency is not limited to men of a certain age or a certain socioeconomic group.

© 2014 Wadsworth, Cengage Learning

Older men who are financially well-off (or are pretending to be) frequently drive around in sports cars: Jaguars, BMWs, Mercedes. They are looking to show their power in society, and their attractiveness comes from the status that they hold.

Younger men frequently go for the "souped up" look with their cars. Some like big American cars, riding low to the ground, with a mechanism to make them bounce. (How cool!) Others go for the foreign cars, especially Hondas, which they customize with all kinds of crazy features like lights and fiberglass body kits. Whether they're driving big American cars or customized Hondas, young men have to have powerful sound systems to complete the effect.

topic:_____

thesis statement: _____

_____

_____

2. Madam C. J. Walker, a pioneer in beauty sales, was an African American woman whose stamina and business sense made her a perfect example of the rags-to-riches story. She was born Sarah Breedlove on a cotton plantation in Louisiana in 1867. Her parents had been slaves and worked as sharecroppers. She was the first member of her family not born a slave. That didn't spare her from hard work, though. At the age of seven, she began working as a washerwoman. After both her parents died, she married a laborer when she was only 14. By the time she was 17, she was a mother. When she was 19, she was already a widowed single mother.

Eventually Sarah did enough white people's laundry to raise the money to send her daughter to college. She moved to St. Louis, and when she was 37, she stopped working as a laundrywoman and decided to sell hair products for African Americans door-to-door. Moving to Denver, she married an ad salesman named C. J. Walker. Together they started a mail-order business. One year later, it was earning $10 a week. Her business was called C. J. Walker Company, and she became known as Madam C. J. Walker. Although $10 a week was a fabulous amount of money at the time, Sarah decided she would travel and sell even more of her products. Recruiting women to work for her, she motivated them with mottos and stories about her success, telling them if she could become rich, they could become rich also.

And rich she did become. In fact, Madam C. J. Walker became a millionaire. Before she died she built herself a mansion with 34 rooms in the suburbs of New York. She also had a swimming pool, a fancy pipe organ, and an elaborate Italian garden. She happily told everybody that her house was designed by a Negro architect.

topic: _____

thesis statement: _____

_____

_____

© 2014 Wadsworth, Cengage Learning

3. More than ever before, the pressure is on teen-aged boys to be buff, and they are turning to steroids to get there. They have to have six-pack abs, good muscular definition, and strong, sculpted bodies. They want to look like the guys on the cover of the wrestling magazines. The question now is how far are they willing to go to get this look? Working out for several hours a day or lifting exceedingly heavy weights and drinking protein powder morning, noon, and night just doesn't work.

   According to the latest national surveys, almost half a million teenagers in the United States use steroids every year. And, according to the National Institute of Drug Abuse, the number of high school sophomores using steroids more than doubled between 1992 and 2000. A Blue Cross Blue Shield survey revealed that steroid use increased 25 percent between 1999 and 2000 among boys between the ages of 12 and 17. Twenty percent of the boys surveyed said they took body-enhancing drugs because they wanted to look stronger.

topic: _____

thesis: _____

_____

Reading 2

Touch It Up! The Art of Making "Beautiful People"

— Lia Trageser

The following reading exposes the elements involved in creating glamorous magazine cover photos. Trageser, a cosmetologist, also explores the true purpose behind the work and expense of producing these images. As you read, think about the photos you have seen on covers. Look for the main ideas of the paragraphs, and think about the overall thesis of the reading.

---

1   A magazine cover photo is a seduction. The reader is drawn in, seduced to desire and to fall in love with the image and all that it suggests. The picture is a sales pitch, but what is being sold? The idea of perfection, of idealized beauty, is held out as something the viewer should pursue. The viewer is led to believe that she could be that beautiful or that he could be that attractive if only the instructions within the magazine are followed. This fantasy sells millions of magazines every day, even though it is just that—a fantasy. Magazine photographs are so highly manipulated that they are no more real than a painting. The art of photo retouching has reached new limits with lighting, makeup, camera angles and techniques, and finally manual and digital manipulation. The pictures are of such high quality that it is difficult to know that one is not looking at reality. Anyone

Lia Trageser, "Touch It Up! The Art of Making People Beautiful". Reprinted by permission of the author.

© 2014 Wadsworth, Cengage Learning

drawn to these glamorous cover pictures should know exactly what she or he is looking at: a piece of art with many distortions and enhancements, created to sell something.

2   Strong emotions can be invoked by a beautiful magazine cover. Desire, envy, joy, inferiority, hope, and self-loathing are all possible from the same shot. A man may see a gorgeous female model and think, "I want her," while a woman may think, "I want to look like her." When looking at a male model, the man may feel, "I could never look like him," and the woman's thoughts may be, "I could never get a man like that. I am hideous." But we all want to try to attain that happy image, even if we need to spend money to do it. Fashion and cosmetics retailers make millions from readers who see the artfully retouched photos and believe that if they purchase the clothes or personal care products or exercise equipment used by the cover model, they will achieve happiness.

3   The perfection of the people in these two-dimensional photographs is irresistible, but it is not real. Flawless bodies, blemish- and wrinkle-free skin, and shiny, flowing hair are all portrayed so invitingly. The man or woman in the photo appears superhuman. Even a fashion model as seemingly perfect as Cindy Crawford is made more so with photo-improvement techniques. Blood vessels in her eyes are erased, pores are removed, and stray hairs are made to disappear. The model may find it hard even to recognize herself. The English actress Kate Winslet was upset by the extent of retouching that was used on a photo of herself on the cover of *GQ* magazine. She complained that she was overly slenderized. She felt misrepresented, knowing that she does not look

AP Photos/Dieu Nalio Chery

Andrew H. Walker/Getty Images

Oprah Winfrey without makeup, and in a touched up photo with makeup.

© 2014 Wadsworth, Cengage Learning

like the photo. The average reader would have no idea that it was not an accurate portrayal and might think Winslet had had great dieting success and try to learn her secret.

4   The whole process begins, of course, with a model who is as near perfect as possible. Here is a person whose proportions and features are genetic anomalies occurring in only one in 1,000 people. Women with long limbs, slim hips, full lips, and large eyes photograph well. Male models with bulky muscles and square jaws project masculinity. The reader may be led to think that what is making this person so attractive is the clothing or cosmetics. A man looking at the cover of *Men's Fitness* may believe that he merely needs to follow the cover model's workout routine in order to look just like him. Both viewers would be overlooking the fact that over 90 percent of the look of the model is effortless. The model was born with certain genes and makes very little effort to achieve the look.

5   Makeup is the next tool in creating the total look. Eyes are made to look larger, and cheekbones are sculpted with shadow and highlight. Lips are made to appear fuller and shinier with lipstick and gloss. Male models do not escape this treatment. Dark undereye circles are concealed, and lashes are lengthened and darkened with mascara. Jaw lines and cheekbones are enhanced with shadow and highlight. Additionally, vast amounts of body makeup are employed to enhance the illusion of perfection in both sexes. Tanner and bronzer are used to darken light skin. Shimmer is used to make muscles stand out and skin look smoother. Full teams of makeup artists, stylists, and hairdressers work on each model.

6   Once the model is ready, the artistry of the photographer begins. Lighting is directed to create or eliminate shadows to hide imperfections. Properly diffused lighting can make skin seem to glow and muscles to ripple. Similarly, positioning the camera just so can make the model seem taller and slimmer. Posing the body can minimize hips, lengthen the neck, and maximize shoulder width. A good stylist and photographer working together can get the model to flex biceps and suck in belly, all the while turning hips and lifting chin, and look perfectly natural doing it.

7   Once the image is burned into film, the retouching artistry commences. Shadows and highlights are enhanced or eliminated. Backgrounds can be blurred, darkened, lightened, or eliminated. Elements of other photographs can be blended into one shot. Parts of the photo can be cropped to emphasize another part. These techniques have been used since the dawn of photography; now, however, the level of expertise using computer technology is astounding.

8   The final step of the image creation is the most magical of all. Digital retouching is the most powerful tool in the artist's arsenal. Using computer software, the artist can make skin look like velvet with no sign of a pore or peach fuzz, never mind a blemish or laugh line. The whites of the eyes are rendered smooth and clear no matter how late the model was up the night before the photo was taken. Hair color may be enhanced, and cleavage may be created with cleverly placed shadows. Body parts can be resculpted, thinning thighs and producing washboard abdominal muscles without a single sit-up. A digital retouch artist can even play Dr. Frankenstein, putting one model's head on another's body. Settings can be changed as well. If the editor decides the photo shot in Miami is not projecting the desired feel, the retoucher can place the model in Paris with the click and drag of a mouse.

9   Once all these elements come together in a magazine cover photo, a powerful piece of art has been born. Months of work and the efforts of many people have gone into one cover; yet with piles of magazines appearing on newsstands every week, the work can seem effortless. If the viewer applies no critical thinking to these images, she or he

© 2014 Wadsworth, Cengage Learning

could believe them to be fact instead of the fanciful art that they are. When a perfect Tom Cruise appears on a *People* magazine cover, a lot of people might think "Tom Cruise is older than I am, but he looks younger. What am I doing wrong?"

10   Readers and consumers of magazines need to be aware that these cover photos are works of art and not goals that they should try to achieve. Because it does not matter what diet, exercise, makeup, or designer clothes you use, you are not going to look like a cover model. Remember—even a cover model does not look like a cover model. Without a team of makeup artists, hairdressers, stylists, photographers, lighting technicians, and photo retouchers, the look of a magazine cover is completely unattainable.

Exercise 6

Work with Words

Use context clues, word-part clues, and, if necessary, the dictionary to choose the best definitions of the italicized words in the following sentences from Reading 2.

1. Anyone drawn to these glamorous cover pictures should know exactly what she or he is looking at: a piece of art with many distortions and *enhancements,* created to sell something. (par. 1)

   enhancements
   a. unnecessary changes
   b. improvements
   c. falsifications

2. Strong emotions can be *invoked* by a beautiful magazine cover. (par. 2)

   Invoked
   a. called up
   b. dampened
   c. improved

3. *Flawless* bodies, blemish- and wrinkle-free skin, and shiny, flowing hair are all portrayed so invitingly. (par. 3)

   flawless
   a. without defect
   b. imperfect
   c. blemished

4. She felt *misrepresented,* knowing that she does not look like the photo. (par. 3)

   misrepresented
   a. not voted on
   b. made to appear as something different
   c. not spoken for on behalf of the people represented

5. Here is a person whose proportions and features are genetic *anomalies* occurring in only one in one thousand people. (par. 4)

   anomalies
   a. common occurrences
   b. regulations
   c. abnormalities

© 2014 Wadsworth, Cengage Learning

6. Months of work and the efforts of many people have gone into one cover; yet with piles of magazines appearing on newsstands every week, the work can seem *effortless.* (par. 9)

   effortless
   a. easy
   b. difficult
   c. deceiving

Exercise 7

Identify Topics, Stated Main Ideas, and Thesis Statements

Choose the best answer to the following multiple-choice questions.

1. What is the best topic for paragraph 4?
   a. human anomalies
   b. near-perfect models
   c. good genes

2. What is the best stated main idea for paragraph 4?
   a. The whole process begins, of course, with a model who is as near perfect as possible.
   b. A man looking at the cover of *Men's Fitness* may believe that he merely needs to follow the cover model's workout routine in order to look just like him.
   c. Male models with bulky muscles and square jaws project masculinity.

3. What is the best topic for paragraph 5?
   a. makeup artists' training
   b. makeup
   c. tanner and bronzer

4. What is the best stated main idea for paragraph 5?
   a. Makeup is the next tool in creating the total look.
   b. Dark under eye circles are concealed, and lashes are lengthened and darkened with mascara.
   c. Jaw lines and cheekbones are enhanced with shadow and highlight.

5. What is the best topic for paragraph 8?
   a. magic and image creation
   b. setting changes
   c. digital retouching

6. What is the best stated main idea for paragraph 8?
   a. The final step of the image creation is the most magical of all.
   b. Digital retouching is the most powerful tool in the artist's arsenal.
   c. Using computer software, the artist can make skin look like velvet with no sign of a pore or peach fuzz, never mind a blemish or laugh line.

7. What is the topic of the reading?
   a. magazines for women
   b. magazine models
   c. magazine cover photos

© 2014 Wadsworth, Cengage Learning

8. Which of the following is the best thesis statement for the reading?
   a. Months of work and the efforts of many people have gone into one cover; yet with piles of magazines appearing on newsstands every week, the work can seem effortless.
   b. The model was born with good genes and makes very little effort to achieve the look.
   c. Anyone drawn to these glamorous cover pictures should know exactly what she or he is looking at: a piece of art with many distortions and enhancements, created to sell something.

Exercise 8

Check Your Understanding

Choose the best answer to the following multiple-choice questions.

1. Which of the following includes the four basic components of a glamorous magazine cover photo?
   a. a good-looking model, with good makeup and an exercise routine to enhance an attractive body
   b. a good-looking model, makeup, photographic artistry, and digital touch-up
   c. a good-looking model, makeup-free skin, photographic artistry, and digital touch-up

2. Kate Winslet was upset because
   a. she didn't feel the cover photo of her on *GQ* was flattering enough.
   b. she was disappointed in the work of the makeup artists.
   c. she was made to look too thin.

3. According to the author, the real purpose behind the creation of these cover photos is to
   a. manipulate the reader into spending money and buying the magazine and the products or services it promotes.
   b. invoke pleasant emotions in the reader.
   c. encourage the reader to follow skin care and exercise tips, especially when they are not costly.

4. Why did the author say a "digital retouch artist can even play Dr. Frankenstein"?
   a. They are so good at what they do that it's difficult for the public to recognize that retouching has taken place.
   b. They can produce a completely new physical image for anybody who can pay for it.
   c. They can put one person's head on another's body, similar to what Dr. Frankenstein did.

Exercise 9

Make Connections and Write

Write short answers to the following questions based on Reading 2, your experience, and your observations. Then, discuss your answers with your class group. Working together, prepare a report for your class as a whole or a written summary for your instructor.

© 2014 Wadsworth, Cengage Learning

1. What magazines are you familiar with that have the kinds of cover photos described in this reading? Give some examples of magazines and of the people featured on the covers.

   _____

   _____

   _____

   _____

2. How do you make choices about what magazines you buy? How does the front cover influence your choices? Explain your answer.

   _____

   _____

   _____

   _____

3. Why do you think the author wants people to be aware of what goes into making a glamorous magazine cover photo? Explain your answer.

   _____

   _____

   _____

   _____

Reading 3 # Body Art

— OLIVIA MAYBERRY

The following reading discusses the practice of decorating the human body from various cultural perspectives. As you read, think about the similarities and differences between the ways people adorn their bodies that you are familiar with and those that are described here.

1   Some years ago, I met a young woman from Belgium named Giselle. She was my friend's son's girlfriend; they had met on the Internet, and she had traveled to France to meet him in person. We were told in advance that she had had a very hard life, and she was

Olivia Mayberry. Written for *Joining a Community of Readers*.

© 2014 Wadsworth, Cengage Learning

"gothic"; I didn't know what that meant, although I had some associations with young people who wear all black and have piercings and rings hanging out of various parts of their faces and bodies. When we came back from a grocery shopping trip, Giselle had arrived. She had very pale skin, a sharp contrast to her dyed black hair. She was very nice about talking to me in French. She spoke slowly, and patiently answered my questions and attempts to make conversation. She did have rings in her nose, lips, tongue, and cheek. What startled me most, though, was what I saw on her back the following day. It was hot and we were walking around some old historic village, so Giselle took off her sweater and was wearing only a skimpy halter top. It was then that I saw the tattoo. At first, from a distance, I thought it was a waterfall coming out of a cave. When I got closer, I could see that it actually was some kind of a wizard with a pointy hat vomiting massive quantities of worms. Yuck.

2   Frankly, I found the tattooed image on this young woman's back appalling. How awful it was to think that she would live the rest of her life with that permanent image! How thankful I was that none of my kids had decided to do such a thing. But how do we, as individuals, decide when something is gross?

3   I started to think about what people do to decorate their bodies. In Western countries, women are generally expected to use makeup, and not so long ago, women squeezed their bodies into incredibly tight corsets to make their waists appear tiny. In ancient Greece, only the wealthiest women were allowed to use makeup. In some African societies, men are the ones who paint their faces to make themselves beautiful. In other African societies, men and women alike cut patterns into their faces and bodies to create scars. Native Americans painted their faces and bodies for a variety of reasons. Tattooing was a common practice in most of Polynesia, and many people all over the world still tattoo their bodies. Giselle's tattoos seemed to be a statement about her pessimism and how ugly the world seemed to her.

4   People practice "body art" all over the world and have done so for millennia; decorating human bodies is done to make oneself more attractive, to observe religious beliefs, to indicate one's social standing, to demonstrate accomplishment, to indicate membership in a certain group, and even to demonstrate rebellion against society. Whether we as individuals like or hate a particular type of body decoration depends on what we have been taught to accept. And what we find acceptable changes over time.

5   The kind of body decoration that we are most familiar with is designed to make individuals more attractive, but in some parts of the world, it's not what we expect. Women wearing makeup or people having plastic surgery to look younger or to have fuller lips or higher cheekbones are examples of decorative body art that is pretty much acceptable to us today. We are no longer surprised by liposuction, the surgery to remove body fat. Facelifts have become commonplace. The procedure to remove wrinkles by injecting Botox, which paralyzes muscles, is widely accepted. Usually the people who subject themselves to these procedures in the search for beauty are women. But the Wodabe men of the Republic of Niger are more concerned than the women of their culture with making themselves attractive. These men are famous for coming together once a year for the *geerewol* festival. In preparation for this event, all the young men who are hoping to get married make a special effort to make themselves beautiful, spending many hours decorating themselves with paint and makeup so they will be as desirable as possible to the women. Their idea of beauty includes having light skin, a high forehead, and a narrow nose. They also darken the area around the eyes and lips to bring out the white of their eyes and teeth.

Polynesia
a group of islands in the South Pacific

Republic of Niger
a country in northwest Africa

© 2014 Wadsworth, Cengage Learning

AP Photos/Christine Nesbitt

Wodabe man preparing for the *geerewol* festival.

Hindu
a person who
follows the main
religion in India
(Hinduism)

New Guinea
an island nation
north of Australia

Sudan
a country in
northeast Africa
south of Egypt

Maori
the native people
of New Zealand

6   Body decoration also frequently conveys religious beliefs. In certain areas of India, Hindu women have elaborate tattoos that illustrate their worship of a particular god from the many in the Hindu religion. Hindu women also paint a red dot on their foreheads as a sign of blessing as well as decoration. In one of the islands of Indonesia, the people tattoo themselves at puberty because "a person's soul would not feel at home in a body that was not artistically 'completed' with fine drawings."[1] So the pursuit of beauty, which assures the goodwill of souls, becomes a lifetime pursuit. In Borneo, New Guinea, tattoos are considered a protective shield against evil and can serve as a link with ancestors, or they can be the mediator between people and the supernatural world.[2]

7   Another function of body decoration can be to represent an individual's status in society. Among the Nuba in southern Sudan, for example, a man's body decoration—nonpermanent paint—can convey his position, age, history, place of origin, and religious faith, in addition to providing a link to his forefathers. The paintings are done by the men themselves, who have developed body and face decoration into a fine art.[3] In Japan, men of certain occupational groups, such as firemen, mailmen, and rickshaw drivers, once had elaborate tattoos covering their whole body, while people in the upper classes looked down upon tattooing. The opposite is true in some Polynesian societies. Among the Maori, for example, tattooing indicated high rank, and only the most powerful people were allowed to have elaborate tattoos.[4]

8   Among Native American peoples of North America body art was practiced for many reasons, but unfortunately, although we have some information and records of its use, there is not enough documentation to completely understand it. When the English colonists first saw the people of the Southeast, they believed that they were fully dressed, when in actuality, they had tattoos over much of their body. Body paint was used by the Plains Indians for a variety of ceremonial occasions with a specific purpose: to bring rain, to prepare for a hunt, to win in battle. Frequently, body decoration indicated an individual's status in his tribe. George Catlin (1796–1872) dedicated

© 2014 Wadsworth, Cengage Learning

Maori Chief, New Zealand, 1923.

Bettmann/Corbis

George Catlin, *Fast Dancer*, a warrior, Ojibwa, 1834.

Smithsonian American Art Museum, Washington, DC / Art Resource, NY

many years of his life to portraying "the living manners, customs, and character of an interesting race of people, rapidly passing away from the face of the earth." [5] It is thanks to Catlin's work that we have hundreds of oil paintings and thousands of pages of sketches and drawings. One of his finest paintings is of Fast Dancer, a warrior painted in 1834.

9   When we look at the photos of body art around the world, they all seem to be part of exotic and distant cultures, but we can find body art in one form or another in our daily lives. Giselle, the Gothic girl from Belgium, is but an extreme example. Most people's tattoos make small, intimate statements. Others—a far smaller group—choose to let everyone see, and perhaps be shocked by, their body decoration.

Notes

1. Karl Gröning, *Decorated Skin: A World Survey of Body Art* (London: Thames and Hudson, 1997), 195.

2. http://www.amnh.org/exhibitions/bodyart (accessed 6/27/06).

3. *Ibid.*

4. Gröning, *Decorated Skin,* 196–198.

5. Quoted in *ibid.,* 38.

© 2014 Wadsworth, Cengage Learning

Work with Words

Use context clues, word-part clues, and, if necessary, the dictionary to write the definitions of the italicized words in the following sentences from Reading 3.

1. Frankly, I found the tattooed image on this young woman's back *appalling*. How awful it was to think that she would live the rest of her life with that permanent image! (par. 2)

   appalling _____

2. Giselle's tattoos seemed to be a *statement* about her *pessimism* and how ugly the world seemed to her. (par. 3)

   statement _____

3. *pessimism* _____

4. People practice "body art" all over the world and have done so for *millennia*. (par. 4)

   millennia _____

5. These men are famous for coming together once a year for the *geerewol* festival. In preparation for this event, all the young men who are hoping to get married make a special effort to make themselves beautiful, spending many hours decorating themselves with paint and makeup so they will be as desirable as possible to the women. (par. 5)

   geerewol festival _____

   _____

6. In Borneo, New Guinea, tattoos are considered a protective shield against evil and can serve as a link with ancestors, or they can be the *mediator* between people and the supernatural world. (par. 6)

   mediator _____

7. Among the Nuba in southern Sudan, for example, a man's body decoration— nonpermanent paint—can convey his position, age, history, place of origin, and religious faith, in addition to providing a link to his *forefathers*. (par. 7)

   forefathers _____

8. Among Native American peoples of North America body art was practiced for many reasons, but unfortunately, although we have some information and records of its use, there is not enough *documentation* to completely under- stand it. (par. 8)

   documentation _____

© 2014 Wadsworth, Cengage Learning

Exercise 11	

Identify Topics, Stated Main Ideas, and Thesis Statements

Choose the best answers to the following multiple-choice questions about Reading 3.

1. What is the best topic for paragraph 5?
   a. familiar body decoration
   b. some expected and unexpected body decorations for beauty
   c. types of plastic surgery to make the body more beautiful

2. What is the best stated main idea for paragraph 5?
   a. The kind of body decoration that we are most familiar with is designed to make individuals more attractive, but in some parts of the world, it's not what we expect.
   b. Women wearing makeup or people having plastic surgery to look younger or to have fuller lips or higher cheekbones are examples of decorative body art that is pretty much acceptable to us today.
   c. The Wodabe men of the Republic of Niger are more concerned than the women of their culture with making themselves attractive.

3. What is the best topic for paragraph 6?
   a. body decoration in India
   b. body decoration of the Hindus
   c. body decoration for religious reasons

4. What is the best stated main idea for paragraph 6?
   a. Body decoration also frequently conveys religious beliefs.
   b. In certain areas of India, Hindu women have elaborate tattoos that illustrate their worship of a particular god from the many in the Hindu religion.
   c. In Borneo, New Guinea, tattoos are considered a protective shield against evil and can serve as a link with ancestors, or they can be the mediator between people and the supernatural world.

5. What is the best topic for paragraph 7?
   a. body decoration to show status
   b. body decoration to show religious faith
   c. body decoration as fine art

6. What is the best main idea sentence for paragraph 7?
   a. Among the Nuba in southern Sudan, for example, a man's body decoration—nonpermanent paint—can convey his position, age, history, place of origin, and religious faith, in addition to providing a link to his forefathers.
   b. Another function of body decoration can be to represent an individual's status in society.
   c. In Japan, men of certain occupational groups, such as firemen, mailmen, and rickshaw drivers, had elaborate tattoos covering their whole body, while people in the upper classes looked down upon tattooing.

7. What is the best topic for Reading 3?
   a. tattoos
   b. tattoos as symbols
   c. body art

© 2014 Wadsworth, Cengage Learning

8. What is the best thesis statement for Reading 3?
   a. Whether we as individuals like or hate a particular type of body decoration depends on what we have been taught to accept.
   b. People practice "body art" all over the world and have done so for millennia; decorating human bodies is done to make oneself more attractive, to observe religious beliefs, to indicate one's social standing, to demonstrate accomplishment, to indicate membership in a certain group, and even to demonstrate rebellion against society.
   c. We can find body art in one form or another in our daily lives.

Exercise 12

Check Your Understanding

Write brief answers to the following questions about Reading 3.

1. Why, according to the author, does Giselle have the tattoo on her back?

   _____

2. Give two examples of cases when only the wealthiest or most powerful people were able to decorate their bodies.

   _____

3. List five reasons why people decorate their bodies.

   _____

   _____

4. What did George Catlin do, and why was his work important?

   _____

   _____

Exercise 13

Make Connections and Write

Write short answers to the following questions based on Reading 3, your experience, and your observations. Then discuss your answers with your class group. Working together, prepare a report for your class as a whole or a written summary for your instructor.

© 2014 Wadsworth, Cengage Learning

1. Give some examples of body art that you like—permanent or temporary—that you or someone you know has or uses.

_____

_____

_____

_____

2. Give some examples of body art that you don't like. Why don't you like it?

_____

_____

_____

_____

3. What do you think about the photo of the Wodabe man preparing for the *geerewol* festival? Do you think he is attractive? What do you think about the sex roles in that society—especially the emphasis on the men making themselves attractive to women? Explain your answers.

_____

_____

_____

_____

4. What are the two people in the chapter opening photo (page 114) trying to communicate with their style of dress? How is it similar to or different from the purposes for the body art shown in the photographs of the Maori chief (page 137) and the Ojibwa warrior (page 137)?

_____

_____

_____

_____

© 2014 Wadsworth, Cengage Learning

| Reading 4 | *The Hidden Costs of That Buff Bod* |

— Mark Santos

In the following reading, Santos examines an aspect of the search to be good-looking that we often overlook: men's efforts to have a "ripped" body. Often, the effort to build muscles leads men to taking serious health risks. In this reading, Santos explores the increasing use of illegal steroids, some of the causes behind it, and some of the dangers it may present.

1   If you have visited a fitness gym over the last 15 years or so, you are sure to have noticed that its clientele has changed. When you enter any Bally's Fitness or 24 Hour Fitness Clubs, you will see increasing numbers of men who are buff. They are not the ordinary buff that comes from a workout regimen with weight lifting. They are the men with rippling abdominal muscles, small waists, and bulging biceps, hamstrings, and quadriceps. In the past, only small numbers of men were obsessed with bodybuilding. Today, with the emphasis that our society and the media place on being fit, and more extremely, on having a muscular body, more men of all ages and backgrounds have become fixated on building their bodies to look stronger, as well as to be stronger, to compete in bodybuilding competitions, or to be better athletes in other sports.

2   These men look strong and healthy, like they are all muscle. They have ideal, if exaggerated, masculine bodies. Clearly, these adolescents and men, ranging in age from 15 to about 40, work out and lift weights. But I begin to suspect that something more is going on. The predominance of muscle mass on these men is simply not attainable by normal means. There is an explanation, however. More and more men and teenage boys also take anabolic steroids to look good, and they are taking serious medical risks to reach their goals.

3   Much of the desire to develop the muscular body by any means necessary is driven by the mass media and commercial images. Dr. Harrison Pope, a Harvard University specialist in steroid abuse, believes a growing number of men feel they never look good enough. He has created a name for this obsession: the Adonis complex. This complex leads to ridiculously overbuilt bodies that Dr. Pope says are everywhere—in Hollywood movies, in action toy figures like G.I. Joe, and on magazine covers. According to him,

mass media
television,
magazines,
movies,
newspapers

> One of the biggest lies being handed to American men today is that you can somehow attain by natural means the huge shoulders and pectorals of the biggest men in the magazines. . . . Generations of young men are working hard in the gym and wondering what on earth they're doing wrong. They don't realize that the "hypermale" look that's so prevalent these days is essentially unattainable without steroids.[1]

4   In the 1970s and 1980s, only a small group of muscle freaks used steroids. Today, the abuse has become more common among ordinary men. Dr. Pope estimates that between one and two million Americans have used or are using steroids.[2] The figures are not hard and fast, though, because men obtain these drugs through illegal

Mark Santos. Written for *Joining a Community of Readers.*

© 2014 Wadsworth, Cengage Learning

venues—on the Internet, on the other side of the border, and from illegally operating labs. The information on who sold what to whom is simply not available because the sale of steroids for the purpose of bodybuilding is not legal. Although the precise statistics are impossible to obtain, most experts are convinced that the number of people using illegal steroids has been increasing.

5   Evidence indicates that the number of adolescents who have been taking illegal steroids is also on the rise. In its study "Monitoring the Future," the National Institute on Drug Abuse found that among high school sophomores, steroid use more than doubled in the United States between 1992 and 2000. Another survey, sponsored by Blue Cross Blue Shield, revealed that for boys between 12 and 17 years old, the use of steroids and similar drugs increased by 25 percent from 1999 to 2000. These boys and adolescents get what they want—buffed-up bodies—but they are also probably getting more than they have bargained for.

6   Anabolic steroids are chemicals that imitate testosterone (a male hormone), which promotes muscle growth and the development of male sexual characteristics, but there are some unattractive side effects as well. Men who take these drugs frequently have huge muscles around their shoulders and have increased bench-press strength. They have less body fat so their waists are smaller and their abdominal muscles are more prominent. In general, all of their muscles are better defined. On the downside, sometimes steroid takers have skin with a reddish glow, a consequence of a rise in blood pressure. They may have increased acne on their back, they may grow extra breast tissue, and their testicles may shrink. [3]

prominent
noticeable, standing out

7   There are some possible serious health effects to unmonitored steroid use. While long-term adverse side effects are not proven, the Drug Enforcement Administration explains that some of the possible serious health problems associated with the abuse of steroids include cardiovascular damage (to the heart and circulatory system), brain damage, and liver damage. The extended list of physical side effects is long: elevated blood pressure and cholesterol levels, severe acne, and premature balding are just a few of the possibilities. For adolescents, taking these hormones might stop the lengthening of bones and result in stunted growth. Some people experience psychotic reactions such as feelings of anger, hostility, and aggression. [4]

8   If you know someone who you suspect is taking steroids, you can help by giving them the information that might save their health or even their life. Every boy and every man should know the hidden cost of getting "the look." The media, instead of promoting the overbuilt look, should be showing us normal, healthy male bodies and alerting us to the dangers of illegal steroid use.

Notes

1. Christopher McDougall, "Buyin' Bulk," *Men's Health,* March 2003, 157–163.

2. *Ibid.*

3. McDougall, "Buyin' Bulk," 161.

4. National Institute on Drug Abuse, "Anabolic Steroid Use," (accessed 6/1/12).

Exercise 14

Work with Words

Use context clues, word-part clues, and, if necessary, the dictionary to write in the appropriate definitions of the italicized words in the following sentences from Reading 4.

© 2014 Wadsworth, Cengage Learning

1. Today, with the emphasis that our society and the media place on being fit, and more extremely, on having a muscular body, more men of all ages and backgrounds have become *fixated* on building their bodies to look stronger, as well as to be stronger, to compete in bodybuilding competitions, or to be better athletes in other sports. (par. 1)

   fixated _____

2. He has created a name for this obsession: the *Adonis complex.* (par. 3)

   Adonis complex _____

3. They don't realize that the "hypermale" look that's so prevalent these days is essentially *unattainable* without steroids. (par. 3)

   unattainable _____

4. The figures are not hard and fast, though, because men obtain these drugs through illegal *venues*—on the Internet, on the other side of the border, and from illegally operating labs. (par. 4)

   venues _____

5. *Anabolic steroids* are chemicals that imitate *testosterone* (a male hormone), which promotes muscle growth and the development of male sexual characteristics, but there are some unattractive side effects as well. (par. 6)

   anabolic steroids _____

6. *testosterone* _____

7. While long-term *adverse* side effects are not proven, the Drug Enforcement Administration explains that some of the possible serious health problems associated with the abuse of steroids include *cardiovascular* damage (to the heart and circulatory system), brain damage, and liver damage. (par. 7)

   adverse _____

8. *cardiovascular* _____

Exercise 15

Identify Topics, Stated Main Ideas, and Thesis Statements

Choose the best answers to the following multiple-choice questions about Reading 4.

1. Which of the following is the best topic for paragraph 3?
   a. media influence
   b. steroids
   c. Dr. Pope

© 2014 Wadsworth, Cengage Learning

2. Which of the following is the best stated main idea for paragraph 3?
   a. Dr. Pope believes a growing number of men feel they never look good enough.
   b. Men don't realize that the "hypermale" look that's so prevalent these days is essentially unattainable without steroids.
   c. Much of the desire to develop the muscular body by any means necessary is driven by the mass media and commercial images.

3. Which of the following is the best topic for paragraph 4?
   a. specialists in steroid use
   b. increase in steroid use
   c. lack of information

4. Which of the following is the best stated main idea for paragraph 4?
   a. In the 1970s and 1980s, only a small group of muscle freaks used steroids.
   b. Dr. Pope estimates that between one and two million Americans have used or are using steroids.
   c. Although the precise statistics are impossible to obtain, most experts are convinced that the number of people using illegal steroids has been increasing.

5. Which of the following is the best topic for paragraph 5?
   a. monitoring the future
   b. adolescents and steroid abuse
   c. lifting weights to change appearance

6. Which of the following is the best stated main idea for paragraph 5?
   a. Evidence indicates that the number of adolescents who have been taking illegal steroids is also on the rise.
   b. In its study "Monitoring the Future," the National Institute on Drug Abuse found that among high school sophomores, steroid use more than doubled in the United States between 1992 and 2000.
   c. Another survey, sponsored by Blue Cross Blue Shield, revealed that for boys between 12 and 17 years old, the use of steroids and similar drugs increased by 25 percent from 1999 to 2000.

7. Which of the following is the best topic for Reading 4?
   a. reasons for and consequences of increased steroid use
   b. teenage boys' steroid use
   c. magazines' portrayal of the ideal male body

8. Which of the following is the best thesis statement for Reading 4?
   a. There are some possible serious health effects to unmonitored steroid use.
   b. Some people [on steroids] experience psychotic reactions such as feelings of anger, hostility, and aggression.
   c. More and more men and teenage boys also take anabolic steroids to look good, and they are taking serious medical risks to reach their goals.

© 2014 Wadsworth, Cengage Learning

Exercise 16

Check Your Understanding

Write brief answers to the following questions about Reading 4.

1. What ideas does the author introduce in paragraph 1?

_____

_____

_____

_____

2. Why is it difficult to get accurate statistics on the use of anabolic steroids?

_____

_____

_____

_____

3. What examples are given to prove the idea that steroid use among adolescents has been increasing?

_____

_____

_____

_____

4. What are some of the negative health effects of anabolic steroid use?

_____

_____

_____

_____

© 2014 Wadsworth, Cengage Learning

Exercise 17

Make Connections and Write

Write short answers to the following questions based on Reading 4, your experience, and your observations. Then discuss your answers with your class group. Working together, prepare a report for your class as a whole or a written summary for your instructor.

1. Do you agree with Santos's idea that men are overly concerned with their body image? What examples can you think of to support your position? (Hint: Think about the people you know and about magazines and television programs.) Explain.

   _____

   _____

   _____

2. How concerned are you personally with your body image? Would you consider doing something that might be dangerous to your health to change your body? Explain and give examples to support your answer.

   _____

   _____

   _____

Language Tip:
Follow Directions

Most people, no matter how well-educated, have difficulty following directions. For some reason we think we understand what we're supposed to do before we listen to or read directions. For example, how often have you filled out a form incorrectly because you didn't follow directions? How often have you answered a test question incorrectly because you didn't take the time to read the question carefully? Let's see how well you follow directions now.

Exercise 18   **Follow Directions**

Carefully follow all of the following directions. Be sure to read *all* the directions (1-7) before you do anything.

1. On a separate piece of paper, write your name in the top right corner.

2. Under your name, write today's date.

© 2014 Wadsworth, Cengage Learning

3. Put a circle around the date.

4. In the bottom right corner, write your birthday.

5. In the middle of the paper, draw a square.

6. Inside the square draw five zeros.

7. Don't do any of the things listed in numbers 1–6. Just sit and fold your hands on your desk.

    How did you do following the directions? Congratulations if you read all the way to step 7 before you began to do anything!

Chapter Review

To aid your review of the reading skills in Chapter 3, study the Put It Together chart.

Put It Together: Topics And Main Ideas	
Skills and Concepts	Explanation
Topics (see page 118)	A topic is a key word or phrase that describes the focus of a reading; it says what the paragraph is about. A topic answers the question "What is the reading about?" in a few words.
Main Ideas (see pages 118, 120–121)	The main idea explains what the author is saying about a topic. It should be stated as a complete sentence.
Stated Main Ideas (see pages 118, 120)	A stated main idea is a sentence in the reading itself that sums up the main idea of the paragraph.
Topic Sentence (see page 120)	A topic sentence is the term used in composition classes for the stated main idea sentence that appears in a paragraph.
Marking Main Ideas (see page 124)	Marking a reading involves identifying and underlining or highlighting main ideas as a technique for remembering and studying.
Central Ideas (see page 126)	The overall general statement or main point the author is making in a reading.
Thesis Statements (see page 126)	The overall general statement or main point the author is making in a persuasive essay.

© 2014 Wadsworth, Cengage Learning

REVIEW SKILLS

Answer the following skills-review questions.

1. Explain how to identify a topic in a paragraph or longer passage.

   _____

   _____

   _____

2. Explain how to identify the main idea or thesis statement in an essay or textbook section.

   _____

   _____

   _____

Write

Write an advertisement for a cosmetics product or procedure in such a way that people would want to buy it. To do this, consider the following:

1. Who are you trying to get to buy this product?

2. What kind of magazine will your advertising copy appear in?

3. Use language and ideas that appeal to people's desire to create an image for themselves.

4. Cut out or draw a picture to accompany your advertisement.

5. Remember, be creative.

COLLABORATE

1. Bring in one magazine with touched-up photos to share with other members of your group. Together, go through the pictures (on the cover, for advertisements, etc.). Choose one photo that you think has been touched up and analyze it, considering the following questions. Then prepare a short report for the class.

   a. List the ways you think the photo has been touched up.

   b. What is the purpose of the photo (to sell something, to convince you to buy the magazine, etc.)? Is the photo effective?

© 2014 Wadsworth, Cengage Learning

2. Bring in a magazine or Internet article (with photos) about any celebrity who is famous because of his or her appearance. Discuss as a group the information in the article that makes it interesting. Be prepared to give a brief report for the class, focusing on:
   a. how the photo creates interest.
   b. other information in the article about appearance that creates interest.

3. Prepare an advertisement for a cosmetics product. As a group, decide on a product that you would like to promote. Prepare an advertising campaign for that product. You can act out a TV commercial in front of the class; video a TV commercial for the class; or design a poster or billboard to advertise the product.

4. Search the Web for information on tattooing. Prepare a report for the class explaining the types of sites available and summarizing some of the information (history, current popularity, pain, risks, and expense).

EXTEND YOUR THINKING

Interview three people about what qualities are attractive. First write five questions that you will ask each person. Be sure to give information about each of your informants (friend, mother, cosmetics salesperson, etc.). After the interviews, share your results with your class group. (The report could be oral but could also be in a chart form.)

 ## WORK THE WEB

1. Do a search on *Google* or another search engine for the documentary "The Story of Cosmetics." Watch it, then write the thesis of the film, and make a list of the main ideas that support the thesis.

2. To explore how people have dressed in the past, go to *Google.com*. Pick a century or civilization for which you want to learn about the dressing customs, then do a search on *Google*. For example, you could type in "19th century fashion" or "19th century men's fashion," or you could type in "Ancient Greek fashion." Select Google Images to find pictures rather than articles. Explore Web sites until you find a picture or pictures of how people dressed. Print the picture. Then, write a short paragraph describing how people dressed. In a second paragraph, discuss whether this style would be considered good-looking today. Explain why or why not.

© 2014 Wadsworth, Cengage Learning

Name _____ Date _____

Behind the Veil

— Roberta Alexander

The following reading discusses attitudes that many Americans have toward certain groups of people in our society. In it, the author shares her experiences of being in public places with her daughter-in-law, who is different and who, based on her appearance, attracts a lot of attention. As you read, think about how you would feel if you were the author's daughter-in-law.

1   A trip to the supermarket is never a normal event with my daughter-in-law, Aasiya. People stare at us. Actually, they stare mostly at her, but also at me. Sometimes the stares reflect their fear and <u>apprehension</u>, as though some harm could come to them by being near us. Sometimes the stares seem to reflect surprise, or astonishment at seeing someone who is different from anyone they have ever seen before. Sometimes the stares reflect what seems to be pity, revealing thoughts of "Oh, that poor woman." Mostly their stares convey a sense of complete <u>disbelief</u>, as if they were wondering how it is possible for them to see such a woman in a supermarket in suburban America. Just today, when Aasiya and I were in the supermarket aisle between the spices and the sugar, a woman came around the corner and was so startled when she saw Aasiya that she jumped back and gasped.

2   When I am with Aasiya in public, I try to act normal and friendly because I know that everyone is looking at us. I smile more than usual. I want everybody to understand that I am not weird, that I am just a normal African American grandmother living in the sub-urbs. But, in spite of all my efforts, when I go to the supermarket with my daughter-in-law, we *are* weird. We probably even provide people something to talk about when they get home to their families.

3   Aasiya is pretty and she is not unlike any other bright 22-year-old woman who has re-cently immigrated to the United States. She has black hair, long and beautiful. She has huge, soft eyes. Her mouth is big and her smile is wide and friendly. She loves to laugh and she loves to act silly. She has had very little traditional schooling as we know it, but she speaks, reads, and writes five languages. She is comfortable around all my highly educated women friends. She easily becomes the life of the party. Aasiya likes to ride the swings in the park, she wants to go to Disneyland, and she loves to eat Hershey's chocolate bars. As the months go by, she is becoming increasingly anxious to visit her mother and family in India.

4   But Aasiya is different. When she goes out in public or when she is around any man who is not an immediate member of her family, she wears a veil. Not just an ordi-nary scarf around her head like many Muslim women do, but a veil—a *nikab*—that covers her entire face, with only a slit for her eyes. She also wears a <u>ubaya</u>, a kind of black robe which completely covers her regular clothes, and comes down almost to her feet. So, if you were to see her on the street, you would not know what she looked like. You would only know that she is completely covered in black. If you ever saw the movie *Star Wars*, you might think that she looks like a miniature Darth Vader with the veil replacing his plastic mask. If you ever saw Aasiya in her *nikab* and *ubaya*, you

Roberta Alexander. Written for *Joining a Community of Readers.*

© 2014 Wadsworth, Cengage Learning

would never know that she is beautiful, and funny, and friendly, and sensitive, and ever so intelligent.

5   People's <u>verbal</u> responses to Aasiya are always interesting, and almost always <u>offensive</u>. People have told her, "You're in America now," and, "Why don't you go back where you come from?" and, "How can she see where she's going?" and, "What kind of an outfit is that?" and, "Look! She's wearing a mask." Children also stare. Aasiya asked me the other day if I can tell when she is smiling by just looking at her eyes while she has her veil on. She wants the children to know that she is smiling at them. Unfortunately, you can't tell when she's smiling.

6   I first met Aasiya two years ago at the Los Angeles International Airport. I had been waiting at the spot where people come walking out after clearing immigration and customs. I had seen Mexican soccer teams, Central American immigrants, Japanese tourists, and people returning from vacations in Singapore. Finally, I saw my son, who was dressed, in my mind, like Lawrence of Arabia, and Aasiya, who was completely covered. She said, "Hi, Mom" and gave me a warm hug. It wasn't until an hour later that I was able to see what she looked like. When we arrived home, Aasiya, in her very limited English, managed to keep up a conversation with all of us, and she even had us laughing about all the things that had happened to her during her first airplane trip. When she volunteered to help cut up the chicken for dinner, she sat on the floor, put the knife against the corner of the wall, holding it down with her foot, and proceeded to cut the chicken pushing the chicken pieces past the knife. We were all shocked, but we didn't say anything because we didn't want her to feel uncomfortable. When we sat down to eat, Aasiya ate everything with her fingers—rice, salad, chicken, vegetables, everything. Then, when she was finished eating, she licked each finger individually to clean it off. Again, I was shocked, but my kids kind of liked this fascinating woman with her interesting habits. No one said anything, nor did we communicate our surprise and discomfort to her.

7   Now, Aasiya is more used to American customs. She doesn't prepare food on the floor, but she is still much more comfortable eating with her hands as people do in India and much of the world. She also has continued to wear her veil and practice her religion.

8   Islam is not much different from other major religions that are familiar to us. It comes from the same tradition as Judaism and Christianity. Muslims believe in one God, and they follow basic rules of morality, which perhaps can best be summed up by the commandment, "Do unto others, as you would have others do unto you." Live a moral life on earth and you will be rewarded by going to heaven. Personally, I don't find any of these beliefs offensive, and although my son converted to Islam and married a Muslim woman, I have accepted his decision, and I love his wife.

9   Unfortunately, I don't think most Americans share my views. I think that Muslims are the new group in this country that is easy to fear, to blame, and to hate. Much of this fear, blame, and hate comes from our ignorance. As a group, they are like anyone else. Period. So often though, the bad guy in the movies looks like an Arab (the way we think Muslims look), the "suspects" for most terrorist acts are Muslims, and by extension, we Americans tend to not trust Muslims. We tend to see them as the enemy, almost the same way that Communists were the enemy during the Cold War, almost the same way that many people thought African-Americans, or Jews, or immigrants were the enemy for much of the twentieth century.

© 2014 Wadsworth, Cengage Learning

10   At the supermarket, people view my daughter-in-law with suspicion. They think she is strange, threatening, mysterious, oppressed, and probably timid. She could be the wife of a "terrorist." Understandably, we fear what we cannot know, and I believe we also fear what we cannot see. However, most people's assumptions about Aasiya could not be farther from the truth. She is confident and smart and she can stand up for herself. She is not <u>subjugated</u> by her husband. She makes her own decisions about how she will dress when she goes out on the street. (The other women in her family do not wear the extreme veil that Aasiya wears.) Nobody tells her what to do. I wish everyone in this country could see her when she gets on the back of the grocery cart and pushes off, racing around the parking lot with her *ubaya* flowing behind her. That image reminds us that there is a completely normal, young, playful woman under all of that black.

11   I grew up in the 1950s, and I got used to being stared at when I was a child. People stared at us because my father was black and my mother was white. It was illegal for interracial couples to marry in California at that time, and it was very unusual to see interracial couples at all. That has changed, but not the mentality that led to the law and to people staring at us. Hopefully we will learn to know and accept the latest group of people who are objects of intolerance. I don't like being stared at in the supermarket, but I am blessed with a beautiful daughter-in-law. For me, she is no longer mysterious. I have learned from her, laughed with her, taught her, and we have both grown as human beings together. I wish everyone could be so lucky.

Use context clues, word-part clues, and if necessary the dictionary to write the definitions of the italicized words.

1. Sometimes the stares reflect their fear and *apprehension*, as though some harm could come to them by being near us. (par. 1)

   apprehension _____

2. Mostly their stares convey a sense of complete *disbelief*, as if they were wondering how it is possible for them to see such a woman in a supermarket in suburban America. (par. 1)

   disbelief _____

3. When she goes out in public or when she is around any man who is not an immediate member of her family she wears a veil. Not just an ordinary scarf around her head like many Muslim women do, but a veil—a *nikab*—that covers her entire face, even her eyes. (par. 4)

   nikab _____

4. She also wears a *ubaya*, a kind of black robe which completely covers her regular clothes, and comes down almost to her feet. (par. 4)

   ubaya _____

© 2014 Wadsworth, Cengage Learning

5. People's *verbal* responses to Aasiya are always interesting, and almost always *offensive*. People have told her, "You're in America now," and, "Why don't you go back where you come from?" (par. 5)

verbal _____

6. *offensive* _____

7. She is confident and smart and she can stand up for herself. She is not *subjugated* by her husband. She makes her own decisions about how she will dress when she goes out on the street. (The other women in her family do not wear the extreme veil that Aasiya wears.) Nobody tells her what to do. (par. 10)

subjugated _____

Choose the best answers to the following multiple-choice questions about the reading.

8. Which of the following is the best topic for paragraph 1?
   a. Aasiya in the supermarket
   b. people's reactions to Aasiya
   c. suburban America

9. What is the main idea for paragraph 1?
   a. People think Aasiya is strange and different and perhaps threatening when they see her.
   b. People are startled when they see Aasiya in the supermarket.
   c. People pity Aasiya.

10. Which of the following is the best topic for paragraph 8?
    a. the similarity of the religions
    b. the belief in one God
    c. the belief in heaven

11. The main idea of paragraph 8 is that
    a. Muslims believe in one God.
    b. Muslims believe that if you live a moral life on earth you will be rewarded by going to heaven.
    c. Islam is not much different from other major Western religions that are familiar to us.

12. Which of the following is the best topic for paragraph 9?
    a. ignorance and fear about Muslims
    b. bad guys in movies
    c. Communists during the Cold War

© 2014 Wadsworth, Cengage Learning

13. The main idea of paragraph 9 is that
    a. because of ignorance, people tend to consider Muslims as the enemy.
    b. Communists were the enemy during the Cold War.
    c. the bad guys in the movies frequently look Arab.

14. The author believes that Aasiya is similar to other bright, young, immigrant women because
    a. Aasiya dresses differently from most Americans.
    b. Aasiya likes to swing in the park, she wants to go to Disneyland, and she misses her family.
    c. Aasiya is beautiful.

15. The emphasis of this reading is that Aasiya is different because
    a. she speaks other languages.
    b. she comes from another country.
    c. she wears the *nikab* and the *ubaya*.

16. The author writes that when she is with Aasiya in public, she tries to act normal and friendly. This is so because
    a. she always acts normal and friendly.
    b. she tries extra hard because she wants people to accept Aasiya and herself, and not to treat them differently.
    c. she knows that she is not really a normal person in any case, so when she and Aasiya go out in public, they are quite a spectacle.

17. The author believes that if
    a. everyone had a Muslim daughter-in-law, everything would be better in this world.
    b. people could only know Aasiya, many of their prejudices and fears about Muslims would disappear.
    c. we are ever to solve our problems, we must stop staring at people in the supermarket.

Write short answers to the following questions based on your reading, your experience, and your observations.

18. Have you ever gotten to know someone who looked very different from you? Explain who the person was and how knowing that person affected you.

_____

_____

_____

_____

© 2014 Wadsworth, Cengage Learning

19. How do you think Aasiya feels when she is in public? What would you do to get people to accept you if you were in her position, assuming that she is not going to change her beliefs or the way she dresses?

_____

_____

_____

_____

20. How do you think Aasiya's experiences have changed after 9/11? Explain, considering people's reactions to the way she dresses.

_____

_____

_____

_____

© 2014 Wadsworth, Cengage Learning

Name _____ Date _____

Armando's Tattoos

— Ivan Ramos

The following reading by a student from San Diego City College describes his friendship with a former gang member. In this reading, Ramos shares his research into the meanings of as well as problems associated with gang tattoos.

1   By the time I met Armando Martínez, he didn't have a promising future. When he walked into class, looking uncertain but smiling, we became instantly aware of his presence. He was tall, over six feet, wearing khaki work pants and a plaid flannel shirt, but what most caught my eye were his tattoos. His head was shaved, and there were letters tattooed into his scalp. There were tattoos on each of his fingers. There were tattoos on the back of his neck. I tried not to stare and not to form any negative impressions. But I knew, as we all did, that this guy was a gangbanger and had probably done some time in prison.

2   When we introduced ourselves on that first day, Mando told us he had recently gotten out of prison and was on parole, but now he was going to school because he wanted to turn his life around. He had been trying to get a steady job, but in spite of constant efforts, he couldn't get one because of his appearance and his background. He also told us he was volunteering at a local elementary school, teaching the kids Nahuatl (the language of the Aztecs) after leading them through exercises to help them settle down. Armando never missed class and was never late. He always did the homework. He always had something to add to the discussion—usually a point of view that none of us had thought about. Each of us students got to know him in a special way. He was self-conscious about his clothes and his appearance, and he was trying to get some different clothes so he wouldn't look like a gangbanger. He became part of our group. We even went to the Latino Film Festival together. Then, at one Tuesday night class, our professor showed up with two strangers. We wondered why they were in class. We soon learned they had come to tell us Mando was dead—gunned down by some gangbanging punk in front of his little sisters. Two years have gone by, but I still miss Armando Martínez.

3   I'm sorry now that I didn't ask him to show me his tattoos and to explain them to me. I'm sure he would have done it. But, somehow, I felt so uncomfortable about them that when I was with him I tried to ignore these markings that were so evident all over his body. I have since understood some things better: Members of gangs get tattoos to identify themselves, and sometimes later in life, if they want to turn their lives around, those tattoos are a source of problems.

4   Members of gangs usually wear a uniform of one kind or another. The Crips and Gangster Disciples in Fayetteville, Tennessee, are a good example. Their gang colors are black, blue, gray, white, and green. Some of the symbols they use are a crown, a six-pointed star, a sword, a pitchfork, and a heart with wings, flames, or horns. The Fayetteville Police also report that these two gangs wear their hats <u>cocked</u> to the right, leave their right shoe untied, and roll up their right pants leg. [1]

Ivan Ramos. Written for *Joining a Community of Readers*.

© 2014 Wadsworth, Cengage Learning

5   Gangs can distinguish themselves from other gangs by their uniforms. In Fayetteville, the Vice Lords and the Flippin Street Posse have a uniform that is different from that of the Crips and Gangster Disciples. Their colors are red and white; their symbols are a five-pointed star, a Playboy bunny, a champagne glass, and a pyramid. They wear their hats cocked to the left, leave their left shoe untied, and roll up their left pants leg. [2]

6   With a little Internet research, you can find some amazing information about how gangs dress, but most of the articles are about their tattoos. The gang tattoos frequently have a code behind them. A teardrop tattoo located near the eye <u>signifies</u> that the person has killed someone or has spent time in prison. A <u>shamrock</u>—the three-leaf clover—is used by the white <u>supremacist</u> gang, the Aryan Brotherhood. Various numbers like 13, 14, 1312, and even telephone area codes such as 818, 714, 213, and 619 are gang codes and often appear on tattoos.

7   Some of the gangs most known for their tattoos and violence are called MS-13 and MS-18. The "MS," which they use in their graffiti and tattoos, stands for "Mara Salvatuche." "Salvatuche" refers to someone from El Salvador. Some say the best translation is Salvadoran Pride. The MS gangs formed mostly in the 1980s during the civil wars in Central America when many refugees fled from the violence of those wars to find a better life in the United States. <u>Ironically</u>, the formation of violent gangs was the result of the search for peace. When the Salvadoran kids were faced with discrimination and contempt in their new home, some of them responded by forming MS. Now the gangs exist in many parts of the United States as well as in El Salvador, to which thousands of the members have been deported.

8   When former gang members like Armando decide to turn their lives around, the tattoos can haunt them, but getting rid of them isn't easy. Employers don't usually hire somebody who has tattoos. Police will stop and question somebody who has gang tattoos much more frequently. To help former gang members get rid of their tattoos and the <u>stigma</u> attached to them, there are programs both in the United States and in Central America. Clinics in Central America and in places like San Luis Obispo,

Gang members with tattoos.

White/PhotoLibrary

© 2014 Wadsworth, Cengage Learning

California, provide tattoo-removing services. It can take dozens of treatments to get all of this body art off. Laser removal is the least painful, but it feels like getting burned or snapped with a rubber band. The other form of removal, infrared light treatments, slowly burns the tattoo off and is so painful that <u>anesthesia</u> is used. [3]

9   Researching gang tattoos and removal techniques brings my thoughts back full circle to my friend Armando Martínez. The last time I saw Mando, his tattoos were gone. As he lay in his casket, his skin was an even gray. In death, the makeup that covered his body had finally <u>obliterated</u> his gang tattoos.

Notes

1. Graham Sweeney, "Police Pronounce Proactive Residents Solution to Gangs," *Fayette County Review,* March 10, at http://www.fayettecountyreview.com/articles/2006/03/10/news/news03.text (accessed 3/11/06).

2. *Ibid.*

3. CBS News, "Getting Rid of Gang Tattoos," July 18, 2002, at http://www.cbsnews.com/stories/2002/07/17/earlyshow/contributors/tracysmith/main515437.shtml (accessed 3/11/06).

Use context clues, word-part clues, and, if necessary, the dictionary to write in the appropriate definitions of the italicized words in the following sentences.

1. The Fayetteville Police also report that these two gangs wear their hats *cocked* to the right, leave their right shoe untied, and roll up their right pants leg. (par. 4)

   cocked _____

2. A teardrop tattoo located near the eye *signifies* that the person has killed someone or has spent time in prison. (par. 6)

   signifies _____

3. A *shamrock*—the three-leaf clover—is used by the white *supremacist* gang, the Aryan Brotherhood. (par. 6)

   shamrock _____

4. *supremacist* _____

5. *Ironically,* the formation of violent gangs was the result of the search for peace. (par. 7)

   ironically _____

6. To help former gang members get rid of their tattoos and the *stigma* attached to them, there are programs both in the United States and in Central America. (par. 8)

   stigma _____

© 2014 Wadsworth, Cengage Learning

7. The other form of removal, infrared light treatments, slowly burns the tattoo off and is so painful that *anesthesia* is used. (par. 8)

anesthesia _____

8. In death, the makeup that covered his body had finally *obliterated* his gang tattoos. (par. 9)

obliterated _____

Choose the best answers to the following multiple-choice questions about the reading.

9. Which of the following is the best topic for paragraph 4?
   a. gang uniforms
   b. the Crips
   c. gang colors

10. Which of the following is the best stated main idea for paragraph 4?
   a. The Crips and Gangster Disciples in Fayetteville, Tennessee, are a good example.
   b. Members of gangs usually wear a uniform of one kind or another.
   c. The Fayetteville Police also report that these two gangs wear their hats cocked to the right, leave their right shoe untied, and roll up their right pants leg.

11. Which of the following is the best topic for paragraph 6?
   a. researching gangs on the Internet
   b. the meaning of the shamrock
   c. the code behind the tattoos

12. Which of the following is the best stated main idea for paragraph 6?
   a. With a little Internet research, you can find some amazing information about how gangs dress, but most of the articles are about their tattoos.
   b. Various numbers like 13, 14, 1312, and even telephone area codes such as 818, 714, 213, and 619 are gang codes and often appear on tattoos.
   c. The gang tattoos frequently have a code behind them.

13. Which of the following is the best topic for paragraph 8?
   a. tattoo removal programs
   b. clinics in Central America and San Luis Obispo, California
   c. discrimination against people with gang tattoos and the difficulties getting rid of them

14. Which of the following is the best stated main idea for paragraph 8?
   a. When former gang members like Armando decide to turn their lives around, the tattoos can haunt them, but getting rid of them isn't easy.
   b. Clinics in Central America and in places like San Luis Obispo, California, provide tattoo-removing services.
   c. To help former gang members get rid of their tattoos and the stigma attached to them, there are programs both in the United States and in Central America.

© 2014 Wadsworth, Cengage Learning

15. What is the least painful method of tattoo removal?
    a. infrared light treatments
    b. scraping
    c. laser

16. What examples are given for places where former gang members can get their tattoos removed?
    a. Fayetteville and Flippin Street
    b. Tampa, Florida
    c. Central America and San Luis Obispo, California

17. Which of the following is the best topic for the entire reading?
    a. meaning of tattoos
    b. gang tattoos
    c. tattoo removal

18. Which of the following is the best thesis statement for the entire reading?
    a. Members of gangs get tattoos to identify themselves, and sometimes later in life, if they want to turn their lives around, those tattoos are a source of problems.
    b. Two years have gone by, but I still miss Armando Martínez.
    c. When the Salvadoran kids were faced with discrimination and contempt in their new home, some of them responded by forming MS.

Write short answers to the following questions based on your reading, your experience, and your observations.

19. How do you think law enforcement officers can use information about gang tattoos?

    _____

    _____

    _____

    _____

20. Do you think it's a good idea for gang members to identify themselves with tattoos? Explain your answer.

    _____

    _____

    _____

    _____

© 2014 Wadsworth, Cengage Learning

4 Unstated Main Ideas

CHALLENGES IN EDUCATION

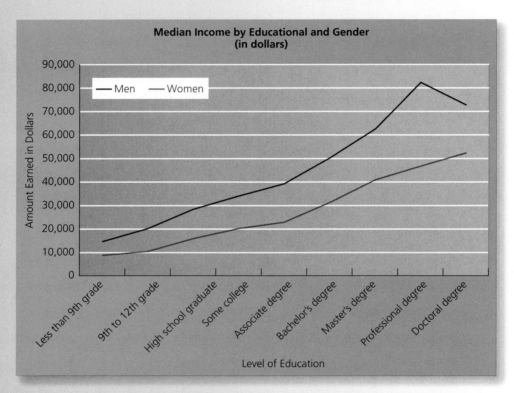

Median Income by Educational and Gender (in dollars)

Source: U.S. Census Bureau, 2004 *Historical Income Tables — People* (Washington, D.C.: U.S. Department of Commerce, 2004), table P-16; also at www.census.gov

- How much money per year do men earn if they don't have a high school diploma, but have completed some high school? Women?

- According to this chart, which category of degree and gender earns the most money per year? What is the difference for women with the same degree?

- How do you think we can explain the difference in earnings between men and women?

- What is the highest degree you are planning to complete? What are your reasons for this choice, keeping in mind that money isn't everything?

Getting Ready to Read

Why do some people do well in school while others do not? What behaviors, both in and out of the classroom, help us to do well in school? What behaviors hold us back? Some people believe that the home environment is most important for preparing students to do well; others believe that what happens in the classroom itself is most important. The answers to these questions are vital to us as individuals and to our society as a whole. After all, the purpose of schools is to help us prepare for life, to fit into our society, and to be productive and aware citizens. How can we be sure that our schools are doing a good job?

In this chapter, you will read and think about student and teacher behaviors and what is necessary for students to be successful. As you do, you will improve your reading skills by learning how to:

- Identify unstated main ideas
- Write main idea, central idea, and thesis sentences in your own words

© 2014 Wadsworth, Cengage Learning

Reading 1

Education in the United States:
They Think I'm Dumb

— MARGARET L. ANDERSEN AND HOWARD F. TAYLOR

TEXT BOOK **This reading is from a college sociology textbook. It begins with the story of a young African-American boy and his experiences with school. As you read, think about what you know about schools, and what you think are some of the successes as well as the problems of our schools.**

pseudonym
false name

1 Ollie Taylor (a pseudonym) is a bright eleven-year-old African American. He is growing up in a two-parent family in Boston. Although he receives considerable encouragement, love, and respect from his family, Ollie Taylor is certain that everything he attempts will fail. He is convinced that he is, in his own words, worthless. Ollie's feelings about himself can be traced directly to his school rather than his family or his peers. In Ollie Taylor's case, the feeling of worthlessness was significantly created by the system of tracking: the grouping, or stratifying, of students within the educational system according to their presumed academic ability.

presumed
supposed

2 In Ollie's own words:
   The only thing that matters in my life is school, and there they think I am dumb and always will be. I'm starting to think they are right. . . . Upper tracks? Man, when do you think I see those kids? I never see them. . . . If I ever walked into one of their rooms, they'd throw me out before the teacher ever came in. They'd say I'd only be holding them back from their learning (Psychologist Tom Cottie, quoting Ollie Taylor [pseudonym]).

3 Stories like Ollie Taylor's are common. His case highlights one of the problems facing the American system of education: Should children be grouped (tracked) according to their ability, allowing them to learn at their most comfortable pace, or should they be grouped simply by age, perhaps impeding the progress of fast learners and setting too quick a pace for the slow learners?

exemplifies
is an example of

4 There are both positive and negative consequences to early tracking of students. . . . Ollie Taylor's case exemplifies the negative consequences, but all is not necessarily bleak for Ollie and those like him. Ollie's case also exemplifies the positive possibilities of getting an education in the United States. As an African American, he is six times more likely to graduate from high school now than in 1940. After earning a high school diploma, he will be more likely to get a good job and less likely to join the ranks of the unemployed. If he completes his education, he will be more likely—though certainly not guaranteed—to earn a sufficient wage.

5 Unfortunately, Ollie's chances of dropping out prior to graduation are fairly high. They are considerably higher than for a white man of his age but significantly lower than for a Hispanic young man of his age. If, however, he does graduate, he will stand a better chance of avoiding the grim path of many urban black and Hispanic male drop-outs and many white youth as well—a path leading to unemployment and possibly drug abuse, poor health, incarceration, and death at an early age.

perpetuation
continuation,
maintaining

6 The education institution in the United States is capable of sending a person down two entirely different paths. One leads to the perpetuation of racial, ethnic,

© 2014 Wadsworth, Cengage Learning

spawns produces

prospects
possibilities

socioeconomic, and gender inequalities in society; the other lessens these inequalities as the individual goes on to a good job, a decent income, and relative happiness. The system of education in this country spawns both outcomes, making or breaking the life prospects of millions of students like Ollie Taylor.

Exercise 1

Recall and Discuss

Answer these questions about Reading 1, and prepare to discuss them in class.

1. How does Ollie Taylor feel about himself as a student, and why does he feel that way?

_____

_____

_____

2. According to the reading, what are the advantages and disadvantages of tracking?

_____

_____

_____

_____

_____

_____

3. Have you had any experiences with tracking? Do you thinking tracking is a good idea? Explain your opinion.

_____

_____

_____

4. How has the education of African-Americans changed since 1940?

_____

_____

_____

© 2014 Wadsworth, Cengage Learning

5. Who do you know or know about who has done really well in the American education system? How do you think that happened?

_____

_____

_____

6. What do you think the schools can do to help students be successful and complete high school? Where else might children get help in addition to school?

_____

_____

_____

Unstated Main Ideas

In Chapter 3 you identified topics and main ideas that were stated directly in the paragraph or passage. The main idea, as you remember, is simply a general statement, or assertion the writer wants to make about the topic. However, as a reader you will find that main ideas are not always so obvious. Sometimes the main idea is not stated at all, and you need to arrive at the main point the writer is trying to make based on the information you are given. Sometimes authors deliberately avoid stating main ideas to force readers to think critically about the information presented and to come to their own conclusions.

unstated main idea the main idea of a reading that the reader must figure out because there is no main idea sentence

To decide on an **unstated main idea**, you should follow three basic steps.

1. Identify the topic.
2. List the points made about the topic.
3. Add up the points listed to arrive at the main idea.

Read the following paragraph and see if you can decide what the unstated main idea is by following these three steps.

per capita
per person
compulsory
required

Forty percent of Finns aged 24 to 65 have a college degree compared with 12 percent in the United States. Understandably, Finns are, per capita, the greatest consumers of literature in the world. School attendance is compulsory up to age 16, an earlier age than in Belgium, but schooling is rigorous. High school students attend classes 38 hours a week, compared with about 25 hours in the United States. Finnish students are also required to take more courses, including two foreign languages. All higher education is free, with most financial support coming from the state and the rest from private industries. (Thio, *Sociology*)

© 2014 Wadsworth, Cengage Learning

1. What is the topic? *education in Finland*
2. What are the points made about the topic?

   - *40 percent of Finns have college degrees versus 12 percent in the United States.*
   - *Finns consume the most literature (read the most) in the world.*
   - *Schooling is rigorous (very demanding).*
   - *High school students are in class 38 hours a week versus 25 hours a week in the United States.*
   - *Finns take more courses, including two foreign languages.*
   - *All higher education is free.*

3. Add up the points listed to arrive at the main idea: *Finland has an outstanding educational system.*

Sometimes authors seem to state more than one main idea within a single paragraph. Sometimes the ideas even contradict each other. As you read you must think actively about the ideas presented. If you are asked to identify the main idea in a paragraph where there appears to be more than one, your statement of the main idea may need to include both ideas. For example, read the following paragraph about the Japanese educational system.

attributed to
achieved by, caused by

The Japanese youngsters' academic excellence cannot be attributed to the schools alone. Japanese mothers play a crucial role in their children's education, not only constantly encouraging hard work but also rendering help with homework. After-school classes, called jukus ("cram shops"), also contribute substantially, as they are attended by more than one-quarter of all primary pupils and more than one-half of all secondary students. Since so many students are involved in this supplementary learning, Francis McKenna concludes that the quality of Japanese schooling is actually lower than popularly believed. (Thio, *Sociology*)

Which of the following is the best topic for this paragraph?
   a. the success of Japanese students and jukus
   b. the success of Japanese students and studying outside school

You should have chosen *b* as the best topic because it includes the idea that Japanese students study in different ways outside of school: with their mothers' assistance as well as in after-school classes (jukus).

Which of the following sentences is the better statement of the main idea of this paragraph?
   a. The success of Japanese students may be due to the time they spend studying outside school rather than to the quality of the schools themselves.
   b. After-school classes are the main reason why Japanese students are so successful academically.

You should have chosen sentence *a* as the better statement of the main idea for the paragraph. Sentence *b* emphasizes the contribution of extra hours to Japanese students' success, but the paragraph as a whole does not try to prove that this is the main reason, or the only reason, for their success. Also, this statement does not include the doubts raised in the last sentence of the paragraph about the quality of regular Japanese schools.

© 2014 Wadsworth, Cengage Learning

Exercise 2

Identify Topics and Unstated Main Ideas

For each of the following paragraphs, choose the topic and the sentence that is the better statement of the paragraph's main idea.

inculcate teach with emphasis

1. The public schools, supported by public funds, have the responsibility to teach skills needed in public life—among them the use of the English language. They also must inculcate an appreciation of all the cultures that have contributed to this country's complex social weave. To set one ethnic group apart as more worthy of attention than others is unjust, and might breed resentment against that group. (Mujica, "Bilingualism's Goal")

   topic
   a. cultural appreciation in U.S. society
   b. English language and cultural appreciation in schools

   main idea
   a. All cultures need to be appreciated by the schools, and all students need to be given a good education that includes English.
   b. Special treatment of one ethnic group is not fair and causes resentment.

lure temptation, attraction

2. [His students'] life stories were amazing, and Crowfoot alone had heard every one. He struck up a conversation with a chunky kid in the front row and found himself listening to the dreams of a Salvadoran boy who hoped someday to become a cop. He complimented the artwork of the student who couldn't seem to shut up in class and found himself the confidant of a frustrated adolescent whose Guatemalan mother so feared the lure of gangs that she wouldn't let him out of the house. Someone stuck a wad of chewing gum into the hair of a tattooed class bully and, as he leaned forward to help remove it, he found himself unexpectedly moved by the gleam of hot tears welling in the boy's eyes. (Hubler, "Fledgling Teacher Gets Tough Lessons, Unexpected Rewards")

   topic
   a. student conversations
   b. surprising student stories

   main idea
   a. There were a lot of students in Crowfoot's class.
   b. Crowfoot learned a lot about his students, and sometimes they did not fit the ideas that he had about them before he knew them better.

phenomenal extraordinary

3. There has been phenomenal growth in the number of children who receive their formal education at home. Today there are about 500,000 such children, compared with only 12,500 in the late 1970s. Most of the homeschooling parents are fundamentalist Christians who believe that religion is either abused or ignored in the public school. Other parents reject public education because of poor academic standards, overcrowding, or lack of safety. Most homeschooling parents have some college, with median incomes between $35,000 and $50,000. Over 90 percent are white. (adapted from Thio, *Sociology*)

© 2014 Wadsworth, Cengage Learning

topic
a. reasons for homeschooling
b. income levels of homeschooled students

main idea
a. More parents are choosing homeschooling for their children, and they are doing so for a variety of reasons.
b. Parents often reject public education because of the problems they observe there: poor academic standards, overcrowding, and lack of safety.

4. On a cloudy winter afternoon, Florann Greenberg, a teacher at P.S. 14 in New York City, noticed that her first-grade class was growing fidgety. One girl, dropping all pretense of work, stared at the snow falling outside the schoolroom windows. Annoyed, Greenberg asked her, "Haven't you seen snow before?" The girl whispered, "No." Her classmates began shaking their heads. Then it dawned on Greenberg: Of course these children had never seen snow; almost all were immigrants from Colombia and the Dominican Republic. Immediately, she changed the lesson plan. New topic: What is snow? How is it formed? How do you dress in the snow? What games do you play? (Gray, "Teach Your Children Well")

dawned on
became apparent to, understood by

topic
a. the need for teacher sensitivity and flexibility
b. children from Colombia and the Dominican Republic

main idea
a. Many children have never seen snow and are surprised and fascinated when they see it in New York City for the first time.
b. Teachers like Florann Greenberg need to recognize the diversity of their students' experience and plan lessons accordingly.

5. Younger students sometimes have emotional problems in their educational environment. The stress of taking exams and of meeting deadlines can cause difficulty for those not used to responsibility and intense work. On the other hand, older students with children or with experience in jobs or the military adapt to pressure and stress more easily. A student who is also the parent of three children, for example, knows that grades, exams, and reports are not the most important aspects of life. Older students are also less likely to be intimidated by instructors or professors. (Levine and Adelman, *Beyond Language*)

topic
a. student age and handling stress
b. younger students and stress

main idea
a. Younger students sometimes have emotional problems in their educational environment.
b. Older students are likely to handle the stress of being a student better than younger students.

© 2014 Wadsworth, Cengage Learning

Reading 2

Fear 101

— JAN JARRELL

In the following reading, Jan Jarrell, an English professor at a community college in California, reflects on why some of her students may be failing or dropping out. She connects her experience to a recent study of community college students across the United States. As you read, identify her thesis and the main ideas, stated or unstated.

1   Today, most high school seniors plan to go to college. They understand that a degree will help them get a better job. It is worth their time, energy, and money. Yet, by age 30, only about 30 percent of adults in the United States have obtained a bachelor's degree. As a college student, you can probably quickly list the reasons why people do not achieve this goal: money problems, family obligations, jobs, relationships, social activities, and personal issues, such as a lack of motivation. But have you ever considered that fear might be stopping people from realizing their dreams? Professor Rebecca D. Cox of Seton Hall University has. In fact, she wrote a book about it: *The College Fear Factor: How Students and Professors Misunderstand One Another.* After interviewing and observing dozens of students and professors at 34 campuses over a five-year period, Cox concluded that fear is often at the heart of student failure.

2   After reading her book, I realize that there are many reasons for this fear; it grows out of a variety of student backgrounds. As a community college professor, the experiences of my own students mirror those that Cox describes in her book.

3   In many ways, I consider Danny to be a typical first-year college student. He had never liked school much. Some electives such as art were okay, but mostly he went to school just to hang out with his friends. He barely graduated from high school, and said he didn't remember writing a single essay in four years. He enrolled in college because there weren't any decent jobs in his community, and he wanted more options in life. He met with a counselor and decided to major in machine technology, though he would have to brush up his math, reading, and study skills first. He was excited when classes began. However, after the first week, he looked through the stack of syllabi he had collected and felt overwhelmed. He told me that he remembers thinking, "I've never been any good at school. Why should that change now? I can't do all of this." During the first month of the semester, a friend got him a part-time job at a warehouse. By midsemester, he had withdrawn from all his classes except one.

first-generation college student the first person in one's family to go to college

4   Brianna's status as a first-generation college student is also common in community colleges. She had done well in high school and felt ready to enroll in college. But her confidence waned when she missed the first meeting of her first class, Psychology 101. It's not that she had forgotten about the class or slept too late or didn't care. In fact, she had even gotten to campus an hour before the start of the class. However, it took her 45 minutes to find a parking space and another 30 minutes to find the classroom. She was too embarrassed to enter the class 15 minutes late. She thought about waiting until after class to explain what had happened to her professor, but she felt too nervous. She figured that the professor would tell her she should have planned to get to campus earlier. She arrived early to the next class session only to discover that the pro

Written by Jan Jarrell. Reprinted by Permission of the author.

© 2014 Wadsworth, Cengage Learning

fessor had already dropped her. In Brianna's words, the professor seemed "too high and mighty" to talk to, and besides, friends had warned her that college professors were really busy and often impatient. She decided to wait until the following semester to take the class. Unfortunately, she had to enroll with the same professor. She felt a knot in her stomach when she walked into class, never spoke to the professor during the whole semester, and ended up with a "D."

5   According to Cox, sometimes students employ counterproductive strategies to manage their fear. These strategies do not help them to achieve their goals. Some students quit to avoid feeling such extreme anxiety. Others sabotage themselves in different ways. My student, Vincent, is a combat veteran who had completed three tours in Iraq before starting college. He had waited until his second year to attempt freshman composition. "I know it's crazy," he stated, "but English really scares me. When I hear the word 'essay,' I just feel like bolting from the classroom." His fear paralyzed him. Although he came every day and was always on time, he **agonized** over his assignments, often turning them in late or not at all. He didn't pass the class, but said he felt good that at least he hadn't dropped. If students do not turn in an assignment, then they do not have to risk failing it. This strategy gives them a more comfortable reason for not passing—it's not that they did poor work, they just didn't complete it.

agonized
struggled

6   I talk to my colleagues all the time and it would be easy for many to conclude that these three students (and others like them) are unmotivated, irresponsible, or lazy. They would see tardiness, absences, and missed deadlines as evidence of these poor qualities. In reality, the fear of failure was simply too crushing. Cox observes that students and professors need to work together in order to overcome this **debilitating** fear. For many students, the first strategy is to acknowledge the fear and make the decision to persevere in spite of it. For professors, recognizing students' fears is important, but they also need to be able to "come down" to the students' level by being friendly and accessible.

debilitating
destructive

7   There are many reasons why a student fails his or her courses or drops out of college altogether. The work of Rebecca Cox sheds light on a core issue that has previously been ignored or even invisible. Bringing this fear out in the open is the first step to diminishing its negative influence and building a foundation for student success.

Exercise 3

Work with Words

Use context clues, word-part clues, and, if necessary, the dictionary to write the definitions of the italicized words in the following sentences from Reading 2.

1. Yet, by age 30, only about 30 percent of adults in the U.S. have *obtained* a bachelor's degree. (par. 1)

   obtained _____

   _____

© 2014 Wadsworth, Cengage Learning

2. But her confidence *waned* when she missed her first class, Psychology 101. (par. 4)

waned _____

_____

3. Others *sabotage* themselves in different ways. (par. 5)

sabotage _____

_____

4. "I know it's crazy," he stated, "but English really scares me. When I hear the word 'essay,' I just feel like *bolting* from the classroom." (par. 5)

bolting _____

_____

5. For many students, the first strategy is to acknowledge the fear and make the decision to *persevere* in spite of it. (par. 6)

persevere _____

_____

6. Bringing this fear out in the open is the first step to *diminishing* its negative influence and building a foundation for student success. (par. 7)

diminishing _____

_____

Exercise 4

Identify Unstated Main Ideas

For each of the following paragraphs from Reading 2, choose the better main idea statement from the two sentences given. The main idea may be stated or unstated in the paragraph.

1. Paragraph 3
   a. Negative experiences in high school can increase a student's anxiety in college.
   b. Danny and many college students never liked school very much.

© 2014 Wadsworth, Cengage Learning

2. Paragraph 4
   a. A professor may drop you if you aren't present on the first day of class.
   b. For many students like Brianna a professor that seems too distant can add to a student's fears.

3. Paragraph 5
   a. Some students quit to avoid feeling such extreme anxiety.
   b. Students use counterproductive strategies to manage their fear.

4. Paragraph 6
   a. Students and professors can work together to overcome the negative impact of fear.
   b. Professors might see these students as unmotivated, irresponsible, or lazy.

5. The thesis of the whole reading:
   a. Fear is an important reason why students fail or drop classes.
   b. By age 30, only about 30 percent of adults in the U.S. have obtained a bachelor's degree.

Exercise 5

Check Your Understanding

Write brief answers to the following questions about Reading 2.

1. List some reasons why people do not finish college.

   _____

   _____

   _____

2. What are some unhelpful fear management strategies mentioned in paragraph 5? Explain and give examples.

   _____

   _____

   _____

   _____

© 2014 Wadsworth, Cengage Learning

Exercise 6

Make Connections and Write

Write short answers to the following questions based on Reading 2, your experience, and your observations. Then discuss your answers with your class group. Working together, prepare a report for your class as a whole or a written summary for your instructor.

1. Describe a situation when you or someone you know experienced the kind of fear discussed in this reading.

_____

_____

_____

2. What are some positive coping strategies that students could use who face the fears discussed in this reading?

_____

_____

_____

3. What do you think is the most important reason why so many people do not realize their goal of getting a college degree? Do you agree with the reading? Why or why not?

_____

_____

_____

_____

Writing Main Idea Sentences

. . . .

unstated main idea sentence your sentence for stating the main idea of a paragraph when the author does not directly state it

To identify an unstated main idea, you may need to write that idea in your own words. This is an **unstated main idea sentence**. To formulate an unstated main idea sentence, follow the steps for finding the main idea, then add one step, as follows:

1. Identify the topic.
2. List the points made about the topic.
3. Add up the points listed to arrive at the main idea.
4. Include the topic in the unstated main idea sentence, which explains what the author is saying about the topic.

© 2014 Wadsworth, Cengage Learning

For example, read the following paragraph.

Among the students in continuing education programs are blue-collar workers seeking a promotion, a raise, or a new career; homemakers preparing to enter the job market at middle age; retired people seeking to pursue interests postponed or dormant during their working years; and people who want to enrich the quality of their personal, family, and social lives. Most of these adults are serious students, as 60 percent are enrolled in a degree program. (Thio, *Sociology*)

dormant
not active

1. What is the topic? *adults returning to school (or more specifically) reasons why adults return to school*
2. What is the main idea? *Adults return to college for many different reasons.*

Because the main idea is not stated in this paragraph, you need to write it in a complete sentence of your own. Notice that the words used for the topic of the paragraph are included in the unstated main idea sentence.

Language Tip: Writing Complete Sentences

When you are asked to write the main idea for a paragraph or for a longer passage you've read, be sure you write that idea as a complete sentence. A complete sentence is a subject and verb combination that can stand on its own. For example, the following group of words is a complete sentence: "I arrived at school early." It has a subject, *I,* and a verb, *arrived,* and it is a complete thought that makes sense by itself. However, if we change this group of words to say, "If I arrive at school early," *I* is the subject, and *arrive* is the verb. But this group of words is still not a complete sentence. The word *If* at the beginning sets up a condition that isn't completed in the sentence. It's not a complete thought, so it's not a sentence. The sentence would be complete if it were worded something like this: "If I arrive at school early, I will have time to review my work." Likewise, "Men riding in a car" and "Because he doesn't like anchovies" are groups of words that do not form complete sentences. They would be sentences if they were worded something like this: "Three men were riding to work in the car," and "James won't eat the pizza because he doesn't like anchovies." Remember, a complete sentence must have a:

1. Subject
2. Verb
3. Complete thought that makes sense
4. Capital at the beginning
5. Period, question mark, or exclamation point at the end

© 2014 Wadsworth, Cengage Learning

Exercise 7   Write Complete Sentences

The following groups of words are not complete sentences. Rewrite each group of words so it forms a complete sentence. The first one has been done for you.

1. People who want to enrich the quality of their personal, family, and social lives

   <u>People who want to enrich the quality of their personal, family, and social</u>

   <u>lives often return to college after many years.</u>

   _____

2. How Matthew earned a degree in mathematics

   _____

   _____

   _____

3. After the final exam was over

   _____

   _____

   _____

4. Since John forgot to bring his watch to class on the day of the test

   _____

   _____

   _____

5. If you want to complete a B.A. degree in only four years

   _____

   _____

   _____

© 2014 Wadsworth, Cengage Learning

6. Who continue to study after high school than in any other country

_____

_____

_____

7. If you don't get your high school diploma

_____

_____

_____

8. Unlike everybody else who had something to say during class

_____

_____

_____

Organize to Learn: Work in Groups

One of the most beneficial ways for many people to organize what they've learned involves working in groups. If you already know that you learn best by discussing what you've read with other people or completing tasks—such as answering questions, organizing ideas graphically or reviewing for a test—with a friend or two, working in groups may be a strategy that you want to use regularly to improve your understanding and ensure that you remember what you've learned. Many people find working in groups an excellent learning and studying technique. Researchers have identified a number of things that help make small groups more effective, whether they are these groups are working together at school or at work.

© 2014 Wadsworth, Cengage Learning

Exercise 8   Work with a Partner or a Group

Working with a partner or a group, answer the following questions and prepare to discuss your answers in class.

1. List the advantages and disadvantages of studying in a group, and steps that you think people in groups could take to make sure that the group functions well.

   Advantages of Working in Groups

   _____

   _____

   _____

   Possible Problems of Working in Groups

   _____

   _____

   _____

   Ways to Make Groups Work Well

   _____

   _____

   _____

2. Employers today say it is important for people to be able to work collaboratively on projects. Why do you think this is true? Give some examples you know of where people have to work in groups on their jobs.

   _____

   _____

   _____

© 2014 Wadsworth, Cengage Learning

Participating in Small Groups

— [ADAPTED FROM] LARRY SAMOVAR

TEXT BOOK The following reading discusses how small work groups function. It also gives some guidelines for how a group of people can work together well. As you read, think about the experiences you have had working in small groups and try to identify the main ideas.

1   Learning to work with other people is one of the most important skills you can develop for your college career and for your lifetime of work. More and more often, students are required to work with their peers—other students in the class—to carry out a variety of tasks. In any of your classes you may be asked to discuss an article together or to review information provided in a lecture. You may even be asked to do a project together or to write a paper together for which you will be graded as a group! Working collaboratively with other people is a skill that will often be required of you in your lifetime of work.

2   There are many advantages to working with other people, because several minds are better than one. At the same time, there can be disadvantages if the group doesn't work well together.

3   Experts who write about small-group communication agree on certain guidelines, or rules, that are important for members of small groups to follow. First of all, *the members of the group must be motivated to do their best for their group.* So it is important that everyone be prepared to contribute as much as he or she possibly can.

4   The two types of roles that all members of the group must play are (1) task roles and (2) supportive roles. *Task roles* are the responsibilities that group members have in order to work together and achieve their goal. *Supportive roles* involve the actions that individual members must take to make sure that everyone in the group gets along and works well together.

5   The two types of roles that you play overlap: One action may fulfill both roles. For example, a group member might say, "That's a good idea. I think we should write it down as part of our answer." This person is helping the group carry out its assignment ("we should write it down as part of our answer") and at the same time is also being supportive of the other members of the group ("that's a good idea").

TASK ROLES

functional
useful

6   If you perform the following functional and task roles, you and your group will benefit.

   a. Your group should decide on the steps you will follow to accomplish the assignment. If you are asked for the causes of a certain problem, concentrate on the causes. Don't allow yourselves to start talking about what might have happened if something had been different.

   b. You need to be an active member of the group. Contribute as much as you can, but be brief and concise. Don't dominate your group by speaking more than everyone else or insisting that all your ideas be used. Make sure everyone has an opportunity to talk.

   c. By asking questions you can be sure that you all understand the discussion in the same way. You might clarify your understanding by posing questions like: "I think

© 2014 Wadsworth, Cengage Learning

Larry Samovar, "Participating in Small Groups," from *Oral Communication: Speaking Across Cultures,* Brown & Benchmark. © 1995. Used with permission. Page Number/s: 7–10

clarify
make clear

that the author is saying that it helps children if they learn how to read in their first language before they try to learn how to read in a language that they don't under-stand. Do you think that was his point?" In this way, you both clarify what the author was saying, and you find out if your group needs to discuss the idea more before you all agree.

    d. Be a leader when your group needs it. Don't expect one member of the group to make all the decisions. Each member of the group can be a leader at different times. No one person has all the answers. That's why you are working in a group.

SUPPORTIVE ROLES

7   There are six maintenance and supportive roles that you should keep in mind when you are working in a group.

    a. All of us are different. Each member of your group will have his or her own person-ality and areas of strengths. Members of your group may also come from different cultural backgrounds. Show respect for everyone in your group.

    b. Even if everything that you say is polite, members of your group will also understand your body language. If you frown or make faces, or look at the ceiling when some-one is talking, that person will understand that you disapprove or you are not inter-ested in what he or she is saying.

    c. Your feedback should be clear. You should give verbal and nonverbal responses when your group members are talking. You can make friendly gestures like smil-ing or nodding your head so they know you are alert. You can also show that you are interested in what they are saying by interjecting supportive sounds ("Uh-huh," "I see what you're saying").

    d. Keep a positive and constructive atmosphere. Tell members of your group when they do something well. Encourage each other. Especially encourage the members of the group who do not speak up as much. They may be just as well prepared, and they may have something valuable to say. But you won't know if you don't give them a chance by encouraging their participation.

    e. Communication is a two-way process. Both the listener and the speaker are responsible. Listeners need to be alert and ask questions if they are unclear about what the speaker is trying to communicate. If there is someone in the group who disagrees with everyone else, make every effort to understand that person's point of view.

    f. You may at times need to (1) seek other people's opinions, (2) help the group decide what to do next, (3) help the group stop and evaluate its progress, (4) recognize when members of the group are close to agreement, and (5) help keep the group spirit up.

Exercise 9

Work with Words

Use context clues, word-part clues, and, if necessary, the dictionary to write the definitions of the italicized words in the following sentences from Reading 3.

    1. More and more often, students are required to work with their *peers*—other students in the class—to carry out a variety of tasks. (par. 1)

    peers _____

© 2014 Wadsworth, Cengage Learning

2. Working *collaboratively* with other people is a skill that will often be required of you in your lifetime of work. (par. 1)

   collaboratively _____

3. Experts who write about small-group communication agree on certain *guidelines,* or rules, that are important for members of small groups to follow. (par. 3)

   guidelines _____

4. Contribute as much as you can, but be brief and *concise.* (par. 6, item b)

   concise _____

5. Your *feedback* should be clear. You should give verbal and *nonverbal* responses when your group members are talking. (par. 7, item c)

   feedback _____

6. *nonverbal* _____

   _____

   _____

Exercise 10

Write the Main Idea in Your Own Words

Write a main idea sentence in your own words for each of the following paragraphs and a thesis sentence for all of Reading 3. The first one has been done for you.

1. Paragraph 6, item b

   Be an active member of your group, but be sure that everyone else has a

   chance to contribute as well.

2. Paragraph 6, item c

   _____

   _____

3. Paragraph 7, item a

   _____

   _____

© 2014 Wadsworth, Cengage Learning

4. Paragraph 7, item b

_____

_____

5. Paragraph 7, item f

_____

_____

6. What is the thesis of Reading 3?

_____

_____

Exercise 11

Check Your Understanding

Write brief answers to the following questions about Reading 3.

1. How do the "task roles" help the groups function?

_____

_____

_____

2. How do the "supportive roles" help the groups function?

_____

_____

_____

Exercise 12

Make Connections: Collaborative Activity

Based on Reading 3, your experience, and your observations, write suggestions for improving the way your class groups function. Your suggestions can be for yourself, for members of your group, or for your class group as a whole. Remember to keep your comments positive.

© 2014 Wadsworth, Cengage Learning

_____

_____

_____

_____

_____

_____

Reading 4

The Pursuit of Just Getting By

— AMY WIDNER

This reading is an article that appeared in the student newspaper at the University of Central Arkansas. It was written by a student, Amy Widner, who subsequently graduated and is now a reporter for the Arkansas Democrat-Gazette. In this article, she challenges students who think it's cool to not really try hard to do well in college.

1   Pretending to be dumb to look cool didn't make sense in high school and it certainly doesn't make sense in college. And yet I can't even begin to count how many times I've overheard fellow students play the how-low-achieving-can-you-go game before class starts.

2   "Hey man, how'd you do on the test?"

3   "Oh, man, I got a D, but I didn't study at all, so I guess it's alright."

4   "Yeah, same here. D is for diploma."

5   While I recognize the various purposes that such a conversation might serve—stress relief, nervous small talk, academic confessionals—an unfortunate, and allegedly unintentional side effect is that it gets on my nerves. These conversations, and their evil twin—the have-you-started-on-that-project-yet conversation—may be commonplace enough that they seem normal, but they indicate some very abnormal thinking.

6   We're in college, and our education is costing someone money. In a time when it has become almost automatic to get an undergraduate degree, it seems like students are losing sight of this. But even if college is starting to feel more like extended high school, procrastinating and trying to get by doing as little as possible does not make sense. We are paying our professors to teach us as much as they can to increase our chances of excelling in the job market. Why avoid those lessons when we, our parents, and even taxpayers are spending so much for us to have access to knowledge?

The Pursuit of Just Getting By Amy Widner from *Arkansas Democrat-Gazette,*
March 2008. Reprinted by permission.

© 2014 Wadsworth, Cengage Learning

7   Professors are not an enemy setting up some kind of obstacle course to be success-fully navigated. The winner is not the person who completes the obstacle course with the least amount of effort. And there is no automatic prize at the end—no cheese, and certainly no job. Skills and knowledge are what help students get jobs in the real world, as well as experience working hard and getting things done on time. None of these things are achieved by avoiding work.

8   Another aspect of this attitude that doesn't make sense is what it assumes about employers. Imagine an employer saying the following: "Hi, I'm an employer. I see you graduated from college. That must mean that you know everything you need to know to work for me, so I won't bother seeing if you have any of the skills needed for this job. I'll go ahead and pay you well while I'm at it, because you graduated from college and that's all I care about."

9   Why does all of this bother me so much? It makes students in general look bad, which decreases trust and professionalism. It shows disrespect to professors and the knowledge they're trying to share. It creates a fake atmosphere in the classroom, where the pursuit of knowledge should be the goal instead of the pursuit of just getting by. It lessens what having a college degree means. It makes college a joke, and I'm not quite ready to believe it is yet.

10   The two students having the conversation above should either be making the most of their education by completing their assignments on time and to the best of their abilities, or should be too ashamed to admit out loud that they are doing other-wise. Procrastination and a poor work ethic should not be what we're practicing in college, because they're not what we should be proud of and, in the end, will not be what we'll be rewarded for. So the next time we're tempted to boast at how little work we got away with on that last assignment or how close to the last min-ute we waited to get something done, remember: We're not fooling anybody but ourselves.

Exercise 13

Work with Words

Use context clues, word-part clues, and, if necessary, the dictionary to choose the best definitions of the italicized words in the following sentences from Reading 4.

1. While I recognize the various purposes that such a conversation might serve—stress relief, nervous small talk, academic confessionals—an unfortunate, and *allegedly unintentional* side effect is that it gets on my nerves. (par. 5)

   allegedly
   a. obviously
   b. supposedly
   c. inaccurately

2. *unintentional*
   a. accidental
   b. unavoidable
   c. deliberate

© 2014 Wadsworth, Cengage Learning

3. We're in college and our education is costing someone money. In a time when it has become almost automatic to get an undergraduate degree, it seems like students are *losing sight* of this. (par. 6)

   losing sight of
   a. having problems with their eyes
   b. forgetting
   c. remembering

4. Another *aspect* of this attitude that doesn't make sense is what it assumes about employers. (par. 8)

   aspect
   a. advantage
   b. limit
   c. side

5. It creates a fake atmosphere in the classroom, where the *pursuit of* knowledge should be the goal instead of the pursuit of just getting by. (par. 9)

   pursuit of
   a. disregard for
   b. division of
   c. search for

6. The two students having the conversation above should either be making the most of their education by completing their assignments on time and to the best of their abilities, or should be too ashamed to admit out loud that they are doing *otherwise*. (par. 10)

   otherwise
   a. differently
   b. separately
   c. likewise

7. Procrastination and a poor *work ethic* should not be what we're practicing in college, because they're not what we should be proud of and, in the end, will not be what we'll be rewarded for. (par. 10)

   work ethic
   a. pay for work
   b. work hours
   c. work habits

8. So the next time we're tempted to *boast* at how little work we got away with on that last assignment or how close to the last minute we waited to get something done, remember: We're not fooling anybody but ourselves. (par. 10)

   boast
   a. report
   b. apologize
   c. brag

© 2014 Wadsworth, Cengage Learning

Exercise 14

Write the Main Idea in Your Own Words

Write a main idea sentence in your own words for each of the following paragraphs and a thesis sentence for all of Reading 4. The main idea may or may not be stated.

1. Paragraphs 1–5

   _____

   _____

   _____

2. Paragraph 6

   _____

   _____

   _____

3. Paragraph 7

   _____

   _____

   _____

4. Write a thesis for the whole reading.

   _____

   _____

   _____

Exercise 15

Check Your Understanding

Write brief answers to the following questions about Reading 4.

1. What does the author mean when she writes, "Professors are not an enemy setting up some kind of obstacle course to be successfully navigated" in paragraph 7? What is an "obstacle course"?

   _____

   _____

© 2014 Wadsworth, Cengage Learning

_____

_____

_____

2. What does the author mean, and to whom is she referring when she says, "We're not fooling anybody but ourselves."

_____

_____

Exercise 16

Make Connections and Write

Write short answers to the following questions based on Reading 4, your own experience, and your observations. Then discuss your answers with your class group. Working together, prepare a report for your class as a whole or a written summary for your instructor.

1. Why do you think some students in college choose to just "get by?"

_____

_____

_____

2. What are your friends' attitudes toward studying? Explain and give examples as the author of this reading does.

_____

_____

_____

3. What is your approach to your studies? Are you a hard worker or are you pursuing just getting by? Explain your answer.

_____

_____

_____

© 2014 Wadsworth, Cengage Learning

Chapter Review

To aid your review of the reading skills in Chapter 4, study the Put It Together chart.

Put It Together: Unstated Main Ideas	
Skills and Concepts	Explanation
Unstated Main Ideas (see pages 166–167)	An unstated main idea occurs when the author does not include a main idea sentence. To determine the unstated main idea, follow three basic steps: 1. Identify the topic. 2. List the points made about the topic. 3. Add up the points listed to arrive at the main idea.
Unstated Main Idea Sentences (see pages 174–175)	An unstated main idea sentence is your sentence for stating the main idea of a paragraph when the author does not directly state it. To write an unstated main idea sentence, you add another step to the preceding three steps. 4. Explain what the author is saying about the topic.
Complete Sentences (see page 175)	To write a complete sentence, remember that it must have a: 1. Subject 2. Verb 3. Complete thought that makes sense 4. Capital at the beginning 5. Period, question mark, or exclamation point at the end

To reinforce your learning before taking the Mastery Tests, complete as many of the following activities as your instructor assigns.

Review Skills

Individually or in a group, read the following paragraph. Then follow the steps in "Put It Together" to write the topic and a complete sentence that states the un-stated main idea for this paragraph.

Revlon, the cosmetics company, is being taught in public schools these days. The corporation provides teachers with a free curriculum that instructs students on "good and bad hair days" and asks them to list three hair products they would absolutely need if stranded on a desert island. Meanwhile, in science class, students can conduct a Campbell Soup "Prego Thickness Experiment" comparing the thickness of Prego versus Ragu spaghetti sauces. They can also learn from the American Coal Foundation that the planet may be helped rather than harmed by increased carbon dioxide, while materials sent by Chevron challenge the existence of global warming. A first grade curriculum uses logo recognition—K-Mart, Pizza Hut, Jell-O, and

© 2014 Wadsworth, Cengage Learning

Target—to teach reading while McDonald's, not to be outdone, asks first graders to design a McDonald's restaurant and instructs them on how to apply to the company for a job. (Kanner, "Today's Class Brought to You By. . .")

topic: _____

_____

unstated main idea sentence: _____

_____

Write

In a paragraph, identify your strengths when working in a group. In a second paragraph, describe ways you think you can improve your group participation.

COLLABORATE

In your group, list as many factors as you can think of in the classroom and outside the classroom that contribute to motivating students and helping them be successful in school. Also, list factors (both inside and outside the classroom) that you think demotivate students, making it difficult for them to succeed in school. Include in your two lists information that you have gathered from Chapter 4, as well as what you know, what you have experienced, and what you have observed. Your instructor may ask you to present your findings to the class.

Inside-the-Classroom Motivators

1. _____

2. _____

3. _____

4. _____

5. _____

Outside-the-Classroom Motivators

1. _____

2. _____

3. _____

4. _____

5. _____

© 2014 Wadsworth, Cengage Learning

Inside-the-Classroom Demotivators	Outside-the-Classroom Demotivators
1. _____	1. _____
2. _____	2. _____
3. _____	3. _____
4. _____	4. _____
5. _____	5. _____

EXTEND YOUR THINKING

Find an article from a newspaper or magazine that (1) describes someone who has overcome a very difficult educational situation or challenge or (2) describes successes or problems in a local school. Clip the article and share it with your class group.

Write a central idea or thesis statement for your article to share with your class group and to turn in to your instructor. Be sure that your thesis statement is (1) a complete sentence and (2) a sentence that includes the important points that add up in your article.

 ## WORK THE WEB

Many newspapers and education research and advocacy groups have companion Web sites with frequently updated articles. To learn more about current issues in education and to practice identifying and writing main ideas, use a search engine such as *Google* to look up the phrase "Issues in Education Articles." Browse the Web sites that appear on the first page of your search. Choose an article, read it, and then answer the following questions. Make a copy of your article to turn in with your answers.

1. What is the title of the article?

   _____

2. What is the topic of the article? (State it in your own words.)

   _____

3. What is the central idea, or thesis, of the article? Be sure to write a complete sentence.

   _____

© 2014 Wadsworth, Cengage Learning

Name _____ Date _____

A Third of the Nation Cannot Read These Words

— Jonathan Kozol

In the following reading, Jonathan Kozol does not state his main idea. He instead tells a story about a man who cannot read, and he allows you, the reader, to draw your own conclusions. As you read, put the pieces of the story together so that you can identify Kozol's unstated central idea, or thesis.

meticulous
very neat

1   He is meticulous and well-defended.

2   He gets up in the morning, showers, shaves, and dresses in a dark gray business suit, then goes downstairs and buys a *New York Times* from the small newsstand on the corner of his street. Folding it neatly, he goes into the subway and arrives at work at 9 A.M.

3   He places the folded *New York Times* next to the briefcase on his desk and sets to work on graphic illustrations for the advertising <u>copy</u> that is handed to him by the editor who is his boss.

4   "Run over this with me. Just make sure I get the <u>gist</u> of what you really want."

5   The editor, unsuspecting, takes this as a reasonable request. In the process of expanding on his copy, he recites the language of the text: a language that is instantly <u>imprinted</u> on the illustrator's mind.

6   At lunch he grabs the folded copy of the *New York Times,* carries it with him to a coffee shop, places it beside his plate, eats a sandwich, drinks a beer, and soon heads back to work.

7   At 5 P.M., he takes his briefcase and his *New York Times,* waits for the elevator, walks two blocks to catch an uptown bus, stops at a corner store to buy some groceries, then goes upstairs. He carefully unfolds his *New York Times.* He places it with mechanical <u>precision</u> on a pile of several other recent copies of the *New York Times.* There they will remain until, when two or three more copies have been added, he will take all but the one most recent and <u>consign</u> them to the trash. . . .

8   He opens the refrigerator, snaps the top from a cold can of Miller's beer, and turns on the TV.

9   Next day, trimly dressed and cleanly shaven, he will buy another *New York Times,* fold it neatly, and proceed to work. He is a rather <u>solitary</u> man. People in his office view him with respect as someone who is self-contained and does not choose to join in casual conversation. If somebody should mention something that is in the news, he will give a dry, sardonic answer based upon the information he has <u>garnered</u> from TV.

10 He is protected against the outside world. Someday he will probably be trapped. It has happened before; so he can guess that it will happen again. Defended for now against <u>humiliation</u>, he is not defended against fear. He tells me that he has recurrent dreams.

11 "Somebody says: WHAT DOES THIS MEAN? I stare at the page. A thousand copies of the *New York Times* run past me on a giant screen. Even before I am awake, I start to scream."

From *Illiterate America* by Jonathan Kozol, © 1985 by Jonathan Kozol.
Used by permission of Doubleday, a division of Random House, Inc.

© 2014 Wadsworth, Cengage Learning

12   If it is of any comfort to this man, he should know that he is not alone. Twenty-five million American adults cannot read the poison warnings on a can of pesticide, a letter from their child's teacher, or the front page of a daily paper. An additional 35 million read only at a level which is less than equal to the full survival needs of our society.

Based on the context clues in the reading and using the dictionary definitions provided, choose the best definitions for the italicized words in the following sentences from the reading.

1. He places the folded *New York Times* next to the briefcase on his desk and sets to work on graphic illustrations for the advertising *copy* that is handed to him by the editor who is his boss. (par. 3)

   copy
   a. an imitation or reproduction of an original
   b. the words to be printed or spoken in an advertisement
   c. suitable source material for journalism

2. "Run over this with me. Just make sure I get the *gist* of what you really want." (par. 4)

   gist
   a. the general idea
   b. the basis for action in a suit

3. The editor, unsuspecting, takes this as a reasonable request. In the process of expanding on his copy, he recites the language of the text: a language that is instantly *imprinted* on the illustrator's mind. (par. 5)

   imprinted
   a. produced (a mark or pattern) on a surface by pressure
   b. created a strong or vivid impression of

4. He carefully unfolds his *New York Times*. He places it with mechanical *precision* on a pile of several other recent copies of the *New York Times*. (par. 7)

   precision
   a. exactness
   b. the exactness with which a number is specified
   c. used or intended for accurate or exact measurement

5. There they [the newspapers] will remain until, when two or three more copies have been added, he will take all but the one most recent and *consign* them to the trash. . . . (par. 7)

   consign
   a. entrust
   b. deliver
   c. commit

6. He is a rather *solitary* man. People in his office view him with respect as someone who is self-contained and does not choose to join in casual conversation. (par. 9)

   solitary
   a. existing, living, or going without others; alone
   b. remote from civilization; secluded

© 2014 Wadsworth, Cengage Learning

7. If somebody should mention something that is in the news, he will give a dry, sardonic answer based upon the information he has *garnered* from TV. (par. 9)

garnered
a. gathered as in a place to store grain
b. acquired

8. Defended for now against *humiliation,* he is not defended against fear. He tells me that he has recurrent dreams. (par. 10)

humiliation
a. act of humiliating
b. shame

Choose the best answers to the following multiple-choice questions about the reading.

9. What would be the best topic for this reading?
   a. the life of a secretly illiterate man
   b. the *New York Times* as status symbol
   c. illiteracy in the United States

10. Which of the following was *not* a main point made about the topic?
   a. The man hides his inability to read in clever ways.
   b. The man is an illustrator.
   c. The man is poor because he can't read.

11. What is the central idea of the whole reading?
   a. A lot of people in the United States can't read well.
   b. It is difficult, and even painful, to have to hide the fact that you can't read.
   c. Eventually people who pretend they can read but cannot will be trapped and discovered.

12. What is the topic of paragraphs 1 through 9?
   a. the daily routine of an illiterate man
   b. the precision of the habits of an illiterate man
   c. the respect that an illiterate man gets from people in his office

13. What is the central idea of paragraphs 1 through 9?
   a. The man is aware of what's happening in the world because he watches television and listens carefully.
   b. The man has habits that make it look as if he can read and that help him find out what he needs to know without reading.
   c. The man reads the *New York Times* every day.

Write brief answers to the following questions about the reading.

14. What is the man in this reading afraid of?

_____

_____

© 2014 Wadsworth, Cengage Learning

15. Why does he carry the *New York Times* around with him all the time?

_____

_____

16. What are his bad dreams about?

_____

_____

17. What is Kozol referring to when he writes, "Someday he will probably be trapped"?

_____

_____

18. How many people in the United States, according to Kozol, had problems reading in the 1990s?

_____

_____

Answer the following questions based on your reading, your experience, and your observations.

19. Have you ever been afraid that someone would find out you don't know something that they expect you to know? Explain.

_____

_____

_____

_____

20. Have you ever helped an adult (or a child) learn to read? Explain how you helped and what the experience was like.

_____

_____

_____

_____

© 2014 Wadsworth, Cengage Learning

© 2014 Wadsworth, Cengage Learning

Name _____ Date _____

How I Learned Physics, and English, and Math, and. . . !

—ANNA ROGERS

In this reading, community college professor Anna Rogers recalls her experiences in junior high, high school, and community college. As you read, think about her thesis and how you would write it in your own words. Also, consider how your experiences in school have been similar or different to hers.

1   In my professional life as a community college English professor I meet new people—students, school administrators, colleagues, and community members—almost every day. I face these people each day knowing that I am living a lie. Since I expect a lot of my students, people expect me to be a model of academic excellence. One look at my transcripts from junior high, high school, and the first three years I spent at the local community college, however, tells a different story. These records are <u>peppered with</u> failing grades and withdrawals. I was the kind of student who should have slipped quietly out of the educational system the first chance I got. And I would have… if it hadn't been for electives. Without them, I would have gotten very little out of high school, and I certainly wouldn't have continued on to college and the life I am living now.

2   In high school, it was classes like painting, ceramics, metal shop, drama, graphic arts, music, woodworking, choir, and drafting that kept me coming back to school day after day. They were a welcome break from classes like trigonometry, chemistry, and, yes, even English. Like many other students, I moved through my core curriculum classes in a haze. My boredom-glazed eyes couldn't <u>detect</u> any difference between the equations we were supposed to be balancing in chemistry and the grammar exercises we were supposed to be doing in English. Nothing in that curriculum sparked my interest enough to get me out of bed in the morning; but drama did. I often wonder how many students now, in this <u>era</u> of cuts to the arts and other electives, just hit snooze, roll over, and go back to sleep.

3   If it were not for these classes, I never would have graduated. Each semester, our school put on a play or musical, and I was always involved. To participate in school productions, students had to maintain a passing Grade Point Average (GPA). Without this requirement, I seriously doubt I would have even known what a GPA was; and it's much less likely that I would have been concerned enough about it to maintain a passing one. For those classes that I didn't pass, and there were a few, the thought of not being able to work on the play the next year got me up early day after day for summer school so that, come fall, there would be nothing standing between me and drama.

4   But drama did more than just keep me in school. At the time I didn't understand the positive influence drama was having on my performance in other classes. It didn't make me a straight A student—at least not while I was in high school—but it did force me to learn the concepts in other classes that I would have ignored otherwise, because it put me in situations where I needed to apply them. The first years that I was involved in the play, I worked behind the scenes designing and building the sets, making costumes, hanging lights, and running sound. This work was largely unsupervised, so student

Written by Anna Rogers. Reprinted by permission of the author.

volunteers had to possess a broad range of skills to complete it. We needed strong math skills to develop and <u>monitor</u> budgets and construct sets. We used the principles of physics to build sets and make sure they were safe to use. Although I might not have turned in my homework, I paid attention when the information I needed for drama came up in my other classes. One semester, I remember sitting on the concrete floor in the theater workshop explaining geometry theorems to my drama teacher so she would understand how much material we needed to build a tent with sloped sides. This was the same semester I got a D in geometry. It was also the semester that, although I got an F in physics, I calculated the number of exchanges we would need in a system of pulleys for one person to be able to raise a 250-pound piece of scenery into the rafters between acts.

theorems
rules in algebra, geometry and other areas of math

5   It was in drama class, not English, that I learned English and established the path for my future. Preparing for performances exposed me to the work of masters of the language. Reciting these pieces and listening to others recite them again and again, I heard and reproduced the cadences of the English language; and I thoroughly learned its structure and grammar in a deeper and much more meaningful way than I would have through the obligatory grammar exercises in my English class. Instead of reading my English textbook, I read plays, poems, and novels. I learned to love language, its sounds, and all the things you could do with it. I loved it particularly because it connected me to a much bigger world than my neighborhood and high school.

6   Perhaps most importantly, drama taught me the skill that I have applied the most over the course of my life. Educators put so much energy and effort into teaching critical thinking, but at the same time, many of the classes where students spontaneously engage in critical thinking are being removed from the curriculum. The subject matter of playwrights is human experience in all of its <u>permutations</u>. Performing on stage required me to understand the motivations of characters and appreciate the complexities of their situations. I learned to <u>empathize</u> with them without necessarily agreeing with their decisions or actions. And, by extension, I learned how to analyze the situations I faced in my own life, how to think through and respond to the decisions and actions of people around me, and how to make decisions and take action on my own. Drama is where this happened for me, but it is only one of many classes where this kind of thinking happens for students.

7   The valuable concepts and skills students learn in these elective classes are so complex and far-reaching that they are nearly impossible to measure through the use of standardized tests. As a result, funding for these classes is being cut, and they are disappearing from the school curriculum. This is a disservice to students.

8   Like so many others, my exit from high school was almost totally unnoticed. With the exception of my drama teacher, I think I was invisible to the rest of the teachers at my high school. None predicted that a bright future awaited me; none of them had any particular interest in finding out where I went or what I would do, because I looked like the kind of student who wouldn't really do much. And I didn't . . . for a few years.

9   But when you have experienced real learning as I had in my drama class, it's very hard to be happy with a <u>dead-end</u> job that never allows you the opportunity to learn new ideas or to think critically. Students who participate in these kinds of classes benefit from them and respond to what they have learned in different ways. What I got

© 2014 Wadsworth, Cengage Learning

from my drama classes was a <u>hunger</u> for a satisfying and meaningful life, so after a few years I went back to school. Although none of my high school teachers would have predicted it, I graduated from the University of California at San Diego at the top of my class, earned a master's degree, and now teach English to college students. And I owe it all to drama class.

Use context clues, word-part clues, and, if necessary, the dictionary to write the definitions of the italicized words in the following sentences from the reading.

1. These records are *peppered with* failing grades and withdrawals. (par. 1)

   peppered with _____

2. My boredom-glazed eyes couldn't *detect* any difference between the equations we were supposed to be balancing in chemistry and the grammar exercises we were supposed to be doing in English. (par. 2)

   detect _____

3. I often wonder how many students now, in this *era* of cuts to the arts and other electives, just hit snooze, roll over, and go back to sleep. (par. 2)

   era _____

4. We needed strong math skills in order to develop and *monitor* budgets and construct sets. (par. 4)

   monitor _____

5. The subject matter of playwrights is human experience in all of its *permutations*. (par. 6)

   permutations _____

6. I learned to *empathize* with them without necessarily agreeing with their decisions or actions. (par. 6)

   empathize _____

7. But when you have experienced real learning as I had in my drama class, it's very hard to be happy with a *dead-end* job that never allows you the opportunity to learn new ideas or to think critically. (par. 9)

   dead-end _____

8. What I got from my drama classes was *a hunger* for a satisfying and meaningful life, so after a few years I went back to school. (par. 9)

   hunger _____

© 2014 Wadsworth, Cengage Learning

Choose the best answers to the following multiple-choice questions about the reading, and write the main ideas and thesis in your own words.

9. What would be the best topic for this reading?
   a. The importance of arts education within the education system
   b. What students learn in drama classes
   c. Cuts to classes in the education system

10. Write the thesis of the reading in your own words.

   _____

   _____

   _____

11. What is the topic of paragraph 4?
   a. Applying subject-matter learning to electives
   b. Use of critical thinking when you face a challenge
   c. Life-long learning strategies

12. Write the main idea of paragraph 4 in your own words.

   _____

   _____

   _____

13. What is the topic of paragraph 6?
   a. the human experience
   b. decisions and actions of people around my life
   c. drama and critical thinking

14. Write the main idea of paragraph 6 in your own words.

   _____

   _____

   _____

15. Which of the following does Rogers *not* mention?
   a. Elective classes help students stay in school.
   b. Students can learn critical thinking in elective courses.
   c. Science classes are ineffective.

16. Rogers says she is living a lie because
   a. she meets new people everyday—students, administrators, colleagues, and community members.
   b. she is now a community college English professor, but she was a terrible student at one time.
   c. electives are important for students to be successful in school.

© 2014 Wadsworth, Cengage Learning

Answer the following questions about the reading.

17. What problem does Rogers see with arts classes in education now?

_____

_____

_____

_____

18. Why does Rogers eventually go back to school and complete her bachelor's degree?

_____

_____

_____

_____

19. Explain an experience in school that has changed you. What was the experience? How did it change you?

_____

_____

_____

_____

20. What experiences have you had in arts classrooms? How do they compare to the ones described by the Rogers?

_____

_____

_____

_____

© 2014 Wadsworth, Cengage Learning

5 Main Ideas and Supporting Details

POPULAR CULTURE

Patrick Corrigan/caglecartoons.com

- What time period does this cartoon depict?
- Why is the mother surprised by what her daughter says?
- What is the unstated main idea of this cartoon?

Getting Ready to Read

Our view of ourselves and where we fit in is increasingly influenced not just by our active experiences, but also by our passive experiences. In everything from action-packed video games to glamour-packed magazines at the checkout counter, we are all bombarded by the same images, the same symbols, the same superheroes, and the same all-stars and screen stars. We enjoy them, and we share our enjoyment of them with most people in our society, and increasingly with people all over the world. This popular culture is mass-produced for us. We no longer create our culture; we consume it. In other words, a small group of people in the entertainment industry determines the popular culture. How many parents are telling the stories that they heard as children to their children? In contrast, how many children know only the stories they've seen streamed on a screen? What cultural traditions have we maintained in our families and in our local communities? What traditions have we lost? Is social networking on Internet sites in danger of replacing real relationships? Have we lost our ability to define our own dreams, even ourselves?

In this chapter, you will read and think about video games, Internet social networking sites, teen magazines, and advertising. In the process, you will learn how to:

- Recognize supporting details for main ideas
- Separate general statements from specific information
- Outline what you have read

© 2014 Wadsworth, Cengage Learning

Video Games: The Reality of the Digital World

—MARLEY PEIFER

A high school sophomore whose friends spend many hours playing video games wrote the following reading. This essay is his analysis of what those games can do to young people. Notice his arguments for why the games are harmful, and consider whether or not you agree with his position.

1   As we get further along in the twenty-first century, technology becomes more advanced and more incorporated into our daily lives. It makes our lives easier, longer, and more luxurious. Different machines have been designed to do just about anything—wash your car for you, do math for you, wash your clothes, and there are even machines that entertain and exhilarate you. They're known as video games. They provide the addicting, time-consuming, and complete waste-of-time digital experiences that glue you to the screen and have you coming back for more. Video games are now replacing reading, art, and other wholesome activities that benefit the mind and body.

2   As these electronic games replace more traditional pastimes, there is a noticeable decrease in the creativity and attention span of the kids who play them. A child, after playing video games for three hours, may have difficulty stopping the game and starting to read a book instead. After being immersed in a fast-paced game, children are often incapable of concentrating long enough to read. They quickly lose attention on the book and begin to fidget with something. While playing the game their mind is bombarded with countless images from the screen, images realistic enough that no imagination is required. However, reading requires imagination and thought to understand and register what is being read. Some children may also have difficulty paying attention to a teacher speaking after playing a video game for a while.

exhilarate
thrill

3   A child who plays video games all the time becomes less social. Instead of going and playing with his friends, he'd rather sit cooped up in his room playing video games on his personal television. These days the typical slumber party, instead of consisting of social activities such as board games or talking, consists of several-hour video

Marley Peifer, "Video Games: The Reality of the Digital World." Marley Peifer. Used with permission.

© 2014 Wadsworth, Cengage Learning

game playing marathons that may last well into the night. In this circumstance, even though the group of friends is spending time together, they are not interacting socially with each other. So actually, there is little difference between this activity and really being alone.

4   As soon as a child starts one of these video games, she may become totally immersed in a world very similar to yet different from the real one. While the video world may look and sound realistic, no one really dies, and you can always start over. Modern video games are designed to cater to your sense of sight, hearing, and even your sense of touch. All these senses are stimulated while you play the game, adding to the sensation of being in a different world. In this different world you can be a hero, you can have amazing and superhuman powers, you can do the impossible, you can beat any odds, and you can do anything. In this digital world, you can do all the things you've always wanted to do but couldn't in the real world. It's no wonder, then, that many people prefer this artificial world to reality. A young boy who is unfit physically may escape his shortcomings in sports by playing video games. In the game he can be an all-star home-run hitter or the MVP (most valuable player) for a World Cup soccer team. However, all the action occurs on the screen, and his actual physical fitness may deteriorate. People who have few talents and don't stand out in the real world can take solace in this digital world where they can excel. It's not surprising that people who play video games a great deal may find the "real world" boring, for they are unable to fly around or shoot people like they can in the game.

5   The amount of time that people waste playing video games is alarming. Many games have 100 or more levels, with each level taking close to an hour to complete. Imagine the constructive things that could be done in the time it would take to beat the game. Recent statistics show that young people between ages 15 and 20 play almost nine hours of video games a week, which in most cases is more time than is spent on homework and reading combined. Actually, since this figure is only an average and includes girls, who do not play nearly as much as boys, the amount of time that serious video game players spend is far more than nine hours a week. In some cases, 20 or 30 hours a week would be more like it.

6   As if the games in general weren't already bad enough, approximately half of all video games have a violent theme. One gruesome example is Sony PlayStation's "Resident Evil." In this game, the objective is to kill all the zombies and other horrible creatures before they dismember you and feast on your flesh. But "Resident Evil" is almost innocent compared to the latest versions of "Grand Theft Auto." In this game, the player "becomes" an escaped convict and gains points for hijacking cars, beating up the driver, running over or crushing pedestrians, picking up prostitutes, and, after having sex (indicated by rocking in the car), killing them. The player is also encouraged to attack and kill policemen and blow up their helicopters. How can someone behave normally after indulging in hours of this carnage? The real answer is they can't. Studies have shown that exposure to these video games causes a great increase in aggressive thinking. It's no wonder an individual who has witnessed countless deaths in a game becomes desensitized and can even consider taking a life as no big deal.

7   In recent years, great leaps forward have been made in technology. Significant advances have been made in the fields of medicine, science, and business. But let's not forget the advances in video games. They're becoming ever more realistic and always faster. So what does the future hold? In the not so distant future we must expect graphics so realistic they can't be differentiated from the real thing. The games will be so in-depth they might take more than a year to beat. Also, virtual reality technology, which is now in a mere embryonic stage, will become so advanced that you might not

cater to
please

take solace
feel better

excel
do well

indulging
allowing or yielding to excessive desires

carnage
slaughter or massacre

© 2014 Wadsworth, Cengage Learning

know whether you're in a game or not. The development of this new breed of super in-depth, super realistic video games could be the downfall of creativity and thought for the future generations. These virtual reality games will constantly be improved on and upgraded, becoming better and more realistic until they will replace our actual experiences with digital ones. Yet, hopefully, we will know when to stop.

Exercise 1

Recall and Discuss

Answer these questions about Reading 1, and prepare to discuss them in class.

1. What are the characteristics of video game playing that cause young people to lose their ability to pay attention to reading or to teachers?

_____

_____

_____

2. Why do children who play video games become less social?

_____

_____

3. List Peifer's main reasons for saying that video games are harmful.

_____

_____

_____

_____

4. What experience do you have either directly or indirectly with video games?

_____

_____

_____

5. Why is the cartoon on page 202 included with this reading?

_____

_____

_____

© 2014 Wadsworth, Cengage Learning

Supporting Details

In Chapters 3 and 4 you learned to identify main ideas in a variety of readings. A main idea is usually presented in a broad or general statement of the main point of the reading—what the reading says about the topic. It is also expressed through **supporting details**, which give additional information and are more specific. Some types of supporting details are:

supporting details details that give you additional information and are more specific than a general statement; examples or additional facts

- *Examples.* If the main idea is *people in the past used to entertain themselves more than we do today,* the supporting details might be examples of how they did that, such as:

  a. singing and playing music
  b. dancing traditional dances
  c. telling stories
  d. drawing
  e. writing poetry

- *Facts.* Facts are forms of information that can be checked for accuracy. If the main idea is *Americans watch more television today than they ever did in the past,* the supporting facts would state how many hours Americans watch television and perhaps how many televisions are in American homes.

- *Reasons.* Reasons answer the question "why." If a main idea is *I hate the shows my friends watch,* some reasons might be that they are silly, they are always about the same thing, and they are childish.

- *Descriptions.* Descriptions help us form pictures in our minds and can help us understand better what the writer is communicating to us. If a main idea is *the children were totally absorbed in the video game,* the writer may describe the scene by saying:

  a. Their concentration was so intense they forgot to blink their eyes.
  b. They hunched over the screen as though their lives depended on their virtual reality triumphs or failures.
  c. They held the excitement of the game in the tension of the muscles on their faces.
  d. They didn't even look up or respond in any way when their mother called them to dinner.

The way a main idea is supported by specific details can be seen in sentences, paragraphs, and longer passages.

RECOGNIZING SUPPORTING DETAILS IN SENTENCES

Some sentences include both a general idea and supporting details. A writer may begin a sentence with a general idea and then give evidence. Normally you won't need to analyze a sentence this way, but you should know that frequently sentences have the same organization as paragraphs and longer readings. For example, read the following sentence:

> Our media culture glorifies violence through the images of violent actions such as assault, beatings, and murders that children see repeatedly in products such as video games, television shows, Hollywood movies, and on the Internet.

What is the general idea of the sentence?

Our media glorifies violence through images and products.

© 2014 Wadsworth, Cengage Learning

What are the supporting details? The supporting details are the responses to the following questions: What kinds of images? What kinds of products? What examples are given?

What kinds of images?

    a. *assault*

    b. *beatings*

    c. *murders*

What kinds of products?

    a. *video games*

    b. *television shows*

    c. *Hollywood movies*

    d. *on the Internet*

Exercise 2

Recognize Supporting Details in Sentences

Read the following sentences and then fill in the blanks about them. What is the general idea? What are the supporting details?

1. A new study has concluded that children who are addicted to video games have symptoms ranging from doing worse in school, lying about how much they play, being unable to stop, spending more time and money on the games, and even stealing games and money to support their habit.

   general idea: _____

   _____

   supporting details:

   a. _____

   b. _____

   c. _____

   d. _____

   e. _____

2. The study suggests that the effects of games on children's lives is widespread and troublesome, because 88 percent of children ages 8 to 18 play the games, and more than 3 million are addicted.

   general idea: _____

   _____

© 2014 Wadsworth, Cengage Learning

supporting details:

a. _____

b. _____

3. Games that children used to play, such as "Hide and Seek" and "Cowboys and Indians," involved running around outside and were not as violent as some of today's video games, such as "Doom" and "Blood."

general idea: _____

_____

supporting details:

a. _____

   • _____

   • _____

b. _____

   • _____

   • _____

SEPARATING GENERAL FROM SPECIFIC

The main idea of a paragraph or the thesis of a persuasive essay is a broad or **general statement**. The details that support it are **specifics**. The more detailed the information, the more specific it is. Let's look at a statement about our shared culture, on the nature of modern life:

general statement the main idea of a paragraph or the broadest central idea of a longer reading

specifics detailed information

> We live our lives by having more indirect, imaginary, and simulated experiences through playing video games, watching television, going to theme parks, going on the Internet, and going to the movies.

The general statement is: *We live our lives by having indirect experiences.* The specific information is the list of types of indirect experiences:

a. *playing video games*
b. *watching television*
c. *going to theme parks*
d. *going on the Internet*
e. *going to the movies*

© 2014 Wadsworth, Cengage Learning

Exercise 3

Recognize General Statements and Specific Details

Read the following sentences, then identify the general statements versus the specific details.

1. Many of the talk shows are "self-help" shows devised to help people attain personal and financial freedom.

   general statement: _____

   specific details:

   a. _____

   b. _____

2. Oprah has a variety of goals for helping people. Helping Habitat for Humanity build houses for the homeless and contributing funds for scholarships are just two of her projects.

   general statement: _____

   specific details:

   a. _____

   b. _____

3. There are so many reality television shows these days that most people can find one they enjoy. The public broadcasting stations offer re-enactments of historical periods where participants live as if they were pioneers for six months; on shows like *Extreme Makeover,* we watch people's appearances radically change, often with the help of plastic surgery; and finally, there are singing competitions such as the most popular show of all, *American Idol.*

   general statement: _____

   _____

   specific details:

   a. _____

   b. _____

   c. _____

© 2014 Wadsworth, Cengage Learning

4. *Extreme Makeover: Home Edition* is a reality television program that builds homes and makes dreams come true for people facing severe hardships and needing help. Some of the families this program has helped include a family who run a camp for severely ill children, the family of a Native American woman who died in Iraq, and victims of Hurricane Katrina who lost everything they had.

general statement: _____

_____

specific details:

a. _____

b. _____

c. _____

RECOGNIZING SUPPORTING DETAILS IN PARAGRAPHS

In paragraphs, the general statement, or the main idea, is often given in the first few sentences, and then the writer supports the idea with more specific details. The best process to follow for finding important supporting details is to:

- Identify the main idea.
- Look for the additional important information about the main idea.

These supporting details could be:

- Examples
- Additional facts
- Reasons
- Descriptions

Read the following paragraph, which is based on Reading 1, about video games.

> There is a noticeable decrease in the creativity and attention span of the kids who play video games for long periods of time. A child, after playing a video game for three hours, may have difficulty stopping the game and starting to read a book instead. After being immersed in a fast-paced game, children are often incapable of concentrating long enough to read. Their attention quickly drifts from the book and they begin to fidget with something. While playing the game their mind is bombarded with countless images from the screen, images realistic enough that no imagination is required. However, reading requires imagination and thought to understand and register what is being read. According to Dr. Daniel Amen, a medical doctor and psychiatrist, scientific studies have shown that violent video games lead to an increase in aggressive activity.
>
> *Peifer, "Video Games"*

© 2014 Wadsworth, Cengage Learning

What is the main idea, or the general statement, of the paragraph?

There is a noticeable decrease in the creativity and attention span of the kids who play video games for long periods of time.

What are the supporting details? That is, how is the main idea supported with specific examples, facts, reasons, or descriptions?

a. *It is difficult for the child to stop playing and to read instead. (example)*
b. *Children don't have the attention span or imagination to enjoy reading. (reason)*
c. *Studies show that violent video games lead to an increase in aggressive activity. (fact)*

Exercise 4   Identify Main Ideas and Supporting Details

For each of the following paragraphs, write the main idea, then list the major supporting details. The first one has been done for you.

1. Video games are not all bad. In fact, there are many benefits to playing these electronic games. Playing increases young people's motor skills. It gives them practice in problem solving. It can improve their ability to see spatial relationships in their minds. It can be therapeutic for children who have attention deficit disorders. Playing video games has been credited with helping the reaction times of senior citizens, and even with leading to higher self-esteem among elderly people. (adapted from Laidman, "Violence, Video Games May Be a Volatile Mix")

   main idea: *There are many benefits to playing video games.*

   supporting details: *Examples of benefits*

   a. *increases motor skills*

   b. *practice in problem solving*

   c. *improves ability to see spatial relationships*

   d. *therapeutic for children with attention deficit disorders*

   e. *helps reaction times of seniors*

   f. *leads to higher self-esteem for elderly*

2. Interactive video games are a huge industry. Annual video game revenue exceeds $18 billion worldwide. U.S. video game revenues of $10 billion per year are double what is spent on movies annually, according to Media Scope, a nonprofit organization concerned with the media's portrayal of, and impact on, children. (Laidman, "Violence, Video Games May Be a Volatile Mix")

   main idea: _____

   supporting details: *Facts about profits*

   a. _____

   b. _____

© 2014 Wadsworth, Cengage Learning

3. Even though the fabulous successes of video games are relatively recent, their history is full of unexpected twists when you think about the companies that have been involved. According to the popular site for video game lovers, http://www.gamespot.com, "Atari was an American company with a Japanese name, and the Japanese company Sega was started by an American. Magnavox, the company that started it all, is owned by Phillips, a company that is over a century old, and Nintendo, the company that made video games popular again, is just as old. And who would have ever thought Sony, the company that invented all types of electronics, from transistor radios to video recorders, would release a video game console that would become its top-selling product of all time?"

main idea: _____

_____

_____

supporting details: <u>Examples of unexpected twists</u>_____

a. _____

b. _____

c. _____

d. _____

_____

4. Great White, a second-rate heavy metal band, allegedly caused a disastrous fire in a Rhode Island nightclub where 97 people died. A week later, sales of the band's albums increased by over 1,000 percent. After John Lennon was murdered, his solo album, which had not been doing well, went to number one on the charts for nine weeks. After Michael Jackson dangled one of his children from a balcony in Berlin and a television special about his bizarre lifestyle aired on national TV, and later, after his death, sales for all of his albums spiked. Tupac Shakur, who was killed in Las Vegas in 1996, sold millions more records after he died than during his life. Perhaps it's human nature to have a fascination with disaster. But one thing is clear: Disasters and odd behavior increase sales of popular music.

main idea: _____

supporting details: <u>Examples of increased sales</u>_____

a. _____

b. _____

_____

© 2014 Wadsworth, Cengage Learning

c. _____

d. _____

5. The American Academy of Pediatrics recommends the establishment of a media rating system and controls that would be family friendly. According to this organization, "American children between 2 and 18 spend an average of 6 hours and 32 minutes each day using media—television, commercial or self-recorded video, movies, video games, radio, recorded music, computers and the Internet." Research shows that exposure to media violence causes a variety of physical and mental health problems, including fear, nightmares, depression, and sleep disturbances. The pediatricians are asking producers not to glorify violence and not to have human targets in the games. They would also like to make it easy for parents to evaluate the content of video games and music lyrics. Finally, they would like the creation of a more positive media for children.

main idea: _____

_____

_____

supporting details:

Concerns:

a. _____

b. _____

Proposed changes:

a. _____

b. _____

c. _____

USING SUPPORTING DETAILS TO FIND THE UNSTATED MAIN IDEA

In Chapter 4 you learned how to find the unstated main idea of paragraphs and the central idea of longer passages: First list the points made about the topic; then add them up to arrive at the main idea. Basically, this process means that you recognize the supporting details in a reading and then, based on those details, you decide what the main idea is. You will be practicing this skill in much of the reading that you will be doing for college classes, as you read for pleasure, and as you read for your professional work.

© 2014 Wadsworth, Cengage Learning

Language Tip:
Facts

Facts are one important type of supporting detail. In general, facts are statements that can be proven, but there are many different kinds of facts, including:

- *Statistics*—provide information in number form
- *Events*—are examples of things that have happened or will happen
- *Dates*—tell when something happened or will happen
- *Descriptions*—explain in a concrete way how something looks, feels, sounds, or smells
- *Lists*—put similar items together to show spatial or time relationships among the items

Exercise 5   Identify the Facts and the Main Idea

Identify what kind of facts are being used in each of these examples: statistics, events, dates, descriptions, or lists. Each example may use more than one kind of fact. Then add up the facts to arrive at the unstated or stated main idea.

1. Rapper Lauryn Hill became the first hip-hop artist to ever win Album of the Year. Actor Warren Beatty crafted his satire *Bulworth* around rap's language of protest. Martha Stewart, the woman who teaches Americans about good taste, appeared at the MTV Music Awards with rapper Busta Rhymes. (Adapted from Scott, "Rap Goes from Urban Streets to Main Street")

   type of facts:_____

   main idea:_____

2. The hip-hop label Def Jam took in nearly $200 million in 1998. Rap sold more than 81 million CDs, tapes and albums in 1998, compared with 72 million for country and western. Rap sales increased 31 percent from 1997–98, in contrast to 2 percent gains for country, 6 percent for rock, and 9 percent for the music industry overall. (Adapted from "Live and Kicking")

   type of facts:_____

   main idea:_____

   _____

   _____

© 2014 Wadsworth, Cengage Learning

3. Once the three networks [ABC, CBS, and NBC] fought only among themselves for audience leadership. . . . But since the early 1980s the Big Three networks have faced five dangerous competitors whose combined and growing strength has stolen many of the networks' viewers. These are
   a. cable television
   b. a growing number of independent TV stations, which have developed strong audience appeal . . .
   c. home video, which viewers watch instead of television
   d. the aggressive young Fox network
   e. appearance in 1995 of two additional broadcast networks, WB Television (Warner Brothers) and UPN, United Paramount Network. (Agee, Ault, and Emery, *Introduction to Mass Communications*)

   type of facts: _____

   main idea: _____

   _____

4. Growth in the gaming industry has been phenomenal, and upon looking back the graphics of the first video games seem very simple and plain—not lifelike at all. Atari's Nolan Bushnell released Pong in 1972 as the world's second stand-up, quarter-based arcade game. Though it was not the first video game ever invented, it launched the commercial video game market. Two small white rectangles represented each player. The players controlled each rectangle, trying to deflect a bouncing ball. The game was similar to table tennis. (Smith and Lam, "Computer and Video Games")

   type of facts: _____

   main idea: _____

Reading 2

Facebook and Internet: With Friends Like These Who Needs Enemies?

— NADIA MANDILAWI

The following reading is about Internet-based social networking sites. As you read, look for the main ideas and the supporting points, and consider your own experiences. Do you agree with the author's thesis? Do you find her supporting points convincing?

Written for *Joining a Community of Readers*. Used by permission of Nadia Mandilawi.

© 2014 Wadsworth, Cengage Learning

1   From the outside of the cafe in downtown Los Angeles, Rosemarie Evans and John Strum look like any other affectionate couple sharing a sandwich and some french fries on a Saturday afternoon. It's a hot day in August, and despite the 103-degree temperature, the two seem comfortable on their date. They readily nod their heads when the waitress asks them if they want dessert. His joke is making her laugh; her hand rests peacefully on his arm. In a long-distance relationship, John is on a visit from Arizona and the two are eagerly planning Rosemarie's first trip to his hometown. The only snag: he actually lives with his wife and two children 110 miles away in San Diego. Later, Rosemarie will learn this. She will also learn that her boyfriend's name is not John, and that he is not the firefighter he told her he was. "John" was an impostor. Sadly, Rosemarie's story comes with a sense of familiarity rather than shock. Like many people in our country, she met her boyfriend on MySpace. As Internet communities like Facebook continue to expand, so do the number of users who create false profiles. Also at risk as these networks grow are rights concerning privacy. It's vital for people to consider not only the benefits of membership, but the heightened risks as well.

2   As a cautious member of Facebook for some time now myself, I enjoy the opportunity it's given me to connect with people I've missed. Since joining the network, I regularly keep in touch with my sister in Colorado. I play Scrabble with a friend in Spain. I know what my former college roommate is currently reading and what her new baby looks like. On a trip from California to New York last year, I surprised an old friend on his birthday after he used Facebook to message me, and several others from around the country, the address for his party. For the first time, I've had the chance to meet family members who live in Iraq because of joining the network. This has been most exciting for me because it has given me the opportunity to view photos of their homes and gain daily contact with them through status updates and messages, none of which would have been possible had I not joined Facebook.

3   The more time I've spent on Facebook, the faster my social network seems to expand, and my experience is not unique. The number of Facebook users is growing astronomically. According to *Time* magazine's online publication, "Facebook is undergoing a huge period of growth. With more than 150,000 new users signing up daily, it is growing three times as fast as [its] rival MySpace."[1] Furthermore, approximately 794 million people were actively using the network in early 2012, and this number is quickly increasing.[2] What started out as a small Web site linking a few friends at Harvard University has turned into the largest social networking site available to people online today. This increased use of Facebook shows us that many people rely on and enjoy what the Internet has to offer.

astronomically
incredibly fast

4   Inevitably, with any community that develops at such a rapid rate, the level of risk intensifies as well. One such risk is the rising number of members like Rosemarie's boyfriend "John," who create false profiles. With MySpace, John was able to be whomever he wanted. He cleverly crafted a profile that seemed authentic. Online, Rosemarie viewed countless photographs of John in Arizona. In these pictures, he posed with family members in front of his house, as well as firefighters he claimed to work with. Rosemarie even watched him accept an award for his work as a firefighter through a YouTube video link he sent her. As the two messaged each other on MySpace daily, John gained a great deal of trust and love from Rosemarie. You can imagine Rosemarie's distress when she learned John was a fake. Luckily for her, this relationship didn't become dangerous. As more users flock to the Internet, the number of people who

© 2014 Wadsworth, Cengage Learning

create false profiles is larger than it was when social networking sites were less popular. Though caution might seem obvious, many of us fail to keep it in mind and we should remember to protect ourselves when we communicate online.

5   Just as we need to be concerned about the accuracy of the profiles of our new "friends," we need to be concerned about the impressions our own profiles create. Did you know that college admissions officers also turn to what is available online when deciding which students to accept? According to a 2011 Kaplan study, one in 4 U.S. college admissions officers admitted to "Facebook surfing" potential applicants before admitting them. In 2008, the same survey showed that only one in 10 college admissions officers were checking Facebook. Posts such as those using vulgar language or photos showing applicants drinking alcohol negatively affect applicants' chances of being accepted.[3]

6   Potential students, I'm sure, had no idea that the pictures or comments they posted on Facebook would be looked at by college officials. Many of us feel the information we post on the network is private, when in fact it is not. Unless we spend time understanding and enforcing the privacy features offered, our information can be accessed by just about anyone, and that is not what most social network users bargain for.

bargain for
expect

7   The Internet and its social networking sites have wonderful benefits, but the risks are high. We need to be mindful of stories like that of Rosemarie and "John," and to recognize that all the information that's out there—like "John's" profile—is not always true, and sometimes the consequences can be serious. As we make decisions about what to believe as well as what we choose to reveal about ourselves on certain Web sites, we should be aware of the consequences involved.

reveal
make known,
make public

Notes

1. Laura Locke, "The Future of Facebook," *Time*, July 17, 2008, at www.time.com/time/business/article/0,8599,1644040,00.html (accessed April 22, 2009).

2. http://www.howmanyarethere.org/how-many-facebook-users-are-there-2012/ (accessed 4/12/11)

3. Ryan Lytle, "College Admissions Officials Turn to Facebook to Research Students." *U.S. News and World Report*, October 10, 2011, at http://www.usnews.com/education/best-colleges/articles/2011/10/10/college-admissions-officials-turn-to-facebook-to-research-students (accessed June 21, 2012).

Exercise 6

Work with Words

Use context clues, word-part clues, and if necessary, the dictionary to write the definitions of the italicized words in the following sentences from Reading 2.

1. They *readily* nod their heads when the waitress asks them if they want dessert. (par. 1)

    readily _____

2. She will also learn that her boyfriend's name is not John and that he is not the firefighter he told her he was. "John" was an *impostor*. (par. 1)

    impostor _____

© 2014 Wadsworth, Cengage Learning

3. As long as MySpace, Facebook, and other networks on the Internet gain popularity, it's vital for people to consider not only the benefits of membership, but the *heightened* risks as well. (par. 1)

vital _____

4. *heightened* _____

5. The more time I've spent on Facebook, the faster my social network seems to expand, and my experience is not *unique*. (par. 3)

unique _____

6. With MySpace, John was able to be whomever he wanted. He cleverly crafted a profile that seemed *authentic*. (par. 4)

authentic _____

7. Unless we spend time understanding and enforcing the privacy features offered, our information can be *accessed* by just about anyone, and that is not what most social network users bargain for. (par. 6)

accessed _____

8. We need *to be mindful* of stories like Rosemarie and "John," and to recognize that all the information that's out there—like "John's" profile—is not always true, and sometimes the consequences can be serious. (par. 7)

to be mindful _____

Exercise 7

Identify Main Ideas and Supporting Details

For the following groups of sentences from, or related to, Reading 2, write "MI" for the main idea sentence and "SD" for the sentences that provide supporting details.

1. ___ a. From the outside of the cafe in downtown Los Angeles, Rosemarie Evans and John Strum look like any other affectionate couple sharing a sandwich and some french fries on a Saturday afternoon.
    ___ b. It's a hot day in August, and despite the 103-degree temperature, the two seem comfortable on their date.
    ___ c. They readily nod their heads when the waitress asks them if they want dessert.
    ___ d. His joke is making her laugh; her hand rests peacefully on his arm.

2. ___ a. I regularly keep in touch with my sister in Colorado.
    ___ b. I play Scrabble with a friend in Spain.

© 2014 Wadsworth, Cengage Learning

___ c. As a cautious member of Facebook for some time now myself, I enjoy the opportunity it's given me to connect with people I've missed.

___ d. I know what my former college roommate is currently reading and what her new baby looks like.

___ e. On a trip from California to New York last year, I surprised an old friend on his birthday after he used Facebook to message me, and several others from around the country, the address for his party.

3. ___ a. "With more than 150,000 new users signing up daily, it is growing three times as fast as [its] rival MySpace."

    ___ b. Furthermore, approximately 794 million people were actively using the network in early 2012, and this number is quickly increasing.

    ___ c. The number of Facebook users is growing astronomically.

    ___ d. It started out as a small Web site linking a few friends at Harvard University.

4. ___ a. With MySpace, John was able to be whoever he wanted.

    ___ b. He cleverly crafted a profile that seemed authentic.

    ___ c. Online, Rosemarie viewed countless photographs of John in Arizona.

    ___ d. In these pictures, he posed with family members in front of his house, as well as firefighters he claimed to work with.

    ___ e. Rosemarie even watched him accept an award for his work as a firefighter through a YouTube video link he sent her.

Exercise 8

Make Connections and Write

Write short answers to the following questions based on Reading 2, your own experience, and your observations. Then discuss your answers with your class group. Working together, prepare a report for your class as a whole or a written summary for your instructor.

1. In your own words, write the central idea, or thesis, of Reading 2.

_____

_____

_____

2. List some benefits and risks for having a social networking page both from the reading and from your own experience.

_____

_____

_____

© 2014 Wadsworth, Cengage Learning

3. Do you use Facebook or any other social networking site? What information do you put on it? With whom do you communicate on it?

_____

_____

_____

4. What do you like best about social networking sites?

_____

_____

_____

5. Do you agree with Mandilawi that revealing too much about yourself can be dangerous? Explain why or why not, and give examples.

_____

_____

_____

Organize to Learn: Outline

When you are reading information that includes a lot of details, it is helpful to organize that information in some way so it will be easier to remember. Making an outline is one good method. Outlines include the most important points of a reading in a way that provides you with a visual framework for studying and remembering information. This framework shows the central idea and important supporting details.

To set up your outline:

1. Identify the topic and the central idea (or thesis for persuasive readings).
2. Identify the supporting points for those ideas.

© 2014 Wadsworth, Cengage Learning

adverse negative

For example, in the following two paragraphs, pay particular attention to (1) the main idea and (2) the supporting details.

The Center for Successful Parenting makes available more than forty years of clinical research on the adverse effects of media violence on the nation's juvenile population. The founders believe that America's children live in a society that glorifies aggressive behavior. Even if children are not influenced to commit violence themselves, they may live in fear of violent acts by their schoolmates, friends, and neighbors. At the same time, children are desensitized to these violent realities. The Center believes that there are two ways to go about changing this situation. One plan is to make all parents and grandparents in America aware of the fact that media violence is a huge and growing problem that must be addressed now. Another plan is to give parents and grandparents some helpful guidelines for helping children to live happy, secure, and safe lives.

There are five ways for parents to help combat the negative effects of media violence in their home. First, provide a Media Free zone in your home where children can read, talk, and play games. Second, do not put a television in your child's bedroom. Third, read to your children. Fourth, refuse to expose younger children to violent content in movies, television shows, and video games. Fifth, check Moviereports.org. Moviereports.org is a Web site run by the Center for Successful Parenting that has reviews of movies and video games for parents to look at before they take their children to a movie or buy them a video game. The reviews are done by experts who look at content in movies and games. The Web site is an excellent resource for those parents who wish to become informed about a movie or game. (Stoughton, "Media Violence and What's Being Done About It")

Now, we'll go through the process of writing an outline for these paragraphs.

1. First we need to ask the question, What is the topic of the reading?

    The Center for Successful Parenting and the effects of media violence on children

2. Next, what is the central idea?

    The Center for Successful Parenting makes available the research on media violence and its effects on children, and it helps parents combat the negative effects of media violence in their home.

3. Finally, what are the important supporting details? In the central idea sentence, we can notice that the first detail is *the effects of violence on children*. So for our outline we could list the supporting details that prove this point. Notice that in an outline we use capital letters (A, B, C, etc.) to signal broad categories and numbers (1, 2, 3 etc.) to indicate supporting details under those categories.

© 2014 Wadsworth, Cengage Learning

A. **The effects of media violence on children**

    1. Children may commit violence or live in fear of violence.
    2. Children are desensitized to violence.

The second point of the central idea sentence is *ways to combat the negative effects of media violence*. So, for our outline we would list the supporting details for that point.

B. **Five ways to combat media violence**

    1. Provide a Media Free zone in your home.
    2. Do not put a television in your child's bedroom.
    3. Read to your children.
    4. Refuse to expose younger children to violent movies, television shows, and video games.
    5. Check Moviereports.org for reviews of movies and video games.

We can put these pieces together to form a single outline of the two paragraphs.

topic: The Center for Successful Parenting and the effects of media violence on children

main idea: The Center for Successful Parenting makes available the research on the effects of violence on America's children, and it helps parents combat the negative effects of media violence in their home.

A. **Effects of violence on children**

    1. Children may commit violence or may live in fear of violence.
    2. Children are desensitized to violence.

B. **Five ways to combat effects of media violence**

    1. Provide a Media Free zone in your home.
    2. Do not put a television in your child's bedroom.
    3. Read to your children.
    4. Refuse to expose younger children to violent movies, television shows, and video games.
    5. Check Moviereports.org for reviews of movies and video games.

Exercise 9 Outline

Read the following paragraphs. Then follow the model for outlining to fill in the spaces of the outline provided for you.

Media violence is an issue that has recently become one of the leading questions in government, the court systems, and our society at large. After recent "school killings," many authorities have begun to question the role the media have played. Studies connect violence in the media with violent behavior exhibited in society. The surgeon general, the attorney general, and the Office of the President all have released statements concerning the

© 2014 Wadsworth, Cengage Learning

negative effect that violence in the media has on our society. The American Medical Association calls "media violence" one of the largest threats to our national health.

"Media violence" is the term given to any form of media that graphically portrays, glorifies, and promotes violence. Action movies, for instance, often portray violence in such a way that it becomes attractive to people, especially the young. Some music lyrics and video games do the same. The media, by glorifying perverse actions, help to encourage aggressive behavior among children and adolescents.

The fact that, as a society, we are surrounded by and fascinated with violence has an effect on the younger population called "desensitization." This term is basically applied to a child or adolescent who, through repeated and prolonged exposure to violence, becomes indifferent to it. It simply becomes a part of his or her life. Study after study has been done to show that exposure to violent media influences human behavior. There is no question about this fact from a scientific standpoint, as it has been proven beyond a doubt. So if this is true, how is society responding? (Stoughton, "Media Violence and What's Being Done About It")

indifferent
having no feeling

topic: _____

central idea: Media violence is a major social issue. _____

A. Media violence — a major social issue

   1. _____

   2. Surgeon general, attorney general, the president—negative effect

   3. _____

   _____

B. Media violence—any medium that graphically portrays, glorifies, and promotes violence

   1. Action movies

   2. _____

   3. _____

C. Media violence — "desensitization" of children

   1. _____

   2. Confirmed by "study after study"

© 2014 Wadsworth, Cengage Learning

© 2014 Wadsworth, Cengage Learning

Reading 3

Teen Girl Magazines: The Good, the Bad, and the Beautiful

— Elena Marie Peifer

In the following reading, Elena Peifer discusses what teen girl magazines mean for adolescent girls—how they influence them for better and for worse. As you read, consider what you know about teenage girls, and analyze whether Peifer's assessments of the magazines and of their reading audience seem justified. Also, note how she develops her thesis and her supporting points.

1   Almost every day the average teenage girl is judged and criticized by other teenage girls on clothes, complexion, hair, makeup, and figure. But where does the teenage girl's idea of beauty come from? One of the answers is magazines. Magazines such as *Teen, Seventeen, YM (Young and Modern),* and *Teen People* have models on every page, pictures of the perfect body, smoothest hair, and flawless features. When we teenage girls see these flawless faces and gorgeous bodies, an idea of the perfect woman gets placed in our heads, and this idea sticks.

2   The ideal of the 110-pound, size-three, C-cup, five-foot nine-inch blond woman is one that many of us will go to extremes to achieve. We will deprive ourselves of food in pursuit of this image. When we can't reach this unrealistic goal, too many of us end up binge eating because we're depressed. Then, in order not to gain weight, we are likely to purge ourselves of the food we consumed. So the destructive cycle of eating disorders begins. As if disrupting our eating habits is not bad enough, we will wear uncomfortable clothes to look "better," high-heeled shoes to look taller, too-tight jeans to look smaller, dyed hair to be blond, and uncomfortably revealing outfits to look more like the young women in the magazines. But why exactly do we teenage girls torture ourselves so to change our looks and try to take on the supposed perfection of the models in magazines? What is in these magazines that appeals so much to girls who are becoming young women?

consumed
ate

disrupting
radically changing

3   Horoscopes, advice, beauty and body tips, questions and answers on all topics, and interesting and informative articles are some of the things you will find in magazines targeted at teenage girls. In some of the many articles they have about anorexia, bulimia, and other eating disorders, the magazines tell about the devastating effects—medical and psychological—of those disorders, along with firsthand accounts of people who have suffered from them. Yet, on just about every page, there are young women who are so thin they look as if they have those very disorders. Other interesting stories that these magazines sometimes have are firsthand accounts of "shopaholics," or compulsive buyers, while on just about every page there are advertisements practically screaming, "Buy, buy, buy." Ads for clothes, bathing suits, makeup, hair care, nail care, and "feminine needs" are everywhere. These ads lead teenage girls to believe that if we manage to obtain all of these products, we will somehow be transformed into the glamorous women in the magazines who, because they are "beautiful," must also be happy. The advertisements thrust on young women the idea that we need—in fact, that we must have—all of these products to be socially accepted.

devastating
extremely damaging

Elena Marie Peifer, "Teen Girl Magazines: The Good, the Bad, and the Beautiful." Used with permission.

4   Although magazines create impossible desires for young women, there are also many features that will help us through this awkward stage of life. In traditional cultures, there are coming-of-age ceremonies that provide very clear guidelines and rituals for how we are supposed to act as we experience our adolescence; however, American girls in our times are left to fend for ourselves during the stage between childhood and womanhood. Magazines such as *Seventeen* have articles about some of the life-altering decisions that must be made during this time, decisions such as whether or not to have sex, do drugs, concentrate in school, and go to college. These articles are supplemented with advice columns with names like "Beauty," "Boys," and "Saying Goodbye," which go over teenagers' problems and their solutions.

life-altering
life changing

5   Sometimes teenagers, like all other people, want to laugh, even if it means laughing at other people's misfortunes. Columns that poke fun at other people are "Trauma-rama," "Most Mortifying Moments," and "Why Me?" It's hard for teenage girls to find our way in life, so we sometimes want to read about someone else who has had bad or embarrassing experiences. More importantly, however, magazines publish articles on hard-to-deal-with, widespread experiences—divorce, domestic violence, difficult breakups, peer pressure, and even rape. These articles show young women that we are not alone in dealing with these problems and refer us to people who can help. Family members are the hardest people to talk to about these problems, and sometimes these articles can explain to teen girls some possible ways to inform our families about what we're going through.

6   With parents, friends, teachers, and peers telling the young women of today who to be and how to act, it is easy for girls to get lost trying to find who we truly are. In the adolescent girl's search for her identity, the teen magazines can be both bad and good. On the one hand, they instill in our minds an unrealistic and unachievable goal of beauty. On the other hand, they help us find ourselves and understand better how to accomplish our goals in life. If we can find a way to tune out the messages from the models and ads, or if the magazines themselves would rule them out, I think these magazines would be mostly beneficial in allowing young women to take advantage of learning from others' mistakes. After all, we would all like to learn from mistakes without making them ourselves.

Exercise 10	**Work with Words**

Use context clues, word-part clues, and, if necessary, the dictionary to write the definitions of the italicized words in the following sentences from Reading 3.

1. The ideal of the 110-pound, size-three, C-cup, five-foot nine-inch blond woman is one that many of us will go to extremes to achieve. [Young women] will deprive themselves of food *in pursuit of* this image. (par. 2)

   in pursuit of _____

2. What is in these magazines that *appeals* so much to girls who are becoming young women? (par. 2)

   appeals _____

© 2014 Wadsworth, Cengage Learning

3. In some of the many articles they have about *anorexia, bulimia,* and other eating disorders, the magazines tell about the devastating effects—medical and psychological—of those disorders along with firsthand accounts of people who have suffered from them. (par. 3)

anorexia and bulimia _____

4. In traditional cultures, there are *coming-of-age ceremonies* that provide very clear guidelines and rituals for how we are supposed to act as we experience our adolescence; however, American girls in our times are left to fend for themselves during the stage between childhood and womanhood. (par. 4)

coming-of-age ceremonies _____

_____

5. If we can find a way to tune out the messages from the models and ads, or if the magazines themselves would rule them out, I think these magazines would be mostly *beneficial* in allowing young women to take advantage of learning from others' mistakes. (par. 6)

beneficial _____

Exercise 11

Identify Main Ideas and Supporting Details

For the following groups of sentences from or related to Reading 3, write "MI" for the main idea sentence and "SD" for the sentences that provide supporting details.

1. ___ a. Teenage girls sacrifice their health and comfort trying to achieve the right look.
   ___ b. Young women will deprive themselves of food in pursuit of this image.
   ___ c. We will wear uncomfortable shoes to look taller, too-tight jeans to look smaller, dyed hair to be blond, and uncomfortably revealing outfits.

2. ___ a. On just about every page there are advertisements practically screaming, "Buy, buy, buy."
   ___ b. Some of the interesting stories that these magazines have are about "shopaholics," or compulsive buyers.
   ___ c. There are important articles from which we can learn a lot, but there are also models and advertisements that seem to represent the unrealistic expectations the articles warn us about.

© 2014 Wadsworth, Cengage Learning

3. __ a. These articles are supplemented with advice columns with names like "Beauty," "Boys," and "Saying Goodbye," which go over teenagers' problems and their solutions.

__ b. Magazines such as *Seventeen* have articles about some of the life-altering decisions that must be made during this time, decisions such as whether or not to have sex, do drugs, concentrate in school, and go to college.

__ c. There are also many features in these teen magazines that can help us through this awkward stage of life.

4. __ a. These articles show young women that they are not alone in dealing with these problems.

__ b. The magazines help girls deal with very real problems.

__ c. Magazines publish articles on hard-to-deal-with, widespread experiences—divorce, domestic violence, difficult breakups, peer pressure, and even rape.

Exercise 12

Outline

Based on Reading 3, choose the best answers to the questions. Then fill in the spaces of the following outline model.

1. What is the topic of the reading?
   a. magazines
   b. teen magazines
   c. teen magazines for girls

2. What is the best thesis statement for the reading?
   a. Teen magazines appeal to girls because they have so many glamorous photos.
   b. If we could find a way to tune out the messages from the models and ads, teen magazines would be mostly beneficial for young women.
   c. Teen magazines contradict themselves.

Now fill in the outline.

topic:_____

main idea:_____

_____

A. Trying to reach the idea of beauty set by the magazines_____

1. Eating disorders (anorexia, binge eating, purging)

2. _____

© 2014 Wadsworth, Cengage Learning

    B. <u>Contradictions between the lessons of the articles and the advertisements</u>

        1. _____

        2. <u>Articles about shopaholics/pictures and ads of things to buy on every page</u>

    C. <u>Good features</u>

        1. <u>Articles about important decisions we have to make</u>

        2. _____

        3. _____

    D. <u>Bad and good sides, but mostly beneficial</u>

        1. <u>Instill in our minds unrealistic goals</u>

        2. _____

Exercise 13

Make Connections and Write

Write short answers to the following questions about magazines and advertisements based on your reading, your experience, and your observations.

1. What kinds of magazines do you read? What kinds of articles and advertisements do they have?

    _____

    _____

    _____

2. Do your magazines have both a positive and a negative side as Peifer states the teenage girl magazines do? Explain.

    _____

    _____

    _____

© 2014 Wadsworth, Cengage Learning

Crack and the Box

— PETE HAMILL

How much time do you spend watching entertainment on your television, or other electronic devices? Do you think you are a television or Internet addict? In the following reading, Pete Hamill compares watching television to being addicted to drugs. What are his points of comparison? Is he convincing? As you read, keep in mind his thesis and his major and minor supporting details. Also, notice we've added footnotes to explain information in the reading that might be unfamiliar to you. Look at the end of the reading to find these explanations.

1   One sad, rainy morning last winter I talked to a woman who was addicted to crack cocaine. She was 22, stiletto-thin, with eyes as old as tombs. She was living in two rooms in a welfare hotel with her children, who were two, three, and five years of age. Her story was the usual tangle of human woe: early pregnancy, dropping out of school, vanished men, smack and then crack, tricks with johns in parked cars to pay for the dope. I asked her why she did drugs. She shrugged in an empty way and couldn't really answer beyond "makes me feel good." While we talked . . . the children ignored us. They were watching television. . . .

2   Television, like drugs, dominates the lives of its addicts. And though some lonely Americans leave their sets on without watching them, using them as electronic companions, television usually absorbs its viewers the way drugs absorb their users. Viewers can't work or play while watching television; they can't read; they can't be out on the streets, falling in love with the wrong people, learning how to quarrel and compromise with other human beings. In short, they are asocial. So are drug addicts.

3   One Michigan State University study in the early 80s offered a group of four- and five-year-olds the choice of giving up television or giving up their fathers. Fully one-third said they would give up Daddy. Given a similar choice (between cocaine or heroin and father, mother, brother, sister, wife, husband, children, job), almost every stone junkie would do the same.

4   There are other disturbing similarities. Television itself is a consciousness-altering instrument. With the touch of a button, it takes you out of the "real" world in which you reside and can place you at a basketball game, the back alleys of Miami, the streets of Bucharest, or the cartoony living rooms of Sitcom Land. Each move from channel to channel alters mood, usually with music or a laugh track. On any given evening, you can laugh, be frightened, feel tension, thump with excitement. You can even tune in *MacNeil/Lehrer*[1] and feel sober.

5   But none of these abrupt shifts in mood is earned. They are attained as easily as popping a pill. Getting news from television, for example, is simply not the same experience as reading it in a newspaper. Reading is active. The reader must decode little symbols called words, then create images or ideas and make them connect; at its most basic level, reading is an act of the imagination. But the television viewer doesn't go through that process. The words are spoken to him or her by Dan Rather or Tom Brokaw or Peter Jennings.[2] There isn't much decoding to do when watching television, no time to think or ponder before the next set of images and spoken words appears

decode
figure out

© 2014 Wadsworth, Cengage Learning

Reprinted by permission of International Creative Management, Inc. © by Pete Hamill.

passive
not active

to displace the present one. The reader, being active, works at his or her own pace; the viewer, being passive, proceeds at a pace determined by the show. Except at the highest levels, television never demands that its audience take part in an act of imagination. Reading always does.

6   In short, television works on the same imaginative and intellectual level as psychoactive drugs. If prolonged television viewing makes the young passive (dozens of studies indicate that it does), then moving to drugs has a certain coherence. Drugs provide an unearned high (in contrast to the earned rush that comes from a feat accomplished, a human breakthrough earned by sweat or thought or love).

alienated from
separated from

7   And because the television addict and the drug addict are alienated from the hard and scary world, they also feel they make no difference in its complicated events. For the junkie, the world is reduced to him or her and the needle, pipe, or vial; the self is absolutely isolated, with no desire for choice. The television addict lives the same way. Many Americans who fail to vote in presidential elections must believe they have no more control over such a choice than they do over the casting of *L.A. Law*.

8   The drug plague also coincides with the unspoken assumption of most television shows: Life should be easy. The most complicated events are summarized on TV news in a minute or less. Cops confront murder, chase the criminals, and bring them to justice (usually violently) within an hour. In commercials, you drink the right beer and you get the girl. Easy! So why should real life be a grind? Why should any American have to spend years mastering a skill or craft, or work eight hours a day at an unpleasant job, or endure the compromises and crises of a marriage?

enhance
improve

9   The doper always whines about how he or she feels; drugs are used to enhance feelings or obliterate them, and in this the doper is very American. No other people on earth spend so much time talking about their feelings; hundreds of thousands go to shrinks, they buy self-help books by the millions, they pour out intimate confessions to virtual strangers in bars or discos. Our political campaigns are about emotional issues now, stated in the simplicities of adolescence. Even alleged statesmen can start a sentence, "I feel that . . . " when they once might have said, "I *think*. . . . " I'm convinced that this exaltation of cheap emotions over logic and reason is one by-product of hundreds of thousands of hours of television.

10   Most Americans under the age of 50 have now spent their lives absorbing television; that is, they've had the structures of drama pounded into them. Drama is always about conflict. So news shows, politics, and advertising are now all shaped by those structures. Nobody will pay attention to anything as complicated as the part played by Third World debt[3] in the expanding production of cocaine; it's much easier to focus on Manuel Noriega,[4] a character right out of *Miami Vice,* and believe that even in real life there's a Mister Big.

11   What is to be done? Television is certainly not going away, but its addictive qualities can be controlled. It's a lot easier to "just say no" to television than to heroin or crack. As a beginning, parents must take immediate control of the sets, teaching children to watch specific television *programs,* not "television," to get out of the house and play with other kids. Elementary and high schools must begin teaching television as a subject, the way literature is taught, showing children how shows are made, how to distinguish between the true and the false, how to recognize cheap emotional manipulation. All Americans should spend more time reading. And thinking.

12   For years, the defenders of television have argued that the networks are only giving the people what they want. That might be true. But so is the Medellín Cartel.[5]

© 2014 Wadsworth, Cengage Learning

Notes

1. *MacNeil/Lehrer* is a program on public television that is now called *The News Hour*. Dan Rather, Tom Brokaw, and Peter Jennings were the best known news anchors in the 1990s and at the beginning of the twenty-first century.

2. Many countries in the Third World owe billions of dollars to American and European banks. Because of having to pay interest on this debt, these countries are becoming poorer, and it is because of poverty that many farmers turn to growing drug-related crops.

3. Manuel Noriega was a dictator of Panama who was involved in drug trafficking.

4. The Medellin Cartel is the most powerful drug ring in Colombia.

Exercise 14

Work with Words

Use context clues, word-part clues, and, if necessary, the dictionary to choose the best definitions of the italicized words in the following sentences from Reading 4.

1. Viewers can't work or play while watching television; they can't read; they can't be out on the streets, falling in love with the wrong people, learning how to quarrel and compromise with other human beings. In short, they are *asocial*. (par. 2)

   asocial
   a. not social or able to get along with people in a variety of ways
   b. not able to go to parties
   c. not able to be in a good argument

2. There are other disturbing similarities. Television itself is a *consciousness-altering* instrument. With the touch of a button, it takes you out of the "real" world in which you reside and can place you at a basketball game, the back alleys of Miami, the streets of Bucharest, or the cartoony living rooms of Sitcom Land. (par. 4)

   consciousness-altering
   a. able to make conscious
   b. able to make unconscious
   c. able to change your consciousness

3. Drugs provide an unearned high (in contrast to the earned rush that comes from a *feat* accomplished, a human breakthrough earned by sweat or thought or love). (par. 6)

   feat
   a. task
   b. extraordinary accomplishment
   c. unearned "high"

© 2014 Wadsworth, Cengage Learning

4. The drug plague also *coincides with* the unspoken assumption of most television shows: Life should be easy. (par. 8)

coincides with
a. conflicts with
b. contradicts
c. corresponds to

5. The doper always whines about how he or she feels; drugs are used to enhance feelings or *obliterate* them, and in this the doper is very American. (par. 9)

obliterate
a. cover up
b. repair
c. destroy

Exercise 15

Identify Main Ideas and Supporting Details

For the following groups of sentences from or related to Reading 4, write "MI for the main idea sentence and "SD" for the sentences that provide supporting details.

1. __ a. Getting information from television is not the same as getting information from books.
   __ b. Reading is active.
   __ c. The reader must decode little symbols called words, then create images or ideas and make them connect.
   __ d. At its most basic level, reading is an act of the imagination.
   __ e. The reader proceeds at his or her pace.
   __ f. The television viewer is passive.
   __ g. The words are spoken to him or her by Dan Rather.
   __ h. There isn't much decoding to do or time to think before the next set of images goes up.
   __ i. The viewer proceeds at the pace set by the show.

2. __ a. The world for the junkie is reduced to his or her need to get high.
   __ b. Because the television addict and the drug addict feel separated from the world, they also feel that they make no difference in the world.
   __ c. The junkie does not think about the world or people in his or her life.
   __ d. The television addict lives just like the junkie.
   __ e. The television addict often doesn't vote for president because he or she feels that voting won't make any difference.

3. __ a. If you drink the right beer, you'll get the girl.
   __ b. Television shows that life should be easy.
   __ c. Cops confront murder, chase criminals, and bring them to justice in one hour.
   __ d. The most complicated events are summarized and simplified on television in a minute or less.

© 2014 Wadsworth, Cengage Learning

Exercise 16

Prepare to Outline

Based on Reading 4, choose the best answers to the questions. Then, follow directions for Item 3.

1. What is the topic of the reading?
   a. Drug addiction
   b. Television as an addiction
   c. The passivity of watching television

2. What is the best thesis sentence for the reading?
   a. Television, like drugs, dominates the lives of its addicts.
   b. Television itself is a consciousness-altering instrument.
   c. Television cannot be considered a psychoactive drug.

3. Make a list of the most important supporting points for Hamill's thesis in Reading 4. _____

   _____

   _____

   _____

   _____

   _____

4. On a separate piece of paper, and using the list you made for item 3, write an outline for Reading 4.

Exercise 17

Make Connections and Write

Write short answers to the following questions based on Reading 4, your experience, and your observations. Then discuss your answers with your class group. Working together, prepare a report for your class as a whole or a written summary for your instructor.

1. When do you watch television or watch television programs on your computer or digital devices? Why do you watch at those hours?

   _____

   _____

   _____

   _____

© 2014 Wadsworth, Cengage Learning

2. Have you ever stopped watching television or entertainment on a digital device for several days or more? What was the experience like?

_____

_____

_____

_____

3. Do you agree with Hamill that television is like drugs? Explain your answer.

_____

_____

_____

_____

4. Why does Hamill title his article "Crack and the Box"?

_____

_____

_____

_____

5. Do you think it's a good idea to restrict the amount of television or entertainment on digital devices that children watch? Explain your answer.

_____

_____

_____

_____

© 2014 Wadsworth, Cengage Learning

Chapter Review

To aid your review of the reading skills in Chapter 5, study the Put It Together chart.

Put It Together: Main Ideas And Supporting Details	
Skills and Concepts	Explanation
Supporting Details (see pages 205–206, 209–210, 212)	Supporting details give additional information about the main idea and are more specific. They can be examples, facts, reasons, and even descriptions.
General Statements and Specific Information (see pages 205–207)	The main idea of a paragraph or essay is a broad, general statement. Specifics are the details that support the general statement.
Outlining (see pages 219–220)	Outlining is a useful technique for organizing information that you need to remember. When you outline, you follow four basic steps: 1. Determine the topic. 2. Determine the main idea(s). 3. Determine the supporting details for the stated or unstated main idea(s). 4. Arrange the information in outline form.

To reinforce your thinking before taking the Mastery Tests, complete as many of the following activities as your instructor assigns.

Review Skills

Complete the following skills-review tasks individually or in a group.

1. What is the difference between a main idea and a supporting detail?

   _____

   _____

   _____

2. Write four sentences about a TV program or a magazine. One sentence should state a main idea, and the other three should give supporting details.

   MI _____

   _____

© 2014 Wadsworth, Cengage Learning

SD _____

_____

SD _____

_____

SD _____

3. When is it helpful for you to outline a reading?

_____

Write

On a separate piece of paper, write a paragraph or more answering the questions.

1. What are your favorite types of Internet entertainment?

2. Do social networking sites create real friends? Do they improve friendship, or distort what it means to be a friend? Explain your answers.

COLLABORATE

Brainstorm in a group the ways that all of us are consumers of mass entertainment. Make a list, and then fill out the following chart on the benefits and disadvantages of each type of entertainment. As a group, try to decide which types of mass entertainment have the most benefits and the fewest disadvantages.

Type of Entertainment	Benefits	Disadvantages
_____	_____	_____
_____	_____	_____
_____	_____	_____
_____	_____	_____
_____	_____	_____
_____	_____	_____

© 2014 Wadsworth, Cengage Learning

EXTEND YOUR THINKING

To answer the following questions, you will have to do a little research. Then prepare to share the information you gather with your class group.

1. Search the Internet, go to a library or store, and browse through some popular magazines. Write down the types of articles and advertisements the magazines include. Use this information to explain who the target audience is.

2. Play a video game. Describe the objectives of the game and the effects the game has on you. Determine in what ways the game is beneficial and in what ways it may be damaging. Explain your reasons.

 ## WORK THE WEB

Reading 3 discusses "teen girl" magazines. Use a search engine such as *Google* to go to the *Seventeen* magazine Web site. Then answer the following questions.

1. Describe the Web site. List some details that explain how the magazine appeals to its audience—teenage girls.

_____

_____

_____

_____

2. A good main idea for a paragraph about *Seventeen's* Web site would be, "The *Seventeen* Web site relies heavily on advertising to make money." List the products promoted by ads when you visited the site. This list provides support for the main idea.

_____

_____

_____

3. Magazines that are written for teenage girls usually have articles about appearance, fashion, and personal problems. Write the titles of articles that you found on the Web site that support this statement.

_____

_____

_____

© 2014 Wadsworth, Cengage Learning

Name _____ Date _____

Fighting over Sneakers

—Richard Campbell

TEXT BOOK **The following reading from a communications textbook discusses the impact that advertising and brand names have had on American young people. The example the author uses is the popularity of certain kinds of basketball shoes and the tactics that some poor young people have used in order to get those very expensive shoes. As you read, think about how important brand names are to you. Also think about some of the most popular brands today. Look for Campbell's thesis for this reading, and consider the details that support his thesis.**

1   During the 1950s and 1960s, most serious basketball players wore simple canvas sneakers—usually Converse or Keds. Encouraged by increasing TV coverage, interest in sports exploded in the late 1960s and 1970s, as did a wildly competitive international sneaker industry. First Adidas dominated the industry, then Nike and Reebok. The Great Sneaker Wars have since continued unabated, although they may have peaked at the 1992 Olympics when pro basketball stars Michael Jordan and Charles Barkley—Nike endorsers—refused to display the Reebok logo on their team jackets at the awards ceremony. Reebok had paid dearly to sponsor the Olympics and wanted the athletes to fall in line. A compromise was eventually worked out in which the two players wore the jackets but hid the Reebok name.

unabated
as strong as ever

2   Although the Olympic incident seems <u>petty</u>, battles over brand-name sneakers and jackets in the 1980s were a more dangerous "game." Advertisers found themselves <u>embroiled</u> in a controversy that, for a time, threw a bright and uncomfortable spotlight on the advertising industry. In many poor and urban areas throughout the United States, kids and <u>rival</u> gangs were fighting over and stealing brand-name sportswear from one another. Particularly coveted and targeted were $100-plus top-of-the-line basketball shoes, especially the Nike and Reebok brands heavily advertised on television. A few incidents resulted in shootings and killings. Articles in major newspapers and magazines, including *Sports Illustrated* ("Your Sneakers or Your Life") <u>took advertisers to task</u>. Especially hard hit was Nike, which by the early 1990s controlled nearly 30 percent of the $5.5 billion world sneaker market. Nike's slogan—"Just do it"—became a rallying cry for critics who argued that while for most middle-class people, the command simply meant get in shape, work hard, and perform, for kids from poorer neighborhoods, "Just do it" was a call to arms: "Do what you have to do to survive."

controversy
public argument

coveted
desired
(something that belongs to someone else)

3   The problem was <u>exacerbated</u> during the 1980s by underlying economic conditions. As the gap between rich and poor grew, advertisements suggested that our identities came from the products that we own. It is not surprising, then, that the possession of a particular brand-name product became increasingly significant for kids who felt they did not own much. Having the "right" sneaker or jacket came to represent a large part of their identities. For some groups and gangs, such possession became a requirement for membership.

4   The controversy over brand-name products has raised serious concerns about the moral responsibilities of agencies and advertisers. On one hand, Nike and other advertisers have become a lightning rod for the problems of a consumer culture that promises the good life to everyone who "just does it." On the other hand, criticisms

© 2014 Wadsworth, Cengage Learning

Richard Campbell, et al, "Fighting over Sneakers" from *Media and Culture,* 5e.
© 2006 by Bedford/St. Martin's. Reproduced by permission of Bedford/St. Martin's.

of advertising have often stopped with the ads and have not examined whether they *cause* the violence or are simply *symptoms* of the <u>inequities</u> in contemporary America. Although many critics <u>vilified</u> Nike at the time, few were willing to discuss the <u>drawbacks</u> of capitalism and consumerism in general.

5   Fights over sneakers and jackets generate significant questions at the heart of our consumer culture. Does brand-name advertising unrealistically raise hopes about attaining the consumer "dreams" that some ads promise? Who should share the ultimate responsibility for violence that takes place in the name of a coveted shoe or jacket? As a society, should we mandate noncommercial messages and public-service announcements that offer alternative visions? While we need to debate these issues vigorously as individuals and as a society, in some communities kids and adults have already acted. Although brand-name products continue to sell well, an alternative attitude rejects such labeling and opts for cheaper generic products and used rummage-sale clothing. Posing a challenge to the advertising industry, this attitude undermines the view that brand-name identification is a requirement of our times.

mandate
require

Use the context clues, word-part clues, and, if necessary, the dictionary to choose the best definition for each of the italicized words in the following sentences from the reading.

1. Although the Olympic incident seems *petty*, battles over brand-name sneakers and jackets in the 1980s were a more dangerous "game." (par. 2)

   petty
   a. unimportant
   b. important
   c. necessary

2. Advertisers found themselves *embroiled* in a controversy that, for a time, threw a bright and uncomfortable spotlight on the advertising industry. (par. 2)

   embroiled
   a. involved in celebration
   b. involved in conflict
   c. confused

3. In many poor and urban areas throughout the United States, kids and *rival* gangs were fighting over and stealing brand-name sportswear from one another. (par. 2)

   rival
   a. friendly
   b. enemy
   c. executive

4. Particularly coveted and targeted were $100-plus top-of-the-line basketball shoes, especially the Nike and Reebok brands heavily advertised on television. A few incidents resulted in shootings and killings. Articles in major newspapers and magazines, including *Sports Illustrated* ("Your Sneakers or Your Life"), *took advertisers to task*. (par. 2)

   took advertisers to task
   a. praised advertisers
   b. criticized advertisers
   c. looked for publicity

© 2014 Wadsworth, Cengage Learning

5. The problem was *exacerbated* during the 1980s by underlying economic conditions. As the gap between rich and poor grew, advertisements suggested that our identities came from the products that we own. (par. 3)

exacerbated
a. relieved
b. made worse
c. complemented

6. Although many critics *vilified* Nike at the time, few were willing to discuss the *drawbacks* of capitalism and consumerism in general. (par. 4)

vilified
a. said bad things about
b. said good things about
c. made suggestions about

7. *drawbacks*
a. advantages
b. disadvantages
c. details

8. On the other hand, criticisms of advertising have often stopped with the ads and have not examined whether they cause the violence or are simply symptoms of the *inequities* in contemporary America. (par. 4)

inequities
a. inequalities
b. wealth
c. high standard of living

For the following groups of sentences, write "MI" for the main idea sentence and "SD" for minor supporting details.

9. ___ a. At that time, the basketball players wore simple canvas shoes, but those times have changed.
___ b. The 1950s and 1960s were simpler times for our athletes and for our young people.
___ c. Today, with the help of advertising, many young people feel that they have to own a pair of expensive Nike or Adidas.

10. ___ a. In many poor and urban areas throughout the United States, kids and rival gangs were fighting, stealing, and sometimes killing for brand name sportswear.
___ b. The battles over brand-name sneakers and jackets became a dangerous game.
___ c. Articles about the incidents appeared in newspapers and magazines, including *Sports Illustrated.*

11. ___ a. As the gap between rich and poor grew, advertisements suggested that our identities came from the products that we own.
___ b. The possession of a particular brand-name product became more important for kids who felt they did not own much.
___ c. Having the right sneaker or jacket was important to these children.

© 2014 Wadsworth, Cengage Learning

12. __ a. Some critics think that advertisers are responsible for our problems as a consumer culture.

    __ b. Young people getting killed for basketball shoes is just one example of the problems that we face.

    __ c. The controversy over brand-name products has raised serious questions about the moral responsibilities of advertisers.

13. __ a. As a society, we should mandate noncommercial messages and public-service announcements that offer alternative visions.

    __ b. In some communities people are taking a stand against brand-name products.

    __ c. These examples show us that we really don't "have to have" those expensive products.

Choose the best answers to the following multiple-choice questions about the reading.

14. What is the main idea, or thesis, of "Fighting Over Sneakers"?
    a. The advertising industry has created a need for brand-name products that has even led to violence.
    b. Nike is a better sneaker than Adidas for aspiring young athletes.
    c. Young people cannot have a good opinion of themselves if they don't own brand-name sneakers and jackets.

15. Which of the following is *not* true about the 1992 Olympics?
    a. Reebok sponsored the Olympics.
    b. Reebok wanted the athletes to wear Reebok jackets.
    c. The athletes were happy to wear the Reebok jackets.

16. What is the primary reason the author gives for why young people feel they must own brand-name sneakers?
    a. The more expensive sneakers help them play better ball.
    b. Having the right sneaker came to represent a large part of their identities.
    c. They can tell the difference between cheap products and well-made products.

17. What idea do you get about advertising from the reading?
    a. Advertising influences our society in bad ways.
    b. Advertising is simply doing an important job informing the consumer.
    c. Advertising helps companies make the profits that they deserve.

18. It is clear that the author believes which of the following?
    a. Consumer culture is healthy and good for the economy.
    b. Consumer culture creates problems.
    c. The answers to the problems of consumer culture are simple.

© 2014 Wadsworth, Cengage Learning

Write short answers to the following questions about advertising and brand name products, based on your reading, your experience, and your observations.

19. What advertisements do you think have influenced you most to buy a brand-name product, or at least to want to buy it? Explain.

_____

_____

_____

_____

20. Why do you think some people spend a lot more money to buy certain brand-name electronics, clothes and shoes, and do you think those products are worth the extra price? Explain.

_____

_____

_____

_____

© 2014 Wadsworth, Cengage Learning

Wii Fun for Everyone!

—ANNETTE LARSON

In the following reading, Annette Larson enthusiastically endorses the Nintendo Wii gaming system. As you read, consider whether you agree with her broad endorsement of this type of gaming. Notice how she explains that the criticisms of video games do not apply to Wii. Focus on how she develops her argument and the details she uses to support her thesis and main ideas.

1   Despite their rising popularity, not all people have been attracted to video games. Many people never spent hours playing the primitive games that first came out on Atari and Nintendo systems. Even the more advanced games and systems that have been produced lately have not appealed to everyone. Grandparents, outdoors types, athletes, retired people, and rural people have traditionally been the part of the population, or <u>demographic</u>, that has been least interested in playing video games, or "gaming" as fans call it. Critics have even attacked gaming, saying that it can lead to <u>antisocial</u> and violent behavior while also being bad for people's health and family relations. If that is so, the Nintendo Wii is a gaming system that will <u>revolutionize</u> the way people play video games, making gaming a healthy, social, and family-friendly activity attractive to everyone.

2   What is Wii anyway? Wii is Nintendo's fifth home gaming system and was released in 2006. The name was chosen because it is simple and easy to pronounce in many languages. Also, according to Nintendo, "Wii sounds like 'we,' which emphasizes that the console is for everyone."[1] One thing that makes Wii different is the <u>range</u> of things you can do with it and the ways in which you have to use your body to make it work. Several wireless handheld controllers and pads or balance boards that you stand on make many sports, exercises, and games more realistic. You actually have to swing or jump to hit a tennis ball, and you have to move your hips to the beat in dancing games. Wii comes with a package of games called Wii Sports that includes tennis, baseball, bowling, golf, and boxing. All of these games were made to be simple and fun to play for nongamers. There are also many other game and fitness packages as well as options for playing with friends and family. Because of its design, the Wii has consistently outsold competing gaming systems around the world.[2]

3   When it designed Wii, Nintendo made a system that would be fun for everyone, including the people who never liked gaming before. In a press conference, Nintendo's president, Satoru Iwata, said, "We're not thinking about fighting Sony, but about how many people we can get to play games."[3] Nintendo is making Wii attractive to a lot more people in a variety of ways. An advertising and public-image campaign targeted nongamers, while the assortment of games, fitness activities, and sports is meant to be fun for all types of people. One TV and Internet ad shows Nintendo representatives visiting American homes with a Wii system and saying, "Wii would like to play." The ad pictures families, urban youth, high school students, Hispanics, African-Americans, and cattle ranchers all enjoying Wii with the Japanese representatives. No language is needed after the first sentence: The joy of Wii is understood by all. The games played in this advertisement are mostly part of the Wii Sports package, which has become the most popular. These games appeal to a wide range of people instead of just hardcore gamers. The Wii Fit package is meant for elderly people, for families, and for those who are interested in various fitness activities offered by the package.

© 2014 Wadsworth, Cengage Learning

Written by Annette Larson. Reprinted by permission of the author.

4   In another part of its promotion campaign Nintendo has focused on older people who have traditionally been nongamers. Nintendo has even given free Wii consoles to senior centers where residents now wait in lines to play.[4] Even 81-year-old Queen Elizabeth has become hooked to Wii after she tried a bowling game on Prince William's system. In Britain people as old as 103 have been reported to be playing the Wii in retirement homes! Obviously, Nintendo has succeeded in making its new system fun for all, including the grandparents of the usual gamers. [5]

5   Wii is the perfect <u>response</u> to critics' claims that gaming is violent, antisocial, and bad for family relationships, as it is proving to be a great social activity to bring families, friends, and communities together. Wii tennis tournaments have been held in bars, stores, and community centers in several countries, attracting large audiences. One bar in New York held a Wii tennis tournament called "Wiimbledon."[6] Senior citizens at retirement homes have even formed virtual-bowling leagues and big social gatherings around Wii Sports competitions.[7] Another benefit of Wii is that most of the Wii games people are playing are not violent at all. The system also has parental controls that allow parents to restrict what games and Web sites their children can go to. Critics can't complain about Wii; it is the ideal social and family-friendly gaming system.

6   Another negative perception of video games is that they are unhealthy because they keep people from playing outside and getting physical exercise. The Wii, however, is actually health-promoting in several ways. Most Wii games require at least some exercise, and there is even a package of games called Wii Fit that focuses specifically on a player's fitness. Wii Fit includes yoga, stretching, strength training, aerobics, and balance games. The system keeps track of players' personal weight, age, and physical activity level to help them design a <u>personalized</u> exercise program. Wii Fit is almost like a combination of a personal trainer and gaming system all in one! Wii is not only healthy for everyday use. It also promises to be a valuable tool for physical therapy treatments for athletes, injured soldiers, and stroke victims.[8] This type of therapy is already being called "Wiihabilitation"!

7   Every day there is more evidence of Wii's positive benefits. It makes gaming fun for people—including the Queen of England—who have never been interested in video games. Scientific studies describe its good <u>outcomes</u>, and seniors, consumer groups, hospitals, and families are all becoming fans. This new gaming system is healthy, social, family-friendly, and amazing fun for everyone!

Notes

1. Simon Carless, "Breaking: Nintendo announces new Revolution name –'Wii,'" April 27, 2006, at http://www.gamasutra.com/php-bin/news_index.php?story=9075 (accessed March 15, 2009).

2. "Nintendo: Consolidated Financial Highlights," January 29, 2009, at http://www.nintendo.co.jp/ir/pdf/2009/090129e.pdf#page=11 (accessed March 15, 2009).

3. Quoted in Anoop Gantayat, "Dragon Quest IX Q and A," at http://ds.ign.com/articles/750/750610p1.html (accessed March 15, 2009).

4. Jennifer Collins, "Seniors Becoming Old Hands at Wii," December 11, 2007, at http://marketplace.publicradio.org/display/web/2007/12/11/old_wii/ (accessed March 15, 2009).

5. Dean Rousewell, "Make Way for the Q Wii N," January 6, 2008, at http://www.people.co.uk/news/tm_headline=make-way-for-the-q-wii-n%26method=full%26objectid=20276099%26siteid=93463-name_page.html (accessed March 15, 2009).

© 2014 Wadsworth, Cengage Learning

6. BBC NEWS, "Wii Players Need to Exercise Too," December 21, 2007, at http:// news. bbc.co.uk/2/hi/health/7155342.stm (accessed March 15, 2009).

7. Collins, "Seniors Becoming Old Hands at Wii."

8. Lindsey Tanner, "Break a Leg? 'Try Wiihabilitation,'" February 8, 2008 at http:// www. msnbc.msn.com/id/23070190/wid/11915829 (accessed March 15, 2009).

Use context clues, word-part clues, and, if necessary, the dictionary to choose the best definition for the meaning of each of the italicized words in the following sentences from the reading.

1. Many people never spent hours playing the *primitive* games that first came out on Atari and Nintendo systems. (par. 1)

   primitive
   a. artistic
   b. simple
   c. difficult

2. Grandparents, outdoors types, athletes, retired people, and rural people have traditionally been the part of the population, or *demographic,* that has been least interested in playing video games, or "gaming" as fans call it. (par. 1)

   demographic
   a. rural people
   b. grandparents
   c. part of a population

3. Critics have even attacked gaming, saying that it can lead to *antisocial* and violent behavior while also being bad for people's health and family relations. (par. 1)

   antisocial
   a. unfriendly
   b. constructive
   c. stubborn

4. Nintendo Wii is a gaming system that will *revolutionize* the way people play video games, making gaming a healthy, social, and family-friendly activity attractive to everyone. (par. 1)

   revolutionize
   a. change
   b. speed up
   c. upset

5. One thing that makes Wii different is the *range* of things you can do with it and the ways in which you have to use your body to make it work. Several wireless handheld controllers and pads or balance boards that you stand on make many sports, exercises, and games more realistic. (par. 2)

   range
   a. place for target practice
   b. variety
   c. group

© 2014 Wadsworth, Cengage Learning

6. Wii is the perfect *response* to critics' claims that gaming is violent, antisocial, and bad for family relationships, as it is proving to be a great social activity to bring families, friends, and communities together. (par. 5)

response
a. argument
b. answer
c. proof

7. The system keeps track of players' *personal* weight, age, and physical activity level to help them design *a personalized* exercise program. (par. 6)

personalized
a. individual
b. group
c. team

8. Scientific studies describe its good *outcomes,* and seniors, consumer groups, hospitals, and families are all becoming fans. (par. 7)

outcomes
a. public events
b. interest groups
c. results

For the following groups of sentences from or related to the reading, write "MI" for the main idea sentence and "SD" for the sentences that provide supporting details.

9. ___ a. The TV and Internet ad shows Nintendo representatives visiting American homes with a Wii system and saying, "Wii would like to play."
___ b. No language is needed after the first sentence: the joy of Wii is understood by all.
___ c. An advertising and public-image campaign targeted nongamers, emphasizing its broad appeal, and in fact, one ad says it all.
___ d. The ad pictures families, urban youth, high school students, Hispanics, African-Americans, and cattle ranchers all enjoying Wii with the Japanese representatives.

10. ___ a. Nintendo has even given free Wii consoles to senior centers.
___ b. Even 81-year-old Queen Elizabeth has become hooked to Wii after she tried a bowling game on Prince William's system.
___ c. In Britain people as old as 103 have been reported to be playing the Wii in retirement homes!
___ d. In another part of its promotion campaign Nintendo has focused on older people, who have traditionally been nongamers.

11. ___ a. Wii is proving to be a great social activity to bring families, friends, and communities together.
___ b. Wii tennis tournaments have been held in bars, stores, and community centers in several countries, attracting large audiences.
___ c. One bar in New York held a Wii tennis tournament called "Wiimbledon."
___ d. Senior citizens at retirement homes have even formed virtual-bowling leagues and big social gatherings around Wii Sports competitions.

© 2014 Wadsworth, Cengage Learning

12. ___ a. Most Wii games require at least some exercise, and there is even a package of games called Wii Fit that focuses specifically on a player's fitness.

    ___ b. The Wii is actually health-promoting in several ways.

    ___ c. Wii Fit includes yoga, stretching, strength training, aerobics, and balance games.

    ___ d. The system keeps track of players' personal weight, age, and physical activity level to help them design a personalized exercise program.

13. ___ a. Wii Fit is almost like a personal trainer and physical therapist combined.

    ___ b. It helps people develop a personalized exercise program.

    ___ c. Studies show that Wii players use more energy than people playing other video games.

    ___ d. It keeps track of the players' weight, age, and physical activity level to help them design their program.

Choose the best answers to the following multiple-choice questions about the reading.

14. What is the main idea, or thesis, of "Wii Fun for Everyone!"?
    a. Wii is the best video game that has ever been sold.
    b. Even though people criticize video games for being antisocial and reducing people's physical activity, Wii is an exception because it is healthy and encourages people to do things together.
    c. As part of its promotion campaign Nintendo has focused on older people, who have traditionally been nongamers.

15. Which of the following is *not* a reason the author gives for buying a Wii.
    a. Wii promotes activity.
    b. Wii is fun.
    c. Wii is inexpensive.

16. The author uses the example of the Queen of England to demonstrate that
    a. she is a video game expert.
    b. older people like the Wii activities.
    c. she is a good sport.

17. The Wii Sports package
    a. is included with the system.
    b. comes at minimal cost.
    c. has been sold out.

Write short answers to the following questions about video games and the Wii gaming system based on your reading, your experience, and your observations.

18. What video games are you familiar with? How do you know about them, and what do you think about them?

_____

_____

© 2014 Wadsworth, Cengage Learning

_____

_____

19. What do you think about this article? Would you buy a Wii home gaming system after reading it? What additional information do you think it should contain? Explain your answer.

_____

_____

_____

_____

20. What are some problems with video games? Answers will vary.

_____

_____

_____

_____

© 2014 Wadsworth, Cengage Learning

CHAPTER

6 Writing Summaries

DRUGS IN OUR SOCIETY

"JUST TELL ME WHERE YOU KIDS GET THE IDEA TO TAKE SO MANY DRUGS."

ScienceCartoonPlus.com

I bought a gun and chose drugs instead.
—*Kurt Cobain*

- List all of the substances you think of as a "drug."

- What do you think the cartoon means? Explain.

- What kinds of drugs do you think are in the medicine cabinet in the cartoon?

- In what ways do drugs make our lives better? In what ways do they make our lives worse? Discuss specific drugs and their positive and/or negative effects.

- What is the meaning of the Kurt Cobain quote?

Getting Ready to Read

Drugs of all kinds are part of our lives. Almost all Americans take drugs at some time. We regularly use and sometimes misuse legal drugs such as prescription medications, alcohol, coffee, and tobacco. And some of us use "illicit" drugs, such as marijuana, cocaine, and methamphetamines. In modern day society, drugs are a complicated issue. Have you ever thought about how the development of new drugs has improved the quality of our lives over the years? Or about how drugs are also capable of worsening the quality of our lives?

In this chapter, you will read and think about some of the consequences of drug use—for better or for worse—in our society. As you do, you will improve your reading skills by learning how to write summaries that capture, in your own words, central ideas and major supporting details. To accomplish this you will improve your reading skills by learning how to

- Distinguish major supporting details from minor supporting details
- Determine if minor supporting details are important to remember
- Mark texts to distinguish major and minor supporting details
- Use outlines to visualize the distinction between major and minor supporting details
- Organize main ideas and supporting details into maps
- Paraphrase and credit other people's words and ideas
- Write summaries that capture, in your own words, main ideas and major supporting details

© 2014 Wadsworth, Cengage Learning

Reading 1

The Buzz Takes Your Breath Away . . . Permanently: Misuse of Prescription Pain Relievers

—[ADAPTED FROM] THE U.S. FOOD AND DRUG ADMINISTRATION AND
THE NATIONAL INSTITUTES OF HEALTH

The following reading examines the severe problems that abuse of prescription pain relievers can cause. As you read, think about how you (or people you know) use these medicines and why you need to know and remember the information in this reading.

YOU'VE HEARD IT BEFORE

1   How many times has someone told you a "party" drug could lead to more serious problems—like addiction, brain damage, or even death? You've probably heard it so many times that it's getting hard to believe, especially when people around you are smoking, drinking, and rolling. But though casual users may not always show obvious signs of the damage their habits can wreak, all drugs—even prescription pain relievers—have real potential for harm. When abused alone, or when taken with other drugs or alcohol, prescription pain medications can kill you; and the death toll from misuse and abuse of prescription drugs is rising steadily.

wreak
cause

WHICH DRUGS TO WATCH OUT FOR AND SIGNS OF OVERDOSE

2   The most dangerous prescription pain relievers are those containing drugs known as opioids, such as morphine and codeine. People take them to feel warm and elaxed. Some common drugs containing these substances include Darvon, Demerol, Dilaudid, OxyContin, Tylenol with Codeine, and Vicodin. Your friends may call these drugs by their street names: *ac/dc, coties, demmies, dillies, hillbilly heroin, o.c., oxy, oxycotton, percs,* and *vics* to name a few. Whatever you call them, remember: If you combine them or take too much, they can be fatal. Some danger signs of overdose from these drugs include: slow breathing, tiny pupils, confusion, fatigue or passing out, dizziness, weakness, apathy, cold and clammy skin, nausea, vomiting, and seizures.

opioids
narcotic drugs
that are usually
prescribed to
manage pain

THE DANGEROUS TREND

3   The United States is in the middle of an epidemic of prescription overdoses. In 2010, 12 million Americans said they were using opioid pain relievers without a prescription. In 2009, hospitals reported almost 500,000 emergency room visits related to the abuse of these painkillers. This costs health insurance companies as much as $72 billion a year in direct costs. In 1999 there were 4,000 deaths related to painkillers, but by 2008 that number had risen to 15,000 deaths. The number of deaths from *all* prescription

Adapted from The U.S. Food and Drug Administration and The National Institutes of Health. U.S. Food and Drug Administration, "Misuse of Prescription Pain Relievers: The Buzz that Takes Your Breath Away… Permanently" (brochure), at http://www.fda.gov/Drugs/ResourcesForYou/ ucm193918.htm (accessed 12/11/11). National Institutes of Health, "Deaths From Abuse of Painkillers Triple in a Decade," at http://www.nim.nih.gov/medlineplus/news/fullstory_118202.html (accessed 12/10/11)

© 2014 Wadsworth, Cengage Learning

drug overdoses has tripled in a decade, peaking at 36,000 fatalities in 2008. The United States suffers more deaths from the abuse of prescription narcotics than deaths from heroin abuse and cocaine abuse combined.

WHO'S USING?

4   Overdose deaths and the abuse of painkillers are not spread equally among the American population. More men than women die of overdoses from prescription painkillers. The rates are highest among middle-aged adults. People living in rural areas are almost twice as likely as city dwellers to overdose on opioid pain relievers, and different ethnic groups have different rates of overdoses as well. The highest overdose rates are among whites and American Indian or Alaska Natives. The estimated numbers for who is abusing painkillers are also telling: one in 10 American Indians and Alaska Natives, one in 20 whites, and one in 30 blacks. Traumatic experiences sometimes lead people to seek escape from their physical and psychological pain through the use, and sometimes, tragically, the misuse of prescription pain relievers. This has become a problem for some veterans returning from the wars in Iraq and Afghanistan.

EASY AVAILABILITY

5   Prescription painkillers have become relatively easy to obtain for a number of reasons. According to Thomas R. Frieden, director of the U.S. Centers for Disease Control, "Enough narcotics are prescribed to give every adult in America one month of prescription narcotics." Some doctors prescribe these medications too easily. Some doctors prescribe large quantities of painkillers to people who don't need them. Some people go from doctor to doctor to get more pills, and some people steal these medicines out of other people's medicine cabinets.

Exercise 1

Recall and Discuss

Answer these questions about Reading 1, and prepare to discuss them in class.

1. List two bits of information that you find most interesting in this reading.

_____

_____

_____

2. How much have prescription drug overdoses increased in a decade? What are some reasons you think this has happened?

_____

_____

_____

_____

_____

© 2014 Wadsworth, Cengage Learning

3. Why do you think the U.S. has more deaths from prescription narcotics than from heroin and cocaine abuse?

_____

_____

_____

_____

_____

4. What reasons can you think of that would explain why different groups (based on age, class, region, and ethnicity) abuse prescription drugs at such different levels? Consider just one or two of the groups to explain the statistics for abuse of these drugs.

_____

_____

_____

5. Which drugs do you think are most harmful in our country? In your community? Explain your answer.

_____

_____

_____

6. What drugs do you think are most beneficial? Explain your answer.

_____

_____

_____

© 2014 Wadsworth, Cengage Learning

Preparing to Write Summaries

summary
shortened form of a reading in words that are different from the author's

Summaries provide the content of a passage, essay, or reading in a shortened form using words different from those the original author used. Students and professionals are often asked to write summaries of important information. You might, for example, be asked to research a topic—such as the health consequences of alcoholism—and report your summarized findings to your fellow students or your employer. Writing a summary is also an excellent way to organize the material in textbooks for future review and test preparation.

If you are summarizing a paragraph, the first step is to identify the main idea. If you are summarizing a longer text, your first task will be to identify the central idea—the overall general statement or main point the author is making, or the thesis of a persuasive essay. Then, you need to identify the levels of supporting details to decide which details to include in your summary.

MAJOR AND MINOR SUPPORTING DETAILS

In addition to recognizing main ideas and supporting details, as you practiced in Chapter 5, it is important to know how to distinguish major supporting details from minor supporting details.

major supporting details
the most important reasons, facts, examples, or descriptions the author gives to support the central idea, statement, or thesis

Major Supporting Details **Major supporting details** are the most important examples, facts, reasons, or descriptions that the author gives to support the central idea, or thesis. Frequently, these major supporting points in an essay, article, or multi-paragraph passage are in the topic sentence of paragraphs.

minor supporting details
additional points that provide more information or examples to support major supporting details

Minor Supporting Details The **minor supporting details** are additional points that support major supporting details. They can give:

1. more information to explain the major supporting details.
2. more examples to illustrate major supporting details.
3. more specifics to make the material more interesting.

In some subjects, minor supporting details offer important information essential to your understanding. For example, when you are studying for a biology exam, you will need to learn and remember minor supporting details. For most articles or textbook readings, however, it is not necessary to remember minor supporting details. For these types of texts, you need to sort through information—to distinguish the major details from the minor details. In other situations, such as when you are reading a magazine article for pleasure or to understand general trends, minor supporting details are extras that may make the reading more pleasurable, more interesting, or more convincing.

WORKING WITH CENTRAL IDEAS AND MAJOR AND MINOR SUPPORTING DETAILS

You can reinforce your understanding of a reading as well as aid your studies by learning to organize information in ways that reflect the relationships between central ideas and major and minor supporting details. To master the material you read you will need to analyze the information. To do this, it is helpful to mark texts, outline content, create maps, and write summaries.

© 2014 Wadsworth, Cengage Learning

MARKING MAJOR AND MINOR SUPPORTING DETAILS

In Chapter 3, you practiced marking main ideas to help you organize to learn. Marking can also help you distinguish major and minor supporting details and remember the major ones. Here is one way to mark a longer reading. First, double underline the central idea or thesis of a whole passage. Next, single underline and identify major supporting details (often the main ideas of paragraphs) with capital letters (A,B,C). Finally, number minor supporting details. You can even put low-ercase letters (a, b, c) in front of more minor supporting details if you decide they are necessary to remember. If you mark your text in this way, or if you develop your own system of marking, you will find it easy to locate important information when you are reviewing or studying for a test. Notice how the passage below is marked.

People use drugs for many different reasons. Drugs can make us feel better physically or enhance our moods or abilities. Because they have positive ef-fects, drugs are frequently prescribed and used. These effects can lead to misuse as well.

The main reason we use drugs may be our expectation to overcome ill-ness and discomfort, or experience pleasure easily and quickly. When we have a headache we take some kind of pill—an aspirin, Excedrin, or Aleve. If we want to change how we feel in general, or to alter our consciousness, it's easy to swallow a pill, drink alcohol, snort cocaine, or inhale marijuana.

Challenges and painful situations in our personal lives can also lead to drug use. Sometimes our families are dysfunctional. Children can be neglected, and family members may abuse one another physi-cally or verbally. We may feel uncomfortable in social situations. We may not have enough money to live comfortably. The list is a long one, but to deal with these stresses, some people may experiment with drugs or use them occa-sionally. Others may take drugs frequently or compulsively.

Exercise 2

Mark Passages

Go back to Reading 1 on pages 250–251. Mark it by following the example above.

USING AN OUTLINE

In Chapter 5, you practiced organizing the information you learn into outlines using letters and numbers to indicate levels of information. Outlining is a great way to see which supporting details are major, which are minor, and how both support the central idea, because an outline shows how the details relate to each other in a spatial way. Here is an annotated visual:

© 2014 Wadsworth, Cengage Learning

topic: expressed in a few words, not a complete sentence, to be used as the title

central idea or thesis: expressed as a complete sentence

A. Major supporting detail

    1. Minor supporting detail
       a. more minor detail
       b. more minor detail

    2. Minor supporting detail

B. Major supporting detail

Look at paragraphs 3 and 4 on pages 250–251 about prescription drug abuse. We can outline the major and minor supporting details in these paragraphs as follows:

topic: Dangerous trends in prescription drug abuse

thesis: Prescription drug abuse and its disastrous consequences are a huge problem.

A. The United States is in the middle of an epidemic of prescription drug overdoses. (major supporting detail for thesis/main idea of the paragraph)

    1. In 2010, 12 million Americans said they were using opioid pain relievers without a prescription.
    2. Caused almost 500,000 emergency room visits in 2009
    3. Costs insurance companies $72 billion per year
    4. All prescription drug use tripled in a decade; 36,000 fatalities in 2008.
    5. Pain killer deaths 1999—4,000; 2008—15,000
    6. More deaths from abuse of prescription narcotics than from heroin and cocaine abuse

B. Overdose deaths and the abuse of painkillers are not spread equally among the American population. (major supporting detail for thesis and main idea of the paragraph)

    1. More men than women die of overdoses from prescription painkillers.
    2. Overdose rates are highest among middle-aged adults.
    3. People living in rural areas are almost twice as likely as people living in other areas to overdose on opioid pain relievers.
    4. Highest rates of overdose deaths: Whites, Native Americans, Alaskan Natives
    5. Abuse of pain relievers by ethnicity
       a. One in 10 American Indians and Alaskan Natives
       b. One in 20 whites
       c. One in 30 blacks
    6. Traumatic experiences, such as war, sometimes lead people to use or abuse pain killers (veterans of wars in Iraq and Afghanistan)

© 2014 Wadsworth, Cengage Learning

Exercise 3

Outline

For the following passage, complete the short outline below by writing in the topic or title, the stated or unstated central idea or thesis, the major supporting details, and the minor supporting details. Some of the information has been provided.

The Science of Drug Addiction

For much of the early twentieth century (1900s), drug addiction was not well understood, but that is beginning to change with the help of recent scientific research.

When scientists began to study addictive behavior in the 1930s, people addicted to drugs were thought to be morally bad and lacking in willpower. Those views shaped society's responses to drug abuse, treating it as a moral failing rather than a health problem. This idea—that drug abuse is a moral failing—led to an emphasis on punishment rather than preventative and treatment programs. Today, thanks to science, our views and our responses to drug abuse have changed dramatically. New and important discoveries about the brain have revolutionized our understanding of drug addiction, and allow us to respond much more effectively to the problem.

As a result of scientific research, we know that addiction is a disease that affects both brain and behavior. We have identified many of the biological and environmental factors and are beginning to search for the genetic variations that contribute to the development of the disease. In fact, drugs can actually change the brain itself, and that can lead to compulsive drug abuse. Scientists use this knowledge to develop effective prevention and treatment approaches that reduce the toll drug abuse takes on individuals, families, and communities. At the National Institute on Drug Abuse (NIDA), we believe that increased understanding of the basics of addiction will empower people to make informed choices in their own lives, adopt science-based policies and programs that reduce drug abuse and addiction in their communities, and support scientific research that improves the Nation's wellbeing.

Adapted from Nora D. Volkow, M.D. Director National Institute on Drug Abuse Revised 2010
http://www.drugabuse.gov/scienceofaddiction/ (accessed 12/28/11)

Topic or title: _____

Central idea: For much of the early twentieth century (1900s), drug addiction was not well understood, but that is beginning to change with the help of recent scientific research.

A. In the 1900s people believed that bad people and people who didn't have self-control became addicted to drugs

    1. _____

    2. New discoveries about the brain have changed our ideas.

    3. _____

© 2014 Wadsworth, Cengage Learning

B. As a result of research, we know that addiction is a disease that affects both brain and behavior.

   1. There are many causes of addiction.

      a. _____

      b. _____

      c. _____

      d. Drugs can affect the brain itself, which can lead to compulsive drug abuse.

   2. Scientists use this knowledge to develop prevention and treatment approaches.

   3. Increased understanding of addiction will have positive effects.

      a. On individuals

      b. _____

      c. On research

Organize to Learn: Make a Map

In addition to outlining, another way to organize information for learning is to create a visual pattern that diagrams information, such as the map shown here. Notice how the information in a paragraph or in a longer passage can be organized visually so that you immediately understand the relationships between the central idea, the major supporting details, and the minor supporting details. As you practice mapping and outlining, you will probably find that you like one technique more than another. Sometimes, though, a map can show some relationships better than an outline. For example, if something is causing something else to happen, you can use arrows to show the cause-and-effect relationship. Some people even draw little cartoons to help them organize and remember information. Now take a look at the sample maps on the next page.

The information from paragraph 4 (page 251) about who in the U.S. is more likely to overdose on prescription medication, mapped in the pattern shown, would look like the map shown on the next page.

In this map, the information is shown in a spatial way. The topic and main idea are at the top. The people with the highest rates of overdoses are listed in 5 boxes. Then the more minor supporting details about rates of *abuse* of painkillers are broken down by ethnic groups.

Each map will look different, because it is shaped to suit the information with which you are working. Some maps will have branches, and some may use arrows.

Map the following paragraphs based on the examples below.

© 2014 Wadsworth, Cengage Learning

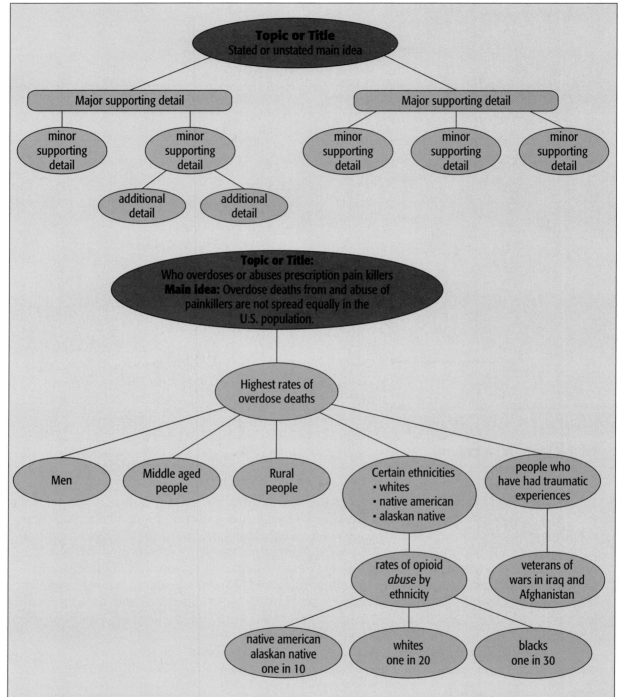

1. A drug is any substance—other than food and water—that, when taken into the body, alters its functioning in some way. Drugs are used for either therapeutic or recreational purposes. *Therapeutic* use occurs when a person takes a drug for a specific purpose such as reducing a fever or controlling a cough. In contrast, *recreational* drug use occurs when a person takes a drug for no purpose other than achieving a pleasurable feeling or psychological state. Alcohol and tobacco are examples of drugs that are primarily used for recreational purposes; their use by people over a fixed age (which varies from time to time and place to place) is lawful. Other drugs—such as some anti-anxiety drugs or tranquilizers—may be used legally only if prescribed by a physician for therapeutic use, but are frequently used illegally for recreational purposes. (From KENDALL, *Sociology in Our Times*, 9e. © 2013 Cengage Learning.

© 2014 Wadsworth, Cengage Learning

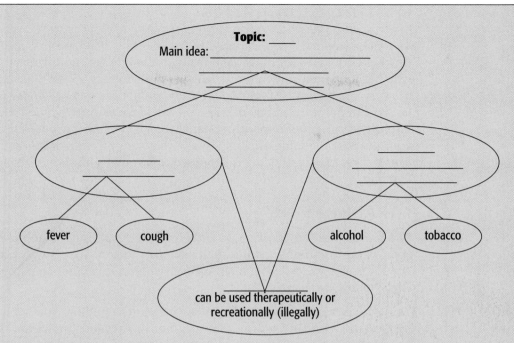

Topic: ____
Main idea: _____
_____
_____

fever   cough   alcohol   tobacco

_____
can be used therapeutically or
recreationally (illegally)

2. *Cannabis* is the hemp plant from which marijuana is derived. It is a mixture of dried leaves, flowers, stems and seeds taken from the plant. Smoking is the usual way to use both marijuana and hashish. When smoked, cannabis has an immediate effect that may last several hours. The desired effects are a mild, relaxed euphoria and increased sensory awareness (vision seems sharper, food tastes better). Unintended effects can include increased heart rate, anxiety, sluggish mental functioning, and reduced memory.

From WEITEN, *Psychology*, 9e. © 2013 Cengage Learning.

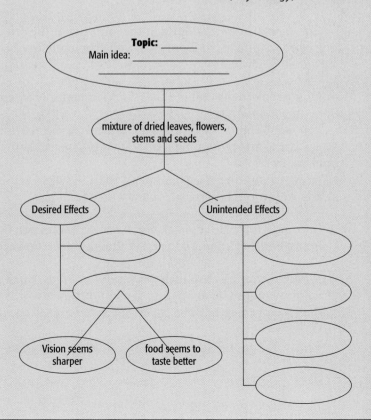

Topic: _____
Main idea: _____
_____

mixture of dried leaves, flowers,
stems and seeds

Desired Effects   Unintended Effects

Vision seems
sharper   food seems to
taste better

© 2014 Wadsworth, Cengage Learning

Writing Summaries

To write a summary, you will need to use the skills you have just practiced: Identify the central idea (or thesis) and major and minor supporting details and decide whether to include any minor details in your summary. Sometimes minor details are very interesting, but very often they are not necessary. Unless you sort out levels of importance among details, you can become overwhelmed. Decide on the importance of minor supporting details based on your purpose for reading and your purpose for summarizing. Usually minor supporting details are not needed because a summary, after all, is supposed to be quite a bit shorter than the original reading.

PARAPHRASING

paraphrase write someone else's idea in your own words

The first step in summarizing an article or longer text is to paraphrase the central idea. **Paraphrasing** is writing someone else's idea in your own words. In some ways it is similar to stating main ideas in your own words. To paraphrase effectively, follow these steps:

1. Read and understand the idea that you want to put into your own words.
2. Try to substitute words that are familiar to you for words that are not familiar.
3. Write down only one or two of the very important words that help explain the idea.
4. Turn your paper over and try to write the sentence in your own words.
5. Don't get discouraged. Paraphrasing is a skill that takes a lot of practice. You won't sound like a professional writer to begin with, but you're not supposed to!

Let's look at a few examples. If the following is the original sentence from someone else's writing, what words will you absolutely need to keep when you rewrite the idea?

Most people in the United States think it is perfectly acceptable to drink alcohol.

You would probably pick *think and drink alcohol*, so you might state this idea in your own words by writing the following: In general, Americans think it is okay to drink alcohol.

Now try another example. Read the following sentence, and decide which words you would keep when you rewrite the idea.

Drinking a few martinis in an elegant bar is impressive, but swigging some wine from a bottle in a paper bag on the street corner is frowned upon.

Which words are absolutely necessary? *martinis, bar, wine, paper bag*
So how might you state this idea in your own words? An example would be: It's bad to drink wine out of a paper bag on the street, but it's okay to drink martinis in a fancy bar.

© 2014 Wadsworth, Cengage Learning

| Exercise 4 | **Paraphrase** |

Rewrite each of the following sentences in your own words. All of these sentences come from a college textbook titled, *Drugs, the Spectrum*.

1. Any substance if used by the wrong person, in the wrong dosage, or at the wrong time or place, can be abused.

   _____

   _____

2. Tobacco prevention programs, especially those that operate outside of schools, seem to be more effective with high-risk youths.

   _____

   _____

3. As early as the 1950s, the tobacco industry was aware that tobacco use was linked to illness.

   _____

   _____

4. Depressed people may smoke as a form of self-medication.

   _____

   _____

5. Gasoline sniffing by children is a prominent factor in lead poisoning, which negatively affects physical and mental growth.

   _____

   _____

6. Determining which depressed individuals will respond to antidepressant medications poses a challenge to physicians.

   _____

   _____

© 2014 Wadsworth, Cengage Learning

7. During times of fatigue and lethargy, people sometimes look for stimulants—substances that will elevate their mood and make them energetic.

_____

_____

_____

8. Legal stimulants such as caffeine and nicotine are the most widely used drugs in the world.

_____

_____

_____

9. It has been shown that as cocaine use went down in the 1990s, educational achievement went up.

_____

_____

_____

10. Because high doses affect judgment and decision-making skills negatively, amphetamines can cause severe behavioral problems.

_____

_____

_____

WRITING THE FIRST SENTENCE OF A SUMMARY

You can begin a summary in different ways, but an effective method gives the central idea (or thesis) and the source of information in the first sentence. Many professors and employers want to know the central idea (or thesis) of the text you're summarizing, who wrote it, and where and when it was published at the very beginning of the summary. Remember, it is very important to use your own words. If you take words directly from another text, you must use quotation marks (" ") and include the source of your information. If you use other people's sentences or phrases without giving them credit, you may be accused of copying, or **plagiarizing**, their work. One of the most important rules in

plagiarizing copying without giving proper credit

© 2014 Wadsworth, Cengage Learning

American colleges and universities is *don't copy other people's work and present it as your own.*

Many students say, "But I can't explain it as well as this writer." This may be true, but the only way you can learn to write better is if you practice, and if you can put an idea into your own words, it proves that you understand that idea. However, if you need to use some of the author's words, put quotation marks around them and give the source.

Once you have figured out how to write the central idea in your own words, you can write the first sentence of the summary by using the phrase, "According to *(name of author)*, in *(his or her)* *(article, passage, or book)* *(title)*, *(central idea in your own words)*."

For example, you may have decided that the central idea of an article, written in your own words, is:

A few centuries ago, people believed that alcoholics simply chose to drink excessively.

Let's say the article you are summarizing is written by Lois White. The title of the article is "The History of Alcohol Use." You would write your first sentence something like this:

According to Lois White, in her article "The History of Alcohol Use," a few centuries ago, people believed that alcoholics simply chose to drink excessively.

Exercise 5

Write Central Idea Sentences for Summaries: Paraphrase and Give Credit

Rewrite the following central idea sentences in your own words. Give credit to the author and refer to the source. Use the format "*According to* _____." The first one is done for you. (These are not real authors or real sources. We've created them to give you practice.)

1. When we have a physical problem, we immediately think that taking some kind of pill or "medicine" will make our discomfort go away. (based on an article by Jeb Maxwell titled "Our Pill Culture")

   According to Jeb Maxwell, in his article "Our Pill Culture," when we have a

   problem with our bodies, we just want to take something that will make

   us feel better.

2. Once we recognize that alcoholism is a disease, we are more likely to try to help alcoholics get treatment. (based on an article by Justin Thomas titled "New Approaches to Overcome Alcoholism")

   _____

   _____

   _____

© 2014 Wadsworth, Cengage Learning

3. Most people use alcohol socially and don't abuse it or become addicted. (based on an article by John Dalton titled "Alcoholism, the Truth")

_____

_____

_____

4. More resources should be used on drug prevention. (based on a book by Howard Zellin titled *The War on Drugs*)

_____

_____

_____

5. The first puff of marijuana will send your children down the wrong path into more and more serious drug abuse. (based on a book by John Smith titled *How to Raise Your Children*)

_____

_____

_____

USING A PROCESS TO WRITE A SUMMARY

To write an effective summary, follow these steps:

1. Carefully read and make sure you understand the material you are going to summarize.
2. Determine the central idea, or thesis. Write that central idea in a sentence using your own words. When you write the central idea sentence, give credit to the author whose work you are summarizing and mention the title of the reading, article, or book.
3. Decide what major supporting details you need to include.
4. Decide whether to include any minor supporting details. Usually you do not need to include this level of detail.
5. Write the summary in your own words, beginning with your central idea sentence and including the major supporting details. Use complete sentences.
6. Remember, it is easier to use your own words if you are not looking directly at the passage while you write. Don't copy! If you use the author's language, be sure to put quotation marks around those words.

© 2014 Wadsworth, Cengage Learning

In a summary, you are giving the information or opinion of another writer in an abbreviated form. You are not giving your own opinion. Unless your instructor asks you to do so, do not inject your ideas into your summary.

Now you know the steps for writing a summary, how to write a central idea sentence in your own words, and how to give credit to the author and source. So now let's practice the steps of writing a summary. Go back to the article titled "The Science of Drug Addiction" on page 256.

What is the central idea of this reading (in your own words)?

People did not understand drug addiction in the early twentieth century.

What are the major supporting details and important minor supporting details (in your own words)?

- *In the 1930s people thought that drug addicts were bad people who didn't have self-control.*
- *People believed that addicts needed to be punished.*
- *Today scientists are learning that addiction is a disease that affects brain and behavior.*
- *Scientists use this information to do a better job reducing drug abuse, with particular focus on prevention and treatment.*
- *Understanding addiction is helpful for decision making on the individual and the community level.*

Using the central idea sentence and the major supporting details, your summary should look something like the following example. Notice how the major supporting details and a couple of examples work to explain the central idea. Notice also that it is important to give the author and the source in the summary.

According to Nora D. Volkow, in the short article, "The Science of Drug Addiction," people did not understand drug addiction in the early twentieth century. People believed that addicts needed to be punished. Today scientists are learning that addiction is a disease that affects brain and behavior. Scientists use this information to do a better job reducing drug abuse, with particular focus on prevention and treatment. Understanding addiction is helpful for decision making on the individual and the community level.

Exercise 6

Write a Summary

Read the following article about tobacco addiction written by Nora D. Volkow, the Director of the National Institute of Drug Abuse. Follow the steps for "Using a Process to Write a Summary" and write your summary on a separate piece of paper.

Tobacco Addiction

Tobacco use kills approximately 440,000 Americans each year, with one in every five U.S. deaths the result of smoking. Smoking harms nearly every organ in

© 2014 Wadsworth, Cengage Learning

the body, causes many diseases, and compromises smokers' health in general. Nicotine, a component of tobacco, is the primary reason that tobacco is addictive, although cigarette smoke contains many other dangerous chemicals, including tar, carbon monoxide, acetaldehyde, nitrosamines, and more.

An improved overall understanding of addiction and of nicotine as an addictive drug has been helpful in developing medications and behavioral treatments for tobacco addiction. For example, the nicotine patch and gum, now readily available at drugstores and supermarkets nationwide, have proven effective for quitting smoking when combined with behavioral therapy.

Advanced technologies make it possible for researchers to observe changes in brain function that result from smoking tobacco. Researchers are now also identifying genes that predispose people to tobacco addiction and predict their response to smoking cessation treatments. These findings—and many other recent research accomplishments—present unique opportunities to discover and develop new treatments for tobacco addiction.

Nora D. Volkow, M.D.Director National Institute on Drug Abuse, Printed 2009
[http://www.drugabuse.gov/researchreports/nicotine/nicotine.html (accessed 12/28/11)]

Reading 2   Drinking: A Double Life

—[Adapted from] Caroline Knapp

The following reading is from Caroline Knapp's autobiographical book, *Drinking: A Love Story,* about her own alcoholism. In this passage she describes some typical behaviors of alcoholics, and she argues that the emotional suffering caused by alcoholism is just as important as its negative economic costs to society.

1   When people talk about the human costs of alcoholism, they tend to focus on numbers: an annual economic drain of $98.6 billion. About 23,000 lives lost to drunk-driving accidents. An additional 30,000 lives lost to other injuries incurred while under the influence. People often forget to consider the psychological and emotional costs of alcoholism (to alcoholics and the people in their lives) that trigger immeasurable pain.

immeasurable
too great to measure, immense

2   My sister called me once in tears, the year our father was dying. "I feel like I'm going to lose everyone I love," she said, "including you. I feel like I'm going to get a phone call in the middle of the night saying you've been killed in a car accident." She didn't say "because you were drunk" but she didn't need to; we both knew. But I brushed it off.

pursue
continue with

3   "Don't be ridiculous," I said. "I'm *fine*. Nothing is going to happen." My tone was more defensive than reassuring, though, and she didn't pursue the subject. She just sniffled into the phone and when we hung up a few minutes later, I felt a little guilty, but mostly annoyed. *Feh*, I thought, dismissing her fears and sadness. *Ridiculous.* Then I opened a bottle of wine. Door shut, case closed.

From *Drinking: a Love Story* by Caroline Knapp, © 1995 by Caroline Knapp. Used by permission of The Dial Press/Dell Publishing, a division of Random House, Inc.

© 2014 Wadsworth, Cengage Learning

4   Al-Anon, the 12-step program for friends and family members of alcoholics, estimates that every alcoholic's drinking affects at least four other people. We worry parents, lovers, coworkers, anyone close who crosses our paths. We lose our tempers with them; we blame them for our troubles; we push them away.

appalled
disgusted, sickened by

5   We never quite let them in or let them know us too well, because we're afraid that if they got too close they would be appalled at what they'd find. So, a great deal of the active alcoholic's energy is spent constructing facades—false appearances. We put forward a front to others so that we look okay, lovable, worthy, and whole. But inside we don't think we are any of those things.

6   Mostly, we lie. That's a statement of fact, not a judgment. Alcoholics lie about big things, and we lie about small things, and we lie to other people, and (above all) we lie to ourselves. Author John Cheever wrote about this in his journals, calling dishonesty "the most despicable trait." He wrote, "You take a nap and claim to be tired from work. You hide a whiskey bottle in the cabinet and claim to be a wiser man than your friends who hide whiskey bottles in the closet. You promise to take a child to the circus and have such a bad hangover that you can't move. You promise to send money to your old mother and do not."

manipulate
falsify

7   Big lies, small lies: It's hard to find an alcoholic who didn't manipulate the truth about *something*, even if it was minor stuff, stuff that really didn't add up to anything at all. My friend Gail used to lie about movies and books. If a group of people at work were talking about something they'd read, she'd chime in instinctively. "Oh, I read that," she'd say, even if she hadn't; or she'd say she *loved* some movie that other people loved, even if she'd never even heard of the movie, let alone seen it. To an outsider this sounds stupid and useless until you consider that people who drink constantly never really get a chance to know how they feel about anything, even things like movies and books. After a while drinkers just fall into the behavior, a way of overcompensating: We learn to pretend we have opinions because deep in our own hearts, we really don't.

overcompensating
an exaggerated attempt to make up for a weakness

8   Linnette, a woman I met in my first year of sobriety, lied so much she thought she was going crazy—the stories she told different people whirled around in the back of her mind. [. . .] She'd tell her mother she needed money to buy protective bars for the windows on her basement apartment and then she'd spend the money on drugs. She'd tell her boss she had to fly home suddenly because her mother had taken ill (she hadn't), and then she'd go on a three-day bender. [. . .] After a while her whole life felt like one huge heap of rationalizations and justifications and stories piled on stories. Linnette, who's 34, is a small woman, about five foot three, with wavy brown hair and wide green eyes. She's pretty in a perky, youthful way, with a bright, almost surprised expression that gives her an innocent look and makes her duplicity seem all the more astonishing.

bender
drunken binge

Exercise 7

Work with Words

Use context clues, word-part clues, and, if necessary, the dictionary to write the definitions of the italicized words in the following sentences from Reading 2.

1. "I'm fine. Nothing is going to happen." My tone was more *defensive* than *reassuring*, though, and she didn't pursue the subject. (par. 3)

   defensive _____

© 2014 Wadsworth, Cengage Learning

2. *reassuring* _____

3. So, a great deal of the active alcoholic's energy is spent constructing *facades*—false appearances. (par. 5)

   facades _____

4. Author John Cheever wrote about this in his journals, calling dishonesty "the most *despicable trait*." (par. 6)

   despicable _____

5. *trait* _____

6. After a while her whole life felt like one huge heap of *rationalizations* and justifications and stories piled on stories. (par. 8)

   rationalizations _____

Exercise 8

Check Your Understanding

Choose the best answers to the following multiple-choice questions about Reading 2.

1. What is the main topic of Reading 2?
   a. the economics of alcohol abuse
   b. the psychological and emotional pain of alcoholism
   c. the 12-step program

2. What is the best statement of the central idea of the reading?
   a. Alcoholism is expensive for our society.
   b. Alcoholism costs the United States about $98.6 billion per year, and about 53,000 lives per year due to drunk driving or other alcohol-related accidents.
   c. People forget to consider the psychological and emotional costs of alcoholism to alcoholics and the people in their lives.

3. Which of the following is the best main idea sentence for paragraphs 2 and 3?
   a. My sister called me once in tears.
   b. Alcoholics, including the author, deny that they have a drinking problem.
   c. Alcoholics never listen to their family members.

4. The writer's sister thought she was going to lose everyone she loved because
   a. she knew her father was dying.
   b. she suspected both of her parents were dying.
   c. she was afraid she would lose not only her father, but also her sister Carolyn (the author) because of Carolyn's alcoholism.

© 2014 Wadsworth, Cengage Learning

5. When her sister called in tears, Carolyn
   a. was sympathetic.
   b. was annoyed.
   c. decided to stop drinking.

6. Which of the following is the best main idea sentence for paragraphs 6 through 8?
   a. Alcoholics lie about all kinds of things.
   b. Linnette told her mother she needed money to buy protective bars for the windows on her basement apartment, and then she'd spend the money on drugs.
   c. Linnette is pretty in a perky, youthful way, with a bright almost surprised expression that gives her an innocent look.

7. Circle the sentence below that contains the minor supporting detail.
   a. My friend Gail used to lie about movies and books.
   b. It's hard to find an alcoholic who didn't manipulate the truth about *something*.
   c. After a while drinkers just fall into the behavior, a way of overcompensating: we learn to pretend we have opinions because deep in our own hearts, we really don't.

8. Circle the sentence below that contains the major supporting detail.
   a. Linnette would tell her mother she needed money to buy protective bars for the windows on her basement apartment and then she'd spend the money on drugs.
   b. She would tell her boss she had to fly home suddenly because her mother had taken ill (she hadn't) and then she would go on a three-day bender.
   c. Linnette lied so much she thought she was going crazy.

Exercise 9

Outline

Complete the following outline for Reading 2.

Topic: _____

Central idea in your own words: _____

_____

A. Alcoholics deny they have a problem.

B. _____

   1. _____

    _____

   2. Put up a front to hide their feelings of inadequacy

© 2014 Wadsworth, Cengage Learning

C. Alcoholics lie about all kinds of things and break promises.

    1. Take a nap and claim to be tired from work

    2. _____

      _____

    3. _____

    4. _____

D. It's hard to find an alcoholic who didn't manipulate the truth about something. (like Gail who lied about movies and books)

    1. Gail's lies

      a. <u>opinions of movies she hadn't seen</u>

      b. <u>opinions of books she hadn't read</u>

E. _____

    1. _____

    2. _____

Exercise 10   Write a Summary

Using the central idea, main ideas, and the important details you identified in Exercise 9, write a four-to-six sentence summary of Reading 2. Remember to use your own words, and refer to the author and the title in your first sentence.

Exercise 11   Make Connections and Write

Write short answers to the following questions based on Reading 2, your own experience, and your observations. Then discuss your answers with your class group. Working together, prepare a report for your class as a whole or a written summary of your discussion for your instructor.

© 2014 Wadsworth, Cengage Learning

1. What experiences have you had with alcohol or with people who drink? Explain your answers.

   _____

   _____

   _____

2. How do you think people begin abusing alcohol? Do you think some people are more likely to become alcoholics than others?

   _____

   _____

   _____

3. Describe an alcoholic you know personally or one you have heard or read about that stopped drinking. How did he or she stop?

   _____

   _____

   _____

4. Do you think alcoholism is a disease? Why or why not?

   _____

   _____

   _____

Reading 3

Peyote: Native "Drug" of North America

— LOGAN MATTHEWS

The following reading discusses the history of ceremonial peyote use among Native Americans. The author is generally favorable toward the use of this drug in religious practices, but it is important to understand that, at times in U.S. history, this use was illegal. Today, members of the Native American Church may legally use peyote under specific circumstances. As you read, think about why eating peyote would be meaningful to their belief system.

© 2014 Wadsworth, Cengage Learning

Logan Matthews. Written for *Joining a Community of Readers*. Used by permission.

indigenous
native, or local

North America
geographical area
including Mexico,
the United States,
and Canada

1   Peyote is a slow-growing spineless cactus from the Chihuahua desert of Southwestern Texas and Northern Mexico. Unlike its fellow desert plants, this little cactus is full of a variety of mind-altering chemicals. The most well-known chemical in peyote, mescaline, chemically attaches to locations in the human brain and causes intense hallucinogenic experiences that typically last 12-18 hours. Users often report seeing bright stripes of color, checkerboard patterns, and kaleidoscope-like geometric shapes.[1] Indigenous people in North America have used peyote in their spiritual practice for centuries and continue to do so today.

2   These indigenous people recognized peyote's potential for ceremonial use thousands of years before the arrival of Europeans. The psychological effects of mescaline must have caused much fascination, amazement, and fear in the first humans to eat peyote. It is understandable how such a powerful plant might influence religious and magical ideas in early Native American societies. Archaeological evidence shows that peyote was indeed used in a ritualistic way. In the Rio Grande region of Texas the small cactus has been found collected and rolled into balls with other herbs in locations with small statues. From dating this evidence, archeologists have concluded that peyote was used ceremonially around 5,000 years ago[2]. Over the centuries, diverse groups of Indians throughout the region have developed different but related cultures of peyote use.

3   The arrival of Spanish conquerors and Catholic priests in the 1500s brought a clash of cultures. The conquerors detested the native religion(s) and the ceremonial use of mind-altering plants. One of the main goals of the Spaniards in the New World was to convert all the natives to Christianity. They believed that the use of peyote and other drugs was a particularly evil aspect of what they already considered a false religion. In their view, eating peyote was as criminal as cannibalism. So they put harsh punishments in place to destroy the culture surrounding these practices. New converts to Christianity were interrogated about their use of the cactus. Despite hundreds of years of persecution and domination by the Spanish, however, the ritualized use of the peyote cactus managed to survive in Mexico, and even to expand.

4   By the late 1800's the culture of peyote practiced in Northern Mexico had spread to tribes further to the North. Native American tribes had been devastated by disease and war. The U.S. government was forcibly relocating them onto reservations. This destructive process led to the loss of many Native American tribes' unique cultures, languages, and traditions. Many tribes embraced the cultural use of peyote because it filled a gap in tribal spiritual life. The Kiowa and Comanche Indians who had been displaced to Oklahoma were central to the development and spread of this religious practice. Soon, many other tribes of the Southwest and Southern plains adopted peyote use. At the turn of the twentieth century, the Native American Church (NAC) was established. It provided a unified religious system that crossed tribal boundaries. It was based on the ceremonial use of peyote. Elements of many traditions contributed to the practices of the NAC, including those of Northern Mexican tribes, Comanche, Kiowa, and even Christianity.

5   The Native American Church and local tribal leaders control peyote rituals to ensure the powerful drug is not misused or used recreationally. A typical modern peyote ritual may be held to celebrate the birth of a baby, to heal a sick person, to commemorate the death of a family member, or for other meaningful events. While the service may vary from tribe to tribe, there are certain unifying elements that date back to the Kiowa and Comanche adaptations of Mexican peyote ceremonies. Experienced practitioners called Roadmen lead modern ceremonies in a tepee or other small building

© 2014 Wadsworth, Cengage Learning

with a central fire. Participants sit in a circle around an altar and use ceremonial objects such as rattles, feather fans, staffs, and drums. Pieces of dried peyote cactus are passed around and consumed while special songs and chants accompany the drumming. The ritual usually goes all night in what might be considered a mix of communal prayer and personal meditation[3]. Participants in the NAC suggest that these rituals benefit individuals and the community through the reduction of problems such as alcoholism, drug addiction, crime, stress, and domestic violence.

6   Native Americans' relationship with peyote has lasted thousands of years, and current trends suggest that relationship will continue for a long time into the future. The Native American Church and the mind-altering peyote cactus played a central role in the formation of a more unified and modern Native American identity. The Native American Church has grown rapidly in the hundred years since its beginning, and now has an estimated 250,000 members[4].

Notes

1. David E. Nichols, "Hallucinogens," *Pharmacology & Therapeutics, 101* no. 2 (2004): 131–81, http://dc112.4shared.com/doc/S9k8XXyB/preview.htm. Retrieved December 16, 2011.

2. M Terry, *et al.,* "Lower Pecos and Coahuila peyote: new radiocarbon dates," *Journal of Archaelogical Science,* (2006) 33:1017-21.

3. Richard Evans Schultes, Albert Hoffman, Christian Ratsch, "Plants of the Gods: Their Sacred, Healing, and Hallucinogenic Powers," (Rochester, VT: Healing Arts Press, 1998).

4. "A Brief History of the Native American Church". Council on Spiritual Practices. http://www.csp.org/communities/docs/fikes-nac_history.html. Retrieved 12/16/2011.

Exercise 12

Work with Words

Use context clues, word-part clues, and, if necessary, the dictionary to write the definitions of the italicized words in the following sentences from Reading 3.

1. Unlike its fellow desert plants, this little cactus is full of a variety of *mind-altering* chemicals. (par. 1)

   mind-altering _____

   _____

2. The most well-known chemical in peyote, *mescaline*, chemically attaches to locations in the human brain and causes intense *hallucinogenic* experiences that typically last 12-18 hours. . (par. 1)

   mescaline _____

   _____

3. *hallucinogenic* _____

   _____

© 2014 Wadsworth, Cengage Learning

4. From this evidence, *archeologists* have concluded that peyote was used ceremonially around 5,000 years ago. (par. 2)

   archeologist _____

   _____

5. One of the main goals of the Spaniards in the New World was t*o convert* all the natives to Christianity. (par. 3)

   to convert _____

   _____

6. New *converts* to Christianity were *interrogated* about their use of the cactus. Despite hundreds of years of *persecution* and domination by the Spanish, however, the ritualized use of the peyote cactus managed to survive in Mexico and even to expand. (par. 3)

   converts _____

   _____

7. *interrogated* _____

   _____

   _____

8. *persecution* _____

   _____

   _____

Exercise 13

Check Your Understanding

Choose the best answers to the following questions about Reading 3.

1. Which of the following is the best topic for Reading 3?
   a. chemical properties of peyote
   b. ceremonial peyote use past and present
   c. Spanish conquest of Mexico

© 2014 Wadsworth, Cengage Learning

2. Which of the following sentences best states the central idea of Reading 3?
   a. Indigenous people in North America have used peyote in their spiritual practice for centuries and continue to do so.
   b. When the Spanish arrived in Mexico they began a harsh campaign to convert the people to Christianity and to wipe out the use of mind-altering drugs.
   c. A typical modern peyote ritual may be held to celebrate a birth of a baby, to heal the sick, to honor someone who has died, or to recognize other important events.

3. The peyote plant probably influenced religious and magical ideas in early Native American cultures because
   a. it is a tiny cactus from the Chihuahua desert.
   b. people became more interested in it when the Spanish tried to wipe out its use.
   c. after eating peyote, people would have visions.

4. Tribes in the United States established the Native American Church and the ceremonial use of peyote
   a. 5,000 years ago.
   b. when the Spaniards first conquered Mexico.
   c. in the late 1800s.

5. Which of the following sentences is the best main idea sentence for paragraph 3?
   a. The Spaniards wanted to convert the native people to Christianity because they believed it was the only true religion.
   b. The Spaniards instituted harsh practices to eliminate the ceremonial use of peyote because they believed it was evil and un-Christian.
   c. New converts to Christianity were interrogated about their use of the cactus.

6. Circle the sentence below that states a major supporting detail.
   a. The Native American Church and the local tribal leaders control the peyote rituals.
   b. A typical modern peyote ritual may be held to celebrate the birth of a baby, to heal a sick person, to commemorate the death of a family member, or for other meaningful events.
   c. Participants sit in a circle around an altar and use ceremonial objects such as rattles, feather fans, staffs, and drums.

7. Circle the sentence below that states a major supporting detail.
   a. Findings from the Rio Grande region of Texas show that the small cactus was collected, rolled into balls with other herbs, and found in locations with small statues.
   b. From dating this evidence, archeologists have concluded that peyote was used ceremonially around 5,000 years ago.
   c. Early Native Americans recognized peyote's potential for ceremonial use thousands of years before the arrival of Europeans.

© 2014 Wadsworth, Cengage Learning

8. Briefly describe why, according to Matthews, the culture of peyote spread to the tribes to the north of Mexico?

_____

_____

_____

_____

_____

_____

9. What do participants believe are the positive influences of using peyote in religious rituals?

_____

_____

_____

Exercise 14 — **Mark Central Idea, Main Ideas, and Important Supporting Details**

Carefully reread Reading 3. Double underline the central idea, underline the major supporting points (the main ideas stated in some of the paragraphs), and number the important minor supporting points within the paragraphs that you think should be included in an outline.

Exercise 15 — **Make an Outline**

On a separate piece of paper, write an outline of Reading 3. Be sure to follow the directions on page 254–255.

Exercise 16 — **Write a Summary**

Write a summary of Reading 3. Remember to use your own words, and to refer to the author and the title in your first sentence.

© 2014 Wadsworth, Cengage Learning

Exercise 17

Make Connections and Write

Write short answers to the following questions based on Reading 3, your experience, and your observations. Then discuss your answers with your class group. Working together, prepare a report for your class as a whole or a written summary for your instructor.

1. Why do you think a hallucinogenic drug would enhance spiritual ceremonies?

   _____

   _____

   _____

   _____

   _____

2. Should the government allow the use of mescaline in religious ceremonies? Why or why not?

   _____

   _____

   _____

   _____

   _____

3. What rituals or ceremonies are included in the religion you practice (or one with which you are familiar)? Why are they important?

   _____

   _____

   _____

   _____

   _____

© 2014 Wadsworth, Cengage Learning

4. How did peyote use change after the conquest? What are some other examples of how religious practices have changed over time? Why did they change?

_____

_____

_____

_____

_____

5. What do participants believe are the positive influences of using peyote in religious rituals? How would you explain these beneficial consequences?

_____

_____

_____

_____

_____

_____

_____

_____

WRITING SUMMARIES FOR NARRATIVES

narrative a spoken or written account of a series of events, of someone's life, or of a work of fiction

autobiography the story of someone's life written by that person

key events the moments in a narrative that provide the major supporting details

At times you will need to summarize a **narrative**—a spoken or written account of a story, a series of events, an **autobiography** or biography, or of a work of fiction. Many people, especially children, tend to give a step-by-step account of what happens in a narrative, often with far too much detail. If you've ever listened to this kind of summary you probably were thinking, "Oh, please stop dragging it out and just get to the point."

To summarize a narrative, such as a person's life story (or part of it), you need to figure out which few **key events** are the most significant—these are the major supporting details of a narrative. These moments are not just interesting highlights; rather, they are points in the story that connect to a broader idea. They might relate to themes such as injustice, struggle, or transformation. Frequently, the author does not present these key moments in the order in which they happened. Even if they are presented in the order in which they happened, it is up

© 2014 Wadsworth, Cengage Learning

to you, in your summary, to figure out how to group these significant events to best emphasize their broader meaning. If you first identify a central idea in the narrative, it will be easier to select the key events (major supporting details and significant minor details) that illustrate that idea. In this way, your summary will be useful to someone reading it. Often, the central idea is not stated directly. Occasionally, variations of the central idea may be repeated several times. Once you have confirmed the central idea and narrowed down the key events, you will be ready to write your summary.

A good example of an autobiographical narrative is Jimmy Santiago Baca's book, *A Place to Stand*. It is a long, fascinating book with a lot of interesting and graphic details. Baca explains in the beginning of the book that he is telling the story of his transformation from criminal to poet. He writes about his time in prison; "I became a different man, not because prison was good for me, but in spite of its destructive forces. In prison, I learned to believe in myself and to dream for a better life." So, we can easily identify the central idea from what Baca writes in the introduction.

The central idea, written as the first sentence of the summary, might be something like:

> According to Jimmy Santiago Baca, in his autobiography, A Place to Stand, he completely changed while he was in prison from a criminal to a poet.

Next, you need to organize the key events or stages of his life—in other words, the major supporting points and important minor details. The basic outline would look something like this:

A. Early life was difficult
  1. abandoned at a young age
  2. alcoholic father
  3. mother ashamed of him because he was dark and looked Mexican

B. Life of addiction and crime
  1. alcohol, drugs
  2. dealing drugs
  3. violence

C. Life in Prison
  1. rebelling against the system
  2. solitary confinement
  3. surviving conflict with other inmates (gangs) and guards

D. Transformation
  1. learning to read and write
  2. writing poetry

At first glance, this outline may seem to include a lot of details, but remember this is a summary of a 200-page book, not a short article. The kinds of details that you would *not* include would be events such as: 1) how Jimmy's mother just dumped the kids at his grandparents' house and went off with her new boyfriend; or 2) for exactly what charges Jimmy was found guilty that resulted in his prison sentence; or 3) the various fights he had with other inmates in the prison. The summary itself would look something like the following:

© 2014 Wadsworth, Cengage Learning

According to Jimmy Santiago Baca, in his autobiography, A Place to Stand, he completely changed while he was in prison from a criminal to a poet. His father was an alcoholic, and his mother was ashamed of him because he was dark and looked Mexican. Ultimately he and his brother were abandoned. He turned to alcohol and drugs and became a drug dealer and a violent man. Baca spends most of the book describing his experiences in prison. He explains how prison culture works, with gangs based on race, corrupt guards, and a kill-or-be-killed mentality. Baca survived the conflicts, but rebelled against the system. He eventually ended up in solitary confinement. Finally, he learned to read and write. Writing poetry allowed him to overcome his past. When he got out of prison, he knew he would make a different future for himself.

Exercise 18

Write a Summary of a Narrative

Read the following story, then follow the steps below to summarize it in your own words.

Auntie's Last Days with Drugs

Elizabeth Martin

Two days after my auntie died of pancreatic cancer, my sister Olivia and I took the bottles of her prescription pain medicine and flushed them down the toilet. We hated that stuff. Auntie didn't have any children, and in many ways she was like a mother, even a "fairy godmother" to us. We were her only family.

Auntie had gotten her diagnosis several months earlier and was constantly nauseated from the chemotherapy drugs the doctors gave her. She lived in a fog of Percocet and morphine, and repeatedly complained that her brain was not clear enough for her to tell us all the things she wanted to say. She hated the drugs and the nausea of the chemo, but the pain was unbearable without them. No matter what we brought her, she refused to eat. We tried everything: carrot juice, fresh chicken noodle soup, vegetable soup, lean pieces of meat, Ensure, even spaghetti. She didn't usually eat more than one forkful. Sometimes she just fell asleep without eating anything. We were getting desperate. She was losing weight fast, and it seemed to us that there wasn't much in life for her to enjoy.

After a while, a friend of mine at the gym told me marijuana helped relieve pain and nausea without making people so drowsy. We were afraid to mention the idea to Auntie because she was so conservative. She was a tea drinker, she never smoked cigarettes, and she usually carried a glass of Seven-Up at social events. Smoking an illegal substance wasn't going to happen. One day, though, we made the suggestion. When she said she would try it, it took us completely by surprise. We didn't even know where to get the stuff or how to smoke it; but, eventually, somebody gave us a "bong"—a contraption that kind of water processes the marijuana and makes it a little easier to smoke.

Auntie was nervous about the whole plan, and insisted that we go onto the back porch with the lights turned off. It was as if she thought the police would come running in and arrest her for smoking the stuff. It was hard to imagine

Auntie's Last Days with Drugs by Elizabeth Martin.

© 2014 Wadsworth, Cengage Learning

the police handcuffing and hauling away a frail old lady who could barely walk. Anyway, it was hard for her to inhale and she was nervously looking around the yard the whole time. She managed to get in a few puffs mixed with some coughs. Then she said she wanted to order some take-out food and go eat at the kitchen table! She hadn't walked out the door of her room, let alone eaten at the table, for several weeks.

She ordered lasagna with a tomato and cheese sauce from our favorite pizza place and ate the whole thing! We were so happy, but Auntie still wasn't done. Over a cup of tea, she began to tell us some of the things she hadn't been able to say because she had been so nauseous and sleepy. She told us she loved us, that our parents had gone through some rough times together, and how she tried to be there for us, to help us through those difficult periods. Then she reminded us of some funny things that had happened over the years (like the times Olivia and I would put on her jewelry and high heels and lip sync and dance to Ray Charles records), so the three of us ended up laughing, crying, and hugging one another.

It was a magical evening, but it was not repeated. Our dear aunt did take a few puffs from her stash from time to time, but she never got her energy back, and she was always afraid that she would get caught. Still, for a few short weeks, she was able to carry on conversations with us. The cancer had spread to other organs. She gave up, went back to bed, and got pumped full of narcotics again. She felt miserable—couldn't eat and couldn't string words together to make a sentence. She was reduced to brief requests like, "water please," "need to go to the bathroom." She was too nauseous and dizzy to sit up or walk a few steps. The worst part was that there was nothing we could do to comfort her.

We were happy to throw the narcotics down the toilet when Auntie passed. She's not nauseous or in pain anymore. We are sad, but at least we had a few decent weeks before she left us.

1. Write the central idea of this reading in your own words.

_____

_____

_____

_____

_____

2. List the three to four key events (major supporting details) that illustrate the central idea.

   A. _____

   _____

© 2014 Wadsworth, Cengage Learning

B. _____

_____

_____

C. _____

_____

_____

3. Using the thesis sentence that you wrote above, and the major supporting details you have identified, write a summary of the reading on a separate piece of paper.. Remember to use your own words, and refer to the author and the title in your central idea sentence. Your summary should be about four sentences long.

Reading 4   # After Drugs and Dark Times, Helping Others

—[ADAPTED FROM] BENEDICT CAREY

The following article, published in the *New York Times* in December 2011, tells the story of Antonio Lambert, a man who has successfully controlled his mood swing problems and crack cocaine addiction. He has even become a counselor for people who have similar problems. As you read, think about the central idea and the key events in his life that support that idea.

1   The taste of cocaine and the slow-motion sensation of breaking the law were all too familiar, but the thrill was long gone. Antonio Lambert was not a young hoodlum anymore, but a family man with a career, and here he was, high as any street user, sneaking into his workplace at nine o'clock at night, looking for—what exactly? He didn't really know.

2   He left the building with a few cell phones (which he threw away) and a feeling that he was slipping, falling back down into a hole. He walked in the darkness, walked with no place to go, and then he began to do what he has taught others in similar circumstances to do: turn, face the problem, and stand back up. "I started talking to myself,

Benedict Carey, "After Drugs and Dark Times, Helping Others". Adapted from *The New York Times* December 20, 2011. © 2011 *The New York Times*. All rights reserved. Used by permission and protected by the Copyright Laws of the United States. The printing, copying, redistribution, or retransmission of this Content without express written permission is prohibited.

© 2014 Wadsworth, Cengage Learning

sensation
feeling

out loud; that's one of my coping strategies, and one reason I relapsed is I had forgotten to use those," said Mr. Lambert, 41, a mental health educator who has a combined diagnosis—*mood disorder* with drug addiction—that is among the scariest in psychiatry. He texted a friend, someone who knew his history, had dealt with similar problems, and who could help talk him back down. And he checked himself into a hospital. "I know when it's time to reach out for help."

peer
a person in a
similar position

3   Mr. Lambert is a self-taught ex-convict who is becoming a prominent peer trainer, giving classes in Delaware and across the country. He is one of a small number of people who have chosen to describe publicly how difficult it is to manage such a severe dual diagnosis. Mr. Lambert, who has climbed out of a deep hole, puts it this way: "There are a lot of people dealing with mental illness, drugs, abandonment, abuse, and they don't think there's a way out. I didn't. I didn't."

4   As he was growing up, he couldn't avoid the older toughs in the Brighton section of Portsmouth, Virginia, and he spent some of his school-age years taking beatings. At least those fights taught him survival skills. Not everything did: He remembers being sexually abused at age six by an older boy in the neighborhood—brutally. He had no one to tell, even if he had known what to say. His mother and father were split, living blocks apart, each a fixture in the neighborhood's social swirl of house parties, bars, card games, and other attractions. His mother was often out, sometimes leaving the boy at a friend's house for "a few hours" that turned into an entire weekend. For much of that time, he waited on the porch.

PATH TO DRUGS AND PRISON

5   Antonio Lambert began to stand his ground on the street, earning a name as an up-and-coming gangster by age 12. He was soon into drugs, first as a courier and then as local muscle, armed and very dangerous. He began using more and more cocaine, crack usually. The skinny boy grew big, strong, and crazy enough that he would ride around on his bike with a sawed-off shotgun on the handlebars, pull up to a group of dealers and throw an empty bag on the ground in front of them, with these instructions: Fill it up. Now. "I would shoot the gun off in the air to show I was serious, then just take the drugs and move on to the next pack of dealers," he said. He was a junior in high school.

6   It couldn't last, and it didn't. He survived several gunfights, taking a bullet behind the ear in one (it is still lodged there), and in another being ambushed from behind and hit in the legs, arms, and pelvis; those bullets were all removed without lasting damage, except for prominent scars. But the police were onto him now, and by 1991, at the age of 21, he was in prison, sentenced to 22 years for malicious wounding with a firearm and other charges.

7   He was not a model prisoner at first. He incited a protest at one institution, after which guards confined him to a "segregation" cell, away from other prisoners, for nearly two years. He began to read in there: the *Encyclopaedia Britannica*, then Robert Ludlum, James Clavell, Sun Tzu, anything he could find. That curiosity nourished a deepening ambition that one day in 2002 turned to conviction. "This young thug I knew from the neighborhood comes in, first day of a life sentence, and he puts his hands up and says, 'Hey, man, I'm here!'—like he's coming into a house party," Mr. Lambert said. "That did it. I knew I had to get out and find a life, something. I didn't know what, or how."

© 2014 Wadsworth, Cengage Learning

8   It was June 2003, and Mr. Lambert was out of prison (having earned time for good behavior) and living in Virginia Beach, close to home but not too close. Married with daughters now, he was becoming particularly skilled at installing and finishing floors. His life looked to be taking some shape, if not yet direction. But the work hours were long, money was very tight, and an argument with his wife reopened his inner struggle with resentment and despair.

9   Down he went, back to the streets of Brighton, crashing at friends' apartments and feeling lost, moody, and desperate for his medication of choice. The gunmetal taste of cocaine was irresistible, and at least it broke the fall. But his mood would return darker, and he would have to get high again. That is how it almost always goes with a dual diagnosis of addiction and a mood disorder. Each problem exacerbates the other, in a cycle that is extremely difficult to break.

BREAKING THE CYCLE

10   Yet Antonio Lambert did break that vicious cycle. Leaving two ounces of cocaine and his pistol in his stepbrother's house one morning, he walked out. He was feeling in some ways more hopeless than he had behind bars—when his cell phone buzzed. It was his mother, and she had just seen something on late-night television: an advertisement for *Teen Challenge USA*, a Christian-based recovery program. She gave him a phone number. He wrote it down, sat on the stoop of a boarded-up house and thought about it for a long time, and then dialed. The man on the other end listened and offered to drop the fee if the young man pledged himself to God. He made the commitment that morning and has been a regular churchgoer since. He completed the program and soon found a job at a warehouse, beginning as a temporary worker and advancing to assistant distribution manager. He was living clean, the family was intact, and a local therapist put him on lithium, a standard treatment for severe mood swings.

intact
together

11   A friend from church told him about a job opening for peer specialists at a local mental health clinic. He was offered the job and took it. "He had the worst cases; he had to go into these high gang areas, places no one else would go," said Sue Bethune, his boss at the time. The work was exhausting, it put him dangerously close to cocaine dealers (hence the later relapse, which resulted in misdemeanor charges), and relations at home were again badly strained. He began to set new goals for himself, and decided he wanted to become a peer trainer. In 2007, he attended a training talk by Mr. Harrington, the chief executive and founder of the national peer association. They stayed in touch, and soon Mr. Harrington called to say he had scheduled Mr. Lambert to give a speech at an event in Michigan. His story told itself, and people in the audience who feared for a loved one with similar problems wanted to hear more. Parents from all walks of life—doctors, clergy members, and coworkers—have pulled him aside to see if he could talk to a son or a daughter. He joined Dr. Harrington to form a company, Recover Resources, which sells peer support manuals, DVDs, and other educational materials.

ONE DAY AT A TIME WITH A SYSTEM AND A FRIEND

12   "You got to understand, for me, right now, what I been through, it's sometimes hard to believe it's all real," Mr. Lambert said. "But I know my own mental illness and my addiction are real; I feel like they're out there right now, doing push-ups, getting ready to take me down again. That's why I got to have my own system for staying strong."

13   That system is based on a close monitoring of his moods, which respond only partly to the medication. It includes self-talk, often in the car or between appointments ("If this car ends up in the wrong part of town, you'll be flat on your face");

© 2014 Wadsworth, Cengage Learning

mime
an acting technique that uses movement and expressions but no words to portray stories or emotions

and performance of mime, which he has done with a troupe and individually, often in churches, complete with makeup, flowing robes and gospel accompaniment. But when Mr. Lambert feels his mind sinking fast, he has to be with someone who understands what he's going through. He feels he needs a peer himself, someone with a history who knows what it looks like—from the inside—to be struggling mentally, deep in trouble, and feeling dead out of options. Someone who can be an advocate, a companion, who can share his or her own story: who can simply be there, if that's what it takes.

14   On a recent Saturday morning, Mr. Lambert was home alone, watching college football, when he felt a pulse of that same darkness and exhaustion that led to his last relapse. "I call it the monster," he said. "I was lying there on the couch, and after a while, the college football was watching me." He called his friend and peer, Justin Thompson, who hurried over with a pair of fishing poles. The two of them fished that afternoon. They fished and had a smoke and talked about nothing much, and neither could say exactly when it happened, but it did. The monster was gone.

Exercise 19

Work with Words

Use context clues, word-part clues, and if necessary, the dictionary to choose the best definitions of the following italicized words from Reading 4.

1. Mr. Lambert is a self-taught ex-convict who is becoming a *prominent* peer trainer, giving classes in Delaware and across the country. (par. 3)

   prominent

   a. well-known
   b. incompetent
   c. world famous

2. He was soon into drugs, first as a *courier* and then as local *muscle*, armed and very dangerous. (par. 5)

   courier

   a. a person who manufactures drugs
   b. a person who transports drugs
   c. a person who works as a spy for the police

3. *muscle*

   a. fibrous tissue in the body that can contract
   b. strong man, enforcer
   c. brains behind the (illegal) operation

4. He survived several gunfights, taking a bullet behind the ear in one (it is still lodged there), and in another being ambushed from behind and hit in the legs, arms and pelvis; those bullets were all removed without lasting damage, except for *prominent* scars. (par. 6)

   prominent

   a. important
   b. noticeable
   c. minimal

© 2014 Wadsworth, Cengage Learning

5. But the police were onto him now, and by 1991, at the age of 21, he was in prison, sentenced to 22 years for *malicious* wounding with a firearm and other charges. (par. 6)

malicious

   a. accidental
   b. clearly justifiable
   c. purposely cruel

6. That curiosity nourished a deepening ambition that one day in 2002 turned to *conviction*. (par. 7)

conviction

   a. guilty verdict of the jury
   b. strong belief
   c. convincing argument

7. Each problem *exacerbates* the other, in a cycle that is extremely difficult to break. (par. 9)

exacerbates

   a. makes worse
   b. affects
   c. improves

8. He was living clean, the family was intact and a local therapist put him on *lithium*, a standard treatment for severe mood swings. (par. 10)

lithium

   a. a street drug that helps with withdrawal symptoms
   b. exercise therapy for mood swings
   c. a prescription drug for mood swings

9. He feels he needs a peer himself, someone with a history who knows what it looks like—from the inside—to be struggling mentally, deep in trouble, and feeling dead out of *options*. (par. 13)

options

   a. choices
   b. good decisions
   c. bad decisions

Exercise 20

Check Your Understanding

Choose the best answers to the following questions about Reading 4.

1. Which of the following is the best topic for Reading 4?
   a. Anthony Lambert's success at quitting drugs
   b. Lambert's day-to-day struggle with addiction and mood swings
   c. peer counseling as an effective way to help addicts

© 2014 Wadsworth, Cengage Learning

2. Which of the following is the best central idea sentence for Reading 4?
   a. Anthony Lambert struggles constantly with his mood disorder and addiction, but he has a system that helps him cope.
   b. Lambert learned to read and turned his life around while he was in prison.
   c. Lambert learned to defend himself in the neighborhood by turning into such a tough kid that even adult criminals were afraid of him.

3. The combined diagnosis of mood disorder with drug addiction is so dangerous because
   a. it means he has two medical problems.
   b. each problem affects the other and makes it worse.
   c. both problems are completely incurable.

4. When the author of Reading 4 writes, "he was slipping, falling back down into a hole" he is probably referring to Lambert's
   a. having taken drugs again to deal with his mood swings.
   b. tendency to fall down when he was on drugs.
   c. conviction that he could change his life.

5. Which of the following things did Lambert *not* do as a kid?
   a. shoot off a sawed-off shotgun to scare people
   b. transport drugs
   c. get respect at school for his academic achievement

6. The combination of learning to read and write in prison, and seeing a young punk he had known from the outside coming in to serve a life sentence as if he was going to a party was
   a. a turning point for Lambert, when he decided he was going to change his life, for sure.
   b. a joke as far as Lambert was concerned because he saw the humor in his prison experience.
   c. depressing for Lambert, who could see no way out for himself.

7. Why does the author describe three different incidents when Lambert either relapsed into taking drugs, or almost relapsed?
   a. to demonstrate that it is impossible to be successful at staying clean if a person has a dual diagnosis of mood swings and addiction
   b. to emphasize that Lambert's system of fighting his mood swings and addiction is so strong that he doesn't have to worry anymore
   c. to emphasize that Lambert's challenge is constant, but that each time he relapsed he used his system to pull himself out of it

8. In paragraph 14, Lambert says, "I call it the monster." What is the "monster?"
   a. his depression and urge to take drugs
   b. his strained relationship with his wife
   c. Saturday college football

For the following groups of four sentences that provide major and minor supporting details for the thesis of the reading, circle the letter of the sentence with the major supporting detail.

9. a. He took beatings during his school-age years.
   b. He was sexually abused at six.
   c. He was neglected by his mother.
   d. He had a difficult childhood.

© 2014 Wadsworth, Cengage Learning

10. a. His system to fight his mood swings and drug abuse includes about three major actions.
    b. He calls a friend who understands his problem.
    c. He self-talks, messages like "If this car ends up in the wrong part of town, you'll be flat on your face."
    d. He closely monitors his moods.

11. a. He became a skilled floor installer.
    b. He had a number of successes in his work.
    c. He became a peer counselor and later a peer counselor trainer.
    d. He became co-owner of a company that provides educational materials for peer support and education.

12. a. He had a relapse and ended up high as any street user, stealing cell phones.
    b. In 2003, after setting up a good life for himself, he was working long hours, money was tight, and he argued with his wife; then he went into a depression and started taking drugs again.
    c. He knows that he can never let down his guard because his mental illness and urge to take drugs can overwhelm him at any time.
    d. He felt the darkness and depression one Saturday morning when he was watching college football.

Exercise 21

Work with Major and Minor Supporting Details

1. Rewrite the central idea that you identified in Exercise 20 in your own words.

   _____

   _____

   _____

2. Review the reading, and then fill in minor supporting details for the following major supporting points in the chart for Reading 4. Notice that the major supporting details are grouped.

   A. Difficult childhood that contributed to his eventual addiction, criminal activities, and prison

   _____

   _____

   _____

© 2014 Wadsworth, Cengage Learning

B. Turning point in prison

_____

_____

_____

C. Professional/ Work Accomplishments

_____

_____

_____

_____

D. His system for fighting his mood swings and crack habit

_____

_____

_____

_____

Exercise 22

Write a Summary

Using the central idea and the major supporting details from Exercise 21, write a summary of Reading 4. Think carefully about the minor supporting details to decide which one or two you will include in the summary. Your summary should be four to six sentences. Remember to use your own words, and to refer to the author and the title in your first sentence.

© 2014 Wadsworth, Cengage Learning

Exercise 23

Make Connections and Write

Write short answers to the following questions based on Reading 4, your experience, and your observations. Then, discuss your answers with your class group. Working together, prepare a report for your class as a whole or a written summary for your instructor.

1. Reviewing the reading, what are the two to three sentences you find most interesting?

_____

_____

_____

_____

Are they sentences that had major supporting details or minor supporting details? Why did you find them interesting?

_____

_____

_____

_____

2. Why do you think seeking the help of a friend is so crucial for Lambert when he's in trouble? Who do you go to when you have problems?

_____

_____

_____

_____

© 2014 Wadsworth, Cengage Learning

3. Have you ever tried to break a bad habit? Were you successful? Describe your experience.

_____

_____

_____

_____

_____

Chapter Review

· ·

To aid your review of the reading skills in Chapter 6, study the Put It Together chart.

Put It Together: Supporting Details	
Skills and Concepts	Explanation
Major Supporting Details (see page 253–254)	Major supporting details are the most important • reasons, • facts, • examples, or • descriptions that the author gives to support the central idea statement or thesis.
Minor Supporting Details (see page 253–254)	Minor supporting details are additional points that give: • More information to explain major supporting details • More examples to illustrate major supporting details • More specifics to make material more interesting It is not usually necessary to remember minor supporting details. As you study, you will need to distinguish them from major supporting details so you won't become overwhelmed.
Marking (see page 254)	Marking involves underlining main ideas and numbering minor supporting details; writing on on a text to help you remember the information.
Outlining (see pages 254–255)	Outlining organizes information you want to learn by using numbers and letters and spatial layout to indicate levels of information.
Mapping (see pages 257–258)	Mapping diagrams the relationships between ideas and information in a visual way.

© 2014 Wadsworth, Cengage Learning

Paraphrasing (see pages 260–261)	Paraphrasing is putting an idea that someone else has written into your own words.
Summarizing (see pages 260, 262, 264–265)	Rewriting what someone else has written in a shorter version and in your own words. Steps for writing a summary: 1. Read and understand the reading you are going to summarize. 2. Determine the central idea or thesis. Write it in your own words, referring to the author and the source of the reading. 3. Decide on which major supporting details to include. 4. Decide whether you need to include minor supporting details. (Usually you do not.) 5. Write the summary in your own words; don't give your opinions unless you are asked. 6. Don't copy, but if you do use the author's words, put them in quotation marks.
Writing Summaries for Narratives (see pages 278–280)	Follow the steps for writing a summary, with a focus on identifying **key events** that help you determine the central idea of the narrative.
narrative	a spoken or written account of a series of events, someone's life, or a work of fiction
autobiography	the story of someone's life written by that person
key events	the moments in a narrative that provide the major supporting details; these are points in the story that connect to a broader idea such as injustice, struggle, or transformation

To reinforce your thinking before taking the Mastery Tests, complete as many of the following activities as your instructor assigns.

Review Skills

. . . .

Complete the following skills-review task individually or in a group. When do you think it is helpful for you to use each of the following techniques for studying?

Outlining

_____

_____

_____

© 2014 Wadsworth, Cengage Learning

Marking the text

_____

_____

_____

Mapping

_____

_____

_____

Summarizing

_____

_____

_____

Write

On a separate piece of paper, write a paragraph or more answering one of the following questions:

1. What do you think is the best way to help prevent the abuse or accidental overdose of prescription medicines?
2. As a parent, how would you handle the question of drinking alcohol?
3. If you were a policy maker (in your community, city, state, or at the federal level), what kind of program would you put in place to deal with drug abuse problems? Be specific about what problems you would be trying to address, and what activities/benefits the program would provide.

© 2014 Wadsworth, Cengage Learning

COLLABORATE

Brainstorm in a group the ways in which drugs can help people. Make a list of the drugs that people in your group identify as most helpful; then fill out the following chart that indicates in what ways these drugs make our lives better.

Name of the Drug	Ways in which it helps people
_____	_____
	_____
_____	_____
	_____
_____	_____
	_____
_____	_____
	_____

EXTEND YOUR THINKING

To answer the following questions, you will have to do a little research. Then, prepare the information you gather to share with your class group.

1. Briefly interview 6-10 people. They can be family members, friends, anybody.
2. Ask them the following two questions, and keep track of how they answer. Do *not* prompt them to think about alcohol or drugs:
   A. What do you do to relieve stress?
   B. What do you do to relax?
3. Organize their answers, listing and grouping the responses (for example, how many exercise, take a nap, meditate, see friends, etc.). Make sure to note the number of people who mention alcohol and/or other drugs. If people say they go to parties or go out to bars or clubs, ask about drinking or using drugs in those situations.

 ## WORK THE WEB

To learn more about different aspects of drugs in our society, use a search engine such as *Google* to go to the official Web site for the Drug Policy Alliance or the National Institute on Drug Abuse. Or, do a Google search on the Native American Church to learn more information about ritual peyote use.

© 2014 Wadsworth, Cengage Learning

Choose an article from the Web site. When you have chosen an article, preview it. Read the article, and then answer the following questions.

1. What is the title of the article? On which Web site did you find it?

   _____

   _____

   _____

2. What is the topic of the article?

   _____

   _____

   _____

3. Write the first sentence of a summary of the article. Remember to use the following structure: "According to [name of author—if no author is given, you can give the name of the Web site] in the online article [title of article], [central idea in your own words].

   _____

   _____

   _____

4. On a separate piece of paper, write a summary of the article in your own words.

© 2014 Wadsworth, Cengage Learning

Name _____ Date _____

The Most Deadly Drug

—Elizabeth Nguyen

In the following essay, Elizabeth Nguyen challenges our society's assumption that it's okay to drink alcohol. She even asserts that, in many ways, alcohol is more dangerous than a lot of illegal drugs. As you read, notice the major and minor supporting details the author uses to support her thesis.

1   The most deadly drug in the United States is not <u>confined</u> to the black market or criminal drug dealers, nor is it confined to inner city back alleys. Its consumption is not limited to socially <u>outcast</u> junkies, and its <u>ill</u> effects are felt in every neighborhood and at every social level. Politicians use it, judges use it, police use it, and doctors use it. Its consumption is promoted at many social and family events, and there is probably some of it in your house right now. The most dangerous drugs are not crack, heroin, or crystal meth, despite the fact that these drugs are among the most demonized. Cannabis, ecstasy, opium, and PCP are not the most dangerous drugs either, even though they receive much media attention, and millions of dollars are spent each year to combat their use. The real killer is alcohol.

demonized
portrayed as wicked or evil

2   Although alcohol is the most culturally and legally acceptable drug in our society, it is also the most dangerous. Its dangers take three major forms. First, alcohol is highly addictive and causes a <u>multitude</u> of physical and mental health problems. Second, its mind-altering effects cause many types of deadly accidents every year. Third, and perhaps most disturbing of all, alcohol is frequently <u>implicated</u> in a variety of violent crimes every year including murder, assault, child abuse, domestic violence, and rape.

3   The most direct dangers of alcohol use come from its addictive nature and its toxic effects on human health. Short-term consequences of the over-consumption of alcohol sometimes include vomiting, passing out, or having a hangover the next day. Excessive drinking in a short period of time can lead to alcohol poisoning and even death. Overdosing on alcohol is more common than most people realize, especially when alcohol is used in combination with other drugs. Long-term use can damage virtually every organ in the human body. The most common long-term health conditions alcohol causes include various cancers, liver diseases, and mental health problems. Alcoholics most commonly die from cancer or liver disease. According to the American Cancer Society, the abuse of alcohol is known to cause seven types of cancer, including mouth cancer, bowel cancer, and liver cancer[1]. Other liver ailments, such as cirrhosis of the liver and fatty liver disease, are also common among alcoholics. Last but not least, alcoholism is associated with a number of mental <u>ailments</u>. In addition to overall brain damage and brain shrinkage, alcoholics face an increased risk of dementia, depression, anxiety disorders, social <u>phobias</u>, and suicidal tendencies. According to the Centers for Disease Control, alcohol caused 79,000 deaths in the United States each year between 2001 and 2005[2]. According to the World Health Organization, the global annual death toll from alcohol is much higher, at 3.5 million[3].

dementia
brain disorder that leads to intellectual decline

4   Alcohol abuse is responsible for many dangerous and deadly accidents each year. The most common include automobile accidents, boating accidents, fires, falls, and

Elizabeth Nguyen. Written for *Joining a Community of Readers*. Used by permission.

© 2014 Wadsworth, Cengage Learning

drowning. Of these, car accidents are the most deadly. Its use is estimated to cause almost half of all automobile fatalities in the United States; and drunk driving is considered the leading cause of death among young Americans. The National Highway Safety and Traffic Administration reported 16,885 drunk driving related deaths in 2005 alone[4]. Drunk driving accidents are not the only accidents caused by alcohol. In the United States, 38 percent of fire fatalities, 49 percent of drownings, and 63 percent of fatal falls occurred while the victims were under the influence of alcohol[5]. Because alcohol slows reaction time, <u>hinders</u> judgment, and reduces <u>inhibitions</u>, it is unsurprising that it leads to many accidents. The mind-altering effects of alcohol are more dangerous than those of many other drugs; and this is especially dangerous because most people take drinking for granted because of its <u>widespread</u> use and acceptance in our society.

5   Due to its effects on the brain and emotions, alcohol is connected to many violent crimes every year. Among college students these crimes are especially noticeable because of the large quantities of alcohol consumed on college campuses. According to the National Institute on Alcohol Abuse and Alcoholism, drunk students between the ages of 18 and 24 assault more than 696,000 of their peers every year. The NIAAA also reports that more than 97,000 students between the ages of 18 and 24 are victims in cases of alcohol-related sexual assault and rape each year. Alcohol has been implicated in 90 percent of student rape cases and 95 percent of violent crimes committed on college campuses. Outside of college campuses, domestic violence, child abuse and neglect, burglary and vandalism are also frequently connected to alcohol use.

6   It is obvious from all the information collected by government agencies and medical researchers that alcohol causes more deaths, disease, and injuries than any of the more notorious illegal drugs. It is therefore the most deadly drug, even though our cultural values and legal system do not reflect this fact. While many people shudder when they think about the dangers of crack, methamphetamines, heroin, marijuana, and LSD, none of these forbidden drugs has a track record that compares with the everyday deadliness of alcohol.

Notes

1   American Cancer Society, "Alcohol Use and Cancer," (http://www.cancer.org/Cancer/CancerCauses/DietandPhysicalActivity/alcohol-use-and-cancer) (accessed 12/08/11)

2   Centers for Disease Control, "Alcohol and Public Health," http://www.cdc.gov/alcohol/ (accessed 12/08/11).

3   World Health Organization, "Alcohol Fact Sheet," http://www.who.int/mediacentre/factsheets/fs349/en/ (accessed 12/02/11).

4   National Highway Safety Traffic Administration, "Alcohol and Highway Safety: A Review of the State of Knowledge," www.nhtsa.gov/staticfiles/nti/pdf/811374.pdf (accessed 10/1/12).

5   Wayne Weiten, Dana S. Dunn, and Elizabeth Yost Hammer, *Psychology Applied to Modern Life: Adjustment in the 21st Century*, 5e, (Wadsworth Cengage Learning, 2012), 151–154.

Use context clues, word-part clues, and, if necessary, the dictionary to write the definition for each of the italicized words in the following sentences from the reading.

© 2014 Wadsworth, Cengage Learning

1. The most deadly drug in the United States is not *confined* to the black market or criminal drug dealers, nor is it confined to inner city back alleys. (par. 1)

   confined _____

2. Its consumption is not limited to socially *outcast* junkies, and its *ill* effects are felt in every neighborhood and at every social level. (par. 1)

   outcast _____

3. *ill* _____

4. First, alcohol is highly addictive and causes a *multitude* of physical and mental health problems. (par. 2)

   multitude _____

5. Third, and perhaps most disturbing of all, is that alcohol is often *implicated* in a variety of violent crimes every year including murder, assault, child abuse, domestic violence, and rape. (par. 2)

   implicated _____

6. Other liver *ailments,* such as cirrhosis of the liver and fatty liver disease, are also common among alcoholics. (par. 3)

   ailments _____

7. In addition to overall brain damage and brain shrinkage, alcoholics face an increased risk of dementia, depression, anxiety disorders, social *phobias*, and suicidal tendencies. (par. 3)

   phobias _____

8. Because alcohol slows reaction time, *hinders* judgment, and reduces *inhibitions*, it is unsurprising that it leads to many accidents. (par. 4)

   hinders _____

9. *inhibitions* _____

   _____

10. The mind-altering effects of alcohol are more dangerous than those of many other drugs, and this is especially dangerous because most people take drinking for granted because of its *widespread* use and acceptance in our society. (par. 4)

    widespread _____

For the following groups of sentences that provide major and minor supporting details for the thesis of the reading, circle the letter of the sentence with the major supporting detail.

© 2014 Wadsworth, Cengage Learning

11. a. The most direct dangers of alcohol use come from its addictive nature and its toxic effects on human health.
   b. Liver ailments, such as cirrhosis of the liver and fatty liver disease, are also common among alcoholics.
   c. Excessive drinking in a short period of time can lead to alcohol poisoning and even death.

12. a. In the United States, 38 percent of fire fatalities, 49 percent of drownings, and 63 percent of fatal falls victims were due to the influence of alcohol.
   b. The National Highway Safety and Traffic Administration reported 16,885 drunk driving related deaths in 2005 alone.
   c. Alcohol abuse is responsible for many dangerous and deadly accidents each year.

13. a. According to the National Institute on Alcohol Abuse and Alcoholism, drunk students between the ages of 18 and 24 assault more than 696,000 of their peers every year.
   b. Due to its effects on the brain and emotions, alcohol is connected to many violent crimes every year.
   c. The NIAAA also reports that more than 97,000 students between the ages of 18 and 24 are victims in cases of alcohol-related sexual assault and rape each year.

Write short answers to the following questions based on the reading.

14. List the mental ailments that alcohol can cause.

_____

_____

_____

_____

15. What is the global annual death toll from alcohol?

_____

Is this statistic a major or minor detail for the reading?

_____

16. List four minor supporting details for the short-term effects of overconsumption of alcohol.

_____

© 2014 Wadsworth, Cengage Learning

17. Why do you think alcohol consumption contributes dramatically to the numbers of victims of assault and rape between the ages of 18 and 24? Explain your answer.

_____

_____

_____

_____

18. If alcohol were more difficult to obtain, do you think its many disastrous consequences would be reduced? Explain your answer.

_____

_____

_____

_____

19. Write the thesis of this reading in your own words.

_____

_____

_____

_____

20. Using the thesis sentence that is identified for you above, and the major supporting details you have identified, write a summary of *The Most Deadly Drug* on a separate sheet of paper. Remember to use your own words, and refer to the author and the title in your central idea sentence. Your summary should be four to six sentences long.

© 2014 Wadsworth, Cengage Learning

Name _____ Date _____

Rethinking the War on Drugs

—[Adapted from] Larry J. Seigel

TEXT BOOK **The following reading from a criminology textbook suggests that the "War on Drugs" has not been successful and that there are better ways to deal with the drug problem in our country. As you read, carefully consider the major and minor supporting details the author provides to support his position.**

1   With so much money to be made from the <u>illicit</u> drug industry, can any strategy reduce the <u>lure</u> of drug trafficking? Despite massive efforts to control drugs through prevention, <u>deterrence</u>, education, and treatment strategies, the fight against substance abuse has not been successful. Policy makers need to consider another approach.

2   The so-called War on Drugs is far too expensive, and the money it costs could instead be spent on education and economic development. Waging this "war" has cost U.S. taxpayers more than $500 billion over the past 20 years. Drug enforcement and treatment now cost federal, state, and local governments about $100 billion per year.[1]

3   Most treatment efforts aimed at convincing known drug users to quit have been unsuccessful. The problem may be that there are multiple, uncoordinated efforts to control drugs. Some rely on enforcement and punishment, while others rely on treatment and rehabilitation. The former efforts require drug users to be secretive so they won't be caught. The latter efforts require users to be open and willing to get treatment.[2]

4   Considering these failures, the only way to deal with the drug problem is through decriminalization of drug offenses. Legalization is necessary, according to drug expert Ethan Nadelmann, because almost all human societies have used <u>mood-altering</u> substances; and people have always wanted, and will find ways of obtaining, psychoactive drugs.[3] Nadelmann heads the Drug Policy Alliance, a national organization dedicated to ending the "War on Drugs," which the Alliance believes has become <u>overzealous</u> in its effort to punish drug traffickers.[4]

5   Nadelmann reminds us that federal, state, and local governments have spent billions of dollars trying to make America drug-free, but spending all this money has not been effective. Heroin, cocaine, methamphetamine, and other illicit drugs are cheaper, purer, and easier to get. Though the United States prosecutes and imprisons more people for drug crimes than ever before, statistics measuring drug use haven't improved. The number of Americans behind bars on drug charges is greater than the number of Europeans <u>incarcerated</u> for all charges; and Europe's population is 500 million larger than ours.[5]

6   Nadelmann also reminds us that the effort to control drugs creates more problems than it solves. <u>Draconian</u> laws keep users in hiding and restrict their access to clean needles. This <u>exacerbates</u> public health problems like HIV and hepatitis C, as addicts often <u>transmit</u> these diseases by reusing and sharing needles. Once infected with a disease, addicts often don't get the treatment they need. When they get caught and go to prison, their families suffer: Children of inmates are at risk of educational failure, joblessness, addiction, and delinquency. In addition, people with serious illnesses like cancer and AIDS may be denied access to their medicines, or even arrested and prosecuted for using medical marijuana.

Larry J. Seigel, *Criminology,* 11e; Wadsworth/Cengage 2012, pp. 507–508.

© 2014 Wadsworth, Cengage Learning

7   Banning drugs creates <u>covert</u> networks of manufacturers and distributors, many of which use violence as part of their standard operating procedures. Although some people believe that drug use is immoral, one has to ask if it is any worse than the unrestricted use of alcohol and cigarettes. Both of these drugs are addictive and unhealthful. Far more people die each year because they abuse these legal substances than are killed in drug wars or from abusing illegal substances.

8   If drugs were legalized, according to Nadelmann, the government could control their price and distribution. This would reduce addicts' cash requirements, so crime rates would drop because users would no longer need so much money to support their habits. Drug-related deaths would decline because government control would reduce needle sharing and the spread of AIDS. Legalization would also destroy drug-importing <u>cartels</u> and gangs. Because drugs would be bought and sold openly, the government would be able to collect taxes on the sale of drugs. Of course, drug distribution would be regulated, like alcohol, keeping drugs away from adolescents, public servants such as police and airline pilots, and known felons.

Notes

1. Office of National Drug Control Policy, "National Drug Control Strategy FY 2009 Budget Summary," February 2008, www.whitehousedrugpolicy.gov/publications/policy/09budget/ (accessed October 1, 2012).

2. Barry Goetz, "Pre-Arrest/Booking Drug Control Strategies: Diversion to Treatment, Harm Reduction and Police Involvement," *Contemporary Drug Problems,* 33 (2006): 473–520.

3. Ethan Nadelmann, "An End to Marijuana Prohibition," *National Review*, July 12, 2004; Peter Andreas and Ethan Nadelmann, *Policing the Glob: Criminalization and Crime Control in International Relations* (London: Oxford University Press, 2006).

4. Drug Policy Alliance, "What's Wrong with the Drug War?" www.drugpolicy.org/drugwar/ (accessed 10/1/12).

5. According to the Drug Policy Alliance, nearly 6 in 10 people in state prison for a drug law violation have no history of violence or high-level drug selling activity. Drug arrests have more than tripled in the last 25 years, totaling more than 1.66 million arrests in 2009. More than four out of five of these arrests were for mere possession. African Americans comprise about 13 percent of the U.S. population and 13 percent of people who use or sell illegal drugs, but make up 37 percent of those arrested for drug law violations and 56 percent of those in state prisons for a drug law violation. Drug Policy Alliance, "Drug War Facts," http://nomoredrugwar.org/drug-war-facts (accessed 12/13/11).

Use context clues, word-part clues, and, if necessary, the dictionary to write the definition for each of the italicized words in the following sentences from the reading.

1. With so much money to be made from the *illicit* drug industry, can any strategy reduce the *lure* of drug trafficking? (par. 1)

   illicit _____

© 2014 Wadsworth, Cengage Learning

2. *lure* _____

3. Despite massive efforts to control drugs through prevention, *deterrence*, education, and treatment strategies, the fight against substance abuse has not been successful. (par. 1)

   deterrence _____

4. Legalization is necessary, according to drug expert Ethan Nadelmann, because almost

5. all human societies have used *mood-altering* substances; and people have always wanted, and will find ways of obtaining, psychoactive drugs. (par. 4)

   mood-altering _____

6. Nadelmann heads the Drug Policy Alliance, a national organization dedicated to ending the "War on Drugs" which the Alliance believes has become *over-zealous* in its effort to punish drug traffickers. (par. 4)

   overzealous _____

7. The number of Americans behind bars on drug charges is greater than the number of Europeans *incarcerated* for all charges; and Europe's population is 500 million larger than ours. (par. 5)

   incarcerated _____

8. *Draconian* laws keep users in hiding and restrict their access to clean needles. (par. 6)

   draconian _____

9. This exacerbates public health problems like HIV and hepatitis C, as addicts often *transmit* these diseases by reusing and sharing needles. Once infected with a disease, addicts often don't get the treatment they need. (par. 6)

   transmit _____

10. Banning drugs creates *covert* networks of manufacturers and distributors, many of whom use violence as part of their standard operating procedures. (par. 7)

    covert _____

11. Legalization would also destroy drug-importing *cartels* and gangs. (par. 8)

    cartels _____

For the following groups of sentences that provide major and minor supporting details for the thesis of the reading, circle the letter of the sentence that states the major supporting detail.

© 2014 Wadsworth, Cengage Learning

12. a. Drug enforcement and treatment now cost federal, state, and local governments about $100 billion per year.
    b. The so-called War on Drugs is too expensive.
    c. Waging this "war" has cost U.S. taxpayers more than $500 billion over the past 20 years.

13. a. Addicts often transmit diseases like HIV and hepatitis C by reusing needles.
    b. People with serious illnesses like cancer and AIDS may be denied access to their medicines, or even arrested for using medical marijuana.
    c. Draconian laws keep users in hiding and exacerbate public health problems.

14. a. The only way to deal with the drug problem is through decriminalization of drug offenses.
    b. Almost all human societies have used mood-altering substances.
    c. People have always wanted, and will find ways of obtaining, psychoactive drugs.

15. a. Crime rates would decline because drugs would be bought and sold openly, and the government would be able to collect taxes.
    b. Drug-related deaths would decline because government control would reduce needle sharing and the spread of AIDS.
    c. If drugs were legalized, according to Nadelmann, the government could control their price and distribution.

Choose the best answers to the following multiple-choice questions about the reading.

16. Which of the following sentences is the best thesis for the reading, "Rethinking the War on Drugs"?
    a. Almost all human societies have used mood-altering substances.
    b. Overly severe laws keep drug users in hiding and exacerbate public health problems.
    c. The fight against substance abuse has been unsuccessful and policy makers should consider legalizing drugs.

17. According to this reading, the current war on drugs has actually
    a. contributed to drug-related deaths.
    b. reduced drug abuse in this country even though it is expensive.
    c. helped reduce the violence surrounding the illegal drug trade.

18. The author suggests
    a. that drug use is immoral.
    b. drug abuse should be accepted by society.
    c. that drug use is not worse than the use of alcohol and cigarettes.

© 2014 Wadsworth, Cengage Learning

19. Do you agree with the thesis of this reading? In what ways do you agree with the thesis of this reading? In what ways do you disagree? Explain your answer.

_____

_____

_____

_____

_____

20. Write the thesis of the reading in your own words.

_____

_____

21. Using the thesis sentence you wrote above, and the major supporting details you have identified, write a summary of Mastery Test 6B on a separate sheet of paper. Remember to use your own words, and refer to the author and the title in your first sentence. Your summary should be four to six sentences.

© 2014 Wadsworth, Cengage Learning

7 Patterns of Organization

FAMILIES

Barack Obama with his single mother

In every conceivable manner, the family is link to our past, bridge to our future.
—*AUTHOR ALEX HALEY*

- Who is in the photograph?

- Does your family look like the family in the photograph? How is it similar? How is it different?

- How would you explain the quotation? Do you agree with it?

- How do you think the quotation might apply to the photo?

- Does the quotation apply to your family and your experiences? In what ways?

Getting Ready to Read

What is a family? What do you think a family should be like? If you think about your own family, your friends' families, and other families you know, you will recognize that there are lots of different kinds of families. Who are the members of these families? You probably know some single-parent families, some blended families, some families that include grandparents, and some families made up of both biological parents and their children.

In this chapter, you will read and think about varieties of family life in the United States. As you do, you will improve your reading skills by learning how to:

- Recognize patterns of organization, including examples, chronological order, definition, comparison and contrast, and cause and effect
- Recognize words and other clues that can help you identify patterns of organization
- Organize what you have read using patterns of organization

© 2014 Wadsworth, Cengage Learning

Reading 1

My Husband's Nine Wives

— Elizabeth Joseph

In the following reading, Elizabeth Joseph writes about her experience in a rather unusual marriage relationship. Her family practices polygamy; that is, her husband had six other wives when she married him, and now he has nine wives. Read to see why she thinks this is an ideal relationship for herself and her children.

1   I married a married man.

2   In fact, he had six wives when I married him 17 years ago. Today, he has nine.

3   In March [1991], the Utah Supreme Court struck down a trial court's ruling that a polygamist couple could not adopt a child because of their marital style. Last month, the national board of the American Civil Liberties Union, in response to a request from its Utah chapter, adopted a new policy calling for the legalization of polygamy.

paradox
something that is different from what is expected

mandates
requires

4   Polygamy, or plural marriage, as practiced by my family is a paradox. At first blush, it sounds like the ideal situation for the man and an oppressive one for the women. For me, the opposite is true. While polygamists believe that the Old Testament mandates the practice of plural marriage, compelling social reasons make the lifestyle attractive to the modern career woman.

5   Pick up any women's magazine and you will find article after article about the problems of successfully juggling career, motherhood, and marriage. It is a complex act that many women struggle to manage daily; their frustrations fill up the pages of those magazines and consume the hours of afternoon talk shows.

monogamous
following the custom of being married to one person

6   In a monogamous context, the only solutions are compromises. The kids need to learn to fix their own breakfast, your husband needs to get used to occasional microwave dinners, you need to divert more of your income to insure that your preschooler is in a good day care environment.

7   I am sure that in the challenge of working through these compromises, satisfaction and success can be realized. But why must women only embrace a marital arrangement that requires so many trade-offs?

8   When I leave for the 60-mile commute to court at 7 A.M., my two-year-old daughter, London, is happily asleep in the bed of my husband's wife, Diane. London adores Diane. When London awakes, about the time I'm arriving at the courthouse, she is surrounded by family members who are as familiar to her as the toys in her nursery.

9   My husband, Alex, who writes at night, gets up much later. While most of his wives are already at work, pursuing their careers, he can almost always find one who's willing to chat over coffee.

10   I share a home with Delinda, another wife, who works in town government. Most nights, we agree we'll just have a simple dinner with our three kids. We'd rather relax and commiserate over the pressures of our work day than chew up our energy cooking and doing a ton of dishes.

11   Mondays, however, are different. That's the night Alex eats with us. The kids, excited that their father is coming to dinner, are on their best behavior. We often invite another wife or one of his children. It's a special event because it only happens once a week.

Elizabeth Joseph, "My Husband's Nine Wives," New York Times, 5/23/91. © 1991 New York Times Co., Inc. Used with permission.

© 2014 Wadsworth, Cengage Learning

12   Tuesday night, it's back to simplicity for us. But for Alex and the household he's dining with that night, it's their special time.

13   The same system with some variation governs our private time with him. While spontaneity is by no means ruled out, we basically use an appointment system. If I want to spend Friday evening at his house, I make an appointment. If he's already "booked," I either request another night, or if my schedule is inflexible, I talk to the other wife and we work out an arrangement. One thing we've all learned is that there's always another night.

14   Most evenings, with the demands of career and the literal chasing after the needs of a toddler, all I want to do is collapse into bed and sleep. But there is also the longing for intimacy and comfort that only he can provide, and when those feelings surface, I ask to be with him.

intimacy
closeness

15   Plural marriage is not for everyone. But it is the lifestyle for me. It offers men the chance to escape from the traditional, confining roles that often isolate them from the surrounding world. More important, it enables women, who live in a society full of obstacles, to fully meet their career, mothering, and marriage obligations. Polygamy provides a whole solution. I believe American women would have invented it if it didn't already exist.

confining
restricting

Exercise 1

Recall and Discuss

Answer these questions about Reading 1, and prepare to discuss them in class.

1. Why does Joseph think that polygamy is an attractive lifestyle for the modern career woman?

   _____

   _____

   _____

2. What does she mean when she says her husband is already "booked"?

   _____

   _____

   _____

3. What does she mean when she says, "Polygamy provides a whole solution"?

   _____

   _____

   _____

© 2014 Wadsworth, Cengage Learning

4. How do women or men you know manage the responsibilities of marriage, family, and career? Contrast their situations with the one Joseph describes.

_____

_____

_____

Patterns of Organization

. . . .

patterns of organization the ways supporting details are put together to support main ideas

In Chapters 5 and 6 you learned to distinguish between main ideas and the many supporting ideas in paragraphs and essays. These supporting ideas are often organized according to certain **patterns of organization**. Writers choose a particular pattern of organization because it helps them present their ideas and information in a clear way. Recognizing these patterns makes it easier for readers to understand what the writer is trying to tell them. Three of the most common ways to organize information are by examples, chronological order, and definition.

EXAMPLES

examples a pattern of organization that provides instances of the main idea, introduced with phrases like for *example* and for *instance*

One of the most commonly used ways to organize information is by **examples**, which explain a more general idea by providing instances of it. In Chapter 5 you learned that examples are one type of supporting detail. One way to present examples is to list and number them. This variation is called **enumeration**.

In Sentences   Examples are easily recognized in sentences where they are introduced by a phrase like "such as" and separated by commas. For instance, read this sentence and identify the different types of families.

enumeration a pattern of organization that lists examples using numbers

> Families in America today include a wide variety of models, such as the traditional <u>extended family</u>, the <u>single-parent family</u>, the <u>nuclear family,</u> and the <u>blended family</u>.

extended family a family that includes grandparents, aunts, and uncles, as well as parents and children

Each of the underlined terms in this sentence is a separate example of a kind of family in today's society. Notice that commas separate the examples here, but in some cases longer examples are separated by semicolons.

Word Clues for Examples   The following groups of words signal that examples are used.

- such as
- for example
- for instance
- moreover
- also
- another

© 2014 Wadsworth, Cengage Learning

Other Clues for Examples The following list provides other types of signals for examples.

- commas
- semicolons
- numbers in parentheses
- letters of the alphabet in parentheses
- bullets

In Paragraphs In a paragraph or a longer passage, an example could be one sentence or several sentences long. Examples in sentences are often used to support the main idea statement of a paragraph. In the following paragraph, the main idea is stated in the first sentence, "Families around the world choose to raise their children in various ways." The writers then use examples from the United States, Western Europe, Africa, and India to support their main idea. Notice that each example is introduced by its location in a different part of the world.

> Families around the world choose to raise their children in various ways. In the United States and in Western European societies, the biological parents traditionally have assumed the responsibilities of child rearing, but this is only one of the many variations in the world. In the Buganda tribe of Central Africa, the biological father's brother is responsible for child rearing. The Nayars of southern India assign this role to the mother's eldest brother. (adapted from Appelbaum and Chambliss, *Sociology*)

Once you recognize that this paragraph is organized to give examples, you can arrange that information into a map showing the major and minor supporting details. In Chapters 5 and 6 you already learned to organize supporting details into maps and outlines. The map of this paragraph would look like this:

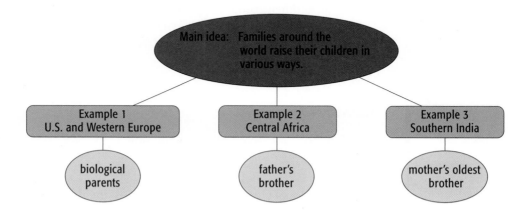

Sometimes writers list examples by number. In the following paragraph, the benefits of extended families are *enumerated*.

> In many parts of the world, the extended family, in which grandparents, aunts, uncles, and children all live together, is the most common family structure. The

© 2014 Wadsworth, Cengage Learning

extended family structure has been successful because it provides many benefits for families such as (1) economic advantages, because it is cheaper to house and to feed many people who all live together; (2) work distribution advantages, because there are more people to share in household tasks such as cooking, cleaning, and taking care of children; and (3) social advantages, because with so many family members around, no family members are lonely or left alone if they need help taking care of themselves due to sickness or old age.

When examples are enumerated, they are easy to outline. For the preceding paragraph, a brief outline might look like this:

topic: benefits of extended families

main idea: The extended family structure has been successful because it provides many benefits for families.

    I. Economic
       A. Cheaper to live together
       B. Cheaper to eat together

    II. Work distribution; share in tasks
       A. Cooking and cleaning
       B. Taking care of children

    III. Social
       A. No one lonely
       B. If sick or old, taken care of

Sometimes authors provide examples in bulleted lists. In the following excerpt, the author presents the sources available to a family caring for an aging parent using *bullets*.

No one can, or should, take care of another person without help. Here are three important sources for finding help:

- Government/community agencies
- Medical facilities and businesses catering to older people and caregivers
- Relatives, friends, coworkers and neighbors

(Smith, *Caring for Your Aging Parents*)

Exercise 2

Identify Examples

In the following paragraphs, underline the main idea. Then on a separate sheet of paper, make a map, outline, or bulleted list that shows the important examples in the paragraph.

1. In traditional European peasant societies, the firstborn son inherited the family land, so second and third sons had to look for other ways to earn a living. In sixteenth-century Spain there were more options open to them. First, they could join the Church. Second, they could become a paid soldier. And finally, they could join the expeditions of exploration to the New World.

© 2014 Wadsworth, Cengage Learning

2. Historically, men's most important role within the family structure was to provide food for the family. This they did by hunting, fishing, and raising sheep or cattle. In addition, they were frequently responsible for the agricultural tasks that required heavy physical labor.

3. First of all, the family, because of the strong feelings it generates, is a powerful source not just of love and care but also of pain and conflict. . . . In most families, there are instances of conflict and violence, such as anger, physical punishment of children, or spouses poking and slapping each other. In fact, the family is one of the few groups in society empowered by law or tradition to hit its members. It is, for example, legal for parents to spank their children as a form of punishment. Moreover, many husbands who strike their wives to "keep them in line" are not arrested, prosecuted, or imprisoned. (Thio, *Sociology*)

CHRONOLOGICAL ORDER

chronological order a pattern of organization that provides information in time order, using words like *then, when, after, before, later,* and *while*

process a series of steps that must be done in a certain order to get the desired result, using words like *first, second,* and *finally*

Chronological order organizes information according to the time at which events occur or occurred. It often shows how something developed over time or explains its history. This pattern is often used to narrate stories and explain the steps in a **process**.

In Sentences   Dates or times may signal chronological order in sentences. For example, the writer of the following sentence is concerned about the changes in the baby boom generation's attitude toward family between the 1960s and the 1970s.

> The large baby boom generation, which had been active in the 1960s, was moving on to marriage and parenthood by the end of the 1970s. (Skolnick and Skolnick, *Family in Transition*)

Process is usually signaled by words like *first, second, after, then,* and *once.* In explaining the writing process, it is important to indicate what a writer does first, as in the following example:

> Once you have brainstormed your ideas, [then] you are ready to sort through them to decide what you want to include in your essay.

Word Clues for Chronological Order and Process   The following words signal time relationships for the chronological order and process patterns of organization.

- first
- second
- next
- then
- when
- after

- before
- later
- while
- once
- finally
- last

© 2014 Wadsworth, Cengage Learning

Other Clues for Chronological Order and Process The following list provides other types of signals for chronological order and process patterns of organization.

- dates (July 1, 2014)
- centuries (fifth century, 1900s)
- decades (1920s)
- days (Wednesday, Thanksgiving)
- time of day (afternoon, 5:30 A.M.)

In Paragraphs Chronological order may also be used to organize information in paragraphs and longer passages. For example, in the following paragraph each sentence begins with dates to keep the reader's focus on the changes in the family from one decade to another. In fact, the main idea of the paragraph is: "The American family has been changing over time" or "The American family has changed since the 1950s." The time clues—which help you figure out the main idea—have been underlined for you.

to epitomize to be the perfect example of something

> During the 1950s the Cleavers on the television show "Leave It to Beaver" epitomized the American family. In 1960, over 70 percent of all American households were like the Cleavers: made up of a breadwinner father, a homemaker mother and their kids. Today, "traditional" families with a working husband, an unemployed wife, and one or more children make up less than 15 percent of the nation's households. (Martin et al., *America and Its Peoples*)

Organize to Learn: Make a Time Line

timeline a table listing important events by dates

One good way to organize information based on chronological order is to use a **time line**, which is a table listing important events by dates. With a time line, you can see the chronological relationship between events. For example, the following paragraph can be organized with a time line:

> According to the U.S. Census Bureau, since the 1950s both men and women have gradually been marrying at a later age. In 1955, the average age to enter a first marriage for a man was 22.6 and for a woman 20.2. By 1970, men's average age was 23.2 and women's was 20.8. Ten years later, in 1980, the average age for men was 24.7 and for women 22.0. This gradual increase continued into the 1990s. In 1995, the average age for a man to enter his first marriage was 26.9 and for a woman it was 24.5. By 2000 the figures were 26.8 and 25.1.

A time line for the information in this paragraph might look like this:

main idea: Since the 1950s, men and women have entered their first marriages later.

© 2014 Wadsworth, Cengage Learning

1955   Men married at age 22.6, women 20.2
1970   Men married at age 23.2, women 20.8
1980   Men married at age 24.7, women 22.0
1995   Men married at age 26.9, women 24.5
2000   Men married at age 26.8, women 25.1

Exercise 3   Make a Time Line

In the following excerpts, underline dates and words or phrases that indicate chronological order. Write the main idea in your own words and complete the time lines.

1. Developed largely after World War I came to an end in 1918, the U.S. custom of dating has spread to many industrial countries. It has also changed in the United States in the last two decades. Before the 1970s, dating was more formal. Males had to ask for a date at least several days in advance. It was usually the male who decided where to go, paid for the date, opened doors, and was supposed to be chivalrous. The couple often went to an event, such as a movie, dance, concert, or ball game.

   Today, dating has become more casual. In fact, the word "date" now sounds a bit old-fashioned to many young people. (Thio, *Sociology*)

   main idea: _____

   _____

   time line:

   1918   _____

   Before 1970s   _____

   Today   _____

2. Families and individual family members have at certain times in history decided to move away from the areas where they were born. In the early 1800s, German peasants began migrating to the United States. In the 1840s, people from Ireland migrated because there was not enough food due to the failed potato crops. Later in the nineteenth century, Scandinavians came. Finally, in the 1890s and early twentieth century, many Eastern European families moved to the "New World," looking for better opportunities.

   main idea: _____

   _____

© 2014 Wadsworth, Cengage Learning

time line:

Beginning of 1800s   _____

1840s   _____

Late 1800s   _____

End of 1800s, early   _____
twentieth century

  _____

3. Family life in China improved during the middle of the twentieth century because more Chinese babies began living past the first year of life. The number of births remained fairly constant, but in the early decades of the twentieth century, 27 to 30 infants died out of 1,000 births. In 1952, 18 infants died out of 1,000 births, and by the early 1970s, that figure had fallen to about 15 per 1,000. (adapted from "China," *Encyclopedia Britannica*)

main idea: _____

_____

time line:

Early twentieth century   _____

1952   _____

1970   _____

4. When a baby cries, parents usually go through a simple trial-and-error process to solve the baby's problem. First, they may check to see if the baby's diaper needs to be changed. If they change the diaper and the baby is still crying, they may next simply pick her up to see if she just wants to change positions or be held. Then, if that doesn't work, they offer her something to eat. Next, if the baby is still crying, they might take her outside in her stroller or for a ride in the car. Finally, if the problem is still not solved, they might decide to call the doctor in case she is getting sick or is in pain.

main idea: _____

_____

time line:

First   _____

Next   _____

© 2014 Wadsworth, Cengage Learning

Then	_____
Next	_____
Finally	_____

L_____

Definitions

definition a pattern of organization that answers the question, "What is it?" or "What does it mean?" using words like *means, refers to, consists of,* and *is*

Definition is a frequently used pattern of organization in college textbooks. It answers the question: "What is it?" or "What does it mean?"

In Sentences A sentence that develops a definition often introduces a term and then explains what it means. For example, the following sentence explains the meaning of *monogamy*. The term is in *italics* to attract our attention to its importance, and the meaning is provided between the dashes.

> *Monogamy*—the marriage of one man to one woman—is the most common form in the world. (Thio, *Sociology*)

Word Clues for Definition The following words indicate a definition will follow.

- means
- refers to
- consists of
- is
- that is
- namely
- in other words

Other Clues for Definition Sometimes definitions are provided in special locations such as

- inside dashes, or
- inside parentheses.

In Paragraphs Sometimes a definition is so complex that it needs a paragraph or more of explanation. For example, in the following excerpt the authors try to define *family*. In fact, the central idea of this excerpt is the definition of the family. Notice that *family* is not an easy word to define, and the authors approach it in several different ways.

> What is a family? In everyday conversation we make assumptions about what families are or should be. Traditionally, both law and social science specified that

© 2014 Wadsworth, Cengage Learning

consist of be made
up of

the family consisted of people related by blood, marriage, or adoption. Some definitions of the family specified a common household, economic interdependence, and sexual and reproductive relations. . . .

constituting forming

Burgess and Locke defined the family as "a group of persons united by the ties of marriage, blood, or adoption; constituting a single household; interacting and communicating with each other in their respective social roles (husband and wife, mother and father, son and daughter, brother and sister); and creating and maintaining a common culture." This definition goes beyond earlier ones to talk about family relationships and interactions. (Lamanna and Riedmann, *Marriages and Families*)

Notice how definition as a pattern of organization can be outlined.

topic: *Definition of the family*

main idea: *A family is defined as people related by blood, marriage, or adoption, although some experts have added additional characteristics to that list.*

Additional characteristics:

    I. *Single household*
   II. *Economic interdependence*
  III. *Sexual and reproductive relations*
  IV. *Communicating with each other in their roles*
   V. *Maintaining a common culture*

Exercise 4

Identify Definitions

Underline the definition of each italicized word. Then complete the maps that follow.

1. A few societies have placed the mother at the head of the family. This type of family is called *matriarchal*. The husband usually goes to live with the wife's family. Women may own the property and pass it on to their daughters. A few tribes today are matriarchies. (Glazer, "Family")

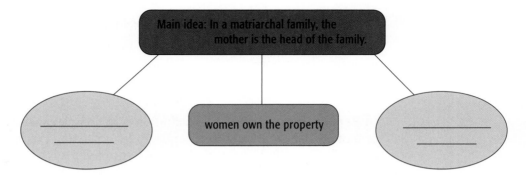

Main idea: In a matriarchal family, the mother is the head of the family.

women own the property

2. There are also norms governing the number of spouses a person may have. *Monogamy*— the marriage of one man to one woman—is the most common form in the world. But many societies, especially small, preindustrial ones, approve of *polygamy*, marriage of one person to two or more people of the opposite sex. It

© 2014 Wadsworth, Cengage Learning

is rare for a society to allow the practice of *polyandry*, marriage of one woman to two or more men. . . . A new variant of polygamy has become increasingly common in the United States. Rather than having several spouses at the same time, many have one spouse at a time, going through a succession of marriage, divorce, and remarriage. Such practice is not really polygamy, but *serial monogamy*, marriage of one person to two or more people but only one at a time. (Thio, *Sociology*)

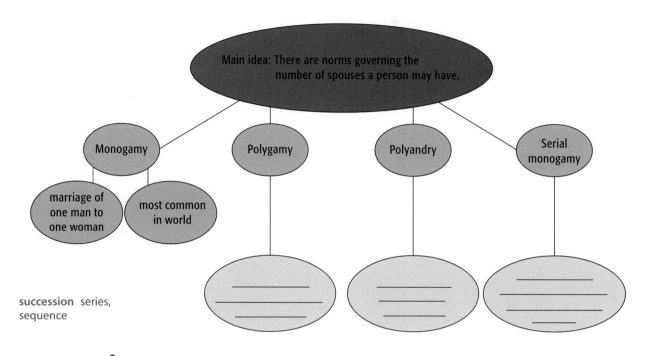

succession series, sequence

© 2014 Wadsworth, Cengage Learning

Exercise 5

Identify Patterns of Organization in Sentences

Decide whether each of the following sentences is organized primarily by examples, by chronological order, or by definition. The first one has been done for you.

1. In the United States and Canada, the term *family* commonly means a group of related persons who share a home. (Glazer, "Family")

   pattern of organization: *definition*

2. The rate of divorce has more than doubled since 1965, peaking in 1979 and dropping slightly since then. (Lamanna and Riedmann, *Marriages and Families*)

   pattern of organization: _____

3. The study of the family does not fit neatly within the boundaries of any single scholarly field: genetics, physiology, archeology, history, anthropology, sociology, psychology, and economics all touch upon it. (Skolnick and Skolnick, *Family in Transition*)

   pattern of organization: _____

4. [Between] 1960 and 1993 the percent of children in one-parent families who were living with a never-married mother grew from 4 percent to 35 percent. (Wolf, *Marriages and Family in a Diverse Society*)

pattern of organization: _____

5. Single-parent families, one-earner nuclear families, two-earner families, and step-families reflect the diversity of American families today.

pattern of organization: _____

6. A society with the women in charge is called *matriarchal* (from words meaning "mother" and "ruler"). (Cavan, "Family")

pattern of organization: _____

Exercise 6

Identify Patterns of Organization in Paragraphs

Decide whether each of the following paragraphs is organized primarily by examples, by chronological order, or by definition. Find the main ideas and write them on the lines provided (they may be stated or unstated). A paragraph may have more than one pattern of organization, so identify the one that is most important for supporting the main idea. The first one has been done for you.

1. Preparing a meal in the nineteenth century was no easy task. Women had to kill and pluck the chickens, remove the scales from fish, roast and grind the coffee, pound sugar, and sift the flour. (adapted from Martin et al., *America and Its Peoples*)

   pattern of organization: <u>Examples</u>

   (This paragraph is chiefly organized to provide examples of the various tasks—such as killing and plucking birds, roasting and grinding coffee, and sifting flour—housewives had to perform 100 years ago.)

   main idea: <u>Housewives had to do a lot of different chores to prepare a</u>

   <u>meal prior to the 1890s.</u>

2. Families have been changing gradually over time, but in much of the world, the changes have followed the same basic steps. When families lived on farms, they were large because people needed children to help them with the work. Mothers spent their time taking care of the household. But in the last few hundred years, people have been moving to urban areas where families have fewer children. Jobs have increasingly become available to women, and fewer women are able to stay at home and pass up the possibility of an added income to help support the family. Today, in most developed countries, the vast majority of women work.

© 2014 Wadsworth, Cengage Learning

pattern of organization: _____

main idea: _____

_____

3. A primary group is a small group marked by close, face-to-face relationships. Group members share experiences, express emotions, and, in the ideal case, know they are accepted and valued. In many ways, teams and families are similar primary groups: joys are celebrated spontaneously, tempers can flare quickly, and expression is often physical. (Lamanna and Riedmann, *Marriages and Families*)

pattern of organization: _____

main idea: _____

_____

4. In American society, life in many families is organized primarily around the *nuclear* family. A nuclear family is made up of parents and their children and spans only two generations. Nuclear families do not include extended family members such as aunts, uncles, and grandparents.

pattern of organization: _____

main idea: _____

_____

5. In a few societies the mother or grandmother has the stronger voice in making decisions. For example, among the Hopi Indians in the Southwestern United States, the women of the family own the land. When a woman marries, her husband moves in with her family or into a house nearby. But the men work the land and also carry out important religious ceremonies. (Cavan, "Family")

pattern of organization: _____

main idea: _____

_____

6. *Cohabitation* refers to two people living together in a sexual relationship without marriage. Two decades ago cohabitation was rare. In 1970 only 11 percent of people who married for the first time had prior experience with cohabitation. Today, almost half of people who enter first marriages have previously cohabited. The U.S. Bureau of the Census estimates that today there are 5 million cohabiting

© 2014 Wadsworth, Cengage Learning

couples in the United States. . . . Of the cohabiting couples, 1.2 million have children under age 15 living with them. (Wolf, *Marriages and Family in a Diverse Society*)

pattern of organization for the first sentence: _____

pattern of organization for the rest of the paragraph: _____

main idea: _____

_____

Language Tip: Transitions

As you have probably already noticed as you learned to identify examples, chronological order, and definitions, certain words provide clues to which pattern of organization is being used. Words like *for example* and *for instance* are signals that the information is organized as supporting examples. Words like *first, then,* and *later* indicate an organization by chronological order. Words like *in other words* and *means* indicate an organization by definitions. These small but important words, called **transitions,** link ideas and show the relationship between ideas. Recognizing common transitions will help you identify patterns of organization.

Watch for the following transitions to help you recognize the introduction of examples.

such as	moreover
for example	also
for instance	another
in addition	

Watch for the following transitions to help you recognize material arranged in chronological order or as steps in a process.

first	before
second	later
next	while
then	once
when	finally
after	last

© 2014 Wadsworth, Cengage Learning

The following transitions help you recognize information organized as a definition.

that is
namely
in other words

Exercise 7   Choose Transitions

Choose the appropriate transitions from the preceding lists to complete the following sentence sets. Answers may vary.

1. *Examples:*

   The average medieval peasant woman had many tasks. ___ _____ she had to care for and raise the children. She _____ had to prepare the limited supply of food for each meal over an open hearth. _____ she did the laundry. _____ keeping her home clean and orderly was difficult because her furniture was limited, and the floor was dirt covered with rushes or straw. The work was never done.

2. *Chronological order:*

   Most medieval European couples married _____ a period of courtship. They may even have had sexual contact before marriage. _____ they had decided to marry, they usually spoke their vows at the door of the village church. _____ the priest pronounced them man and wife. _____ the feast called a "bride ale" began.

3. *Definitions:*

   In family conversations it's important to be forthright as well as sensitive to the feelings of others; _____ you must be honest, but also thoughtful.

Mixed and Paired Patterns of Organization

You have already learned to recognize and analyze examples, chronological order, and definition as patterns of organization. Now you will become familiar with paired, or complex, patterns: (1) comparison and contrast, and (2) cause and effect. These patterns are complex because they pair two different ideas.

© 2014 Wadsworth, Cengage Learning

Don't confuse paired patterns with mixed patterns. Keep in mind that very few passages are organized one way and only one way. In your reading you are likely to find a paragraph that has some dates in it and is organized chronologically, but also provides a definition. Or you may find a paragraph that explains a process but emphasizes the comparisons and contrasts between two processes. Almost everything you read will be a mixed pattern.

A paired pattern, on the other hand, is one with two elements that work together. A paired pattern involves the pairing of two different ideas.

Comparison and Contrast

comparison and contrast
a pattern of organization that answers the question, "How are two things alike or different?"

Comparison and contrast is a common paired pattern of organization. It answers the question: "How are two things alike or different?" To see how this pattern works, read the following excerpt, which compares how families use the television and other media. In the first paragraph you will notice two very different approaches to television use. This paragraph emphasizes the *contrast* between them. The second paragraph emphasizes the *similarities* of entertainment choices that families make.

> In the United States today, families basically have two contrasting attitudes toward television. Many families allow the television to be on at any time of the day or night. Very often, members of these families watch television alone or don't interact with other family members while they are watching. The TV is used to have some kind of background noise in the house, or as a kind of electronic babysitter. Parents often turn it on to entertain "bored" children. In contrast, other families strictly control when the television will be watched and what programs can may be watched. Often these families watch programs together and discuss them together. In these homes, the TV is rarely on if nobody is watching it. Instead of using it as an electronic babysitter, parents insist that children read or play actively rather than sit in front of a screen.

> Regardless of their contrasting attitudes toward television viewing, families in America are choosing television and other passive activities, such as movie viewing, video games, and surfing the Web, with unprecedented regularity. These activities are similar in their inactivity. Family members—young and old—watch rather than do. These passive forms of entertainment dull, rather than encourage, family interaction and community involvement.

unprecedented
unmatched, extraordinary

The main idea of the first paragraph, expressed in the first sentence, clearly sets up the comparison/contrast pattern of organization.

> In the United States today, families basically have two contrasting attitudes toward television.

The phrase "two contrasting attitudes" tells us that the two types of attitudes are different from each other. Then the paragraph goes on to present different behaviors for each attitude toward television. This information can be charted in the following way.

Contrasts of Family Attitudes Toward Television	
Open Television Use	Restricted Television Use
Allow the television to be on at any time of the day or night	Strictly control when the television will be watched and what will be watched
Watch television alone or don't interact with other family members while they are watching	Watch programs together and discuss them
Use the television for background noise	Do not leave the television on if nobody is watching
Use the television as an electronic babysitter	Do not use it as a babysitter, but insist that children read or play actively

The second paragraph introduces other forms of family entertainment—movies, video games, and the Web—describing them as similar. Like television viewing, these activities are passive.

In Sentences Writers can use comparison and contrast in sentences to tell the reader both differences and similarities. For example, a writer might explain the *similarities* in two families' TV habits as follows:

> *Both* families enjoyed spending time together on Sunday afternoons watching football or baseball games on television.

In this sentence *both* indicates that the two families have been compared and that they have something in common—their TV habits.

On the other hand, a writer might explain the *differences* between two families' TV habits.

> My family left the television on all evening, whether anyone was watching or not, *but* I noticed my best friend's family turned the television on only for special programs on PBS or the Discovery Channel.

In this sentence, two different TV habits are presented: the writer's family and her friend's family. The word *but* is a signal that a contrast is coming.

Word Clues for Comparison Watch for clues that can help you recognize comparisons or contrasts in sentences or longer passages. Some are transitions, which are words that link ideas.

Comparisons use the following words and phrases.

- also
- both
- similarly
- alike
- as (the same as, as big as, as small as)

- same
- in comparison
- similar to
- at the same time

© 2014 Wadsworth, Cengage Learning

Word Clues for Contrasts   *Contrasts* use the following words and phrases.

- but
- yet
- although
- while
- instead of
- unlike

- in contrast
- on the other hand
- however
- different from
- than (more than, less than, happier than)

In Paragraphs   In paragraphs, a writer can develop a number of points of comparison or contrast, all supporting one main idea. Consider all of the different kinds of things that are being compared and contrasted in the following paragraph, which describes two types of families—the slave family and the plantation master's family.

> While slave parents who were able to spend time with their children loved them as much as the plantation masters loved their children, the slave family was as different from the master's family as anyone can possibly imagine. Of course, the master's family was well-fed, well-dressed, and lived in a beautiful home. In contrast, the slave families lived on an absolute minimum of food, were often provided one set of clothes for a year, and lived in shacks. The master's children were waited on hand and foot by slave mothers, whose own children had no one to tend to them. The chances were that the master's family was a nuclear family, which lived together until the children grew up and started their own families. In contrast, the slave family could be broken up at any time through the sale of the father, mother, or children.

The main idea of this paragraph appears in the second half of the first sentence:

> . . . the slave family was as different from the master's family as anyone can possibly imagine.

The author does recognize that there is one similarity between the families when she states, "slave parents who were able to spend time with their children loved them as much as the masters loved their children." However, if we look carefully at the rest of the paragraph, we can see that all the supporting details involve ways that these families are *different*. The emphasis, then, is on the *contrast* between the two types of families. These contrasts could be charted in the following way:

Contrasts between Master and Slave Families	
Master Families	Slave Families
Well-fed	Lived on an absolute minimum of food
Well-dressed	Were often provided one set of clothes for a year
Lived in beautiful homes	Lived in shacks
Stayed together	Easily separated by a sale

© 2014 Wadsworth, Cengage Learning

The author continues to give examples of contrasts throughout the rest of the paragraph. When you look closely at this passage, you find the clue words *different from*, *in contrast*, and *while*.

Exercise 8

Understand Comparison and Contrast

The following excerpts all contain comparisons and/or contrasts. Read each one and then answer the questions that follow. The first one has been done for you.

1. We know much more now than we did even a few years ago about how the human brain develops and what children need from their environments to develop character, empathy, and intelligence. (Clinton, *It Takes a Village*)

   List the two things being compared:

   a. *what we know now about the human brain and children's needs*

   compared to

   b. *what we knew a few years ago about these topics*

2. It is less respectable in Hispanic culture for a married woman to work outside the home than in either African-American or non-Hispanic white culture. (Wolf, *Marriages and Families in a Diverse Society*)

   The attitude toward married women working outside the home is being compared in

   a. _____

   to

   b. _____

3. Compared to families with young children, families with adolescents have been neglected. Even for the affluent sector, little work has been done on strengthening support networks for families during the stress of the great transition from childhood to adulthood. Still less attention has gone into strengthening networks for families who live in poverty or culturally different situations. Although adolescents are moving toward independence, they are still intimately bound up with the family, which is much more important to them than is evident. This is especially true in early adolescence. For that reason, we need to pay attention to the ways in which family relationships can be utilized to help adolescents weather the conditions of contemporary life. (Hamburg, "The American Family Transformed")

   This paragraph wants readers to focus on the needs of

   a. families with _____

   rather than

   b. families with _____

   In the middle of the paragraph, the author points out a contrast about adolescents.

   c. adolescents _____

   but

   d. _____

© 2014 Wadsworth, Cengage Learning

Organize to Learn: Make a Circle Diagram

A useful way to check your comprehension after you've read a comparison-and-contrast paragraph or longer passage is to make a circle diagram of the information presented. Follow these simple steps:

1. Determine the main idea.
2. Decide what is being compared or contrasted.
3. Write what is being compared or contrasted above the circles. This will serve as the topic as well as the title of the entire diagram.
4. At the top of each circle put the names of what is being compared or contrasted. If there are similarities between the items, the circles will overlap. The overlapped area could have a heading such as "Similarities" or "Reasons in Common."
5. Determine the points on which the items are being compared.
6. List the differences for each point in the correct circle.
7. List the similarities for both in the section where the circles overlap.

Read the following paragraph about two different attitudes toward having large families.

> People around the world have children for many of the same reasons. Most of us want to live into the future through our children and grandchildren. And babies and children are just plain lovable. According to sociologists, however, it is important to understand that people's reasons for having huge families in poor countries and for having small families in wealthy countries depend largely on the society itself. First, in poor countries, families tend to be larger because being a parent is very important and gives the father and mother status in the community. Second, children are considered a blessing. And finally, children can help the family economically when they are old enough to work and can support their parents when they can no longer take care of themselves. In more wealthy societies, parenthood status is not as important. There is frequently very little support from other family members or community for raising the children. And, finally, it is expensive to raise children. So it is easy to understand why people in certain countries of Europe and North America as well as Japan have fewer children, while people in parts of Asia, Latin America, and Africa do the opposite.

Looking carefully at what is being compared or contrasted, we can identify *family size*, and we can identify the fourth sentence as the main idea:

> It is important to understand that people's reasons for having huge families in poor countries and for having small families in wealthy countries depend largely on the society itself.

Now we are ready to set up the chart with the points of similarities or differences. (In this case, of course, differences are emphasized.)

© 2014 Wadsworth, Cengage Learning

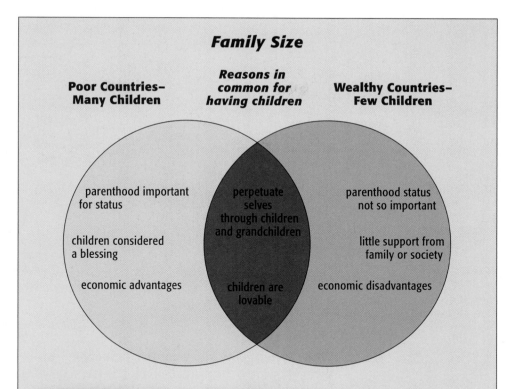

Family Size

**Poor Countries–
Many Children**

*Reasons in
common for
having children*

**Wealthy Countries–
Few Children**

parenthood important
for status

perpetuate
selves
through children
and grandchildren

parenthood status
not so important

children considered
a blessing

little support from
family or society

economic advantages

children are
lovable

economic disadvantages

Exercise 9   Make Circle Diagrams

Read the following three excerpts. The first compares and contrasts some
of the experiences of children in two-parent versus single-parent families.
The emphasis is on single-parent families; the comparison with two-parent
families is sometimes implied rather than directly stated. As you read this excerpt, watch for the different points of comparison so you can complete the
accompanying circle diagram. Then read the other excerpts and complete
the circle diagram provided for them.

1. [There are] . . . positive signs as well as drawbacks in one-parent families.
   One-parent families grant children more autonomy than two-parent families. That is, they allow children to make more decisions and have more control over their lives. This autonomy can have negative consequences when
   a teenager decides to put activities with peers ahead of studying. However,
   one-parent families also require responsibility for household chores from
   children of all ages. Children in one-parent families perform more housework
   than children in two-parent families. It has been suggested that single parents make an unspoken tradeoff in which personal autonomy is granted in
   return for help in running the household. Moreover, children in one-parent
   families tend to be more androgynous than children in two-parent families, in
   that they learn aspects of both traditional male and traditional female roles.
   Boys often learn to cook, and it is not unusual for teenage girls to work on
   Saturdays to earn spending money. These characteristics—household responsibility and androgyny—which one-parent families tend to foster in children,
   can be viewed as positive adaptations to new circumstances. (Wolf, *Marriages
   and Families in a Diverse Society*)

© 2014 Wadsworth, Cengage Learning

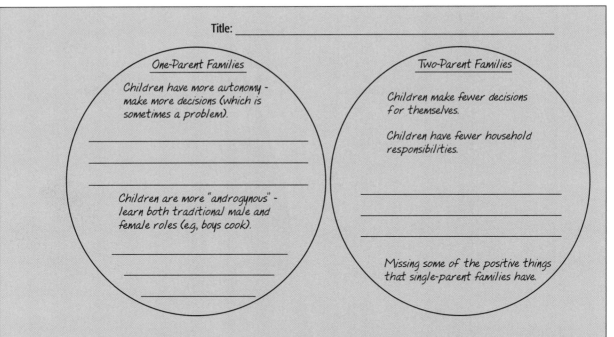

Title: _____

One-Parent Families

Children have more autonomy - make more decisions (which is sometimes a problem).

_____
_____
_____

Children are more "androgynous" - learn both traditional male and female roles (e.g., boys cook).

_____
_____
_____

Two-Parent Families

Children make fewer decisions for themselves.

Children have fewer household responsibilities.

_____
_____
_____

Missing some of the positive things that single-parent families have.

2. While slave parents who were able to spend time with their children loved them as much as the plantation masters loved their children, the slave family was as different from the master's family as anyone can possibly imagine. Of course, the master's family was well fed, well-dressed, and lived in a beautiful home. In contrast, the slave families lived on an absolute minimum of food, were often provided one set of clothes for a year, and lived in shacks. The master's children were waited on hand and foot by slave mothers, whose

Title: _____

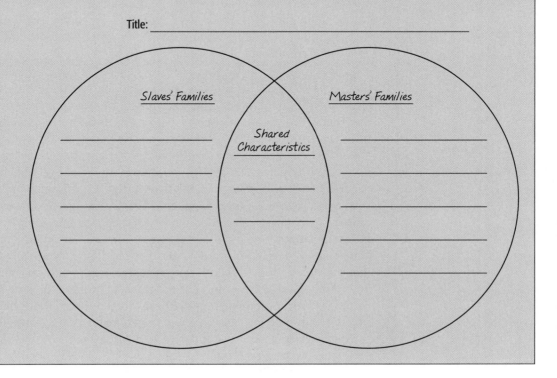

Slaves' Families

_____
_____
_____
_____

Shared Characteristics

_____
_____

Masters' Families

_____
_____
_____

© 2014 Wadsworth, Cengage Learning

own children had no one to tend to them. The chances were that the master's family was a nuclear family, which lived together until the children grew up and started their own families. In contrast, the slave family could be broken up at any time by the sale of the father, mother, or children.

3. In most countries, women prefer to marry older men, and there is a good reason for this. Older men usually have more resources or are richer. American men who are 30 years old earn an average of $14,000 more per year than men who are 20. In some societies, men do not have an important status until they are in their late 20s or early 30s. Men in their late 20s are stronger than younger men, which would have been important to women when men hunted for food. There are, however, some exceptions to the rule of women preferring to marry older men. In some Chinese villages women who are 17 marry boys of 14. In these cases, however, it is already clear that the boys will be wealthy, for they will inherit land and money from their families. These boys already have social status, and their physical strength is not important.

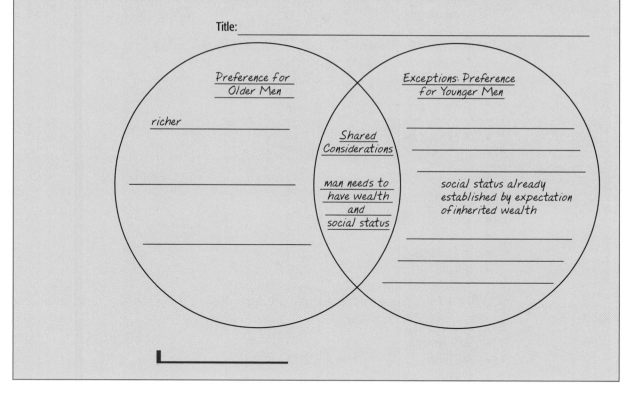

Title: _____

Preference for Older Men

richer
_____
_____
_____

Shared Considerations

man needs to have wealth and social status

Exceptions: Preference for Younger Men

_____
_____
_____

social status already established by expectation of inherited wealth

_____
_____
_____

© 2014 Wadsworth, Cengage Learning

cause and effect
a pattern of organization that answers why something is and explains results

Cause and Effect

The **cause-and-effect** pattern of organization answers two types of related questions. Causes answer *why* something is the way it is, or "What happened to make something the way it is?" Effects usually explain the *results* of some action. They answer the question: "What were the consequences of something that happened?"

In Sentences A single sentence may use either cause or effect or both. For example, a writer might say:

> The high rate of divorce today is caused by a lack of family values.

This writer is trying to explain *why* divorce rates are so high. He might go on to say:

> These high divorce rates have obvious negative effects on young people's attitudes toward marriage.

In this second sentence, the writer is focusing on one of the *results* of divorce. Since cause and effect are such closely related ways of thinking about things, they may be combined in the same sentence or certainly in the same paragraph. For example, both cause and effect appear in the following:

> The high rate of divorce today is caused by a lack of family values, and it has obvious negative effects on the attitudes of young people toward marriage.

Word Clues for Causes Watch for the following word clues that help you recognize cause statements in sentences or longer passages:

- because
- since
- the factors are
- is caused by
- the reason why

Some are verbs:

- contributes to
- leads to
- changes
- influences
- affects

Word Clues for Effects *Effects* are also signaled by word clues. Some are transitions:

- as a result
- therefore
- consequently
- thus
- so
- the effects are
- results

In Paragraphs Longer explanations of causes and effects may take a paragraph or more. Sometimes one effect has many causes, and each needs to be examined in

© 2014 Wadsworth, Cengage Learning

order to understand how a change occurs. All these causes are supporting points for the main idea of a paragraph.

For example, the main idea of a paragraph might be that there is no one reason why a couple decides to divorce; rather, many issues lead to this decision. The rest of the paragraph provides the supporting points, which are the many reasons why people choose to divorce. Also, one cause may have many effects, and each effect needs to be explained. For example, a divorce may have many effects, including money problems for both partners, feelings of anger and sorrow, a need to move, and the emotional responses of children.

In cause-and-effect paragraphs writers may also need to analyze a "chain" of interrelated causes and effects that unfold over time. Sometimes the writer will examine both immediate and underlying causes, or immediate and long-range results.

| Exercise 10 | ## Understand Cause and Effect |

Read the following excerpt on the entry of mothers into the workplace. The author explains why women have made this choice. Then answer the following questions. Clue words have been underlined to assist you.

> Another <u>factor reshaping</u> family life has been a massive influx of mothers into the workforce. As late as 1940, less than 12 percent of white married women were in the workforce; today the figure is nearly 60 percent, and over half of all mothers of preschoolers work outside the home. The major <u>forces</u> that have <u>propelled</u> women into the workforce include a rising cost of living which spurred many families to seek a second source of income; increased control over fertility through contraception and abortion, which <u>allows</u> women to work without interruption; and rising education levels, which <u>lead</u> many women to seek employment for intellectual stimulation and fulfillment. (Martin et al., *America and Its Peoples*)

1. What is the topic of the paragraph? Write it as a title. _____

   _____

2. What are three reasons (causes) why women have entered the workforce in such large numbers?

   a. _____

   b. _____

   c. _____

3. To further explain each of the reasons for women entering the work place, the author gives an effect of each. Fill in the accompanying chart with the causes you listed for question 1 and the effect for each. One cause and its effect have been filled in for you.

© 2014 Wadsworth, Cengage Learning

Cause	Effect
a. Rising cost of living	a. Made it necessary for women to bring a second income into the family
b. _____	b. _____
c. _____	c. _____

4. Read one more cause-and-effect paragraph, and then provide the topic as the title, write or copy the main idea, and fill in the missing cause and missing effect in the chart that follows.

The status of women [in China] has been changed greatly. The marriage law promulgated in 1950 advocates equality of men and women and freedom of marriage; parents no longer arrange marriages. Nurseries, kindergartens, public canteens, and homes for the aged have been widely established, gradually relieving women from family work and enabling them to participate in production. ("China," *Encyclopedia Britannica*)

title: _____

main idea: _____

Cause	Effect
a. _____	a. Marriages are no longer arranged by parents.
b. Nurseries and available care for the aged	b. _____

© 2014 Wadsworth, Cengage Learning

Organize to Learn: Make a Concept Map

As you know, one good way to organize what you have read is to make a map of the information. These maps are sometimes called *concept maps* because they visually show the relationships among all the important ideas, or concepts, in a reading. Maps can be drawn in many sizes and shapes depending on the information being covered. For cause and effect, you probably want to indicate how the two are related. That is, you want the map to clearly show how the cause leads to the effect. This can be done by map layout, making it flow in a certain direction. The direction of flow can be emphasized with the use of arrows.

Exercise 11   Make a Concept Map

The map shown below is based on the first excerpt in Exercise 15. In this case the box on the far right is the result, and the arrows pointing to it are the three major effects of changes on women. On the far left are the causes for the effects that you identified in question 2 of Exercise 15. Complete this concept map using your answers from question 2 of Exercise 15.

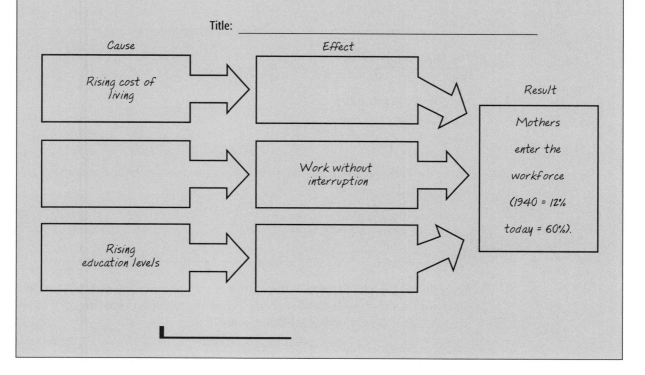

Title: _____

Cause
- Rising cost of living
-
- Rising education levels

Effect
-
- Work without interruption
-

Result
- Mothers enter the workforce (1940 = 12% today = 60%).

© 2014 Wadsworth, Cengage Learning

© 2014 Wadsworth, Cengage Learning

Exercise 12

Identify Patterns of Organization in Sentences

Decide whether each of the following sentences is organized primarily by *comparison and contrast* or by *cause and effect*. Write out the clues that helped you identify the pattern of organization. The first one has been done for you, and an explanation follows.

1. As a result of their parents' inability to preserve their marriages or to marry at all, almost a quarter of U.S. kids live in single-parent households, the majority headed by females. (Black, "Single-Parent Family")

   pattern of organization: <u>*cause and effect*</u>

   clues: <u>"As a result"</u>

   (This sentence is obviously organized by cause and effect because it states that single-parent homes are the result of parents' "inability to preserve their marriages or to marry at all." The phrase "as a result" at the beginning of the sentence gives you a definite clue that an effect will follow.)

2. The rates of college attendance for African-American and Latino men have been decreasing; at the same time, the numbers of white men at tending college are also going down.

   pattern of organization: _____

   clues: _____

3. The fact that so many black men are more likely to serve time in prison has a devastating effect on the black families and communities.

   pattern of organization: _____

   clues: _____

4. Unlike the 1950s, when most college students were men, today the majority of college students are women.

   pattern of organization: _____

   clues: _____

5. According to Dr. Jerry M. Lewis—the author of a significant work on families called *No Single Thread*—healthy spouses complement, rather than dominate, each other. (Curran, "What Good Families Are Doing Right")

   pattern of organization: _____

   clues: _____

6. If every parent spent a few minutes less a day on work-related tasks and instead spent that time with his or her child, children would benefit and families would be stronger.

pattern of organization: _____

clues: _____

Exercise 13

Identify Patterns of Organization in Paragraphs

For each of the following paragraphs, write out the main idea on the line provided. Decide whether each paragraph is organized primarily by *comparison and contrast* or by *cause and effect*. Write the clues that helped you identify the pattern of organization. The first one has been done for you, and an explanation follows.

1. The increase in divorce has contributed to the feminization of poverty, the growing impoverishment of women and their children. Female-headed families represent one-fourth of all families with children, yet they constitute over half (54 percent) of all poor families with children. Divorce often results in sharp downward social mobility for women with children. The poverty rate among single-mother families runs 45 percent, compared to a 6 percent poverty rate for two-parent families and an 18 percent poverty rate for single-father families. (Wolf, *Marriages and Families in a Diverse Society*)

main idea: "The increase in divorce has contributed to the feminization

of poverty, the growing impoverishment of women and their children."

pattern of organization: Cause and effect

clues: "Has contributed to," "results in"

(The primary pattern of organization is cause and effect because the author's main purpose is to look at one result of increased divorce rates: poverty, particularly for women and children. Clues include "contributed to" in the first sentence and "results in" in sentence 3. Most of the rest of the paragraph gives statistics to show just how severe the problem of poverty is for divorced women and their children.)

encounters
comes across

2. The family is the first environment where an individual encounters drug use. Parents who smoke, drink alcohol, or use other drugs will affect the formation and development of their children, even before they are conceived or born. Studies have found that the father's exposure to harmful substances at work, smoking cigarettes, drinking alcohol, and using other drugs, may contribute to low birth

© 2014 Wadsworth, Cengage Learning

fetal
related to a baby
developing during
pregnancy

weight and other malformations in the baby. Young women, especially of low socioeconomic status, who abuse drugs and alcohol tend to be malnourished and lack access to prenatal health care—factors which can contribute to later fetal malformations during pregnancy. Families can also be gravely damaged or destroyed by excessive use of psychoactive substances by family members. The damage can result from the immediate effects of drug use, such as violence associated with intoxication, or from long-term effects, such as economic problems, discord, and breakdown in communication resulting from drug dependence and impaired health. (Hsu, "Drug Use and the Family")

main idea: _____

_____

pattern of organization: _____

clues: _____

kin
relativesrelated to
a baby developing
during pregnancy

3. In American society, life in many families is organized primarily around the *nuclear family*. A nuclear family is made up of parents and their children and spans only two generations. In contrast, traditional societies consider the *extended family* to be of primary importance. The extended family includes those kin who extend outward from the nuclear family, such as grandparents, aunts, and uncles. Extended kin relationships have always been central in immigrant families that are coping with a new environment, but have diminished in importance among white middle-class families. However, today, extended kin relationships are once more growing in importance. . . . One-third of African-American families and one-fourth of white families include other adults in the household. Most often this other adult is a relative. (Wolf, *Marriages and Families in a Diverse Society*)

main idea: _____

_____

pattern of organization: _____

clues: _____

4. Most women in the labor force work primarily because the family needs the money and secondarily for their own personal self-actualization. Because of the decline in real family income, most families find it essential for both parents to work to support them at a level that used to be achieved by one wage-earner, and in many families two earners are required to keep the family out of poverty. Most divorced, single, and widowed mothers must work to avoid poverty. (Scarr, Phillips, and McCartney, "Working Mothers and Their Families")

© 2014 Wadsworth, Cengage Learning

main idea: _____

_____

pattern of organization: _____

clues: _____

Summary Chart: Patterns of Organization

Pattern of Organization	Characteristics	Clues
Examples	Gives instances or examples	Transitions: *such as, for example, for instance, in addition, moreover, also, another* Other clues: Commas and semicolons separate examples; when examples are listed, they are sometimes signaled by numbers, letters, or bullets.
Chronological order and process	Organizes information by time or in a certain order, as in a process	Transitions: *first, second, next, then, when, after, before, later, while, once, finally, last* Other clues: dates (1942, October, etc.), centuries (1400s), decades (1920s), days (Tuesday, Halloween), time (9 A.M., evening)
Definition	Answers the questions: "What is it?" or "What does it mean?"	Word clues: *means, refers to, consists of, is, that is, namely, in other words* Other clues: Sometimes definitions are provided between dashes or in parentheses.
Comparison and contrast	Answers the question: "How are two things alike or different?"	Transitions for comparisons: *also, both, similarly, alike, as, same, in comparison, similar to, at the same time* Transitions for contrasts: *but, yet, although, while, instead of, unlike, in contrast, on the other hand, however, different from, than (more than, less than, happier than)*
Cause and effect	Answers the questions: "What happened to make something the way it is?" and "What were the consequences of something that happened?"	Word clues for causes: *because, since, the factors are, is caused by, reason why, contributes to, leads to, changes, influences, affects* Word clues for effects: *as a result, therefore, consequently, thus, so, the effects are, results*

© 2014 Wadsworth, Cengage Learning

© 2014 Wadsworth, Cengage Learning

Reading 2   How to Meet a Mate

— VIRGINIA MAGGIO

The following reading reviews the ways that people have met life partners in the past and explains how the meeting process is changing in the twenty-first century. As you read, think about your own experiences and those of people you know, considering in what ways they are similar to the people discussed in the reading.

1   Cindy Williams is 25 years old. She has been busy working and going to college part-time since she graduated from high school, seven years ago. She is going to get her teaching credential in a few months, and she already has a full-time job lined up as a bilingual Spanish-English second grade teacher at an elementary school close to her apartment. Cindy is very satisfied with her accomplishments because she has managed to get her degrees without borrowing a lot of money and without help from her parents. There's only one part of her life that she has not attended to, or at least that's how she feels. She does not have a partner, and she is beginning to think about finding someone to share her life with, someone who would be fun, caring, and supportive—someone she might eventually marry and start a family with.

2   Unfortunately, Cindy has not been meeting interesting men lately, but she is not alone. A brief look at the demographics of marriage indicates where part of the problem lies: The marriage age of both men and women has been increasing. Now, the average age of a woman on her wedding day is 25 and for men it's closer to 27. Professional women and men, however, tend to start thinking about marrying and beginning a family much later—well into their 30s—because they are attending college and establishing themselves in their careers before devoting their energies to finding a mate and starting a family. But once men and women are in their late 20s or 30s, it becomes harder to meet the "right" person because the social contacts are not there. These people are no longer in school, they are very involved in their careers, and their social networks tend to weaken over time. Like Cindy, they find it's just hard to meet people.

3   In the past, regardless of social class, marriages were arranged, usually by the couple's parents, based on economic and sometimes on political interests. The clearest examples of this were royal marriages. To guarantee the political and economic strength of the royal family and the court, arrangements were made for the children of kings and queens to marry each other. One of the most famous examples was Catherine of Aragon's marriage to Henry VIII in the early sixteenth century. This conjugal union combined the might of the Spanish empire with the English throne, a fabulous consolidation of power. (After 18 years of marriage, Henry divorced Catherine because she didn't provide him with a male **heir** to the throne.) Among lower classes, matchmaking was very practical as well, if not as celebrated as for royalty. The financial situation of the families was always considered, such as whether the groom's family owned land or livestock that would ensure the bride's standard of living or even enrich it. Other considerations included the need for a woman to assist the groom's mother with domestic chores and the need to have healthy children to help work the fields or to help their parents in their trades.

4   By the twentieth century, the idea of companionship marriage, based on a couple's feelings for one another, was becoming more common. Arranged marriages were

heir
successor, someone to take over a position (such as king)

Virginia Maggio. Written for *Joining a Community of Readers*.

replaced by individuals' meeting, becoming interested, and eventually falling in love and getting married, or more recently just living together. Young people met one another through their friends or families, at college, at religious events, at community events, at gatherings at friends' homes, or even at singles bars. But in the twenty-first century, these venues for meeting people have become less and less useful for singles around the country. Life has become more anonymous, our society has become more mobile, and frequently friends and family are not around. But we are surrounded by messages about dating—"reality dating" on television, advice columns in newspapers, books, and movies—all seeming to tell us how to find the right partner. Now people are looking for new ways to meet a partner: newspaper singles ads, dating services, and, perhaps most important, online dating sites.

5   All of the recent ways to meet people emphasize efficiency. With online services, you first decide what characteristics you want in a partner. Next, you shop around through the computer databases for people who meet these characteristics, and perhaps have a background check done. Once you've found people who meet your requirements, you exchange messages, by phone or e-mail. Then, only after having weeded out the unsuitable candidates, you set up a time and place to meet. In this way, the process is faster, "qualifications" or background information have been verified (depending on the service you're using), and all that's left to do is meet in person to find out if there's any "chemistry." Singles who prefer this method of meeting people say they save time and can actually learn more about a person than they could by meeting at a party.

6   At one time, it was thought that only losers used online dating services. But times are changing, and several million Americans have decided it's a good way to meet someone. In 2003, more than 45 million people visited online dating sites per month, 10 million more than visited those sites during the year before. Subscribers to Web dating sites were already spending some $100 million or more per quarter, and the majority of the subscribers to the leading sites said they were looking for a relationship.[1]

7   A simple Internet search reveals thousands of online dating services. There's a dating service to meet almost any interest. [2] For example, for African Americans there's BlackPlanetLove.com and BlackVoices.com. [3] For older singles who are interested in building new relationships, there is Happilysingle.com. For young, urban subscribers, there are TONY.com (Time Out New York), Nerve.com, and Boston.com. For Jewish singles, there's JDate.com. Some sites, such as Eharmony.com, say they take a "more scientific approach to the matchmaking process" by having subscribers fill out a long questionnaire. [4]

8   Today, singles have their pick of ways to meet a potential partner. They can go the old-fashioned way of going to socials and getting friends to introduce them. Or they can use some of the recent developments like online dating services. People just need to decide what they feel comfortable with. Saying, "I just can't find anybody I like" sounds more like an excuse. After all, there are millions to choose from, and they're just a click away.

Notes

1. Amy Harmon, "Online Dating Sheds Its Stigma as Losers.com," *New York Times*, June 29, 2003.

2. Barbara Dafoe Whitehead, *Why There Are No Good Men Left,* (New York: Broadway Books, 2003).

3. Nikitta A. Foston, "I Met My Husband Online!" *Ebony,* April 2003.

4. Harmon, "Online Dating."

© 2014 Wadsworth, Cengage Learning

Exercise 14

Work with Words

Use context clues, word-part clues, and, if necessary, the dictionary to choose the best definitions of the words that are italicized in the following sentences from Reading 2.

1. A brief look at the *demographics* of marriage indicates where part of the problem lies: The marriage age of both men and women has been increasing. (par. 2)

   demographics
   a. population statistics
   b. difficulties
   c. graphic images

2. One of the most famous examples was Catherine of Aragon's marriage to Henry VIII in the early sixteenth century. This *conjugal union* combined the might of the Spanish empire with the English throne, a fabulous *consolidation* of power. (par. 3)

   conjugal union
   a. union membership
   b. marriage
   c. agreement

3. *consolidation*
   a. loss
   b. strengthening
   c. weakening

4. But in the twenty-first century these *venues* for meeting people have become less and less useful for singles around the country. (par. 4)

   venues
   a. organizations
   b. singles bars
   c. places

5. Life has become more *anonymous*, our society has become more *mobile*, and frequently friends and family are not around. (par. 4)

   anonymous
   a. without a name, impersonal
   b. pleasant
   c. inevitable

6. *mobile*
   a. cell phone
   b. a toy for babies
   c. characterized by moving

Exercise 15

Check Your Understanding

Based on Reading 2, choose the best answers to the following questions.

1. What is the best topic for the reading?
   a. Cindy Williams
   b. women's marriage age
   c. meeting partners

© 2014 Wadsworth, Cengage Learning

2. What is the best central idea statement for the reading?
   a. Cindy Williams's problems are typical.
   b. Women are marrying later in life now.
   c. The rules for meeting partners are changing.

3. What is the best main idea sentence for paragraph 3?
   a. In the past, regardless of social class, marriages were arranged, usually by the couple's parents, based on economic and sometimes political interests.
   b. To guarantee that the political and economic strength of the royal house was maintained, arrangements were made for the children of kings and queens to marry each other.
   c. After 18 years of marriage, Henry divorced Catherine because she didn't provide him with a male heir to the throne.

4. What reasons does the author give for people needing to find new ways to meet a mate?
   a. People are not interested in marrying anymore.
   b. People are waiting longer to get married and are having difficulties meeting a partner.
   c. People are getting divorced, so they find themselves looking for a mate when they are older.

5. What's the best main idea statement for paragraph 7?
   a. A simple Internet search reveals thousands of online dating services.
   b. There's a dating service to meet almost any interest.
   c. For older singles who are interested in building new relationships, there is Happilysingle.com.

Exercise 16

Identify Patterns of Organization

Identify the primary pattern of organization (examples, chronological order or process, definition, comparison and contrast, or cause and effect) for the following paragraphs from Reading 2.

1. Paragraph 2
   a. examples
   b. cause and effect
   c. definition

2. Paragraph 3
   a. cause and effect
   b. definition
   c. comparison and contrast

3. Paragraph 5
   a. cause and effect
   b. Comparison and contrast
   c. process

© 2014 Wadsworth, Cengage Learning

4. Paragraph 7
   a. examples
   b. process
   c. comparison and contrast

Exercise 17

Make Connections and Write

Write short answers to the following questions based on Reading 2, your experience, and your observations. Then, to extend the exercise, discuss your answers with your class group. Working together, prepare a report for your class as a whole or a written summary for your instructor.

1. List the ways you or your friends have met people. Explain how some of those experiences worked.

   _____

   _____

   _____

   _____

2. What do you think is the best way for people in their 20s to meet? Explain your answer.

   _____

   _____

   _____

   _____

3. Have you ever used an online dating service? If yes, describe that experience. If no, would you consider using one? Why or why not?

   _____

   _____

   _____

   _____

© 2014 Wadsworth, Cengage Learning

Reading 3

The Slave Family

— [ADAPTED FROM] ROBERT A. DIVINE, T. H. BREEN,
GEORGE M. FREDRICKSON, AND R. HAL WILLIAMS

TEXT BOOK **The following reading, adapted from an American history textbook,** *America Past and Present,* **explores the African-American family during slavery. It considers the importance of the family structure as a system of support during a period of intense oppression, and describes how the family functioned differently depending on the particular circumstances of their enslavement.**

---

solidarity
standing together
kinship
family ties

1   The African-American church gave slaves a chance to create and control a world of their own. It was a source of resistance to the dehumanizing effects of enslavement. It helped create a sense of community, solidarity, and self-esteem among slaves. The other institution that prevented slavery from becoming completely demoralizing was the African-American family. Slaves had a strong and enduring sense of family and kinship. But the nature of the families or households on particular plantations or farms varied according to local circumstances.

2   On large plantations with relatively stable slave populations, a majority of slave children lived in two-parent households, and many marriages lasted for as long as 20 to 30 years. They were more often broken up by the death or sale of one of the partners than by voluntary separation. Here mothers, fathers, and children were closely bonded, and parents shared child-rearing responsibilities (within the limits allowed by the masters). Some masters encouraged their slaves to be faithful to their marriage partners because they believed that stable unions produced more children, thus increasing their slave force.

3   But in areas where most slaves lived on farms or small plantations, and in areas of the upper South where the trading and hiring out of slaves was frequent, a different pattern seems to have prevailed. Under these circumstances, slaves frequently had spouses who lived on other plantations or farms some distance away. When they lived separately, the ties between husbands and wives were looser and more fragile.

norm
expected pattern
of behavior

4   Since husbands and wives lived far from one another, female-headed families became the norm, and responsibility for child-rearing was given to the mothers, assisted in most cases by female relatives and friends. Mother-centered families with weak conjugal ties were a natural response to the infrequent presence of fathers and the possibility of their being moved or sold beyond visiting distance. Where the breakup of marriages by sale or relocation could be expected at any time, it did not pay to put all of one's emotions in the marriage relationship.

5   Whether the basic family form was nuclear (mother, father, and children) or matrifocal (female-headed), the ties that it created were precious to its members. Masters acquired a great deal of control over their slaves by threatening to break up the family through sale.

6   The terrible anguish that usually accompanied the breakup of families through sale showed the depth of kinship feelings. Masters knew that the first place to look for a fugitive was in the neighborhood of a family member who had been sold away. After emancipation, thousands of freed slaves wandered about looking for spouses, children, or parents from whom they had been forcibly separated years before. The famous

Divine, Robert A.; Breen, T. H.; Fredrickson, George M.; Williams, R. Hal, *America past and present,* 6e, ©2002. Printed and Electronically reproduced by permission of Pearson Education, Inc., Upper Saddle River, New Jersey.

© 2014 Wadsworth, Cengage Learning

spiritual "Sometimes I Feel Like a Motherless Child" was far more than an expression of religious belief. It also reflected the tragedies of many slaves who lost family members, never found them again, and never learned what happened to them.

7   Kinship ties were not limited to blood relations. When families were broken up by sale, individual members who found themselves on plantations far from home were likely to be "adopted" into new kinship networks. Orphans or children without parents were quickly accepted and cared for in new families.

8   Kinship provided a model for personal relationships and the basis for a sense of community. All the slaves on a plantation were, in one sense, members of a single extended family, as their forms of address clearly show. Elderly slaves were addressed by everyone else as "uncle" and "aunty," and younger unrelated slaves commonly called each other "brother" or "sister." Slave culture was a family culture, and this was one of its greatest sources of strength and cohesion. The kinship ties meant slaves could depend on one another in times of trouble. The kinship network also provided a vehicle for the transmission of African-American folk traditions from one generation to the next. Together with slave religion, kinship gave African-Americans some sense that they were members of a community, not just a collection of individuals victimized by oppression.

9   Uncertain as it may have been, the family and kinship structure as well as the religion of the North American slaves made survival possible and helped develop an African-American identity that would be a source of strength in future struggles. Although slave culture did not normally lead to violent resistance to the slaveholders' regime, the inner world that slaves made for themselves gave them the spiritual strength to defeat the masters' efforts to take over their hearts and minds. After emancipation, this cultural heritage would combine with the tradition of open protest created by rebellious slaves and free black abolitionists to inspire new struggles for equality.

cohesion
act of sticking together

Exercise 18

Work with Words

Use context clues, word-part clues, and, if necessary, the dictionary to choose the best definitions of the words that are italicized in the following sentences from Reading 3.

1. It was a source of resistance to the *dehumanizing* effects of enslavement. (par. 1)

   dehumanizing _____

2. Slaves had a strong and *enduring* sense of family and kinship. (par. 1)

   enduring _____

3. But in areas where most slaves lived on farms or small plantations, and in areas of the upper South where the trading and hiring out of slaves was frequent, a different pattern seems to have *prevailed*. (par. 3)

   prevailed _____

4. Mother-centered families with weak *conjugal* ties were a natural response to the *infrequent* presence of fathers and the possibility of their being moved or sold beyond visiting distance. (par. 4)

   conjugal _____

© 2014 Wadsworth, Cengage Learning

5. *infrequent* _____

6. Whether the basic family form was nuclear (mother, father, and children) or *matrifocal* (female-headed), the ties that it created were precious to its members. (par. 5)

   matrifocal _____

7. After *emancipation*, thousands of freed slaves wandered about looking for spouses, children, or parents from whom they had been forcibly separated years before. (par. 6)

   emancipation _____

8. All the slaves on a plantation were, in one sense, members of a single extended family, as their *forms of address* clearly show. Elderly slaves were addressed by everyone else as "uncle" and "aunty," and younger unrelated slaves commonly called each other "brother" or "sister." (par. 8)

   forms of address _____

   _____

9. The kinship network also provided a *vehicle for the transmission* of African-American folk traditions from one generation to the next. (par. 8)

   vehicle for the transmission _____

10. Together with slave religion, kinship gave African-Americans some sense that they were members of a community, not just a collection of individuals *victimized* by oppression. (par. 8)

    victimized _____

Exercise 19

Check Your Understanding

Choose the best way to complete the following statements about Reading 3.

1. Why were marriages weaker when slaves lived on farms or small plantations?
   a. The husbands and wives didn't love each other as much.
   b. There was no one to raise the children.
   c. Members of families often lived far from each other and the sale or relocation of family members could happen at any time.

2. When the author states, "all the slaves on a plantation were, in one sense, members of a single extended family," he is referring to
   a. the marriages of slaves to one another on the same plantation.
   b. the acceptance of everyone in the community as family, whether or not they were related through blood.
   c. the African tradition of ancestor worship.

© 2014 Wadsworth, Cengage Learning

3. What is the best topic for paragraph 2?
   a. causes for slave families to break up
   b. slave families on large plantations
   c. child-rearing responsibilities among slaves

4. What is the best main idea statement for paragraph 2?
   a. Families were more often broken up by the death or sale of one of the partners than by voluntary separation.
   b. Mothers, fathers, and children were closely bonded, and parents shared child-rearing responsibilities.
   c. On large plantations with relatively stable slave populations, a majority of slave children lived in two-parent households, and marriages lasted as long as 20 or 30 years.

5. What is the best topic for the reading?
   a. stable slave families
   b. variety and importance of slave families
   c. religion and family of U.S. slaves

6. What is the best central idea statement for the reading?
   a. Family and kinship ties, although frequently threatened, helped slaves survive the effects of enslavement.
   b. On large plantations with relatively stable slave populations, a majority of slave children lived in two-parent households.
   c. The African-American church was a source of resistance to the dehumanizing effects of slavery.

Exercise 20   **Identify Patterns of Organization**

Identify the pattern(s) of organization for the following paragraphs.

1. Paragraph 2
   a. examples
   b. chronological order
   c. comparison and contrast

2. Paragraphs 2 and 3 together
   a. chronological order
   b. comparison and contrast
   c. definition

3. Paragraph 8
   a. process and comparison and contrast
   b. examples and cause and effect
   c. chronological order and definition

4. What are the primary patterns of organization for the whole reading?
   a. cause and effect and comparison and contrast
   b. chronological order and definition
   c. cause and effect and chronological order

© 2014 Wadsworth, Cengage Learning

Exercise 21

Make Connections and Write

Write short answers to the following questions based on Reading 3, your experience, and your observations.

1. What were the reasons slave families were broken up during slavery?

   _____

   _____

   _____

   _____

2. How do you think the uncertainties of slavery affected interactions within families? Explain your answer.

   _____

   _____

   _____

   _____

3. What are some of the reasons that families get broken up today? Consider how problems beyond families' control affect the ways that families function.

   _____

   _____

   _____

   _____

Exercise 22

Make a Chart, Circle Diagram, or Outline

Use a separate sheet of paper to respond to the following items.

1. Design a circle diagram or chart to compare and contrast slave families on large, stable plantations, and those on farms and smaller plantations.

2. Design an outline of the entire reading. Remember, you may not need to include the information from every paragraph in your outline.

© 2014 Wadsworth, Cengage Learning

Chapter Review

To aid your review of the reading skills in Chapter 7, study the Put It Together Chart.

Put It Together: Patterns of Organization

Skills and Concepts	Explanation
Patterns of organization (see pages 310 and 339)	Patterns of organization are the ways details are arranged to support main ideas.
Examples (see pages 310–312)	Examples as a pattern of organization give one or more instances and are introduced with phrases like *for example* and *for instance*. Sometimes examples are enumerated—listed with numbers or with bullets.
Chronological order and process (see pages 313–315)	Chronological order organizes information in time order and uses words like *then, when, after, before,* and *later*, as well as dates and times (Monday, March 1950, 1975, etc.). Process is a series of steps that must be done in a certain order to get the desired result and uses words like *first, second,* and *finally*.
Definition (see pages 317–318)	Definition as a pattern of organization organizes information to answer the question, "What is it?" and uses words like *means, refers to,* and is.
Comparison and contrast (see pages 324–326)	Comparison and contrast answers the question: "How are two things alike or different?" They are introduced by words like *similarly* and however.
Cause and effect (see pages 331–335)	Cause and effect answers the questions: "Why is something the way it is?" and "What were the results or consequences of something that happened?" Causes are introduced with phrases like *the reason why,* and effects follow words like *as a result*.
Transitions (see pages 322-323)	Transitions are words that link ideas or show the relationship between ideas.
Time lines (see page 314–315)	Time lines are study aids that visually organize information in chronological order or as steps in a process.
Circle diagrams (see pages 328)	Circle diagrams organize comparisons and contrasts. They can consist of two separate circles, which would emphasize the contrasts, or of overlapping circles, which would illustrate similarities in the overlapping section and differences in the parts of the circles that don't overlap.
Concept maps (see page 335)	Concept maps visually show the relationships among the important ideas, or concepts, in a reading, often using arrows.

To reinforce your thinking before taking the Mastery Tests, complete as many of the following activities as your instructor assigns.

© 2014 Wadsworth, Cengage Learning

Review Skills

List the clues that signal each of the following patterns of organization:

1. Examples: _____

2. Chronological order or process: _____

3. Definition: _____

4. Comparison and contrast: _____

5. Cause and effect: _____

Write

1. Write about your family history in a paragraph or short essay that you organize by chronological order.

2. Write a cause-and-effect paragraph or a short essay explaining what you think makes a family successful.

COLLABORATE

1. Share your family history with your class group. Create a time line for each family that members of your group describe. Indicate where your families were in the same years. Discuss the results. Working together, prepare a summary of family history findings to submit to your instructor.

2. Share your writing on the characteristics of a successful family with your group, and discuss your ideas. Then put your ideas together to list the characteristics of a successful family and the characteristics of an unsuccessful family. Are there any overlaps? You can illustrate your information as two separate lists or set it up as a circle diagram. Share comparisons with your class group. Design a circle diagram or compile your lists all together.

EXTEND YOUR THINKING

1. Find an article about families in a newspaper or magazine. Read it carefully. Write out the central idea, the most important pattern of organization, and the clues you used to identify it. Then map, outline, or make a time line or circle diagram of your article. Bring the article and your paper to class to share with your class group or to turn in to your instructor.

2. Interview the oldest person you know (a grandparent, great-grandparent, neighbor, etc.). Ask that person what life was like in his or her family when he or she was young. You might ask things like: (a) Where did you live, in

© 2014 Wadsworth, Cengage Learning

the city or in the countryside? (b) Who were the members of a typical family household? (c) Who did what kinds of work in and outside of the home? (d) What were the roles of men and women in raising the children? (e) How did someone meet the person he or she would marry? (f) What was life like for people who didn't marry?

Write a paragraph or short essay in which you summarize what you learned about family life in the past. You may choose to organize part or all of your essay as chronological order (or process), cause and effect, or comparison and contrast as your pattern of organization.

 ## WORK THE WEB

Genealogy is the study of family and the identification of ancestors. The Internet can be a useful tool in finding information about your ancestors, but it is always advisable to carefully evaluate the Internet sites that you are using. It is a good idea to check if the site is mainly trying to sell you something expensive, if it is infrequently updated, or if many of the links are "broken."

Use a search engine such as Google to find "World-Wide Genealogy Resources". Open the link for "World Genealogy Free Genealogy Resources." This page lists many resources for research.

1. Scroll down and look at the page closely. How is the information on this page organized? Be specific.

   _____

   _____

   _____

   _____

2. You'll notice that some countries have many links and some have very few or might not be listed at all. Why do you think that is?

   _____

   _____

   _____

   _____

© 2014 Wadsworth, Cengage Learning

3. Click on a few places your ancestors came from or that interest you for any reason. What information did you find? If there were problems with the links, describe what you found.

_____

_____

_____

_____

_____

4. Some Americans don't know where their ancestors come from. What are some possible reasons for the lack of this information?

_____

_____

_____

_____

_____

© 2014 Wadsworth, Cengage Learning

The Choices My Family Makes

—Fatima Khan

The following reading by a young Pakistani-American woman explains some of the family and religious life choices she has made for herself. As you read, think about the impact immigrating to a new country has on family life and the kinds of choices it forces the younger members of the family to make as they grow up. Consider how the author uses patterns of organization to support her ideas.

1 My family is from the Punjab region of Pakistan, but I have grown up in the United States. If you know anything about our customs in Pakistan and the customs in the United States, you will understand that there are lots of <u>conflicting</u> pressures on me every day: My strict Muslim parents want me to follow their rules; my friends at school have completely different "rules." Because I have participated in both cultures, I can see life from both sides. After much thought, I have decided to follow in my sisters' footsteps and <u>observe</u> my parents' traditional expectations. I believe that observing my family's traditional customs is better for me than adopting and following the customs of the United States. And, what that actually <u>entails</u> will probably surprise you.

2 First, I have decided to wear a scarf on my head at all times and always to be very modest in my dress. I wear Pakistani clothes for women, which are long tops, kind of a cross between a blouse and a dress, over a special kind of pants. My friends at school think I'm rather foolish to dress this way. They, on the other hand, wear all kinds of things that my family thinks are outrageous. They show their bellies because they have low-waisted pants. They show their breasts because they wear low-cut blouses. It seems as if there is very little of their bodies that they don't show. My parents think only bad girls or girls headed in a bad direction would dress this way because my family is so <u>prudish</u> about the human body. This opinion fits in with their <u>puritanical</u> views in general. I don't agree with my family about everything, though. I don't judge people or my friends by the way they dress. I am close to my friends and I know they are good people. They are thoughtful, funny, helpful, and smart. Because I respect my friends and their culture, I expect them to <u>reciprocate</u> by respecting me, my religion, and my choices about my own lifestyle.

3 Once I am a certain age, I will not go to parties or do anything with any men other than my father or my husband. Rather, I will go to parties with women only. Muslim women's parties are actually more fun as far as I'm concerned than American parties. We dress up for our parties for one another and because we want to, not because we want to impress the men who are there. And we have so much fun. It's our time to just cut loose, laugh, be silly, and play. At the last party I went to there was a foosball table, and you should have heard all of us fancy ladies with high heels and all kinds of jewelry—teams of three on each side of the table—howling about the game: "Hit it! Hit it!" "Oh, man. We are soooo bad." "Move over. Let me play." "Hah!!! I got it. I got a goal!" (My brother was upset because he heard us howling with laughter from way down the street, but he couldn't join us.) I think our parties are fun because we're not thinking about men. Men don't <u>dominate </u>the conversation. Men don't decide what we're going to do next. Men don't decide what we're going to eat.

4 In my experience, in parties with both sexes, there's a completely different atmosphere. In mixed parties, we worry about how the men see us. We often sit silently

Fatima Khan. Written for *Joining a Community of Readers*.

© 2014 Wadsworth, Cengage Learning

while the men are showing off how much they know about some boring topic. We say or do things to please the men, and sometimes the women end up in another room—or more likely the kitchen—talking to one another by ourselves anyway.

5   Finally, I have decided to have an arranged marriage. When I tell my friends about that, they are really amazed. I have seen lots of examples of very successful arranged marriages. My older sister Najat married the husband my parents picked for her, and she has been married for 15 years. Her husband respects her and they are very much in love. Then, there's my other sister, Sofía. The husband my parents picked for her is a very nice guy and now they have three children and are as happy as they can be. Probably the best example for me of a successful arranged marriage is that of my parents. They've been married for 35 years. During that time they have suffered many hardships, and they left Pakistan to live in America, but they have become strong together, and they raised five daughters and three sons. Now, they have eight grandchildren. Our whole family is very close.

6   When people in my culture arrange a marriage, everything takes place in a certain way and in a certain order. First, the boy's parents send a note to the girl's parents saying they would like the daughter to marry their son. Then the girl's parents write a note back saying, essentially, "We'll give you an answer in a certain amount of time." After that, the girl's parents ask their daughter if she wants to get married to this person. If she says "yes," they send a cake and note back saying, essentially, "Yes. It's okay for us." Then, the relationship starts. So on holidays the families send food to one another. The couple doesn't go out with each other, but with whole groups of friends. They usually don't even talk to each other. Sometimes, the engaged couple waits for a few years, but sometimes it's all done in two weeks. Some girls can be engaged as early as the age of 10. (Sometimes the engagement breaks.) As the final step in the process, the families set the wedding date. The girl's parents pay for the furniture and clothes. The boy's parents buy the house and pay for the wedding.

7   For people who live in the United States, all of this can be different. Most Pakistani-Americans marry people they know who live here, but some, like me and my sisters, worry so much about having to change our habits that we choose to find a husband back in Pakistan. People back home who know us call my parents all the time to find out if they can marry one of my sisters or me. It's great because we get to take our pick. We have all chosen not to take big chances on our husbands. We want to marry people we know, so most of us are marrying cousins from back home. This idea surprises most Americans, and they think of it as some terrible kind of <u>incest</u>, but the practice of marrying cousins is extremely common worldwide. When we marry a cousin, we know that he practices our religion the same way we do, and we know he likes Pakistani food and for us to dress in Pakistani clothes. Another advantage of marrying a cousin is leverage. Since they are in our family, we know that the family will be able to pressure them to be good to us. We worry about these things because we know some girls who have married men who later beat them up and abused them. It's easy for us to find a good man from Pakistan because so many men over there dream of coming to the United States to live where life is better.

8   Most of my Pakistani-American friends are <u>becoming</u> more <u>acculturated to</u> life in the United States. They like to do things the way Americans do. They like to shop in the malls, socialize with boys or men, and eat American food. I respect their choices. I also hope for the same things as most American women. I want to get a good college education and a good job. I love America and the freedom I have here, but I also choose to stay within my family's customs and traditional culture.

leverage
influence, power

© 2014 Wadsworth, Cengage Learning

Based on context clues, word-part clues, and, if necessary, the dictionary, choose the best definition for each of the italicized words in the following sentences from the reading.

1. If you know anything about our customs in Pakistan and the customs in the United States, you will understand that there are lots of *conflicting* pressures on me every day: My strict Muslim parents want me to follow their rules; my friends at school have completely different "rules." (par. 1)

   conflicting
   a. different and opposite
   b. similar
   c. difficult

2. After much thought, I have decided to follow in my sisters' footsteps and *observe* my parents' traditional expectations. (par. 1)

   observe
   a. contradict
   b. watch
   c. follow

3. I believe that observing my family's traditional customs is better for me than adopting and following the customs of the United States. And, what that actually *entails* will probably surprise you. (par. 1)

   entails
   a. restricts, forbids
   b. limits
   c. means, involves

4. My parents think only bad girls or girls headed in a bad direction would dress this way because my family is so *prudish* about the human body. (par. 2)

   prudish
   a. excessively modest
   b. flamboyant
   c. disapproving

5. This opinion fits in with their *puritanical* views in general. (par. 2)

   puritanical
   a. permissive
   b. extremely strict in religious views
   c. extremely harsh

6. Because I respect my friends and their culture, I expect them to *reciprocate* by respecting me, my culture, and my choices about my own lifestyle. (par. 2)

   reciprocate
   a. return the feeling
   b. deny the feeling
   c. reject the feeling

© 2014 Wadsworth, Cengage Learning

7. Men don't *dominate* the conversation. (par. 3)

   dominate
   a. listen to
   b. share
   c. control

8. This idea surprises most Americans, and they think of it as some terrible kind of *incest* , but the practice of marrying cousins is extremely common worldwide. (par. 7)

   incest
   a. the practice of marrying someone from another town
   b. the practice of marrying someone from the same family
   c. the practice of marrying outside of one's immediate circle of friends

9. Most of my Pakistani-American friends are becoming more *acculturated to* life in the United States. (par. 8)

   becoming acculturated to
   a. beginning to practice a new culture
   b. beginning to practice a combination of cultures
   c. continuing to practice the old culture while living in a different place

Choose the best answer to the following multiple-choice questions.

10. Choose the best topic for the reading.
    a. Learning to become an American
    b. Preserving customs while living in a new country
    c. Striving to fit in

11. Choose the best central idea sentence for this reading.
    a. If you know anything about our customs in Pakistan and the customs in the United States, you will understand that there are lots of conflicting pressures on me every day: My strict Muslim parents want me to follow their rules; my friends at school have completely different "rules."
    b. Most of my Pakistani-American friends are becoming more acculturated to life in the United States.
    c. I believe that observing my family's traditional customs is better for me than adopting and following the customs of the United States.

12. The primary pattern of organization for paragraph 5 is
    a. examples.
    b. chronological order.
    c. comparison and contrast.

13. Choose the best topic for paragraph 5.
    a. Arranged marriages
    b. My sisters' marriages
    c. Pakistani customs

14. Choose the best main idea sentence for paragraph 5.
    a. I have seen lots of examples of very successful arranged marriages.
    b. Our whole family is very close.
    c. I have decided to have an arranged marriage.

© 2014 Wadsworth, Cengage Learning

15. What is the primary pattern of organization for paragraph 6?
    a. Cause and effect
    b. Chronological (or process) order
    c. Definition

16. Choose the best topic for paragraph 6.
    a. The order of events in arranging a marriage
    b. A Pakistani-style wedding
    c. Setting the wedding date

17. Choose the best main idea sentence for paragraph 6.
    a. First, the boy's parents send a note to the girl's parents saying they would like the daughter to marry their son.
    b. When people in my culture arrange a marriage, everything takes place in a certain way and in a certain order.
    c. The couple doesn't go out with each other, but with whole groups of friends.

Write short answers to the following questions based on your reading, your experience, and your observation.

List Khan's reasons for retaining the religious customs of her family.

_____

_____

_____

_____

19. What does Khan disagree with her family about?

_____

_____

_____

_____

20. What choices do you think immigrant families have to make or should make when they come to live in the United States? Explain your answer.

_____

_____

_____

_____

© 2014 Wadsworth, Cengage Learning

Name _____ Date _____

Marriage, Childbirth, and Child-Rearing

—[Adapted from] James M. Henslin

TEXT BOOK The following reading, adapted from a sociology textbook, describes the patterns that we follow when we make choices about whom to marry, when to have children, and how to raise those children. As you read, think about how "love" as well as the life choices we make are influenced by circumstances.

MARRIAGE

is preceded by
follows, comes after

socially channeled
influenced by age, education, social class, and race ethnicity

1   In the <u>typical</u> case, marriage in the United States is preceded by "love," but <u>contrary to</u> folklore, whatever love is, it certainly is not blind. That is, love does not hit people willy-nilly, as if Cupid had shot darts blindly into a crowd. If it did, marital patterns would be unpredictable. An examination of who marries whom reveals that love is socially channeled.

THE SOCIAL CHANNELS OF LOVE AND MARRIAGE

2   When we marry, we generally think that we have freely chosen our spouse. With few exceptions, however, our choices follow highly predictable social channels relating to age, education, social class, and race-ethnicity. For example, a Latina with a college degree whose parents are both physicians is likely to fall in love with and marry a Latino slightly older than herself who has graduated from college. Similarly, a girl who drops out of high school is likely to fall in love with and marry a man who has done the same.

3   Sociologists use the term _homogamy_ to refer to the tendency of people who have similar characteristics to marry one another. Homogamy occurs largely as a result of _propinquity_, or spatial nearness. That is, we tend to "fall in love" with and marry people who live near us or whom we meet at school, church, or work. The people with whom we associate are far from a random sample of the population, for social filters produce neighborhoods and schools (as well as churches, temples, and mosques) that follow racial-ethnic and social class lines.

4   As with all social patterns, there are exceptions. Although 94 percent of Americans who marry choose someone of their same racial-ethnic background, 6 percent do not. Because there are 60 million married couples in the United States, those 6 percent add up, totaling three and a half million couples.

5   One of the more dramatic changes in U.S. marriage is a sharp increase in <u>interracial</u> marriages. We can trace this change back to the radical changes during the 1960s. Among the many changes <u>ushered in</u> during this period was the breaking of the "color line" in courtship.

CHILDBIRTH

6   Education and income are important in determining how many children women have. Women who graduate from college, for example, are less likely to give birth than those who don't go to college. Even women who drop out of college have fewer children than women who have never taken a college course. It is similar with income. In general, the higher a woman's family income, the fewer children she has.[1]

7   What happens when the baby arrives? The popular image is that it makes a couple deliriously happy. The facts are somewhat different.

© 2014 Wadsworth, Cengage Learning

Henslin, _Sociology: Down To Earth Approach_, 7e © 2005. Reproduced by permission of Pearson Education, Inc.

MARITAL SATISFACTION

8   Sociologists have found that after the birth of a child conflict usually increases while marital satisfaction decreases.[2] To understand why, you need to remember that a <u>dyad</u> (just two persons) provides greater intimacy than a <u>triad</u> (after adding a third person, interaction must be shared). In addition, the birth of a child unbalances the roles that the couple has worked out.[3] Think about the implications for marriage of coping with a fragile newborn's 24-hour-a-day needs of being fed, soothed, and diapered—while having less sleep and more expenses.

SOCIAL CLASS

9   Sociologist Lillian Rubin compared 50 working-class couples with 25 middle-class couples. [4] She found that social class made a significant difference in how couples adjust to the arrival of children. For the average working-class couple, the first baby arrived just nine months after marriage. They hardly had time to adjust to being husband and wife before they were thrust into the demanding roles of mother and father. The result was financial problems, bickering, and interference from in-laws. The young husbands weren't ready to "settle down," and they resented getting less attention from their wives. A working-class husband who became a father just five months after getting married made this telling remark to Rubin: "There I was, just a kid myself, and I finally had someone to take care of me. Then suddenly, I had to take care of a kid, and she was too busy with him to take care of me."

10   In contrast, the middle-class couples postponed the birth of their first child, giving them more time to adjust to each other. On average, their first baby arrived three years after marriage. Their greater financial resources also worked in their favor, making life a lot easier and marriage more pleasant.

CHILD-REARING

11   Who's minding the kids while the parents are at work? A generation ago such a question would have been ridiculous, for the mother was at home taking care of the children. However, that assumption <u>no longer holds</u>. With three of five U.S. mothers working for wages, who is taking care of the children?

MARRIED COUPLES AND SINGLE MOTHERS

12   Overall the child-care arrangements for married couples and single mothers are similar. For each group, about one of three preschoolers is cared for in the child's home. The main difference is the role of the child's father while the mother is at work. For married couples, almost one in four children is cared for by the father, while for single mothers this figure drops to only one in fourteen. Often grandparents step in to fill the gap left by the absent fathers.

DAY CARE

13   About one in six children is in day care. Apparently only a minority of U.S. day care centers offers high-quality care as measured by stimulating learning activities, safety, and emotional warmth. A primary reason for this dismal situation is the low salaries paid to day care workers, who earn an average of only $12,000 a year. [5]

© 2014 Wadsworth, Cengage Learning

SOCIAL CLASS

socialize
train

conformity
following the
norms, behaving
as expected

14   Social class makes a huge difference in child-rearing. Sociologist Melvin Kohn found that parents socialize their children into the <u>norms</u> of their work worlds. [6] Because members of the working class are closely supervised and are expected to follow explicit rules, their concern is less with their children's motivation and more with their outward conformity. Thus they are more apt to use physical punishment. In contrast, middle-class parents, who are expected to take more initiative on the job, are more concerned that their children develop curiosity, self-expression, and self-control. In disciplining their children, they are more likely to withdraw privileges or affection than they are to use physical punishment.

15   Social class also makes a difference in how parents view child development. [7] Lower-class parents think of children as developing naturally, while middle-class parents think that children need a lot of guidance if they are to develop correctly. Consequently, lower-class parents set limits on their children and then let them choose their own activities, while middle-class parents try to involve their children in leisure activities that develop their thinking and social skills.

Notes

1. *Statistical Abstract of the United States,* 2002 (Washington, D.C.: U.S. Bureau of the Census, 2002), table 82.

2. Martin King Whyte, "Choosing Mates—The American Way," *Society,* March–April 1992, 71–77; Chloe E. Bird, "Gender Differences in the Social and Economic Burdens of Parenting and Psychological Distress," *Journal of Marriage and the Family* 59 (August 1997): 1–16; Stacy J. Roberts and Paul R. Amato, "Have Changes in Gender Relations Affected Marital Quality?" *Social Forces* 79 (December 2000): 731–48.

3. Donna G. Knauth, "Predictors of Parental Sense of Competence for the Couple during the Transition to Parenthood," *Research in Nursing and Health* 23 (2000): 496–509.

4. Lillian Breslow Rubin, "Worlds of Pain," in *Marriage and Family in a Changing Society,* ed. James M. Henslin, 4th ed. (New York: Free Press, 1992), 44–50.

5. *Statistical Abstract of the United States,* 2002, tables 546, 547.

6. Melvin L. Kohn, Kazimierz M. Slomczynski, and Carrie Schoenbach, "Social Stratification and the Transmission of Values in the Family: A Cross-National Assessment," *Sociological Forum* 1 (1986): 73–102.

7. Annette Lareau, "Invisible Inequality: Social Class and Child-Rearing in Black Families and White Families," *American Sociological Review* 67 (October 2002): 747–76.

Based on context clues, word-part clues, and, if necessary, the dictionary, write the meaning of each of the italicized words in the following sentences from the reading.

1. In the *typical* case, marriage in the United States is preceded by "love," but *contrary to* folklore, whatever love is, it certainly is not blind. (par. 1)

   typical _____

2. *contrary to* _____

© 2014 Wadsworth, Cengage Learning

3. Sociologists use the term *homogamy* to refer to the tendency of people who have similar characteristics to marry one another. (par. 3)

   homogamy _____

   _____

4. Homogamy occurs largely as a result of *propinquity,* or spatial nearness. That is, we tend to "fall in love" with and marry people who live near us or who we meet at school, church, or work. (par. 3)

   propinquity _____

   _____

5. One of the more dramatic changes in U.S. marriage is a sharp in crease in *interracial* marriages. (par. 5)

   interracial _____

6. Among the many changes *ushered in* during this period was the breaking of the "color line" in courtship. (par. 5)

   ushered in _____

7. To understand why, you need to remember that a *dyad* (just two persons) provides greater intimacy than a *triad* (after adding a third person, interaction must be shared). (par. 8)

   dyad _____

8. *triad* _____

9. A generation ago such a question would have been ridiculous, for the mother was at home taking care of the children. However, that assumption *no longer holds.* (par. 11)

   no longer holds _____

10. Sociologist Melvin Kohn found that parents socialize their children into the *norms* of their work worlds. (par. 14)

    norms _____

Choose the best answer to the following multiple-choice questions.

11. When the author writes that love is "certainly . . . not blind," he means that
    a. people fall in love with another person from similar circumstances.
    b. love is clear-headed and analytical.
    c. we fall in love with people willy-nilly.

12. According to Henslin, which of the following sets of people are most likely to get married?
    a. a black woman and white man
    b. a Latino medical doctor and Latina lawyer
    c. a high school dropout and a college-educated person

13. The primary pattern of organization for paragraph 2 is
    a. chronological order.
    b. examples.
    c. definition.

© 2014 Wadsworth, Cengage Learning

14. Which of the following is the best main idea statement for paragraph 2?
    a. Our marriage choices follow predictable patterns regarding age, education, social class, and race-ethnicity
    b. A Latina with a college degree is likely to marry a Latino slightly older than herself who has graduated from college.
    c. A girl who drops out of high school is likely to fall in love with and marry a man who has done the same.

15. The primary pattern of organization for paragraph 3 is
    a. definition.
    b. chronological order.
    c. comparison and contrast.

16. The primary patterns of organization for paragraph 8 are
    a. chronological order and process.
    b. cause and effect and definition.
    c. examples and comparison and contrast.

17. The primary patterns of organization for paragraphs 9 and 10 are
    a. definition and process.
    b. chronological order and examples.
    c. cause and effect and comparison and contrast.

18. Which of the following is the best main idea statement for paragraphs 9 and 10?
    a. Middle class couples have more trouble adjusting to the arrival of a newborn.
    b. Working class couples have very little trouble adjusting to the arrival of a newborn.
    c. Working-class couples tend to have more difficulties in adjusting to the arrival of a newborn than middle-class couples.

Write short answers to the following questions based on your reading, your experience, and your observations.

19. Think about your friends and family and yourself, if you are married. Did you follow patterns of homogamy for choosing your life mate? Did the people you know do the same? Explain your answer.

    _____

    _____

    _____

20. Considering the discussion of child-rearing in paragraphs 12 through 15, what do you think are some of the most important things to consider about raising a child? Explain your answer.

    _____

    _____

    _____

© 2014 Wadsworth, Cengage Learning

8 Inferences

COMING OF AGE

John Powell Photographer / Alamy

"I get a little down, but I'm very good at hiding it. It's like I wear a mask. Even when the kids call me names or taunt me, I never show them how much it crushes me inside. I keep it all in."
—FROM AN INTERVIEW OF 14-YEAR-OLD ADAM IN WILLIAM POLLACK'S REAL BOYS

- What does the 14-year-old mean when he says he wears a "mask"? Why does he wear a mask?

- What image of themselves are the young men in the photo trying to give?

Getting Ready to Read

Adolescence is a crucial period in everyone's life. It is when we "come of age," when we form our understanding of the world around us and our relationships to people. Many societies have special "coming of age" ceremonies, but in others there is no clear moment when the child turns into an adult. There are no clear rules for how parents and children are supposed to behave during this "growing up" process. Researchers have been studying the adolescent years of boys and girls—young men and women—to try to develop some guidelines that will help them through this difficult passage to adulthood. Teenagers will be making crucial decisions about their attitudes toward education, their friends and families, drugs, sex, their bodies, violence, their work, their lifestyle goals, and their communities. We need to ask ourselves how we can best prepare ourselves and our children to make good choices for now and for the rest of their lives. What can and should parents do? Schools? Communities? The government?

In this chapter, you will read about the challenges for parents and young people during these crucial years. In the process, you will improve your reading skills by learning how to:

- Recognize inferences in visual aids
- Recognize inferences in reading
- Look for clues that inferences are based on

© 2014 Wadsworth, Cengage Learning

The Boy Code: "Everything's Just Fine"

— WILLIAM POLLACK

The following reading is from the best-selling book *Real Boys* by William Pollack, who is a Harvard Medical School child psychologist and researcher. In his book, he addresses many of the problems boys have as they grow up to become men. He believes that boys are in serious trouble, including many boys who seem to be doing fine. As you read, think about why the boy in the story might be in trouble and why he is acting as he does.

1   Adam is a fourteen-year-old boy whose mother sought me out after a workshop I was leading on the subject of boys and families. Adam, she told me, had been performing very well in school, but now she felt something was wrong.

2   Adam had shown such promise that he had been selected to join a special program for talented students, and the program was available only at a different—and more academically prestigious—school than the one Adam had attended. The new school was located in a well-to-do section of town, more affluent than Adam's own neighborhood. Adam's mother had been pleased when her son had qualified for the program and even more delighted that he would be given a scholarship to pay for it. And so Adam had set off on his new life.

3   At the time we talked, Mrs. Harrison's delight had turned to worry. Adam was not doing well at the new school. His grades were mediocre, and at midterm he had been given a warning that he might fail algebra. Yet Adam continued to insist, "I'm fine. Everything's just fine." He said this both at home and at school. Adam's mother was perplexed, as was the guidance counselor at his new school. "Adam seems cheerful and has no complaints," the counselor told her. "But something must be wrong." His mother tried to talk to Adam, hoping to find out what was troubling him and causing him to do so poorly in school. "But the more I questioned him about what was going on," she said, "the more he continued to deny any problems."

4   Adam was a quiet and rather shy boy, small for his age. In his bright blue eyes I detected an inner pain, a malaise whose cause I could not easily fathom. I had seen a similar look on the faces of a number of boys of different ages, including many boys in the "Listening to Boys' Voices" study. Adam looked wary, hurt, closed-in, self-protective. Most of all, he looked alone.

malaise
discomfort

fathom
understand

5   One day, his mother continued, Adam came home with a black eye. She asked him what had happened. "Just an accident," Adam had mumbled. He'd kept his eyes cast down, she remembered, as if he felt guilty or ashamed. His mother probed more deeply. She told him that she knew something was wrong, something upsetting was going on, and that— whatever it was—they could deal with it, they could face it together. Suddenly, Adam erupted in tears, and the story he had been holding inside came pouring out.

6   Adam was being picked on at school, heckled on the bus, goaded into fights in the schoolyard. "Hey, White Trash!" the other boys shouted at him. "You don't belong here with *us*!" taunted a twelfth-grade bully. "Why don't you go back to your own side

From *Real Boys: Rescuing Our Sons from The Myths of Boyhood* by William Pollack, © 1998 By William Pollack. Used by Permission of Random House, Inc.

© 2014 Wadsworth, Cengage Learning

of town!" The taunts often led to physical attacks, and Adam found himself having to fight back in order to defend himself. "But I never throw the first punch," Adam explained to his mother. "I don't show them they can hurt me. I don't want to embarrass myself in front of everybody."

7   I turned to Adam. "How do you feel about all of this?" I asked. "How do you handle your feelings of anger and frustration?" His answer was, I'm sad to say, a refrain I hear often when I am unable to connect to the inner lives of boys.

8   "I get a little down," Adam confessed, "but I'm very good at hiding it. It's like I wear a mask. Even when the kids call me names or taunt me, I never show them how much it crushes me inside. I keep it all in."

9   "What do you do with the sadness?" I asked.

10   "I tend to let it boil inside until I can't hold it any longer, and then it explodes. It's like I have a breakdown, screaming and yelling. But I only do it inside my own room at home, where nobody can hear. Where nobody will know about it." He paused a moment. "I think I got this from my dad, unfortunately."

11   Adam was doing what I find so many boys do: he was hiding behind a mask, and using it to hide his deepest thoughts and feelings—his real self— from everyone, even the people closest to him. This mask of masculinity enabled Adam to make a bold (if inaccurate) statement to the world: "I can handle it. Everything's fine. I am invincible."

persona
a public role or personality

feigned
pretended

bravado
show of false bravery

12   Adam, like other boys, wore this mask as an invisible shield, a persona to show the outside world a feigned self-confidence and bravado, and to hide the shame he felt at his feelings of vulnerability, powerlessness, and isolation. He couldn't handle the school situation alone—very few boys or girls of fourteen could—and he didn't know how to ask for help, even from people he knew loved him. As a result, Adam was unhappy and was falling behind in his academic performance.

13   Many of the boys I see today are like Adam, living behind a mask of masculine bravado that hides the genuine self to conform to our society's expectations; they feel it is necessary to cut themselves off from any feelings that society teaches them are unacceptable for men and boys—fear, uncertainty, feelings of loneliness and need.

14   Many boys, like Adam, also think it's necessary that they handle their problems alone. A boy is not expected to reach out—to his family, his friends, his counselors, or coaches—for help, comfort, understanding, and support. And so he is simply not as close as he could be to the people who love him and yearn to give him the human connections of love, caring, and affection every person needs.

15   The problem for those of us who want to help is that, on the outside, the boy who is having problems may seem cheerful and resilient while keeping inside the feelings that don't fit the male model—being troubled, lonely, afraid, desperate. Boys learn to wear the mask so skillfully—in fact, they don't even know they're doing it—that it can be difficult to detect what is really going on when they are suffering at school, when their friendships are not working out, when they are being bullied, becoming depressed, even dangerously so, to the point of feeling suicidal. The problems below the surface become obvious only when boys go "over the edge" and get into trouble at school, start to fight with friends, take drugs or abuse alcohol, are diagnosed with clinical depression or attention deficit disorder, erupt into physical violence, or come home with a black eye, as Adam did. Adam's mother, for example, did not know from her son that anything was wrong until Adam came home with an eye swollen shut; all she knew was that he had those perplexingly poor grades.

© 2014 Wadsworth, Cengage Learning

© 2014 Wadsworth, Cengage Learning

Exercise 1

Recall and Discuss

Answer these questions about Reading 1, and prepare to discuss them in class.

1. Why was Adam selected to join a special program for talented students?

_____

_____

_____

2. What problems did Adam encounter in his new school?

_____

_____

_____

3. Why did Adam not tell his mother what was happening at the new school?

_____

_____

_____

4. Do you think it was a good idea for Adam to "wear a mask"? Why or why not?

_____

_____

_____

Recognizing Inferences

infer read between the lines to understand what a speaker or writer is saying indirectly

Like Adam, often writers (and speakers) do not state everything directly. Instead, they give you clues—pieces of information—so that you can make some reasonable assumptions or guesses about what they are trying to say. To understand this kind of communication, you must **infer**, or "read between the lines," think about what is being said, and come to your own conclusions. A writer or speaker who says something indirectly is *implying* meaning, and the reader or listener is *inferring* the meaning from the clues that are given.

   In Reading 1, Adam's mother inferred that something was wrong from the clue of her son's poor grades. The second clue was unmistakable—a black eye.

Like Adam's mother, you make inferences every day of your life. The clues for these inferences often come from your understanding and experience and the situation around you. As an example, let's say you're watching a baseball game, the bases are loaded, and the team member who is up to bat strikes out. She says, "Oh, that's just great!" You will of course know, from inference, that she really means, "That's just terrible!"

context a situation that provides clues for inferring meaning

You base your inference on clues in the situation and on your own experience in similar situations. These situations are the **context**. In Chapter 2, you learned that context clues can help you guess a word's meaning from its surroundings. Context clues can help you with inferences, too. At the baseball game you know from the context—striking out when the bases are loaded—that the batter is upset, and she is using the word "great" to mean the opposite, "terrible." You no doubt received extra visual clues from the expression on her face and from the way she acted. She probably looked distressed instead of happy, and her body language probably showed disappointment instead of triumph.

Sometimes inferences can help you predict what will happen next in a situation or a story. For example, if your boss just saw you arriving 20 minutes late for work for the third time this week and he says with a frown, "See me in my office," what do you infer—or predict—he will say to you? It's not likely he's going to praise you! You know that being on time is expected in most jobs, plus you noticed his frown. Those context clues will lead you to infer that he is unhappy with your actions.

MAKING INFERENCES FROM VISUAL CLUES

As the preceding examples—Adam's black eye, your boss's frown—show, the inferences you make every day are often based on visual clues. To see how this works, examine the photograph below. Now, circle the letters of the following inferences that you can reasonably make based on what you can observe in the picture. (You may choose more than one.)

a. The girls in the picture are cousins.
b. The girls in the picture are friends.
c. The girls are happy because they did well on their exams.
d. The girls are happy.
e. The girls have been shopping.

© 2014 Wadsworth, Cengage Learning

Kaz Mori /Getty Images

You should have chosen *b, d,* and *e* as inferences you can reasonably make based on the photograph. From the picture alone, we don't have enough information to assume the girls are cousins (*a*), or that they are happy because they did well on exams (*c*). On the other hand, we can infer that they are friends (*b*) and happy (*d*) because they are close together, even touching, and they are smiling. We can also infer that they have been shopping (*e*) because of the big bags they have.

Visual aids in readings, such as photographs and captions, can provide you with a great deal of information. Always pay attention to them. Study the faces, the posture, and the dialogue, if any.

Exercise 2

Make Inferences from Visual Clues

Examine the photograph below and the cartoon on page 371. Then circle the letters of all the inferences you can reasonably make. You may choose more than one inference for each.

1. Photograph
   a. There is a respectful relationship between the teenage boy and the man.
   b. The boy is not happy with something the man is saying.
   c. There seems to be a disagreement between them.
   d. The man is attempting to assert his authority over the teenager.
   e. The man is the teenager's father.

Angela Hampton Picture Library / Alamy

2. Cartoon
   a. The woman in the picture is probably the young man's mother.
   b. These two people are at home.
   c. The young man is ignoring the woman.
   d. These two people don't love each other.
   e. The woman wants the young man to do his homework.

© 2014 Wadsworth, Cengage Learning

"I bet if I was an I-pod you'd
listen to me!"

MAKING INFERENCES WHILE READING

Writers help us make inferences in many ways. Sometimes they present us with a lot of detailed information and then expect us to reach the same conclusions they did by inference. You practiced this skill of making inferences in Chapter 4 when you learned how to identify unstated main ideas in what you read. Read the following excerpt from a news story to see what you might reasonably infer.

> WASHINGTON—[In Washington, D.C.] police have no gasoline for their cruisers. Health clinics have run out of drugs. Six blocks from the White House, firefighters ride trucks with no ladders and buy their own boots.
>
> Potholes blister Embassy Row. The decrepit water-treatment plant threatens to spew sewage into the Potomac. Earlier this year, inmates set fire to their cells after the prison ran out of food. (Montgomery, "Short of Funds, the Nation's Capital Is Falling Apart")

What can we reasonably infer from this information?

Washington, D.C. is having serious trouble maintaining regular city services.

In this case, this inference would also be the main idea for this passage. It is unstated, but the examples, or clues, in the article add up to this conclusion. What clues do we have to make this inference?

1. *Police don't have gasoline.*
2. *Health clinics don't have drugs.*
3. *Firefighters don't have ladders or boots.*

© 2014 Wadsworth, Cengage Learning

4. The streets have potholes.
5. The water-treatment plant doesn't work.
6. Prison inmates ran out of food.

This long list of examples points to the conclusion that things are falling apart in that city.

You can also infer that these conditions are particularly disgraceful because they are occurring in our nation's capital. This understanding is implied more subtly. The writer states that "six blocks from the White House" firefighters don't have the proper equipment. The firefighters' problems are no doubt true all over the city, but it looks worse when we realize how close this is to the home of the president of our country. Also, there are potholes on Embassy Row. If there are potholes in the finest streets— where ambassadors from countries all over the world reside—that is very embarrassing. From the details the writer includes and the way she states them, we can probably also conclude that she thinks these problems in our nation's capital should be remedied.

Exercise 3

Recognize Inferences in Paragraphs

Read the following passages about the difficulties as well as some of the positive aspects of growing up in our communities and attending our schools. Then circle the letter in front of each statement that you decide is a reasonable inference from what you have read. There may be more than one inference. The first question is explained for you.

1. Even celebrities sometimes quietly give of themselves behind the scenes. In Joe Dumars's life, basketball and community responsibility came together early on. The Detroit Pistons guard grew up in Natchitoches, La., the youngest of seven children. One day his father, a truck driver, cut an old door in half, nailed a bicycle rim to it and transformed the neighborhood. "We had the biggest yard, a basketball hoop, and it was just a magnet for all the kids in the area," he remembers. "It was always crowded, but everyone was made to feel welcome. My mother, Ophelia, made sure of that." (Alter, "Everyday Heroes")

   a. Dumars's father made a basketball hoop and a backboard out of an old door and a bicycle rim.
   b. Joe Dumars was the youngest of seven children.
   c. Dumars's father knew his son would be a basketball star when he grew up.
   d. Dumars's yard became a kind of neighborhood center.

   (Statements a and d are the only reasonable inferences from the information provided in the paragraph. We are told that Dumars's father "cut an old door in half" and "nailed a bicycle rim to it." In the next sentence we discover that there was a basketball hoop in the yard, and we infer that this must have been what his father built. Statement d is supported by the clues that the basketball hoop "transformed the neighborhood," was "a magnet for all the kids in the area," and "it was always crowded, but everyone was made to feel welcome." Statement b is not an inference because it is a fact directly stated in the paragraph. There is not enough information in the paragraph to support statement c. His father might have hoped that Dumars would become a basketball star, but no information in the paragraph tells us that.)

2. In Denmark, a small Scandinavian country, parents have an interesting attitude toward teenagers and alcohol. Most families allow their teenagers to drink small

© 2014 Wadsworth, Cengage Learning

amounts of alcohol at family dinners and at social occasions. This practice seems to make the consumption of alcohol a normal part of life, and Danish parents believe that if alcohol is not forbidden to their children, their children will not sneak off to drink alone. In addition, families, schools and Danish society in general all participate in the following tradition: When a class graduates from high school, they celebrate by visiting each of the classmates' homes to have a drink. Of course, after visiting between 15 and 30 classmates' homes, you can imagine the condition of the students! To ensure the students' safety, the school organizes the activity by providing the class with a bus and a chauffeur to drive it.

   a. Teenagers are probably in fewer drunk-driving accidents in Denmark than in the United States.
   b. Danish teenagers are different from teenagers in other parts of the world.
   c. Danish high school graduates get drunk after their graduation ceremony.
   d. Probably not many auto accidents in Denmark are caused by drunk students who are celebrating their high school graduation.

3. Frequently the children in middle- and upper-middle-class suburbs are busy people. They often leave school to be driven hurriedly to soccer or lacrosse practice three times a week and then to a game once a week on the weekend. They also very often take music lessons once a week near their home or across town, but they need to practice in between lessons, of course. In addition, they may study judo, karate, sewing, or they may be active in church youth organizations.

   a. These children are probably driven around by parents.
   b. These children probably take the bus to all these activities.
   c. There's a good chance that these children don't have very much free time to play.
   d. These children study whenever they're not at organized activities.

4. Everything seemed fine for Camara when he came to this country from Kingston, Jamaica, several years ago. He was living with his mother and stepfather, taking tough courses and getting top grades at Thomas Jefferson. But after a bitter fight with his parents, he found himself out on the street. For four days, he lived and studied on the subway at night, getting off to go to school during the day.

   This would throw most kids for a loop. Even if they're not getting on well with their mothers and fathers, young people depend on parents to provide food and shelter and a certain degree of emotional support and stability. But after people at Thomas Jefferson helped Camara get settled in a homeless shelter, he pulled his grades back up, studied for his SATs, and applied for college admission. Rather than devastating him, the experience of being alone, with nowhere to spend the night but a subway car, seems to have strengthened Camara's resolve to study and make something of himself. (Shanker, "A Real Role Model")

   a. Camara's parents knew he could do well out on his own, so they threw him out of the house while he was still in high school.
   b. Camara had a special kind of inner drive and determination to be successful in school despite the circumstances of his life.
   c. Most young people who have the same problems as Camara are not as successful as he was.
   d. Camara's parents were unable to take care of him.

© 2014 Wadsworth, Cengage Learning

5. Since math is stereotyped as a male domain, boys benefit more than girls from math classes—they are spoken to more, are called on more, and receive more corrective feedback, social interaction, individual instruction, and encouragement. They learn more than what is in the textbook. By contrast, girls are mostly consigned to learning by rote the math in the text, with little exposure to extracurricular math and science. (Thio, *Sociology*)

   a. Boys probably do better in math under these circumstances than do girls.
   b. Girls and boys are treated differently because they are perceived differently.
   c. Because boys are naturally better in math, they should get more attention than girls in math class.
   d. Feedback, individual instruction, and encouragement would make anybody good in math.

6. SOUTH BRUNSWICK, N.J. A tied soccer game between 8- and 9-year-old boys ended in a brawl among their parents yesterday after a disagreement over where a coach was standing, police said. A shootout was to take place between the teams—one from Staten Island, N.Y., and the other from North Hunterdon—but before it could, a Staten Island coach argued that a North Hunterdon coach shouldn't be allowed to stand behind the goal.

   shootout a way to break a tie in tournament soccer games; each team gets five direct kicks on goal

   The argument escalated into a fistfight with as many as a dozen parents and coaches involved. No children were involved, South Brunswick police officer Jim Ryan said. Even after police arrived, parents were still yelling at each other, he said. Ryan said a coach and a parent claimed to have been assaulted, but no one was seriously injured or arrested, police said. Both teams were escorted from the field, and neither was declared the game winner, Ryan said.

   The fight was the latest case of parental rage at youth sporting events this year [2000]. In August, a hockey dad was indicted on manslaughter charges in the beating death of another father at a game in Massachusetts, and a baseball coach was accused of breaking an umpire's jaw after a disputed call in Florida in June. ("Parents in Brawl at Kids' Soccer Game")

   a. The Staten Island coach was right.
   b. The parents can get more worked up at the sporting events than their children.
   c. The children don't care about winning the game.
   d. The children are influenced by the way their parents are acting at these games and will eventually have more violent reactions at sports events themselves.

7. Often the children of immigrants who have lived in the United States for a while rebel against their parents' old-fashioned values and rules. Some Vietnamese mothers, for example, would like their daughters to date—once they are in their twenties and old enough to date—only Vietnamese men who would agree to having their wife's mother live with them if the couple gets married. (Adapted from Pipher, *Reviving Ophelia*)

   a. Young American men would not likely want their mothers-in-law to live with them.
   b. These Vietnamese mothers probably don't want their daughters to become too Americanized.
   c. These mothers' expectations could be considered unreasonable in an American cultural context.
   d. The daughters of Vietnamese immigrants need to be more obedient.

© 2014 Wadsworth, Cengage Learning

Organize to Learn: Separate Personal Opinion from Reasonable Inferences

Quite naturally, you will have your own feelings and opinions about what you read. Did the behavior of the soccer parents (Exercise 3, number 6) disgust you? Did you have a strong reaction to the ideas of the Vietnamese mothers (Exercise 3, number 7)? Your feelings and opinions are valid responses to what you read, but you must not let them get in the way of understanding what the author is saying or implying. If you do not keep personal opinion separate from reasonable inferences, you risk listening to yourself instead of learning from, or "listening" to, the author.

For example, in Exercise 3, number 4, the author writes,

> But after a bitter fight with his parents, he found himself out on the street. For four days, he lived and studied on the subway at night, getting off to go to school during the day.

What was your opinion about these events? It might have been something like one of the following:

1. Parents should never throw their children out, no matter how big the disagreement.
2. He should have taught his parents a lesson by just hiding out for a while so they could worry about him.
3. Why should he still care about doing well in school? His parents obviously don't care what happens to him.
4. I know what it is like to be on the streets when you are a kid; it can really be tough.
5. I don't approve of the parents' throwing their child out of the house, but I understand how parents' exasperation with teenage acting out can make them take drastic steps.

You may have had these or other opinions about Camara's situation, and that's fine. As you learned in the *PRO* reading system, you should always be involved with what you read. Reflect on what you've read, make connections with your prior reading and experiences, and form your own opinions about it. The only caution is to not confuse *your* opinions with inferences suggested by the author. The way to do that is to stick to the clues. For any reasonable inference that you make, be sure there are clues in the reading that lead to that inference.

Read the following paragraph and then see if you know which of the statements that follow is a personal opinion and which is a reasonable inference. In the blank put an "I" for an inference and "O" for a personal opinion.

© 2014 Wadsworth, Cengage Learning

Authorities have become convinced that reformatories have failed as rehabilitation centers and instead have become crime schools in which teenagers learn how to become more effective criminals. A study conducted by the U.S. Department of Justice showed that 49.7 percent of all juveniles in detention facilities had been arrested six or more times. Half of that number had been arrested eleven or more times. Acting on this belief, the Commonwealth of Massachusetts closed all five of its reform schools and placed its young criminals in small, community-based programs. (Newton, *Teen Violence: Out of Control*)

___ The number of juveniles who are repeatedly arrested and returned to reformatories indicates that reformatories are failing to achieve their goal of deterring young people from returning to crime.

This inference is reasonable based on the clues: "49.7 percent of all juveniles in detention facilities had been arrested six or more times"; half of those people "had been arrested eleven or more times"; and "reformatories have failed as rehabilitation centers."

___ It's obvious that many of these juveniles cannot be helped, and they should simply be treated as adults in the courts.

Although the paragraph clearly seems to say that reformatories do not keep the majority of youths from committing additional crimes, there are no clues that prove that the youths simply cannot be helped by any means, and there is no mention of adult courts. This statement is clearly an opinion, perhaps based on other data and experience.

Exercise 4   Identify Personal Opinion or Reasonable Inference

Continue to identify personal opinions and reasonable inferences about the paragraph in the box above. Write "O" for opinion or "I" for reasonable inference. Remember, a reasonable inference has supporting clues in the excerpt itself.

_____ 1. The community-based programs in Massachusetts are definitely the best way to deal with youthful offenders.

_____ 2. The Commonwealth of Massachusetts believed that placing young criminals in small, community-based programs would be more effective than placing them in reform schools.

_____ 3. The State of New York has the best reform schools in the country.

_____ 4. Teenagers who serve time in reformatories often commit crimes after they're released.

_____ 5. Juvenile delinquents should receive the same sentences as adults.

_____ 6. Juvenile crime is a problem in the United States today.

© 2014 Wadsworth, Cengage Learning

FINDING INFERENCES IN LONGER PASSAGES

Inferences in longer passages are sometimes easier to identify than those in short passages because there are more clues. You still go through the same process, which is similar to finding unstated main idea in a paragraph; only in a longer reading you will be finding the central idea or thesis: Add up the information you are given directly, consider all the clues you are given about what is implied, and then infer what the writer is saying. In narratives, or stories, clues will lead you to predict what will happen next. These clues include what has already happened and the character of the people in the story, but your own experiences will help you predict, too.

Reading 2

Codes of Conduct

— GEOFFREY CANADA

The following reading tells how Geoffrey Canada and his brothers learned to resolve a conflict with some other boys in their neighborhood. Canada's mother taught her children an important lesson on the day he describes. As you read, see if you can predict how the conflict will be resolved. What do you think his mother wanted her children to learn from this experience? Mark some clues as you read.

1   Down the block from us was a playground. It was nearby and we didn't have to cross the street to get there. We were close in age. My oldest brother, Daniel, was six, next came John who was five, I was four, and my brother Reuben was two. Reuben and I were unable to go to the playground by ourselves because we were too young. But from time to time my two oldest brothers would go there together and play.

2   I remember them coming inside one afternoon having just come back from the playground. There was great excitement in the air. My mother noticed right away and asked, "Where's John's jacket?"

3   My brother responded, "This boy . . . this boy he took my jacket."

4   Well, we all figured that was the end of that. My mother would have to go and get the jacket back. But the questioning continued. "What do you mean, he took your jacket?"

5   "I was playing on the sliding board and I took my jacket off and left it on the bench, and this boy he tried to take it. And I said it was my jacket, and he said he was gonna take it. And he took it. And I tried to take it back, and he pushed me and said he was gonna beat me up."

6   To my mind John's explanation was clear and convincing; this case was closed. I was stunned when my mother turned to my oldest brother, Daniel, and said, "And what did you do when this boy was taking your brother's jacket?"

7   Daniel looked shocked. What did he have to do with this? And we all recognized the edge in my mother's voice. Daniel was being accused of something and none of us knew what it was.

8   Daniel answered, "I didn't do nuthin; I told Johnny not to take his jacket off. I told him."

From *Fist Stick Knife* by Geoffrey Canada. © 1995 by Geoffrey Canada. Reprinted by Permission of Beacon Press, Boston.

© 2014 Wadsworth, Cengage Learning

9   My mother exploded. "You let somebody take your brother's jacket and you did nothing? That's your younger brother. You can't let people just take your things. You know
I don't have money for another jacket. You better not ever do this again. Now you go
back there and get your brother's jacket."

10   My mouth was hanging open. I couldn't believe it. What was my mother talking
about, go back and get it? Dan and Johnny were the same size. If the boy was gonna
beat up John, well, he certainly could beat up Dan. We wrestled all the time and occasionally hit one another in anger, but none of us knew how to fight. We were all equally
incompetent when it came to fighting. So it made no sense to me. If my mother hadn't
had that look in her eye, I would have protested. Even at four years old I knew this
wasn't fair. But I also knew that look in my mother's eye. A look that signified a line not
to be crossed.

11   My brother Dan was in shock. He felt the same way I did. He tried to protest. "Ma, I
can't beat that boy. It's not my jacket. I can't get it. I can't."

12   My mother gave him her ultimatum. "You go out there and get your brother's jacket
or when you get back I'm going to give you a beating that will be ten times as bad as
what that little thief could do to you. And John, you go with him. Both of you better
bring that jacket back here."

13   The tears began to flow. Both John and Dan were crying. My mother ordered them
out. Dan had this look on his face that I had seen before. A stern determination showed
through the tears. For the first time I didn't want to go with my brothers to the park.
I waited a long ten minutes and then, to my surprise, John and Dan triumphantly
strolled into the apartment. Dan had John's jacket in his hand.

(TO BE CONTINUED)

Exercise 5

Identify Inferences

Use the clues from Reading 2 to support your answers to each of the following
questions about inferences.

1. Why did the boys' mother send them back to get the jacket themselves?

   _____

   _____

2. Why did she make the oldest son, Daniel, get the jacket even though it
   wasn't his?

   _____

   _____

3. Why were the boys scared about going back to the playground?

   _____

   _____

© 2014 Wadsworth, Cengage Learning

4. How do you think they got the jacket?

_____

_____

5. Write your personal opinion of this situation. Was the mother right or wrong to send her sons back to get the jacket?

_____

_____

Now read the rest of the story to find out what happened and to check if your inferences about what happened are correct. See if the rest of the story changes your personal opinion about whether the mother was right or wrong.

Codes of Conduct (*Continued*)

14   My mother gathered us all together and told us we had to stick together. That we couldn't let people think we were afraid. That what she had done in making Dan go out and get the jacket was to let us know that she would not tolerate our becoming victims. I listened unconvinced. But I knew that in not going with Dan and John I'd missed something important. Dan was scared when he left the house. We were all scared. I knew I could never have faced up to that boy. How did Dan do it? I wanted to know everything.

15   "What happened? How did you do it? Did you have to fight? Did you beat him up?" I asked. Dan explained that when he went back to the playground the boy was still there, wearing John's jacket. He went up to him and demanded the jacket. The boy said no. Dan grabbed the jacket and began to take it off the boy. Dan was still crying, but the boy knew it was not from fear of him. A moment of resistance, but Dan's determination prevailed. The boy grew scared and Dan wrestled the jacket free. He even managed a threatening "You better never bother my brother again" as the boy fled.

16   Dan's description of the confrontation left me with more questions. I was trying to understand why Dan was able to get the jacket. If he could get it later, why didn't he take it back the first time? How come the boy didn't fight? What scared him off? Even at four years old I knew I needed to know these things. I needed some clues on which I could build a theory of how to act. Dan's story couldn't help me much. It took many years of playing and hanging on the streets of the South Bronx before I began to put together the pieces of the theory. The only real lesson I learned from the jacket episode was if someone takes something from you, don't tell your mother you lost it, otherwise you might be in danger of getting your face punched in by some boy on the streets of New York City. This was a valuable bit of understanding for a four-year-old in the Bronx.

© 2014 Wadsworth, Cengage Learning

Exercise 6

Work with Words

Use context clues, word-part clues, and, if necessary, the dictionary to write the definitions of the italicized words in the following sentences based on or related to Reading 2.

1. Daniel looked shocked. What did he have to do with this? And we all recognized the *edge* in my mother's voice. (par. 7)

   edge _____

2. But I also knew that look in my mother's eye. A look that *signified* a line not to be crossed. (par. 10)

   signified _____

3. My mother gave him her *ultimatum*. "You go out there and get your brother's jacket or when you get back I'm going to give you a beating that will be ten times as bad as what that little thief could do to you." (par. 12)

   ultimatum _____

4. I waited a long ten minutes and then, to my surprise, John and Dan *triumphantly* strolled into the apartment. Dan had John's jacket in his hand. (par. 13)

   triumphantly _____

5. A moment of resistance, but Dan's determination *prevailed*. The boy grew scared and Dan wrestled the jacket free. (par. 15)

   prevailed _____

Exercise 7

Check Your Inferences

Write brief answers to the following questions about Reading 2. Use the clues you identified in the story to support your answers.

1. Why did the author's mother tell her boys that she didn't want people to think they were afraid?

   _____

   _____

   _____

© 2014 Wadsworth, Cengage Learning

2. Why did the boy let Dan get the jacket back without a fight?

_____

_____

_____

3. Why do you think Dan was crying if it was not from fear of the boy?

_____

_____

_____

4. Why did the author infer at that time that if someone takes something from you it is better not to tell your mother that you lost it?

_____

_____

_____

Exercise 8

Make Connections and Write

Write short answers to the following questions based on Reading 2, your experience, and your observations. Then, discuss your answers with your class group. Working together, prepare a report for your class as a whole or a written summary for your instructor.

1. What do you think it was like for the boys' mother to be raising them alone as a single parent? How do you think she felt?

_____

_____

_____

© 2014 Wadsworth, Cengage Learning

2. Do you think their mother did the right thing under the circumstances? Explain your answer.

_____

_____

_____

3. Do you think the author, now an adult, thinks his mother did the right thing under the circumstances? Explain your answer.

_____

_____

_____

Language Tip: Imagery and Connotation

Imagery

Good writers and good speakers often use language that makes their ideas stronger by affecting our senses—that is, by making us see pictures in our minds or imagine how something feels or smells. For example, in "Codes of Conduct" Canada writes,

> "My mother *exploded*. 'You let somebody take your brother's jacket and you did nothing?'"

The word *exploded* gives us a visual picture of how upset the mother was when the boys said they did nothing about the stolen jacket. We know she didn't actually "blow up"; she was just very angry at the boys' lack of action.

Sometimes, also, writers do not make their point directly. The reader has to picture the images to figure out exactly what is being said. For example, what do you think teenagers in a gang mean when they say:

> "I would rather *be judged by twelve* than *carried by six*."

What are the clues and visual images (pictures formed in your mind) in the sentence?

© 2014 Wadsworth, Cengage Learning

"Judged by twelve" means face a trial (there are twelve people on a jury). *"Carried by six"* refers to being in a coffin. Six people (pallbearers) carry the coffin.

The entire statement means that I would rather be arrested for a crime than be killed.

Connotation

Words also convey positive and negative feelings, or emotions, in addition to their dictionary definition. If you look up the word *work* in the dictionary, you will find it defined as "physical or mental effort or activity," "labor," and "employment or job." This word does not have positive or negative feelings attached to it. But if you add the word *busy* in front of the word *work,* the term has a negative feel. *Busy work* conveys work that is not meaningful, work that is done just to appear busy, to fill time. But *rewarding work* has a positive connotation, or feeling. As you read, be aware of the *connotations,* or feelings, of words. They will help you infer the writer's meaning, too.

Exercise 9   Understand the Language of Imagery

In the following sentences, some examples of language that use imagery have been italicized. Explain (1) what visual images are formed when we read these words and (2) what the words actually mean in the sentence.

1. The "man's world" outside the home was viewed as a *harsh and heartless jungle* in which men need to be strong, ambitious, and aggressive. (Thio, *Sociology*)

   visual image: _____

   meaning: _____

2. For four days, he lived and studied on the subway at night, getting off to go to school during the day. This would *throw most kids for a loop.* (Shanker, "A Real Role Model")

   visual image: _____

   meaning: _____

3. "An eye for an eye. A tooth for a tooth." *(The Bible)*

   visual image: _____

   meaning: _____

   _____

© 2014 Wadsworth, Cengage Learning

4. "We had the biggest yard, a basketball hoop, and it was just a *magnet* for all the kids in the area," he remembers. (Alter, "Everyday Heroes")

   visual image: _____

   meaning: _____

5. My mother gathered us all together and told us we had *to stick together*. (Canada, "Codes of Conduct")

   visual image: _____

   meaning: _____

6. But I also knew that look in my mother's eye. A look that signified *a line not to be crossed*. (Canada, "Codes of Conduct")

   visual image: _____

   meaning: _____

7. In Vietnamese culture, families are seen as *shelter from the storm*. Adolescents don't rebel, but rather *are nested* in extended families that they will be with forever. (Pipher, *Reviving Ophelia*)

   shelter from the storm

   visual image: _____

   _____

   meaning: _____

8. *are nested*

   visual image: _____

   meaning: _____

Exercise 10   **Recognize the Connotations of Words**

Read the following paragraph about work and decide whether each of the uses of the word *work* has a positive or negative connotation. Write a plus (+) if the connotation is positive and a minus (−) if the connotation is negative.

© 2014 Wadsworth, Cengage Learning

"Work" is a word we all use freely. It has many different connotations. We might do a "good day's work." We have people in our organization who are "workaholics" and "workhorses." We "work a problem through." We "work out" on a dance floor or athletic field. (Roth, "The True Nature of Work")

_____   1. good day's work
_____   2. workaholic
_____   3. workhorse
_____   4. work a problem through
_____   5. work out

Reading 3   # Boys Today Are Falling Behind

— WILLIAM POLLACK

In recent years, we have heard a lot about how girls tend to do well in school until they start middle school, and then they start performing poorly in math and science. In response to this information, schools across the country are trying to address the problems of educating our girls. Some people feel that, while girls do face discouragement in our classrooms, we should not forget that boys also have many problems in our educational institutions. The following reading, from Pollack's book, *Real Boys,* examines some of these questions. As you read, notice the details that Pollack uses to strengthen his thesis. Also, what supporting inferences can you make from the author's use of the story about Sal?

---

1   While it may seem as if we live in a "man's world," at least in relation to power and wealth in adult society, we do not live in a "boy's world." Boys on the whole are not faring well in our schools, especially in our public schools. It is in the classroom that we see some of the most destructive effects of society's misunderstanding of boys. Thrust into competition with their peers, some boys invest so much energy into keeping up their emotional guard and disguising their deepest and most vulnerable feelings, they often have little or no energy left to apply themselves to their schoolwork. No doubt boys still show up as small minorities at the top of a few academic lists, playing starring roles as some teachers' best students. But, most often, boys form the majority of the bottom of the class. Over the last decade we've been forced to confront some staggering statistics. From elementary grades through high school, boys receive lower grades than girls. Eighth-grade boys are held back 50 percent more often than girls. By high school, boys account for two-thirds of the students in special education classes. Fewer boys than girls now attend and graduate from college. Fifty-nine percent of all master's degree candidates are now women, and the percentage of men in graduate-level professional education is shrinking each year.

2   So, there is a gender gap in academic performance, and boys are falling to the bottom of the heap. The problem stems as much from boys' lack of confidence in their ability to perform at school as from their actual inability to perform.

vulnerable
unprotected, easily hurt

gender gap
difference in expectations and/ or success of men and women

© 2014 Wadsworth, Cengage Learning

From Real Boys: Rescuing Our Sons from The Myths of Boyhood by William Pollack, © 1998 By William Pollack. Used by Permission of Random House, Inc.

3   When eighth-grade students are asked about their futures, girls are now twice as likely as boys to say they want to pursue a career in management, the professions, or business. Boys experience more difficulty adjusting to school, are up to ten times more likely to suffer from "hyperactivity" than girls, and account for 71 percent of all school suspensions. In recent years, girls have been making great strides in math and science. In the same period, boys have been severely lagging behind in reading and writing.

BOYS' SELF-ESTEEM—AND BRAGGING

4   The fact is that *boys' self-esteem as learners is far more fragile than that of most girls*. A recent North Carolina study of students in grades six to eight concluded that "boys have a much lower image of themselves as students than girls do." Conducted by Dr. William Purkey, this study contradicts the myth that adolescent boys are more likely than girls to see themselves as smart enough to succeed in society. Boys tend to brag, according to Purkey, as a "shield to hide deep-seated lack of confidence." It is the mask at work once again, a façade of confidence and bravado that boys erect to hide what they perceive as a shameful sense of vulnerability. Girls, on the other hand, brag less and do better in school. It is probably no surprise that a recent U.S. Department of Education study found that among high school seniors fewer boys than girls expect to pursue graduate studies, work toward a law degree, or go to medical school.

5   What we really need for boys is the same upswing in self-esteem as learners that we have begun to achieve for girls—to recognize the specialized academic needs of boys and girls in order to turn us into a more gender-savvy society.

6   Overwhelmingly, recent research indicates that girls not only outperform boys academically but also feel far more confident and capable. Indeed the boys in my study reported, over and over again, how it was not "cool" to be too smart in class, for it could lead to being labeled a nerd, dork, wimp, or fag. As one boy put it, "I'm not stupid enough to sit in the front row and act like some sort of a teacher's pet. If I did, I'd end up with a head full of spitballs and then get my butt kicked in." Just as girls in co-educational environments have been forced to suppress their voices of certainty and truth, boys feel pressured to hide their yearnings for genuine relationships and their thirst for knowledge. To garner acceptance among their peers and protect themselves from being shamed, boys often focus on maintaining their masks and on doing whatever they can to avoid seeming interested in things creative or intellectual. To distance themselves from the things that the stereotype identifies as "feminine," many boys sit through classes without contributing and tease other boys who speak up and participate. Others pull pranks during class, start fights, skip classes, or even drop out of school entirely.

yearnings
desires

SCHOOLS AND THE NEED FOR GENDER UNDERSTANDING

7   Regrettably, instead of working with boys to convince them it is desirable and even "cool" to perform well at school, teachers, too, are often fooled by the mask and believe the stereotype, and this helps to make the lack of achievement self-fulfilling. If a teacher believes that boys who are not doing well are simply uninterested, incapable, or delinquent and signals this, it helps to make it so. Indeed when boys feel pain at school, they sometimes put on the mask and then "act out." Teachers, rather than exploring the emotional reasons behind a boy's misconduct, may instead apply behavioral control techniques that are intended somehow to better "civilize" boys.

© 2014 Wadsworth, Cengage Learning

8   Sal, a third-grader, arrived home with a note from his teacher. "Sal had to be disciplined today for his disruptive behavior," the teacher had written. "Usually he is a very cooperative student, and I hope this behavior does not repeat itself."

9   Sal's mother, Audrey, asked her son what he had done.

10   "I was talking out of turn in class," he said.

11   "That's it?" she asked. "And how did your teacher discipline you?"

12   "She made me stay in during recess. She made me write an essay about why talking in class is disruptive and inconsiderate." Sal hung his head.

13   "I was appalled," recalls Audrey. "If the teacher had spent one minute with my child, trying to figure out why he was behaving badly, this whole thing could have been avoided." The teacher had known Sal to be "a very cooperative student." It seems that, the night before, Sal had learned that a favorite uncle had been killed in a car crash. "I told my son that I understood that he was having a really hard day because of his uncle, but that, even so, it's wrong to disrupt class. He was very relieved that I wasn't mad," Audrey said. "The episode made me think about how boys get treated in school. I think the teacher assumed that Sal was just 'being a boy.' And so, although what he really needed was a little understanding and extra attention, instead she humiliated him. It reminded me to think about how Sal must be feeling when something like this happens, because he often won't talk about what's bothering him unless we prompt him to."

Exercise 11   Work with Words

Use context clues, word-part clues, and, if necessary, the dictionary to choose the best definitions of the italicized words in the following sentences from Reading 3.

1. Boys on the whole are not *faring* well in our schools, especially in our public schools. It is in the classroom that we see some of the most destructive effects of society's misunderstanding of boys. (par. 1)

   faring
   a. doing
   b. attending
   c. fighting

2. *Thrust* into competition with their peers, some boys *invest* so much energy into keeping up their emotional guard and disguising their deepest and most vulnerable feelings, they often have little or no energy left to apply themselves to their schoolwork. (par. 1)

   thrust
   a. invited
   b. crushed
   c. thrown

3. *invest*
   a. use money to make more money
   b. use, devote time
   c. withhold

© 2014 Wadsworth, Cengage Learning

4. A recent North Carolina study of students in grades six to eight concluded that "boys have a much lower image of themselves as students than girls do." Conducted by Dr. William Purkey this study *contradicts* the myth that adolescent boys are more likely than girls to see themselves as smart enough to succeed in society. (par. 4)

contradicts
a. agrees with
b. repeats
c. disagrees with

5. Boys tend to brag, according to Purkey, as a "shield to hide deep-seated lack of confidence." It is the mask at work once again, a *façade* of confidence and bravado that boys erect to hide what they perceive as a shameful sense of vulnerability. (par. 4)

façade
a. genuine quality
b. artificial front
c. extravagant parade

6. To *garner* acceptance among their peers and protect themselves from being shamed, boys often focus on maintaining their masks and on doing whatever they can to avoid seeming interested in things creative or intellectual. (par. 6)

garner
a. reject
b. isolate
c. gain

© 2014 Wadsworth, Cengage Learning

Exercise 12

Recognize the Connotations of Words

Read the following sentences from Reading 3, noticing the italicized words. Each of these words has certain connotations. Choose the best descriptions of the definitions and connotations of these words as they are used in the sentences.

1. Over the last decade we've been forced to confront some *staggering* statistics. From elementary grades through high school, boys receive lower grades than girls. (par. 1)

staggering
a. uncertain; negative connotation
b. surprising, astonishing; negative connotation
c. overwhelming; positive connotation

2. When eighth-grade students are asked about their futures, girls are now twice as likely as boys to say they want to *pursue* a career in management, the professions, or business. (par. 3)

pursue
a. capture aggressively; negative connotation
b. strive to attain; positive connotation
c. avoid; negative connotation

3. In recent years, girls have been making great *strides* in math and science. In the same period, boys have been severely *lagging behind* in reading and writing. (par. 3)

strides
   a. resistance; negative connotation
   b. difficult choices; negative connotation
   c. steps forward; positive connotation

4. *lagging behind*
   a. failing to keep up; negative connotation
   b. decreasing gradually; positive connotation
   c. lingering or delaying; negative connotation

5. Indeed the boys in my study reported, over and over again, how it was not "*cool*" to be too smart in class, for it could lead to being labeled a nerd, dork, wimp, or fag. (par. 6)

cool
   a. appearing enthusiastic; positive connotation
   b. appearing unconcerned; positive connotation
   c. appearing unconcerned; negative connotation

6. If a teacher believes that boys who are not doing well are simply uninterested, incapable, or *delinquent* and signals this, it helps to make it so. (par. 7)

delinquent
   a. a debt that is past due; negative connotation
   b. guilty of an offense; negative connotation
   c. incapable; negative connotation

Exercise 13

Identify Inferences and Main Ideas

Choose the best answer to the following multiple-choice questions based on Reading 3.

1. What is the best main idea statement for paragraph 3?
   a. Boys today face more obstacles than girls for being successful in school.
   b. Boys are up to 10 times more likely to suffer from "hyperactivity" than girls.
   c. Boys are severely lagging behind girls in reading and writing.

2. Which is the best main idea statement for paragraph 4?
   a. Girls brag less and do better in school.
   b. Fewer boys than girls expect to pursue graduate studies, work toward a law degree, or go to medical school.
   c. Boys' self-esteem as learners is far more fragile than that of most girls.

Based on the following sentences or groups of sentences from or about the reading, choose the reasonable inferences. (There may be more than one.)

© 2014 Wadsworth, Cengage Learning

3. Just as girls in coeducational environments have been forced to suppress their voices of certainty and truth, boys feel pressured to hide their yearnings for genuine relationships and their thirst for knowledge. To garner acceptance among their peers and protect themselves from being shamed, boys often focus on maintaining their masks and on doing whatever they can to avoid seeming interested in things creative or intellectual. To distance themselves from the things that the stereotype identifies as "feminine," many boys sit through classes without contributing and tease other boys who speak up and participate. Others pull pranks during class, start fights, skip classes, or even drop out of school entirely.

   a. A likely consequence of these behaviors is doing poorly in school.
   b. Boys are not interested in learning like girls are.
   c. One of the reasons boys are not doing well in school is because they are trying to be cool.
   d. Boys feel pressured to hide their yearnings for genuine relationships and their thirst for knowledge. ·

4. Sal, a third-grader, arrived home with a note from his teacher. "Sal had to be disciplined today for his disruptive behavior," the teacher had written. "Usually he is a very cooperative student, and I hope this behavior does not repeat itself."
   Sal's mother, Audrey, asked her son what he had done.
   "I was talking out of turn in class," he said.
   "That's it?" she asked. "And how did your teacher discipline you?"
   "She made me stay in during recess. She made me write an essay about why talking in class is disruptive and inconsiderate." Sal hung his head.
   "I was appalled," recalls Audrey. "If the teacher had spent one minute with my child, trying to figure out why he was behaving badly, this whole thing could have been avoided." The teacher had known Sal to be "a very cooperative student." It seems that, the night before, Sal had learned that a favorite uncle had been killed in a car crash.

   a. Sal doesn't usually speak out of turn in class.
   b. The teacher did not care about why Sal was speaking out of turn.
   c. The teacher did not find out why Sal was speaking out of turn.
   d. The teacher will probably be more critical of Sal for the rest of the semester.

Exercise 14

Make Connections and Write

Write short answers to the following questions based on Reading 3, your experience, and your observations. Then, discuss your answers with your class group. Working together, prepare a report for your class as a whole or a written summary for your instructor.

1. Think about your experiences in school. Who, as you recall, had more difficulty doing well as a group—girls or boys? Explain your answer. What kinds of difficulties did they have, and why do you think that was so?

© 2014 Wadsworth, Cengage Learning

_____

_____

_____

2. What experiences did you have while growing up that would lead you to think you had it easier or harder because you were a boy or a girl?

_____

_____

_____

Reading 4

A Minefield: Teenagers and Racism on the U.S.–Mexico Border

— ENRIQUE DÁVALOS

The following reading was written for _Joining a Community of Readers_. In it, Mexican historian and border resident Enrique Dávalos explores the events of the summer of 2000 in San Diego, when a group of high school boys attacked Mexican workers who lived in a makeshift encampment made of cardboard boxes, crates, and scraps in the canyons near a well-to-do suburb. As you read, consider the reasonable inferences that can be made based on Dávalos's use of supporting details. Also, notice the use of imagery in this reading, beginning with the title. Consider how the imagery makes the reading even more effective.

initiatives
a system in California by which citizens can get a "proposition" on the ballot with a certain number of signatures of registered voters; if it is approved in an election, it becomes law

1   For several years, the political climate in southern California has been increasingly influenced by anti-immigrant attitudes. Mexicans and people of Mexican descent have frequently felt as if they are under attack in a state that once belonged to Mexico.
    Politicians have taken advantage of anti-immigrant feelings and have stirred up the antagonisms when it suited them to do so. (The same politicians, on other occasions, court the vote of the growing Latino population.) A variety of recent initiatives, turned into laws, were designed to deny public health services and even school enrollment to migrants and their children. Once famed for its orange groves and mild weather, California now has a cultural landscape that resembles a minefield, planted with land mines of hatred and racial intolerance, and we are beginning to reap the harvest.

Enrique Dávalos. Reprinted by Permission of the Author.

© 2014 Wadsworth, Cengage Learning

2   In the beginning of the millennium, in San Diego County, during the summer of 2000, a group of teenagers violently attacked a few elderly Mexican migrant workers. These children, boys between 14 and 17 years old, lived in an upper-middle-class neighborhood and attended one of the most prestigious high schools in San Diego. They became "hate" criminals and almost murderers. We have to learn from this experience to deactivate the mines before more racial hatred explodes, destroying our kids.

3   Let's see what the group of teenagers did when they attacked the camp of migrants on July 5, 2000. According to the reports of the local newspaper, the *San Diego Union Tribune*, a group of eight adolescents drove a van to several migrant encampments near their neighborhood and conducted three raids over a period of two hours. It was "a very brutal, violent, cowardly attack," the San Diego police chief said. Some of the workers were hospitalized, and the teenagers even tried to hide the body of a man that they believed they had killed. All the victims were elders ranging in age from 64 to 69. They were beaten with pipes and rocks and shot with pellet guns. Some migrants confronted the attackers with machetes. The youths shouted racial slurs during the beating, and according to authorities, they asked them to show proof they were legal residents. Those who did not show documents were beaten.

epithet
an abusive term

4   Chief of police David Bejarano said that the attackers "wanted them [the workers] to go back to Mexico." Some spray-painted graffiti messages appeared in the camp, including "We're still here! KKK," "Jesus loves U," and some racial epithets. A red-and-yellow swastika was also painted. Police are not sure, however, whether the attackers were responsible for the graffiti because other young men had been seen around the encampment.

derogatory
insulting

5   After the police captured the teenagers, prosecutors said the boys admitted that they thought it was "cool to shoot beaners," a common derogatory term used against Mexicans. One of the adolescents added that he was tired of listening to people speaking Spanish around him.

6   According to journalist Jeff McDonald, the students responsible for the attack lived in a suburb of San Diego, Rancho Peñasquitos, which is full of SUVs (sports utility vehicles), "soccer moms," playgrounds, and parks. Two-thirds of the families are Caucasian, and 31 percent are Asian. "Nearly three-fourths of the residents report household incomes between $60,000 and $150,000, far higher than the San Diego–wide average," said McDonald. Most of the assailants attended Mt. Carmel High School, one of the county's highest performing schools academically. In contrast, their migrant victims lived in improvised camps near the Evergreen Nursery where they worked. They earned a minimal wage with no benefits. They could not afford housing in this country, and our laws don't require employers to provide homes for their workers. Some of the migrant workers had homes in Tijuana, Mexico, where they went on the weekends. Even in their precarious situation, they belonged to the neighborhood. "I have lived in Rancho Peñasquitos for 12 years," writes Kate Martin, and "I have grown up in the presence of these men in our community. These men are a familiar part of the community—the crowd every morning under the State Route 56 overpass, the occasional face in line with me at VONS [the local grocery store], the tireless man at the door asking for work."

stupefaction
astonishment

7   The attack against the migrants caused confusion and stupefaction in the adult community, although it was not a big surprise to students of local high schools. The parents of the young attackers were shocked, their lawyers said. "It saddens me that these boys may have such degree of hate in them," wrote a Rancho Peñasquitos neighbor

© 2014 Wadsworth, Cengage Learning

(Ivonne Chau). However, some students affirmed, after the arrest, that they had "heard about students teasing migrant workers and stealing their bicycles" and that "at least one Latino student had been the victim of a race-motivated beating." Another student told reporters, "I wasn't very surprised; I can see them doing that." In fact, racial tension was not something unknown in Mt. Carmel High School. In the previous spring (2000), students and teachers organized several meetings to discuss ways to stop racial and ethnic insults on campus.

8   The students arrested had different personalities and belonged to different kinds of families. According to Jeff McDonald, some of them lived in broken families, but others were from more stable families. Some of them were known to pick fights and threaten other students at school. One of them already had a juvenile record, and another was attending an alternative high school for students with discipline problems. However, one of the arrested students played football and the guitar. Some neighbors declared that one of the group was "the nicest guy, never violent—kind of shy. He was just like any other teenager, really." In the same way, another neighbor said about another of the teenagers involved in the attack that he was "very friendly. Even now, when he's riding his bike he says hello." Considering the variety of personal situations, it is difficult to explain the attack based only on the psychology, the "natural rebelliousness" of adolescents, or on the specific family problems of these young people. It is frightening to accept, but the attack has broader social and cultural roots.

9   For example, the legal process against the arrested students has brought to light and magnified the racial tension that already existed in San Diego. The teenagers were charged with robbery, assault, and a hate crime. The prosecutor asked that they be tried as adults, which would mean a more severe sentence if they are convicted. However, the parents of the arrested boys, while emphasizing that they were sorry about what their boys had done, also insisted, "Our children are not adults." The issue is controversial, especially after most Californians voted for a new law (Proposition 21, which passed in the fall of 1999) that allows the prosecuting attorney to decide if criminal minors should be tried as adults. Lawyers and parents of Rancho Peñasquitos' students are challenging this law. Earlier it was applied against some African-American and Latino youths with no media attention. "Why is the law unconstitutional when it is used against whites?" asked a student from a local community college with a mostly African-American and Latino population. The irony is that people in Rancho Peñasquitos mostly voted for Proposition 21, never thinking that it might be used against their own children. "It is ironic," wrote Ronda Trapp, "that now that these kids from 'good' families, who go to 'good' schools in a 'good' community, have been charged as adults, others who likely voted for Prop. 21, now argue that it is unconstitutional and morally wrong." At the moment (September 13, 2000), a San Diego judge approved that the eight teenagers be tried as adults; but their parents were ready to appeal.

10   Several people and organizations in San Diego condemned the attack and pointed out that it is just the tip of the iceberg. Sonia Perez, from the National Council of La Raza, mentioned that a national study had found an increase in the number of hate crimes committed against Latinos nationwide. In San Diego, one of these attacks was perpetrated in 1994 by four Marines, members of an elite, SWAT-type military police, said Claudia Smith of California Rural Legal Assistance. She added that Latinos in San Diego are harassed every day: "It would be rare to talk to a group of migrant farm workers and not have them tell you of experiences when bottles were thrown at them from passing vehicles, epithets hurled at them."

© 2014 Wadsworth, Cengage Learning

11   It is disturbing that this wave of racism is poisoning the youth. The Anti-Defamation League has reported that in San Diego the assailants in about half of the hate crimes against Latinos are 20 years old or younger. "The reality is we're seeing younger and younger kids who feel this is an okay thing to do, to beat someone because of their difference[s]," said Jack McDevitt, director of the Center for Criminal Justice Policy Research at Northeastern University in Boston. Racial discrimination is illegal, and assault is illegal. But it is not illegal to joke or be sarcastic about racial differences. How do children perceive racial attitudes and comments from their parents in neighborhoods like Rancho Peñasquitos? What do they learn from attitudes of disgust and indifference toward people who are different? "It is easy to ignore those dark faces, to mutter an exasperated groan each morning while driving under the Route 56 overpass, to close a door on pleading hands, to turn away, to ignore great poverty," wrote Kate Martin, resident of Rancho Peñasquitos. Children are very sensitive. Adults may joke and feel contempt for Mexican migrants, but they should realize that what they feel and think is what their children will put into actions. The attack in Rancho Peñasquitos is a warning.

12   Finding a solution is not easy. How do we create a culture where our children and all members of our communities are safe? How do we clean up the landscape that has been planted with mines of hatred and social intolerance? It is never easy to remove land mines or to deactivate them. They are usually hidden, difficult to find, and dangerous to handle.

13   Children are children, and they should not be tried as adults. However, the perpetrators of the hate crimes committed in Rancho Peñasquitos deserve a severe punishment. Will an experience in prison change the racist perceptions of the teenagers about Mexicans and other minorities? Probably not. Perhaps it would be more useful, as Jacqueline Giles said, that "the perpetrators and their parents should be required to learn Spanish, study Mexican history and culture and perform enough hard, manual labor to bring them to understand that the men whom they held in contempt and brutalized are real people deserving of respect." Perhaps after that experience, they will be able to understand why one of the Mexican workers assailed, Mr. Alfredo Ayala, 64, said that even though his attackers did not show any mercy, he held no anger toward them. He only felt sorry for their families.

Sources

Ivonne Chau, "Letters," *San Diego Union Tribune,* July 21, 2000.

Jacqueline Giles, "Will Prison Teach Teens Tolerance?" *San Diego Union Tribune,* July 21, 2000.

Kate Martin, "Fight Racism by Fighting Indifference," *San Diego Union Tribune,* July 27, 2000.

Jeff McDonald, "Some Suspects in Camp Attack Had Troubled Pasts," *San Diego Union Tribune,* July 22, 2000.

"Mt. Carmel High Has a Way to Go Despite Its Many Triumphs," *San Diego Union Tribune,* July 18, 2000.

Dong-Phuong Nguyen, "Local Attack Mirrors Rise in Reported U.S. Hate Crime," *San Diego Union Tribune*, July 21, 2000.

Alex Roth, "Teen Admitted Role in Attack, Affidavit Says," *San Diego Union Tribune,* July 26, 2000.

Alex Roth, Joe Hughes, Kim Peterson, and Leonel Sanchez, "Police Arrest Seven Teens in Attacks at Migrant Camp," *San Diego Union Tribune*, July 18, 2000.

Ronda Trapp, "Letters," *San Diego Union Tribune,* July 24, 2000 .

© 2014 Wadsworth, Cengage Learning

Exercise 15

Understand the Language of Imagery

In the following sentences from Reading 4, some examples of language that use imagery have been italicized. Explain (1) what visual images are formed when we read these words and (2) what the words actually refer to or mean in the sentence.

1. Once famed for its orange groves and mild weather, California now has *a cultural landscape that resembles a minefield, planted with land mines of hatred and racial intolerance, and now we are beginning to reap the harvest.* (par. 1)

   visual image: _____

   _____

   meaning: _____

   _____

2. We have to learn from this experience to *deactivate* the mines before the racial hatred *explodes,* destroying our kids. (par. 2)

   visual image: _____

   _____

   meaning: _____

   _____

3. How do we clean up *the landscape that has been planted* with mines of hatred and social intolerance? (par. 12)

   visual image: _____

   meaning: _____

4. It is frightening to accept, but the attack has broader social and *cultural roots.* (par. 8)

   visual image: _____

   meaning: _____

5. For example, the legal process against the arrested students has *brought to light and magnified* the racial tension that already existed in San Diego. (par. 9)

   visual image: _____

   meaning: _____

© 2014 Wadsworth, Cengage Learning

6. Several people and organizations in San Diego have condemned the attack and pointed out that it is just the *tip of the iceberg.* (par. 10)

visual image: _____

_____

meaning: _____

7. It is disturbing that this *wave* of racism is poisoning the youth. (par. 11)

visual image: _____

meaning: _____

Exercise 16

Check Your Understanding and Identify Inferences

Choose the best way to complete the following statements about Reading 4.

1. In paragraph 1, we can reasonably infer that the author believes that
   a. the anti-immigrant feelings in California are setting the stage for problems for the young people there as well as for the society as a whole.
   b. Mexicans and people of Mexican descent should not feel as though they are being attacked.
   c. politicians are clearly not to blame for the anti-immigrant attitudes in California.

2. We could reasonably infer that the migrant workers lived in encampments
   a. because they preferred to live outdoors.
   b. because it was illegal to rent apartments to them in Rancho Peñasquitos.
   c. because they could not afford housing in Rancho Peñasquitos.

3. In paragraph 8, we can reasonably infer that the author believes that
   a. the attackers were poor and viciously attacked the workers because they were rich.
   b. the boys come from different backgrounds so it's difficult to give a single simple reason for why they were involved in the attack.
   c. the natural rebelliousness of teenage boys explains the attack.

4. From paragraph 11, we can reasonably infer that the author believes that
   a. the adolescents are carrying out racist attacks because their parents make comments about the immigrants that show contempt for them.
   b. the adolescents are carrying out racist attacks even though their parents have tolerant attitudes for the most part.
   c. there is no explanation for why these boys carried out their attack against the immigrants.

© 2014 Wadsworth, Cengage Learning

5. Jacqueline Giles (par. 13) suggests that "the perpetrators and their parents should be required to learn Spanish, study Mexican history and culture and perform enough hard, manual labor to bring them to understand that the men whom they held in contempt and brutalized are real people deserving of respect." We can reasonably infer that Giles believes that

   a. learning the language of another people teaches you to understand their situation.

   b. understanding another culture's language and history and experiencing doing hard physical labor leads to tolerance and respect.

   c. the schools have failed these adolescent boys.

Exercise 17

Check Your Understanding: Chronological List

Write a chronological list that includes the most important events that take place in Reading 4, in order.

_____

_____

_____

_____

_____

_____

_____

_____

Exercise 18

Make Connections and Write

Write short answers to the following questions about Reading 4 based on your reading, your experience, and your observations. Then, discuss your answers with your class group. Working together, prepare a report for your class as a whole or a written summary for your instructor.

© 2014 Wadsworth, Cengage Learning

1. What solutions does Dávalos give for handling the court case and punishing the boys who committed the hate crime?

_____

_____

_____

_____

2. How do you think the case of the boys should be handled? Should they be tried as adults? If the boys are convicted, what type of sentence should they receive? Explain.

_____

_____

_____

_____

3. Do you think these boys were wearing the "tough guy" mask? Explain.

_____

_____

_____

_____

4. Do you think the actions of these boys come from their personal problems or from problems in society? Explain.

_____

_____

_____

_____

© 2014 Wadsworth, Cengage Learning

Chapter Review

To aid your review of the reading skills in Chapter 8, study the Put It Together chart.

Put It Together: Inferences	
Skills and Concepts	**Explanation**
Inference (see pages 368–372, and 375–377)	An inference is something a writer implies but does not state directly. You have to read between the lines to understand what the writer is saying indirectly.
Imagery (see page 382–383)	Imagery refers to the mental pictures or images that form in our minds created by the written word.
Connotation (see page 382–383)	A connotation is the emotion associated with a word.

To reinforce your thinking before taking the Mastery Tests, complete as many of the following activities as your instructor assigns.

Review Skills

Answer the following skills-review questions individually or in a group.

1. Why is it important to distinguish between your personal opinion and reasonable inferences?

_____

_____

_____

_____

2. What clues do you look for when you are "reading" a photograph or a cartoon?

_____

_____

_____

_____

© 2014 Wadsworth, Cengage Learning

3. How does an author's use of imagery and word connotations help make reading more interesting for the reader?

_____

_____

Write

Find a newspaper or magazine article about the achievements or problems of adolescents. Write a brief summary of the article. Then use your skill at recognizing inferences to conclude your summary with what the author thinks are the causes of adolescents' behavior.

COLLABORATE

Bring your newspaper or magazine articles about adolescents to class to share with your class group. Discuss what the articles have in common. Then complete the accompanying chart.

Types of Adolescents (girls, boys, kids with problems, achievers)	**Achievements or Problems**	**Causes**
_____	_____	_____
_____	_____	_____
_____	_____	_____
_____	_____	_____
_____	_____	_____
_____		

EXTEND YOUR THINKING

Visit a high school, juvenile detention center, community club, or activity for young people. Develop a list of questions you would like to ask based on the readings in this chapter. Interview a counselor, law officer, club leader, or coach about juvenile behavior. Bring the information you learn back to class to share with your fellow students and instructor.

WORK THE WEB

As you have learned in this chapter, there are many things a writer may not say directly that we can infer as readers. Other forms of communication, including songs, depend on inferences, too. In the following exercise, you will practice your skills identifying imagery and inferring what a writer means through the analysis

© 2014 Wadsworth, Cengage Learning

of song lyrics. There are many Web sites that provide the lyrics to popular songs. Use a search engine such as *Google*. Enter the name "Bruce Springsteen," the title "The River," and the word "lyrics."

1. In the beginning of the song "The River," the narrator describes where he comes from. What can you infer from the first verse of the song? What does it mean that he was raised to do what his "daddy" did?

_____

_____

_____

_____

2. What important details do we learn about his wedding, and what do those details tell us?

_____

_____

_____

_____

3. What do you learn about the narrator's work situation, and how is that important to the story?

_____

_____

_____

_____

4. The central visual image in this song is the river itself. What does he go down to the river for? What changes about the river by the end of the song? What might the river represent in his life?

_____

_____

_____

_____

© 2014 Wadsworth, Cengage Learning

Name _____ Date _____

When Money Is Everything, Except Hers

— DIRK JOHNSON

In the following newspaper article, Dirk Johnson shows what it is like for a young person to grow up poor in the middle of a prosperous neighborhood. Johnson points out that adolescence can seem so much worse for kids who are not like their peers—especially when those peers taunt and isolate them. As you read, pay attention not only to how Johnson uses inferences to tell Wendy's story, but also to how his imagery paints a clear picture of her life. Do you think the solutions offered by the counselor at the end of the reading adequately address the problem at hand?

1   DIXON, ILL. Watching classmates strut past in designer clothes, Wendy Williams sat silently on the yellow school bus, wearing a cheap belt and rummage-sale slacks. One boy stopped and yanked his thumb, demanding her seat. "Move it, trailer girl," he sneered.

2   It has never been easy to live on the wrong side of the tracks. But in the economically robust 1990s, with sprawling new houses and three-car garages sprouting like cornstalks on the Midwestern prairie, the sting that comes with scarcity gets rubbed with an extra bit of salt. Seen through the eyes of a 13-year-old girl growing up at Chateau Estates, a fancy name for a tin-plain trailer park, the rosy talk about the nation's prosperity carries a certain <u>mocking</u> echo.

3   The everyday discussion in the halls of Reagan Middle School in this city about 100 miles west of Chicago touches on computer toys that can cost $1,000, family vacations to Six Flags or Disney World, and stylish clothes that bear a Nike emblem or Tommy Hilfiger's <u>coveted</u> label. Unlike young people a generation ago, those today must typically pay fees to play for the school sports teams or band. It costs $45 to play in the youth summer soccer league. It takes money to go skating on weekends at the White Pines roller rink, to play laser tag or rock-climb at the Plum Hollow Recreation Center, to mount a steed at the Horseback Riding Club, . . .[or] to go shopping for clothes at the Cherryvale Mall.

4   To be without money, in so many ways, is to be left out. "I told this girl: 'That's a really awesome shirt. Where did you get it?'" said Wendy, explaining that she knew it was out of her price range, but that she wanted to join the small talk. "And she looked at me and laughed and said, 'Why would you want to know?'" A lanky, soft-spoken girl with large brown eyes, Wendy pursed her lips to hide a slight overbite that got her the nickname Rabbit, a humiliation she once begged her mother and father to avoid by sending her to an orthodontist.

5   For struggling parents, keenly aware that adolescents agonize over the social <u>pecking order</u>, the styles of the moment and the face in the mirror, there is no small sense of failure in telling a child that she cannot have what her classmates take for granted. "Do you know what it's like?" asked Wendy's mother, Veronica Williams, "to have your daughter come home and say, 'Mom, the kids say my clothes are tacky,' and then walk off with her head hanging low."

Dirk Johnson, "When Money Is Everything, Except Hers." From *The New York Times*, October 14, 1998. © 1998 *The New York Times*. All Rights Reserved. Used by Permission and Protected by the Copyright Laws of the United States. The Printing, Copying, Redistribution, or Retransmission of this Content Without Express Written Permission is Prohibited.

© 2014 Wadsworth, Cengage Learning

6   This is not the desperate poverty of Chicago housing projects, where the plight of empty pockets is worsened by the threat of gangs and gunfires. Wendy lives in relative safety in a home with both parents. Her father, Wendell Provow, earns $9 an hour as a welder. Her mother works part-time as a cook for Head Start, the federal education program. Unlike students in some urban pockets, isolated from <u>affluence</u>, Wendy receives the same education as a girl from a $300,000 house in the Idle Oaks subdivision. The flip side of that coin is the public spectacle of economic struggle. This is a place small enough where people know the personal stories, or, at least, repeat them as if they did.

7   Even in this down-to-earth town, where a poor boy nicknamed Dutch grew up to become president, young people seem increasingly enchanted with buying, having, spending and status. R. Woodrow (Woody) Wasson, the principal at Reagan Middle School, makes it a point to sit down with every child and ask them about their hopes and dreams. "They want to be doctors, lawyers, veterinarians and, of course, professional athletes," said Mr. Wasson, whose family roots here go back to the 19th century. "I don't remember the last time I heard somebody say they wanted to be a police officer or a firefighter. They want to do something that will make a lot of money and have a lot of prestige."

8   He said a teacher in a nearby town has been trying to recruit high school students for vocational studies to become tool-and-die artisans, a trade that can pay $70,000 a year. "The teacher can't fill the slots," Mr. Wasson said. "Nobody's interested in that kind of work."

9   It is not surprising that children grow up believing that money is so important, given the relentless way they are targeted by marketers. "In the past, you just put an ad in the magazine," said Michael Wood, the director of research for Teen-Age Research Unlimited, a marketing consultant in suburban Chicago. "Now savvy marketers know you must hit them at all angles—Web sites, cable TV shows, school functions, sporting events." He noted the growth of cross-promotions, like the deal in which actors on the television show "Dawson's Creek," which is popular among adolescents, wear clothes by J. Crew and appear in its catalogue.

10   But young people get cues in their everyday lives. Some spending habits that would once have been seen as <u>ostentatious</u>—extravagant parties for small children, new cars for teenagers—have become familiar trappings for middle-class comfort. The stock market, although it is sputtering now, has made millionaires of many people in Main Street towns. Building developers have recently won approval to build a gated community, which will be called Timber Edge.

11   "Wendy goes to school around these rich kids," her mother said, "and wonders why she can't have things like they do." A bright girl with a <u>flair</u> for art, writing, and numbers, Wendy stays up late most nights, reading books. *The Miracle Worker* was a recent favorite. But when a teacher asked her to join an elevated class for algebra, she politely declined. "I get picked on for my clothes and living in the trailer park," said Wendy, who never brings anyone home from school. "I don't want to get picked on for being a nerd, too."

12   Her mother, who watched three other daughters drop out of school and have babies as teenagers, has told Wendy time and again: "Don't lose your self-esteem."

13   One time a boy at school was teasing Wendy about her clothes—"they don't even match," he laughed—and her humble house in the trailer park. She listened for a while. He kept insulting her. So she lifted a leg—clothed as it was in discount jeans from the Farm & Fleet store—and kicked him in the shins. He told the authorities. She

© 2014 Wadsworth, Cengage Learning

403

got the detention. It became clear to Wendy that the insults were not going to stop. It also became clear that shin-kicking, however deserved, was not going to be the solution.

14   She went to a guidance counselor, Cynthia Kowa Basler, a dynamic woman who keeps close tabs on the children, especially girls who fret about their weight and suddenly stop eating lunch. "I am large," she tells the girls, "and I have self-esteem."

15   Wendy, who knew that Mrs. Basler held sessions with students to increase their self-confidence, went to the counselor. "I feel a little down," Wendy told her. The counselor gathered eight students, including other girls like Wendy, who felt embarrassed about their economic station.

16   In this school named for Ronald Reagan, the students were told to study the words of Eleanor Roosevelt. One of her famous quotations was posted above the counselor's desk: "No one can make you feel inferior without your <u>consent</u>." As a group, the students looked up the definition of inferior and consent. And then they read the words out loud.

17   "Again," the counselor instructed.

18   "Louder," the counselor insisted. Again and again, they read the inspirational words.

19   In role-playing exercises, the children practiced responses to taunts, which sometimes called for nothing more than a shrug. "Mrs. Basler told us to live up to our goals—show those kids," Wendy said. "She told us that things can be a lot different when you're grown up. Maybe things will be the other way around then." Wendy smiled at the notion.

20   Life still has plenty of bumps. When Wendy gets off the school bus—the trailer park is the first stop, so everyone can see where she lives—she still looks at her shoes. She still pulls her shirt out to hide a belt that does not quite make the grade. And she still purses her lips to hide an overbite. But her mother has noticed her smiling more these days. And Wendy has even said she might consider taking an advanced course in math, her favorite subject. "I want to go to college," Wendy said the other day. "I want to become a teacher."

21   One recent day, she popped in to the counselor's office, just to say hello, then walked back down the halls, her arms folded around her schoolbooks. Mrs. Basler stood at the doorway and watched her skip away, a student with so much promise, and so many obstacles. For the girl from Chateau Estates, it is a long way from the seventh grade to college. "She's going to make it," the counselor said, with a clenched fist and a voice full of hope.

Use context clues, word-part clues, and, if necessary, the dictionary to write the definitions of the italicized words in the following sentences from the reading.

1. Seen through the eyes of a 13-year-old girl growing up at Chateau Estates, a fancy name for a tin-plain trailer park, the rosy talk about the nation's prosperity carries a certain *mocking* echo. (par. 2)

   mocking _____

2. The everyday discussion in the halls of Reagan Middle School in this city about 100 miles west of Chicago touches on computer toys that can cost $1,000, family vacations to Six Flags or Disney World and stylish clothes that bear a Nike emblem or Tommy Hilfiger's *coveted* label. (par. 3)

   coveted _____

© 2014 Wadsworth, Cengage Learning

3. For struggling parents, keenly aware that adolescents agonize over the social *pecking order*, the styles of the moment and the face in the mirror, there is no small sense of failure in telling a child that she cannot have what her class-mates take for granted. (par. 5)

pecking order _____

4. Unlike students in some urban pockets, isolated from *affluence*, Wendy re-ceives the same education as a girl from a $300,000 house in the Idle Oaks subdivision. (par. 6)

affluence _____

5. Some spending habits that would once have been seen as *ostentatious* —ex-travagant parties for small children, new cars for teenagers—have become familiar trappings for middle-class comfort. (par. 10)

ostentatious _____

6. A bright girl with a *flair* for art, writing, and numbers, Wendy stays up late most nights, reading books. (par. 11)

flair _____

7. One of her famous quotations was posted above the counselor's desk: "No one can make you feel inferior without your *consent.*" (par. 16)

consent _____

For the following sentences or groups of sentences from or about the reading, choose the reasonable inferences that you can make from the information and clues presented. There may be more than one reasonable inference. Circle the letter in front of the statements that you decide are reasonable inferences from the passage.

8. Watching classmates strut past in designer clothes, Wendy Williams sat si-lently on the yellow school bus, wearing a cheap belt and rummage-sale slacks.
   a. Wendy Williams didn't feel like part of the group of classmates.
   b. Wendy's parents' income was the same as the other students' parents.
   c. Wendy was probably poorer than the other students.
   d. Wendy was proud of who she was.

9. "I told this girl: 'That's a really awesome shirt. Where did you get it?'" said Wendy, explaining that she knew it was out of her price range, but that she wanted to join the small talk. "And she looked at me and laughed and said, 'Why would you want to know?'"
   a. Wendy wanted to know where the girl bought the shirt so she could get one like it.
   b. Wendy was just trying to be friendly with the girl.
   c. The girl insulted Wendy with her answer, "Why would you want to know?"
   d. Behind the girl's words "Why would you want to know?" was the thought, "You wouldn't be able to afford it anyway."

© 2014 Wadsworth, Cengage Learning

10. This is not the desperate poverty of Chicago housing projects, where the plight of empty pockets is worsened by the threat of gangs and gunfires.
    a. Most poor people are violent.
    b. In housing projects, violence frequently makes the experience of poverty much worse.
    c. Wendy's poverty does not affect her safety.

11. But when a teacher asked her to join an elevated class for algebra, she politely declined. "I get picked on for my clothes and living in the trailer park," said Wendy, who never brings anyone home from school. "I don't want to get picked on for being a nerd, too."
    a. You are considered a "nerd" if you take advanced classes.
    b. Only "nerds" take advanced classes.
    c. Wendy thinks that only "nerds" take advanced classes.

12. She went to a guidance counselor, Cynthia Kowa Basler, a dynamic woman who keeps close tabs on the children, especially girls who fret about their weight and suddenly stop eating lunch. "I am large," she tells the girls, "and I have self-esteem."
    a. Girls who stop eating lunch have self-esteem problems
    b. Cynthia Basler frets about her weight.
    c. Cynthia Basler does not allow her weight to affect her self-esteem.

In the following sentences, some examples of language that use imagery have been italicized. Explain (1) what visual images are formed when we read these words and (2) what the words actually mean in the sentence.

13. But in the economically robust 1990s, with *sprawling new houses and three-car garages sprouting like cornstalks* on the Midwestern prairie, *the sting* that comes with scarcity gets *rubbed with an extra bit of salt.*

    sprouting like cornstalks on the prairie

    visual image: _____

    meaning: _____

14. *the sting . . . rubbed with an extra bit of salt*

    visual image: _____

    meaning: _____

15. One boy stopped and yanked his thumb, demanding her seat. "Move it, *trailer girl,*" he sneered.

    trailer girl

    visual image: _____

    meaning: _____

© 2014 Wadsworth, Cengage Learning

16. Life still has *plenty of bumps.*

    plenty of bumps

    visual image: _____

    meaning: _____

Write short answers to the following questions based on your reading, your experience, and your observations.

17. What was your experience growing up? Was your family well-off? Middle-class? Poor? Explain what life was like for you as a teenager and how your family's financial position influenced it.

    _____

    _____

    _____

    _____

18. What do you think of Johnson's statement that "young people seem increasingly enchanted with buying, having, spending and status." Do you agree or disagree with him? Explain why.

    _____

    _____

    _____

    _____

19. Explain the following quotation from Eleanor Roosevelt in your own words: "No one can make you feel inferior without your consent." Do you agree with the quotation? How does it apply to the reading? Explain your answer.

    _____

    _____

    _____

    _____

© 2014 Wadsworth, Cengage Learning

20. Is Wendy Williams's problem a personal problem or a problem in our society? Explain your answer.

_____

_____

_____

_____

© 2014 Wadsworth, Cengage Learning

Name _____ Date _____

Worshipping the Gods of Thinness

— MARY PIPHER

The following reading from Mary Pipher's critically acclaimed book, *Reviving Ophelia,* **explores our society's obsession with thinness and the effect it has on adolescent girls. What can you infer from her statements? Do you agree with her conclusions?**

1   Beauty is the defining characteristic for American women. It's the necessary and often sufficient condition for social success. It is important for women of all ages, but the pressure to be beautiful is most <u>intense</u> in early adolescence. Girls worry about their clothes, makeup, skin and hair. But most of all they worry about their weight. Peers place an enormous value on thinness.

2   This emphasis on appearance was present when I was a girl. Our high school had a "gauntlet" that we girls walked through every morning. It consisted of all the boys lined up by their cars along the sidewalk that led into the front doors. We walked past them to catcalls and remarks about our breasts and legs. I wore a girdle made of thick rubber to flatten my stomach on days I dressed in straight skirts.

3   But appearance is even more important today. Three things <u>account for</u> the increased pressure to be thin in the 1990s. We have moved from communities of <u>primary relationships</u> in which people know each other to cities full of <u>secondary relationships</u>. In a community of primary relationships, appearance is only one of many dimensions that define people. Everyone knows everyone else in different ways over time. In a city of strangers, appearance is the only dimension available for the rapid <u>assessment</u> of others. Thus it becomes incredibly important in defining value.

4   Secondly, the <u>omnipresent</u> media consistently portrays desirable women as thin. Thirdly, even as real women grow heavier, models and beautiful women are portrayed as thinner. In the last two decades we have developed a national cult of thinness. What is considered beautiful has become slimmer and slimmer. For example, in 1950 the White Rock mineral water girl was 5 feet 4 inches tall and weighed 140 pounds. Today she is 5 feet 10 inches and weighs 110 pounds.

5   Girls compare their own bodies to our cultural ideals and find them wanting. Dieting and dissatisfaction with bodies have become normal reactions to puberty. Girls developed eating disorders when our culture developed a standard of beauty that they couldn't obtain by being healthy. When unnatural thinness became attractive, girls did unnatural things to be thin.

6   In all the years I've been a therapist, I've yet to meet one girl who likes her body. Girls as skinny as chopsticks complain that their thighs are flabby or their stomachs puff out. And not only do girls dislike their bodies, they often loathe their fat. They have been <u>culturally conditioned</u> to hate their bodies, which are after all themselves. When I speak to classes, I ask any woman in the audience who feels good about her body to come up afterward. I want to hear about her success experience. I have yet to have a woman come up.

7   Unfortunately girls are not <u>irrational</u> to worry about their bodies. Looks do matter. Girls who are chubby or plain miss much of the American dream. The social desirability research in psychology documents our prejudices against the unattractive, particularly the obese, who are the social lepers of our culture. A recent study found that 11 percent

From *Reviving Ophelia* by Mary Pipher, Ph.D., © 1994 by Mary Pipher, Ph.D.
Used by Permission of G.P. Putnam's Sons, a Division of Penguin Group (Usa) Inc.

© 2014 Wadsworth, Cengage Learning

of Americans would abort a fetus if they were told it had a tendency to obesity. By age five, children select pictures of thin people when asked to identify good-looking others. Elementary school children have more negative attitudes toward the obese than toward bullies, the handicapped or children of different races. Teachers underestimate the intelligence of the obese and overestimate the intelligence of the slender. Obese students are less likely to be granted scholarships.

8   Girls are terrified of being fat, as well they should be. Being fat means being left out, scorned and <u>vilified</u>. Girls hear the remarks made about heavy girls in the halls of the schools. No one feels thin enough. Because of guilt and shame about their bodies, young women are constantly on the defensive. Young women with eating disorders are not all that different from their peers. It's a matter of degree. Almost all adolescent girls feel fat, worry about their weight, diet and feel guilty when they eat. In fact, girls with eating disorders are often the girls who have bought the cultural messages about women and attractiveness hook, line and scales. To conform they are willing to make themselves sick.

9   Particularly in the 1980s and 1990s, there's been an explosion of girls with eating disorders. When I speak at high schools, girls surround me with confessions about their eating disorders. When I speak at colleges, I ask if any of the students have friends with eating disorders. Everyone's hand goes up. Studies report that on any given day in America, half our teenage girls are dieting and that one in five young women has an eating disorder. Eating disorders are not currently the media-featured problem they were in the 1980s, but <u>incidence</u> rates are not going down. Eight million women have eating disorders in America.

Use context clues, word-part clues, and, if necessary, the dictionary to write the definitions of the italicized words in the following sentences from the reading.

1. It is important for women of all ages, but the pressure to be beautiful is most *intense* in early adolescence. (par. 1)

   intense _____

2. Three things *account for* the increased pressure to be thin in the 1990s. (par. 3)

   account for _____

3. We have moved from communities of *primary relationships* in which people know each other to cities full of *secondary relationships*. In a community of primary relationships, appearance is only one of many dimensions that define people. Everyone knows everyone else in different ways over time. In a city of strangers, appearance is the only dimension available for the rapid assessment of others. (par. 3)

   primary relationships _____

4. *secondary relationships* _____

5. In a city of strangers, appearance is the only dimension available for the rapid *assessment* of others. (par. 3)

   assessment _____

© 2014 Wadsworth, Cengage Learning

6. Secondly, the *omnipresent* media consistently portrays desirable women as thin. (par. 4)

omnipresent _____

7. They have been *culturally conditioned* to hate their bodies, which are after all themselves. (par. 6)

culturally conditioned _____

_____

8. Unfortunately girls are not *irrational* to worry about their bodies. Looks do matter. (par. 7)

irrational _____

9. Being fat means being left out, scorned and *vilified*. (par. 8)

vilified _____

10. Eating disorders are not currently the media-featured problem they were in the 1980s, but *incidence* rates are not going down. (par. 9)

incidence _____

In the following sentences, some examples of language that use imagery have been italicized. Explain (1) what visual images are formed when we read these words and (2) what the words actually mean in the sentences.

11. Girls *as skinny as chopsticks* complain that their thighs are flabby or their stomachs puff out. (par. 6)

visual image: _____

meaning: _____

12. The social desirability research in psychology documents our prejudices against the unattractive, particularly the obese, who are the *social lepers* of our culture. (par. 7)

visual image: _____

meaning: _____

13. In fact, the girls with eating disorders are often the girls who have bought the cultural messages about women and attractiveness *hook, line and scales*. (par. 8)

visual image: _____

meaning: _____

© 2014 Wadsworth, Cengage Learning

411

For the following sentences or groups of sentences from the reading, choose the reasonable inferences that you can make from the information and clues presented. There may be more than one. Circle the letter in front of the statements that you decide are reasonable inferences from the passage.

14. Our high school had a "gauntlet" that we girls walked through every morning. It consisted of all the boys lined up by their cars along the sidewalk that led into the front doors. We walked past them to cat calls and remarks about our breasts and legs. I wore a girdle made of thick rubber to flatten my stomach on days I dressed in straight skirts.
    a. The author looked forward to walking the "gauntlet."
    b. The author dreaded walking the "gauntlet."
    c. Most of the other girls were probably also self-conscious about walking the "gauntlet."

15. Girls as skinny as chopsticks complain that their thighs are flabby or their stomachs puff out.
    a. Girls have a good sense of how thin they really are.
    b. Girls think they are fat even when they are not.
    c. Girls understand that it is unhealthy to try to meet the skinny standard of beauty.

16. Teachers underestimate the intelligence of the obese and overestimate the intelligence of the slender.
    a. Teachers may be partly to blame for the way girls feel about their bodies.
    b. Teachers are good at estimating the intelligence of their students accurately.
    c. Teachers are likely to have prejudices against the obese as much as anyone else in the society.

17. Almost all adolescent girls feel fat, worry about their weight, diet and feel guilty when they eat.
    a. The author believes it is unfortunate that girls worry about their weight so much.
    b. The author usually recommends that girls lose weight so that they will feel better about themselves.
    c. The author agrees that the girls should feel guilty when they eat, especially if they are already overweight.

Write short answers to the following questions based on your reading, your experience, and your observations.

18. List the pressures on adolescent girls that Mary Pipher believes lead them to eating disorders.

    _____

    _____

    _____

    _____

© 2014 Wadsworth, Cengage Learning

19. What do you think other people infer about a person from his or her weight? Explain your answer.

_____

_____

_____

_____

20. What steps would you propose be taken to make it possible for adolescent girls to feel good about their appearance? Explain your answer.

_____

_____

_____

_____

© 2014 Wadsworth, Cengage Learning

9 Critical Reading

SOCIAL CONNECTEDNESS AND COMMUNITY

Kim Karpeles / Alamy

I get by with a little help from my friends.
—THE BEATLES

- What does the quotation mean? Does it apply to your life?

- What are the people in the photo doing? What kind of event are they attending?

- Who do you think benefits from the activities in the picture?

Getting Ready to Read

We humans are social creatures. We generally like to be with and do things with other people. We like to have connections with other people, and we naturally form communities of many kinds. Usually we think of our community as being our neighborhood, but there are other communities as well: communities of friends, family, colleagues in our workplaces, people who share common interests, students, and classmates in this course—your own community of readers. The communities we are part of can also become negative influences in our lives, like gangs. The idea of community involvement can include our participation in neighborhood, local, state, and even national government. It can even include recognizing that we are all a part of a global community. Our connectedness with people around us influences our lives in many ways. How can we develop strong ties within our various communities that can help us in positive ways? At the same time, how can we be sure to stay away from social connections that are negative?

In this chapter, you will read about communities, community involvement, and social connectedness in many forms. In the process, you will improve your reading skills by learning how to:

- Distinguish between facts and opinions
- Recognize an author's worldview, point of view, and purpose
- Draw conclusions after considering the facts and the opinions of others

© 2014 Wadsworth, Cengage Learning

Thank You, M'am

— LANGSTON HUGHES

Langston Hughes (1902–1967) is one of the most important African American writers of the twentieth century. He wrote poetry, plays, and short stories as well as nonfiction focusing on the experiences of black people in the United States. As you read the following short story, think about how the two main characters treat each other. Hughes published this story in 1959. Now, more than one-half century later, do you think what happens in this story could still happen?

1   She was a large woman with a large purse that had everything in it but a hammer and nails. It had a long strap, and she carried it slung across her shoulder. It was about eleven o'clock at night, dark, and she was walking alone, when a boy ran up behind her and tried to snatch her purse. The strap broke with the sudden single tug the boy gave it from behind. But the boy's weight and the weight of the purse combined caused him to lose his balance. Instead of taking off full blast as he had hoped, the boy fell on his back on the sidewalk and his legs flew up. The large woman simply turned around and kicked him right square in his blue-jeaned sitter. Then she reached down, picked the boy up by his shirt front, and shook him until his teeth rattled.

After that the woman said, "Pick up my pocketbook, boy, and give it here."

She still held him tightly. But she bent down enough to permit him to stoop and pick up her purse. Then she said, "Now ain't you ashamed of yourself?"

Firmly gripped by his shirt front, the boy said, "Yes'm."

5   The woman said, "What did you want to do it for?"

The boy said, "I didn't aim to."

She said, "You a lie!"

By that time two or three people passed, stopped, turned to look, and some stood watching.

"If I turn you loose, will you run?" asked the woman.

10   "Yes'm," said the boy.

"Then I won't turn you loose," said the woman. She did not release him.

"Lady, I'm sorry," whispered the boy.

"Um-hum! Your face is dirty. I got a great mind to wash your face for you. Ain't you got nobody home to tell you to wash your face?"

"No'm," said the boy.

15   "Then it will get washed this evening," said the large woman, starting up the street, dragging the frightened boy behind her.

He looked as if he were fourteen or fifteen, frail and willow-wild, in tennis shoes and blue jeans.

The woman said, "You ought to be my son. I would teach you right from wrong. Least I can do right now is to wash your face. Are you hungry?"

"No'm," said the being-dragged boy. "I just want you to turn me loose."

"Was I bothering *you* when I turned that corner?" asked the woman.

"Thank You, M'am" From *Short Stories* by Langston Hughes. © 1996 by Ramona Bass and Arnold Rampersad.
Reprinted by Permission of Hill and Wang, a Division of Farrar, Straus and Giroux, Llc.

© 2014 Wadsworth, Cengage Learning

20   "No'm."

"But you put yourself in contact with *me,*" said the woman. "If you think that that contact is not going to last awhile, you got another thought coming. When I get through with you, sir, you are going to remember Mrs. Luella Bates Washington Jones."

Sweat popped out on the boy's face and he began to struggle. Mrs. Jones stopped, jerked him around in front of her, put a half nelson about his neck, and continued to drag him up the street. When she got to her door, she dragged the boy inside, down a hall, and into a large kitchenette-furnished room at the rear of the house. She switched on the light and left the door open. The boy could hear other roomers laughing and talking in the large house. Some of their doors were open, too, so he knew he and the woman were not alone. The woman still had him by the neck in the middle of her room.

She said, "What is your name?"

"Roger," answered the boy.

25   "Then, Roger, you go to that sink and wash your face," said the woman, whereupon she turned him loose—at last. Roger looked at the door—looked at the woman— looked at the door—*and went to the sink.*

"Let the water run until it gets warm," she said. "Here's a clean towel."

"You gonna take me to jail?" asked the boy, bending over the sink.

"Not with that face, I would not take you nowhere," said the woman. "Here I am try- ing to get home to cook me a bite to eat, and you snatch my pocketbook! Maybe you ain't been to your supper either, late as it be. Have you?"

"There's nobody home at my house," said the boy.

30   "Then we'll eat," said the woman. "I believe you're hungry—or been hungry—to try to snatch my pocketbook!"

"I want a pair of blue suede shoes," said the boy.

"Well, you didn't have to snatch *my* pocketbook to get some suede shoes," said Mrs. Luella Bates Washington Jones. "You could of asked me."

"M'am?"

The water dripping from his face, the boy looked at her. There was a long pause. A very long pause. After he had dried his face and not knowing what else to do, dried it again, the boy turned around, wondering what next. The door was open. He could make a dash for it down the hall. He could run, run, run, *run!*

35   The woman was sitting on the day bed. After a while she said, "I were young once and I wanted things I could not get."

There was another long pause. The boy's mouth opened. Then he frowned, not knowing he frowned.

The woman said, "Um-hum! You thought I was going to say *but,* didn't you? You thought I was going to say, *but I didn't snatch people's pocketbooks.* Well, I wasn't going to say that." Pause. Silence. "I have done things, too, which I would not tell you, son— neither tell God, if he didn't already know. Everybody's got something in common. So you set down while I fix us something to eat. You might run that comb through your hair so you will look presentable."

In another corner of the room behind a screen was a gas plate and an icebox. Mrs. Jones got up and went behind the screen. The woman did not watch the boy to see if he was going to run now, nor did she watch her purse, which she left behind her on the day bed. But the boy took care to sit on the far side of the room, away from the purse, where he thought she could easily see him out of the corner of her eye if she

© 2014 Wadsworth, Cengage Learning

wanted to. He did not trust the woman *not* to trust him. And he did not want to be mistrusted now.

"Do you need somebody to go to the store," asked the boy, "maybe to get some milk or something?"

40   "Don't believe I do," said the woman, "unless you just want sweet milk yourself. I was going to make cocoa out of this canned milk I got here."

"That will be fine," said the boy.

She heated some lima beans and ham she had in the icebox, made the cocoa, and set the table. The woman did not ask the boy anything about where he lived, or his folks, or anything else that would embarrass him. Instead, as they ate, she told him about her job in a hotel beauty shop that stayed open late, what the work was like, and how all kinds of women came in and out, blondes, redheads, and Spanish. Then she cut him a half of her ten-cent cake.

"Eat some more, son," she said.

When they were finished eating, she got up and said, "Now here, take this ten dollars and buy yourself some blue suede shoes. And next time, do not make the mistake of latching onto *my* pocketbook *nor nobody else's*—because shoes got by devilish ways will burn your feet. I got to get my rest now. But from here on in, son, I hope you will behave yourself."

45   She led him down the hall to the front door and opened it. "Good night! Behave yourself, boy!" she said, looking out into the street as he went down the steps.

The boy wanted to say something other than, "Thank you, m'am," to Mrs. Luella Bates Washington Jones, but although his lips moved, he couldn't even say that as he turned at the foot of the barren stoop and looked up at the large woman in the door. Then she shut the door.

Exercise 1

Recall and Discuss

Answer these questions about Reading 1, and prepare to discuss them in class.

1. What are the characters' names? Why do you think the woman in the story tells the boy her full name, including the "Mrs."?

   _____

   _____

   _____

   _____

2. What happens in this story?

   _____

   _____

   _____

   _____

© 2014 Wadsworth, Cengage Learning

3. Why doesn't the woman ask the boy about his life?

_____

_____

4. What does the woman want the boy to learn?

_____

_____

5. Why do you think it was so important for the boy to buy the blue suede shoes that he was going to steal money to do it? What kind of shoes would a teenage boy today most likely want to have?

_____

_____

_____

_____

_____

6. How does Roger's attitude change in paragraph 38? How does he want Mrs. Jones to think about him?

_____

_____

_____

7. What lessons do you think Hughes wants us to get from the story?

_____

_____

_____

_____

_____

© 2014 Wadsworth, Cengage Learning

8. Do you think the events of this story are likely to happen today? Explain your answer.

_____

_____

_____

_____

_____

Critical Reading

The theme of this chapter is social connectedness. Think about the way the characters in Langston Hughes's short story are connected. Mrs. Luella Bates Washington Jones is the apparent victim; Roger tries to snatch her purse. But she turns the situation around by catching Roger. Instead of calling the police, she chooses to treat him as if he were her own son and teach him a lesson through her words, her kindness, and her generosity. By making these choices, she demonstrates a sense of responsibility toward others.

Thinking critically about this short story helps us understand the lesson Hughes wanted to teach. To make good choices, we, like Mrs. Luella Bates Washington Jones, need to think critically about what happens in our lives. Mrs. Jones clearly had ideas about young people in her neighborhood that led her to make her choices with the boy; she felt responsible for him. She was not afraid of him, so she decided to take him home, learn why he tried to steal from her, and teach him a lesson about life. To make good choices in life we must be critical thinkers, and critical reading is an important part of that challenge.

Learning to be a critical reader (and thinker) is one of the most important skills you can develop. **Critical reading** is essential for your academic work, but it is also essential in your day-to-day life, in your work life, and in your ability to understand the world around you. As you have worked your way through this textbook, you have consistently responded to many questions that made you think about what you have read. In the "Make Connections" exercises, you have practiced applying what you already know—your experiences and observations—to the readings. Additional important skills for reading critically are distinguishing between fact and opinion, recognizing the author's worldview, point of view, and purpose, and coming to your own conclusions. As a critical reader, you don't accept everything in print as truth. Rather, you use your critical thinking skills to form your own conclusions.

critical reading recognizing an author's purpose or point of view, distinguishing between fact and opinion, and, after careful thought, coming to your own conclusions

Facts and Opinions

As an active reader, you must be alert and involved in every part of the reading process—preparing to read, checking your understanding, making connections to what you already know, and thinking about what you know and what new

© 2014 Wadsworth, Cengage Learning

information you are getting from the reading. The new information you are acquiring may or may not fit with the information you have learned or experiences you have had in the past. Making connections—using all the information available to you—is essential to being a critical reader. Part of this process involves distinguishing between facts and opinions.

FACT

fact a piece of information or a statement that can be checked or proven

A **fact** is a piece of information or a statement that can be checked or proven. The easiest facts to recognize include data such as statistics, events, and dates. One example of a fact is: "People over 65 are twice as likely to vote as college-age adults." If you read this fact in a textbook, you assume it is correct because it can be checked and proven through the reports on voter turnout.

OPINION

opinion a belief or feeling about something that reflects how we interpret facts

An **opinion** is an interpretation of facts. One example of an opinion is: "People over 65 are more likely than any other age group to vote because the rules for voting are unfair for younger people." Opinions don't necessarily provide facts, but they sometimes include facts as support. The fact is "people over 65 are more likely than any other age group to vote." The opinion is "because the rules for voting are unfair for younger people." Table 9.1 provides a concise explanation of facts and opinions.

Table 9.1   Facts and Opinions

Facts	Opinions
Information that can be checked and proven: Statistics, events, dates	An interpretation of information: Thoughts, beliefs

Language Tip: Word Clues for Recognizing Opinions

Language clues can help you distinguish fact from opinion. An opinion might be introduced with statements such as "I think" or "I believe." In addition, words that indicate approval or disapproval are clues that an opinion is being expressed. Examples of these words are "good," "awful," "ridiculous," and "unfair." There are many words in the English language that indicate the expression of an opinion. These are called judgment words.

good	wonderful	beautiful	difficult
awful	disgusting	ridiculous	terrific
interesting	boring	bad	fantastic
fair	unfair	discouraging	encouraging

© 2014 Wadsworth, Cengage Learning

Exercise 2   **Use Word Clues for Fact and Opinion**

On the lines that follow, using the word clues for opinions, write five opinions about problems in your community or school. Then write five facts about the same subject that would support each opinion.

Opinions

1. _____

2. _____

3. _____

4. _____

5. _____

Facts

1. _____

2. _____

3. _____

4. _____

5. _____

RECOGNIZING FACT AND OPINION

Facts and opinions are frequently combined in the same sentence because the opinion expresses the author's interpretation of facts or uses facts as supporting evidence. For example, "Barack Obama won the 2008 presidential election because he is black." A different opinion based on the same fact is, "Barack Obama won the 2008 presidential election because he had better ideas than John McCain." The fact in both of these statements is that Barack Obama won the 2008 presidential election. The interpretations of why he won, however, are different.

For practice, mark the following sentences as facts (F) or opinions (O). If opinions and facts are in the same sentence, mark the sentence as fact and opinion (F+O).

_____ 1. George W. Bush was president of the United States from 2001 to 2009.

_____ 2. President Bush said there were weapons of mass destruction in Iraq, and that we needed to invade that country to keep the world safe.

© 2014 Wadsworth, Cengage Learning

_____ 3. In a time of war, people should not criticize their country because it will help the enemy.

_____ 4. President Bush never should have started the war in Iraq because the Iraqis didn't have weapons of mass destruction.

Sentences 1 and 2 are facts. Although sentence 2 may have incorrect information, it is true that President Bush said there were weapons of mass destruction in Iraq. Sentence 3 is an opinion. Some people will agree with it, and some people will disagree. Sentence 4 has a fact (the Iraqis didn't have weapons of mass destruction) to support the opinion (President Bush never should have started the war).

<table>
<tr><td>**Exercise 3**</td></tr>
</table>

Recognize Facts and Opinions

All of the following sentences or groups of sentences deal with our participation as voters in a larger community—at the local, municipal, state, or federal levels. Indicate whether the statement is a fact (F) or an opinion (O). Write F+O if the statement includes both a fact and an opinion.

_____ 1. Compared to a century ago . . . a smaller percentage of today's eligible citizens actually do vote. (Macionis, *Sociology*)

_____ 2. People over 65, however, are twice as likely to vote as college age adults (half of whom never even registered before the 2000 election). (Macionis, *Sociology*)

_____ 3. People earning more than $75,000 are twice as likely to vote (75 percent voted in 2000) as people earning between $5,000 and $10,000 (41 percent voted). (Macionis, *Sociology*)

_____ 4. People don't vote in high numbers because they are content with their lives. (adapted from Macionis, *Sociology*)

_____ 5. Many Americans are so deeply dissatisfied with society that they doubt elections make any real difference. (adapted from Macionis, *Sociology*)

_____ 6. The United States is basically democratic because voting offers everyone a voice, and no one group or organization dominates society. (adapted from Macionis, *Sociology*)

_____ 7. The United States is not democratic because a small percentage of the people dominates the economy, government, and military. (adapted from Macionis, *Sociology*)

_____ 8. Although the right to vote is one foundation of U.S. democracy, 48 of the 50 states (all except Vermont and Maine) have laws that bar felons—people convicted of serious crimes—from voting. (Macionis, *Sociology*)

_____ 9. Most states don't allow felons to vote because criminals shouldn't have that privilege.

_____ 10. Not allowing felons to ever vote discriminates against an important sector of the U.S. population.

© 2014 Wadsworth, Cengage Learning

Worldview, Point of View, and Purpose

Thinking critically involves understanding an author's worldview, point of view, and purpose for writing. Once you have these skills, you will better be able to evaluate the opinions of others and form your own opinions.

WORLDVIEW

worldview
a belief system,
the way we
understand the
world

Each of us has a **worldview** that reflects our belief system and is the basis for the way we understand the world. This worldview is influenced by many things, such as:

- Our economic position in society, such as wealthy, poor, middle class, on welfare, or unemployed
- Our jobs and level of education
- Our sex and sexual orientation
- Where we come from: the inner city, the suburbs, a rural area, or a different country
- Our ethnicity and religion, such as African American, Hispanic/Latino, or Anglo-Saxon and Catholic, Jewish, Hindu, Protestant, or Muslim
- Our experiences in life
- Our friends and families and their opinions
- The media we read, watch, or listen to

Authors also have worldviews that influence their writing, and it is important for you as a reader to recognize an author's worldview. Knowing "where the author is coming from" will help you think critically about what he or she has to say.

POINT OF VIEW

point of view
our attitude or
position about a
subject, issue, or
event

The author's worldview usually strongly influences his or her **point of view**—the opinion or attitude the author expresses about a subject, event, or issue. For example, from his writing and from what we know about his life, we know Langston Hughes believed that people in neighborhoods need to be interconnected. As a black man, he also believed that black children don't always get justice from the police or in the court system. So he created a heroine who accepts responsibility for a young man who might otherwise have committed a crime, and she turns the young man's life around. The heroine in the story reflects Hughes's point of view, or opinion, about how teenagers should be treated. While your point of view (opinion) may be different from an author's, you want to be sure to recognize the author's point of view.

PURPOSE

author's purpose
author's reason
for writing: the
most common
general purposes
are to inform,
persuade, and
entertain

The **author's purpose** is the author's reason for writing. If you know an author's worldview, it can help you recognize the author's point of view (opinion). The author's point of view usually influences his or her purpose in writing. The three primary reasons for published writing are to **inform**, to **entertain**, and to **persuade**. Textbooks usually inform—that is, they provide information. Fiction and poetry usually entertain—that is, make reading enjoyable. Newspaper editorials or letters to the editor usually try to persuade—that is, influence us

© 2014 Wadsworth, Cengage Learning

inform provide information

entertain make reading enjoyable

persuade influence us to agree with an opinion or point of view

to agree with a point of view. Frequently, these three purposes are combined. In Reading 1, for example, the author wants to entertain us with the short story, but he is also trying to persuade us about the ways in which people should interact with one another. (He wants to persuade us that adult members of the community should take some responsibility for young people, even if they are not their own children.) When an author is trying to persuade, you need to consider a few questions carefully:

- What is the author trying to persuade you to believe?
- What in your experience and observations makes you agree with the author?
- What in your experience and observations makes you disagree with the author?

Exercise 4

Recognize Worldview and Point of View

Read the paragraph and then write answers to the questions that follow.

Mrs. Gonzalez is a single mother of three teenagers. She was born in a small town in Mexico, but now she lives in Chicago. Every morning she leaves the house at 6 AM to catch the bus to go to work across town. She cleans houses all day and returns home at around 6 PM. By the time she gets home, she is exhausted and impatient. She expects her daughter, Inés, to keep the house clean and to cook dinner, but she doesn't ask her sons, Marco and Ivan, to do anything. Mrs. Gonzalez is not happy when Inés complains about having to do all the work because, as a mother, she believes she has to train her daughter to do the work around the house. Inés's friends, however, are not required by their mothers to do housework, so Inés feels her mother is unfair. Inés's brothers, who were born in the United States, like Inés, don't say anything, but they don't volunteer to help their sister either.

1. What influences on Mrs. Gonzalez's worldview can you identify in the paragraph?

_____

_____

_____

_____

2. What is Mrs. Gonzalez's point of view about who should work in the house?

_____

_____

_____

© 2014 Wadsworth, Cengage Learning

3. What influences on Inés's worldview can you identify?

_____

_____

_____

_____

_____

4. What is Inés's point of view about who should work in the house?

_____

_____

_____

5. What influences on Marco and Ivan's worldview can you identify?

_____

_____

_____

_____

6. What is Marco's and Ivan's point of view about who should work in the house?

_____

_____

_____

_____

© 2014 Wadsworth, Cengage Learning

Exercise 5

Recognize Worldview, Point of View, and Purpose

Read the following two passages from a political science textbook that represent opposite points of view about the police and the criminal justice system. Then, answer the questions that follow.

Conservative

In the United States, most criminals are not caught because the police face so many restrictions on how they may do their jobs. For example, liberal judges have limited the police in how or when they can search or question suspects. When criminals are arrested, they frequently are not convicted because of a thousand and one legal technicalities. Sometimes the case against an obviously guilty individual is thrown out because the police didn't follow some small detail of procedure. If the defendant is found guilty, it is often as a result of a plea bargain to a lesser charge.

Liberal

The crime problem has *not* gotten worse because criminals have too many rights, and people who are guilty of committing a crime get off on some technicality. These rights are not "rights for criminals"; they are rights for all citizens. In dictatorships—police states—the authorities can do whatever they like. All citizens, innocent and guilty alike, are victimized. Police power must be carefully controlled by law. Police power without any limitation endangers our liberty. So requiring that the police need to get a warrant before searching someone's home or that police may not use a rubber hose to obtain a confession protects us all. ([adapted from] Shalom, *Which Side Are You On?*)

1. What is the conservative point of view of our criminal justice system?

_____

_____

_____

_____

_____

2. What experiences can you think of that would lead someone to have a conservative point of view of our criminal justice system?

_____

_____

_____

_____

_____

© 2014 Wadsworth, Cengage Learning

3. What is the liberal point of view of our criminal justice system?

_____

_____

_____

_____

_____

4. What experiences can you think of that would lead someone to have a liberal point of view of our criminal justice system?

_____

_____

_____

_____

_____

5. What is the author's purpose for the passage labeled "Conservative"?

_____

_____

_____

_____

6. What is the author's purpose for the passage labeled "Liberal"?

_____

_____

_____

_____

7. Which passage do you agree with most? Explain why you have developed your point of view based on your worldview, your experiences, your knowledge, and your observations.

_____

_____

© 2014 Wadsworth, Cengage Learning

© 2014 Wadsworth, Cengage Learning

Exercise 6

Recognize Purpose

Read the following sentences to determine the author's purpose in each.

1. Since the mid-1960s, voting has decreased by about 25 percent.
   a. inform
   b. persuade
   c. entertain

2. If you don't serve your time as a juror, you can't expect our legal system to be fair.
   a. inform
   b. persuade
   c. entertain

3. A person who kills someone in a bar fight is a greater threat to society than a business executive who refuses to spend money to make his factory a safe place to work.
   a. entertain
   b. persuade
   c. inform

4. Violent crime rates in the United States are far higher than those in other countries.
   a. entertain
   b. persuade
   c. inform

5. The high rates of violent crime prove that the United States needs to have stricter gun control laws.
   a. entertain
   b. persuade
   c. inform

Drawing Conclusions

conclusion
a judgment or decision reached after careful thought

Drawing conclusions is "adding up" all you know about a reading and making some decisions about it. A **conclusion** is a judgment or decision that you reach after careful thought. Read the following passage and consider how the teenager in the story came to his conclusions.

At age 9, William Dunckelman visited a nursing home and was struck by how much an elderly resident appreciated having a chance to chat. Born with an autoimmune disorder that causes stomach, vision and skin problems, Dunckelman, 15, understood the isolation felt by the aged. "Physical pains aren't the only ones," says the Houma, Louisiana, high school sophomore. "There are emotional needs."

With the help from parents William Sr., 50, and Geralyn, 47, he runs Project FAME (Fine Arts Motivating the Elderly), which distributes books, DVDs, CDs and art supplies to nursing homes. Starting with a few local facilities, Dunckelman has sent $200,000 worth of donated goods to seniors in 40 states. And he still finds time to volunteer after school at several Houma nursing homes. "He could be doing a lot of other things," says one resident he visits, Virgi Rogers, 77. "But he's showing us he cares." That didn't stop during Hurricane Katrina, when Dunckelman helped provide food and water to evacuees and comforted those in distress. "You can touch someone's life," he says, "with just a kind word." ("Kids Who Care," *People Magazine*)

From this passage we recognize that William Dunckelman came to the conclusion he could cheer up seniors who live in nursing homes by supplying them with art projects and also by visiting and showing them he cares. Why did he come to his conclusion and act on it? One factor would have been his personal worldview, which was influenced by his having a disorder that causes stomach, vision, and skin problems. These problems made him better able to understand the isolation and loneliness of the aged. He also recognized that "physical pains aren't the only ones; there are emotional needs." Finally, then, his conclusion would have been influenced by his worldview, which was shaped by his experience and by visiting a nursing home when he was young.

| Exercise 7 |

Check Your Understanding and Draw Conclusions

Read the following paragraphs about "The State of Child Care in America" from Vermont Senator Bernie Sanders's Web site. Then answer the questions that follow.

1   Everyday in this country, 13 million children under age six are cared for by someone other than their own parents, in a child care center or by a family care provider. In the United States today, 70% of women with children under age six are in the workforce. In 1969, only 23% of women in this category were participating in the workforce.

2   There are currently 63 million women in the workforce, up 9 million from just 10 years prior. While our economy has undergone an historic change regarding the role of women in the workforce, we have done little to respond to the fact that most two-parent families can no longer afford to stay at home with their children. These same families, however, struggle to find and pay for quality child care. Families who can afford quality child care pay an average of $5,500 per child annually and up to $10,000 for such care. In 49 states, the average cost of child care is higher than the cost of public college tuition.

3   Child care providers themselves are grossly underpaid, and most lack health and pension benefits. In an effort to keep parent fees as low as possible, 31 states require no training in early childhood care and education, and few have comprehensive health and safety regulations. As a result, many low- and middle-income families have no choice but to place their children in lower cost, often lower quality care.

4   To raise awareness of the crisis in child care, I joined with several . . . colleagues in March 2001 to form the bipartisan Congressional Child Care Caucus. The Caucus's mission is to generate Congressional and national awareness of the crisis in child care and to create support for a nonpartisan child care agenda which will ensure access to quality and affordable child care for all American children.

© 2014 Wadsworth, Cengage Learning

Now read and try to answer the following questions to trace how Sanders came to his conclusions and to decide whether you agree.

1. What is the central idea of the passage?

_____

_____

2. List four facts that the author uses as supporting details for the central idea.

   a. _____

   b. _____

   c. _____

   _____

   d. _____

3. What pattern of organization does the author mostly use? (comparison and contrast, chronological order, or cause and effect)

_____

4. What can you reasonably infer from paragraph 3? Explain.

_____

_____

_____

_____

5. What opinions are presented?

_____

_____

_____

© 2014 Wadsworth, Cengage Learning

6. What is the author's point of view and purpose for writing?

_____

_____

7. What conclusions does Sanders draw? How does he act on his conclusions?

_____

_____

_____

8. What is your opinion about this passage? Do you agree or disagree with the author? Base your answer on your reading, your observations, and your experience.

⌐‾‾‾‾‾‾‾‾‾‾

When you read, you need to draw your own conclusions based on how well the author's conclusions fit with your own experiences and also on how convincing you find the author's use of facts, opinions, and examples. Drawing your *own conclusions* is a skill you will use for your whole life when you read, when you think, when you talk, and (hopefully) before you act. You go through this process all the time.

A goal of this textbook has been to help you set this process in motion when you read. The steps are listed in the following chart.

Summary Chart: The Steps in Critical Reading

1. Figure out the central idea of a passage (stated or unstated).
2. Recognize the supporting details that a writer uses to support his or her conclusion.
3. Understand the pattern(s) of organization the author uses so that you can recognize how the author frames his or her argument.
4. Make reasonable inferences regarding the author's assumption about information that may not be stated directly. These assumptions usually reflect the author's worldview.
5. Distinguish between facts and opinions.
6. Recognize the author's worldview, point of view, and purpose.
7. Recognize the author's conclusions.
8. Evaluate those conclusions, deciding if you agree with them and whether or not they might be useful in your own circumstances.
9. Draw your own conclusions based on your reading, your observations, and your experience.

© 2014 Wadsworth, Cengage Learning

Exercise 8

Draw Conclusions

Carefully read the following passage from a sociology textbook. Then answer the questions about the passage.

1   Shortly after midnight on a crisp March evening in 1964, a car pulled to a stop in the parking lot of a New York apartment complex. Kitty Genovese turned off the headlights, locked the doors of her vehicle, and headed across the blacktop toward the entrance to her building. Seconds later, a man wielding a knife lunged at her, and as she shrieked in terror, he stabbed at her repeatedly. Windows opened above, as curious neighbors looked down for the cause of the commotion. But the attack continued—for more than thirty minutes—until Genovese lay dead in the doorway. The police never identified her assailant, but they did discover a stunning fact: Not one of the dozens of neighbors who witnessed the attack on Kitty Genovese went to her aid or even called the police.

2   Decades after this tragic event, we still face the question of what we owe others. As members of modern societies, we prize our individual rights and personal privacy, but we sometimes withdraw from public responsibility and turn a cold shoulder to people in need. When a cry for help is met with indifference, have we pushed our modern idea of personal autonomy too far? In a cultural climate of expanding individual rights, can we keep a sense of human community?

3   People expect the system to work for them, but they are reluctant to support the system. For example, while we believe in the principle of trial by a jury of one's peers, fewer and fewer people today are willing to perform jury duty. At the same time, people are quick to accept government services, but they don't like to pay for these services with taxes.

4   Some sociologists suggest that the solution to this problem lies in recognizing that "strong rights presume strong responsibilities" (Etzione, 2003). Or, put another way, an individual's pursuit of self-interest must be balanced by a commitment to the larger community.

Adapted from Macionis, *Sociology*

indifference lack of concern

autonomy independence, not depending on anyone else

1. What is the central idea of this passage?
   a. Strong rights presume strong responsibilities.
   b. Nobody helped Kitty Genovese.
   c. People are quick to accept government services, but they don't like to pay for these services with taxes.

2. What fact does the author use as a supporting point?

   _____

   _____

   _____

© 2014 Wadsworth, Cengage Learning

3. What problem is identified in this reading?

_____

_____

_____

4. What examples of our responsibilities as citizens does the author give?

_____

_____

5. This passage comes from a textbook. What is the textbook author's purpose for this passage?

_____

_____

_____

_____

6. Do you agree with the point of view that "strong rights presume strong responsibilities"? Explain your answer.

_____

_____

7. What conclusion can you draw from this passage?

_____

_____

Reading 2

The Key to Good Health and Lifelong Happiness

— CHRISTY L. BALL

In this reading, Christy Ball makes a strong argument about habits that will lead to good health and happiness. As you read, identify her central idea and the support she provides to convince the reader. Also, think about how what Ball describes applies to you or people you know.

© 2014 Wadsworth, Cengage Learning

1   Wake Forest University head baseball coach Tom Walter first met 18-year-old Kevin Jordan during routine recruitment in 2010. Recruiting Jordan, an outfielder from Columbus, Georgia, whose impressive skills had attracted the attention of the illustrious New York Yankees, was a no-brainer for Coach Walter. But Jordan's dreams of playing college baseball and perhaps the big leagues one day took an unexpected major blow when, in the final months of his senior year, he began to experience flu-like symptoms and lost 30 pounds. After a battery of tests, doctors found that Jordan suffered from ANCA vasculitis, an autoimmune disease in which his own white blood cells began attacking his tissues. Soon after diagnosis, one of Jordan's kidneys began to fail, and the once fit athlete didn't respond to regular dialysis treatment. By the time his first college course began, doctors found that his kidney was barely functioning at 8 percent and he needed an immediate transplant. Jordan's blood type of O negative made it difficult to find a match. Then, in a gesture fit for a *Lifetime* movie special, Coach Walter stepped up to the plate and made an offer. He'd give Jordan his kidney.[1]

2   "This is something I would have done for any of my ballplayers," Coach Walter said. "There's not a kid on this team, or a kid that I've ever coached, that I wouldn't have done this for." Jordan felt the improved function of his organs and strength returning to his body almost immediately after surgery.[2] This story does more than warm the heart; it is an example of the physical and psychological benefits of group membership, social interaction, and social connectedness.[3] It also demonstrates how the benefits are reciprocal. Jordan is not only going to live a much longer, healthier life, the happiness he feels from his coach's gift will last him a lifetime. Coach Walter is not only going to have a star player on his team, he's going to benefit from the knowledge that his sacrifice extended the lifetime of a very promising young man.

3   Joining a team, league, or social group won't just give you something to do; it might make life worth living altogether. In fact, more and more we see that participating in social activities with your peers, friends, neighbors, and relatives can be good for both your physical and mental health. The problem is that many Americans turn to prescription drugs to solve issues that a change in social behaviors would likely ameliorate.

SOCIAL CONNECTEDNESS: THE PHYSICAL AND PSYCHOLOGICAL BENEFITS

4   Spending time with others is good for our mental, emotional, and physical health, plain and simple. Research clearly shows that the quality and quantity of our relationships will be a major determining factor in the length and quality of our life. The more we connect with others, the less we experience everyday ailments like the common cold, life-threatening diseases like cancer, or quality-of-life issues like memory loss. In fact, cultivating meaningful relationships and participating in regular group activities may actually *improve* our health and *increase* our lifespan.[4]

5   Researchers for the Harvard School of Public Health found that socially isolated people are twice as likely to develop dementia linked to Alzheimer's disease as those who maintain close relationships.[5] In other words, there might be something to that old adage "if you don't use it, you lose it," since people who engage in regular social activities experience the slowest rate of memory decline and greater fulfillment in later life. Researchers for Brigham Young University found that men and women suffering from terminal disease have a 50 percent increased likelihood of survival with stronger social relationships than those without;[6] and another study, which examined the role spouses play in helping patients survive major surgery, found a similar conclusion with respect to recovering from heart surgery.[7]

Written by Christy L. Ball. Reprinted by Permission of the Author.

© 2014 Wadsworth, Cengage Learning

BUT WHY?

6   There are many reasons why having strong relationships with others can help you live a longer, happier life. First, there are practical reasons. When you need advice on how to discipline your teenager or change a tire, or when you need a lift to work or a little extra cash for gas, having close ties with your coworker or neighbor might make that possible. If you regularly play cards, bowl in a league, or shoot hoops, and one Friday you don't make it to the game because you slipped a disc at home, somebody will likely notice. But, perhaps more importantly, there are health reasons. Studies show that lonely people are more likely to have self-destructive habits like drinking, smoking, and overeating, or psychiatric problems like depression, bulimia, and anxiety.[8] On the other hand, people who live in tight-knit communities that are richly connected tend to help each other navigate and sometimes avoid these issues completely.

tight-knit
close

7   The psychological benefits of social connectedness are perhaps the most interesting and profound reasons for forming close relationships. In one study, researchers found young women with breast cancer live longer when they increase their support networks. Reaching out to other people enhances patients' coping skills and ability to handle stress, provides them with much-needed emotional support, and expands their opportunities for sharing all kinds of information.[9]

8   Fifty years of public health research has proven that social connectedness affects all aspects of our physical and psychological health. There is clear, indisputable evidence that socially isolated people are at least twice as likely to die from all causes, compared with those who participate in regular social activities in their community.

CASE IN POINT: THE ROSETO EFFECT

9   There has been much discussion in medical circles about what is now called the "Roseto Effect."[10] During a study that was done over a period of 25 years, researchers noted how Italian immigrants living in Roseto, Pennsylvania, spent a large part of their day socializing with family, neighbors, and other townspeople. A hundred years after they settled, Rosetans maintained the same family unity and community interaction they had before emigration.[11] Researchers realized there was just one major difference between Rosetans and their neighbors. Even though they smoked more, drank more, ate worse, and worked just as hard as people in nearby towns in the mid-part of the twentieth century, Rosetans lived longer and healthier lives because of the social nature of the town. Hanging out on the front porch by day, participating in social clubs by night, and insisting upon a tight-knit community in which individuals did not flaunt their wealth and resources actually made Rosetans healthier.

10   Unfortunately, by the 1980s, suburbanization and social changes in the town transformed Roseto from a place where very few inhabitants experienced heart attacks to one where the incidents of heart attacks matched the national average. A push for the "American Dream" of personal wealth and individualistic happiness began to take shape in the youth culture, and soon the town was mimicking the same negative behaviors and ideals that have led to social isolation throughout the rest of America: namely a white-picket-fence mentality that divides community members and separates what's mine from what's yours. The example of Roseto and its well-documented decline in health continues to instruct us on the importance of placing relationships with people over the pursuit of materialism.

materialism
excessive focus on owning more and more things

© 2014 Wadsworth, Cengage Learning

THE KEY TO HAPPINESS

11   If you're feeling low, lost, alone, or sad, your doctor will likely prescribe one of the countless antidepressants on the market to help you medicate the problem. Indeed, these drugs may help you feel better. But taking prescription drugs can yield any number of unwanted side effects and cost you obscene amounts of money. The one sure fire way we know that we can feel better is through developing meaningful relationships that bring us joy, insight, and a reprieve from our negative inner dialogues.

12   To be sure, the connections we make with others may actually help our bodies handle stressful situations and fight off disease entirely. So, the question becomes: Why should I pay for artificial, temporary healthiness and "happiness" when I can have the real kind that will sustain me for a lifetime?

Notes

1. Ryan McGee, "Coach Steps Up with Kidney Donation," *ESPN.com*, Feb. 8, 2011 (accessed July 2, 2012).

2. Jay Byusbee, "Wake Forest Baseball Coach Donates Kidney to Player Suffering Rare Condition," *The Post Game,* Feb. 8, 2011 (accessed July 2, 2012).

3. Robert Putnam, *Bowling Alone: The Collapse and Revival of American Community* (New York: Simon & Schuster, 2000).

4. Julianne Holt-Lunstad, Timothy B. Smith, and J. Bradley Layton, "Social Relationships and Mortality Risk: A Meta-Analytic Review," *PloS Med* 7.7 (July 2010): e1000316.

5. Karen A. Ertel, M. Maria Glymour, and Lisa F. Berkman, "Effects of Social Integration on Preserving Memory Function in a Nationally Representative U.S. Elderly Population," *American Journal of Public Health* 98.7 (July 2008): 1215–1220.

6. Julianne Holt-Lunstad, Timothy B. Smith, and J. Bradley Layton. "Social Relationships and Mortality Risk: A Meta-Analytic Review." *PloS Med* 7.7 (July 2010): e1000316.

7. Ellen L. Idler, David A. Boulifard, and Richard J. Contrada. "Mending Broken Hearts: Marriage and Survival Following Cardiac Surgery," *Journal of Health and Social Behavior,* 53.1 (Mar. 2012): 33–49.

8. Jeong Won Jahng, Sang Bae Yoo, Vitaly Ryu, and Jong-Ho Lee, "Hyperphagia and Depression-Like Behavior by Adolescence Social Isolation in Female Rats," *International Journal of Developmental Neuroscience* 30.1 (Feb. 2012): 47–53.

9. Ann F. Chou, Susan L. Stewart, Robert C. Wild, and Joan R. Bloom, "Social Support and Survival in Young Women with Breast Carcinoma," *Psycho-Oncology* 21.2 (Feb. 2012): 125–133.

10. Brenda Egolf, Judith Lasker, Stewart Wolf, and Louise Potvin, "The Roseto Effect: A 50-Year Comparison of Mortality Rates," *American Journal of Public Health* 82.8 (Aug. 1992): 1089–1092.

11. Stewart Wolf and John G. Bruhn, *The Power of Clan: The Influence of Human Relationships on Heart Disease* (New Brunswick, NJ: Transaction, 1993).

© 2014 Wadsworth, Cengage Learning

Exercise 9

Work with Words

Use context clues, word-part clues, and, if necessary, the dictionary to write in the definitions of the italicized words in the following sentences from Reading 2.

1. Recruiting Jordan, an outfielder from Columbus, Georgia, whose impressive skills had attracted the attention of the *illustrious* Yankees, was a no-brainer for Coach Walter. (par. 1)

   illustrious _____

   _____

2. After a battery of tests, doctors found that Jordan suffered from ANCA vasculitis, an *autoimmune* disease in which his own white blood cells began attacking his tissues. (par. 1)

   autoimmune _____

   _____

   _____

3. It also demonstrates how the benefits are *reciprocal*. (par. 2)

   reciprocal _____

   _____

4. The problem is that many Americans turn to prescription drugs to solve issues that a change in social behaviors would likely *ameliorate*. (par. 3)

   ameliorate _____

   _____

5. In fact, *cultivating* meaningful relationships and participating in regular group activities may actually improve our health and increase our lifespan. (par. 4)

   cultivating _____

   _____

6. For example, in a recent study on the value of social behaviors and how relationships affect memory, researchers for the Harvard School of Public Health found that socially isolated people are twice as likely to develop *dementia* linked to Alzheimer's disease as those who maintain close relationships. (par. 5)

   dementia _____

   _____

7. In other words, there might be something to that old *adage* "if you don't use it, you lose it," since people who engage in regular social activities experience the slowest rate of memory decline and greater fulfillment in late life. (par. 5)

   adage _____

   _____

8. Hanging out on the front porch by day, participating in social clubs by night, and insisting upon a tight-knit community in which individuals did not *flaunt* their wealth and resources actually made Rosetans healthier. (par. 9)

   flaunt _____

   _____

9. If you're feeling low, lost, alone, or sad, your doctor will likely prescribe one of the countless *antidepressants* on the market to help you medicate the problem. (par. 11)

   antidepressants _____

   _____

   _____

10. The one sure fire way we know that we can feel better is through developing meaningful relationships that bring us joy, insight, and a *reprieve* from our negative inner dialogues. (par. 12)

    reprieve _____

    _____

Exercise 10

Check Your Understanding

Choose the best way to complete the following statements about Reading 2.

1. Coach Walter donated his kidney to Kevin Jordan, but the two only knew each other because
   a. they were neighbors.
   b. they worked at the same place.
   c. Jordan joined the college baseball team.

2. Which of the following is the best central idea statement for the reading?
   a. Coach Walter gave his kidney to one of his baseball players, Kevin Jordan, even though he had just met Jordan.
   b. Joining a team or social group is a great way to spend your free time.
   c. Participating in social activities can have positive physical and mental effects.

© 2014 Wadsworth, Cengage Learning

3. Many studies were done about the inhabitants of Roseto, Pennsylvania, because medical experts discovered that
   a. Rosetans were descendants of people who came from the same town in Italy.
   b. Rosetans lived longer, healthier lives compared to people in neighboring towns even though their diet was worse.
   c. Rosetans were materialistic.

4. Instead of building significant relationships with others within their community, many Americans turn to _____ for happiness.
   a. prescription drugs
   b. television
   c. shopping

5. Lonely people experience more _____ than socially active people.
   a. financial burdens
   b. accidents
   c. disease and depression

Exercise 11

Recognize Author's Purpose

Choose the best way to complete the following statements about the author's purpose in Reading 2.

1. The author's purpose for describing the connection of Coach Walter to Kevin Jordan in the first two paragraphs is to
   a. involve the reader with a story that illustrates the central idea of the reading.
   b. persuade the reader to join a baseball team.
   c. directly state the central idea of the reading.

2. The author's purpose for describing the research related to Roseto, Pennsylvania, is to
   a. evoke anger in the reader by demonstrating that your health may depend on where you live.
   b. insult Americans in general because they don't follow the simple traditions followed by the people of Roseto.
   c. provide support for the conclusion that social connections and social isolation affect health.

3. The author's purpose for the entire reading is to
   a. alert the reader about healthcare costs in the United States.
   b. inform the reader about the health effects of social connections and social isolation.
   c. entertain the reader.

4. The author's purpose in including notes at the end of the reading is to
   a. entertain the reader.
   b. show where her information comes from.
   c. make the reading longer.

© 2014 Wadsworth, Cengage Learning

Exercise 12

Distinguish Facts and Opinions and Draw Conclusions

Write answers to the following questions. Then, discuss your answers with your class group. Working together, prepare a report for your class as a whole or a written summary for your instructor.

1. Write a conclusion you can make after reading the information in Reading 2. Write this conclusion as an opinion.

   _____

   _____

2. Write three facts from Reading 2 that support the conclusion you wrote in question 1.

   a. _____

   b. _____

   c. _____

3. Do you think your conclusions are the same as the author's? Explain your answer.

   _____

   _____

4. What other possible conclusion(s) can be drawn from Reading 2? (Provide at least one).

   _____

   _____

Exercise 13

Make Connections and Write

Write answers to the following questions. Then, discuss your answers with your class group. Working together, prepare a report for your class as a whole or a written summary for your instructor.

1. What kinds of social connections do you have? List them.

   _____

   _____

   _____

© 2014 Wadsworth, Cengage Learning

2. How do your relationships with other people affect your sense of well-being? Do they affect your health? Explain your answer.

_____

_____

_____

3. What opportunities for socializing are available on your campus? What effects might participating in these activities (sports, events, clubs, etc.) have on student health?

_____

_____

_____

4. How do you think Internet social networking has contributed to or taken away from our need to be socially connected?

_____

_____

_____

Reading 3   A Gang, a Murder. Then What?

— Cynthia Roberts

The following reading traces the story of Tony Hicks. It tells how, in a split second, a poorly made decision changed his entire life. While Hicks's story is familiar, what happened afterward is more unusual. As you read, consider the points of view and conclusions of the various people in the story.

1   Having close connections in your community and with a tight-knit group of friends or associates is usually a good thing. It has even been proven that these relationships are actually good for your health. [1] But social connectedness can take many forms. Some are positive; others are negative. Our relationships to people in our community can lead us in good directions: helping one another, enjoying one another's company, and supporting one another. But sometimes these same social connections can be negative. Members of the Mafia have close relationships, but their purpose for existence and their shared goals are criminal. Another example of negative social connectedness that is closer to most of us is gangs.

Cynthia Roberts, "A Gang, a Murder. Then What?". Reprinted by Permission.

© 2014 Wadsworth, Cengage Learning

2   Why do so many young people in our communities join gangs? Sometimes they join because of pressure from their friends and, on occasion, from their families. At other times they join because they're looking for something that's missing in their lives: a strong family or community support structure and a sense of self-esteem. After their initial recruitment into a gang, they "earn" their membership and respect from their "homies." This "rite of passage" is usually violent. Sometimes it entails committing a crime; usually it means committing a violent crime against an innocent victim or against a member of another gang. Sometimes it even means committing murder. Gang members usually end up serving time in prison and/or eventually becoming victims of gang violence themselves.

A MURDER

3   Tony Hicks's experience is in many ways typical of gang members. His mom was 15 years old when he was born. As a kid, he was bounced around from place to place. He lived for many years in Los Angeles where he saw his favorite cousin's bullet-ridden body shortly after he was murdered in a gang shooting. Eventually, his mother sent Tony to live with his grandfather in San Diego. But Tony was an angry boy. He was angry because his father had been abusive and then was no longer around. He was angry because his mother didn't know how to be a mom. He was angry about his situation. He was angry and lonely, too. When he was 14, he began to rebel against his grandfather. On January 21, 1995, he ran away from home and left a note to his grandfather that read, "Daddy, I've run away. Love, Tony." He sought the solace of his friends—gang members. He planned to replace his broken family for a community of friends—the gang.

4   The sequence of events on that same night forever changed Tony's life. During the day, Tony, Antoine (the leader of the gang), and two other gang members smoked pot and drank alcohol. In the evening, they were hungry and decided to order pizzas. "Jacking the pizza guy" was the test that all gang members had to face. The friends had no money, so they gave a fake address. Tariq Khamisa, a San Diego State student, was the pizza delivery man. When he showed up with the pizza and was taking it out of the trunk, he could hear someone cock a gun. He turned around to see the barrel of the gun pointed at his face. Tony held the gun and was surrounded by other gang members. Tony demanded the pizzas and some money. Tariq refused. His friends screamed at him to shoot. Tony hesitated, but pulled the trigger. Tariq collapsed to the ground.

5   With that split-second decision, the course of Tony's life was changed forever; Tariq's life was lost. The following year Tony was the first 15-year-old to be tried and convicted as an adult under a newly passed California law. He received a 25-year-to-life sentence after pleading guilty to first-degree murder.

FORGIVENESS

devastated
overwhemed,
destroyed

6   Although Tony faced the consequences for his actions very early in life, his experience was still typical of a gang member. What is not typical is what happened after the murder of Tariq Khamisa. Tariq's father, Azim, was so devastated by his son's death that he couldn't function. He didn't eat or sleep for days. As a Muslim, he found help and support at his mosque. Eventually, after much prayer and meditation, Azim Khamisa realized that to find peace he must forgive Tony for murdering his son. He also realized that Tariq was not the only victim that night. Tony was also a victim of gangs and a culture of violence that is so prevalent in some communities.

7   Azim decided to dedicate his life to changing this culture of violence. His first step was to forgive Tony. His next step was to get together with Tony's grandfather, Ples

© 2014 Wadsworth, Cengage Learning

Felix. The two men found they had much in common. Tony learned about his grandfather and Tariq's father becoming friends, and he referred to them in his emotional and remorseful speech at his trial, when he was sentenced:

8   Good Morning Judge:

On January 21, 1995, I shot and killed Tariq Khamisa, a person I didn't even know and who didn't do anything wrong to me. On April 11, 1996, I pled guilty to first-degree murder because I am guilty. I wanted to save the Khamisa family and my family from further pain.

From my grandfather, I have learned about the Khamisa family and their only son, Tariq. I have learned about the love they have for him. . . . They have tried to explain to me the compassion the Khamisa family has for me.

I still don't know why I shot Tariq. I didn't really want to hurt him or anyone else. I'm sorry. I'm sorry for killing Tariq and hurting his family. I'm sorry for the pain I caused for Tariq's father, Mr. Khamisa. I pray to God every day that Mr. Khamisa will forgive me for what I have done, and for as long as I live I will continue to pray to God to give him strength to deal with his loss.

My grandfather promised me that he will be Mr. Khamisa's friend and help him in any way he can for the rest of his life. I am very sorry for what I have done. Thank you for giving me the chance to speak. [2]

COMMUNITY

9   Khamisa and Felix knew that they couldn't bring Tariq back to life and they couldn't save Tony from spending a life in prison. But they decided to dedicate their lives to save other lives and keep other children in our communities from following Tony's path. They founded the Tariq Khamisa Foundation (TKF). Now they "speak to elementary and middle school children about gangs, violence, revenge, and the importance of becoming 'peacemakers.'" One of the programs that TKF also sponsors is the Violence Impact Forum (VIF). In the Foundation's Web site, this program is described as

a unique and powerful school-based violence prevention education program for students in the 4th–7th grades. The VIF assembly includes a high-impact video with powerful speakers and lively student audience participation. The program focuses on the personal story of Tariq Khamisa and Tony Hicks and the lifelong consequences of one deadly choice.

VIF panelists include Azim Khamisa, Ples Felix, plus former male and female gang members who share the stark reality of gangs and prison life. Students learn a powerful lesson about the destructive impact of gangs and violence and the importance of making peaceful, positive choices. Students also witness "forgiveness in action" by seeing Azim and Ples sitting together on stage. This is often the first time that many children have been shown that there are alternatives to revenge and retaliation.[3]

10   The Violence Impact Forum has five key messages: (1) Violence is real and hurts everyone. (2) Actions have consequences. (3) Youth can make good and nonviolent choices. (4) Youth can work toward forgiveness as opposed to seeking revenge. (5) Everyone deserves to be loved and well treated. [4]

11   Through their work Khamisa and Felix have reached 350,000 children, and millions more have heard their story. Their violence prevention programs started in San Diego, but have now been replicated in Atlanta and Chicago. [5]When Tony gets out of prison in 2021, they hope that he will join them in their work, a dream that Tony now shares. When Tony's dream comes true, he will have a new set of friends and relationships and a new set of social connections. This time the community Tony finds will be positive.

© 2014 Wadsworth, Cengage Learning

Notes

1. Robert D. Putnam, *Bowling Alone: The Collapse and Revival of American Community* (New York: Simon & Schuster, 2000): 326–335

2. Tony's Sentencing Speech." *Ending the Cycle of Violence Student Workbook*. http://www.aquariusproductions.com/PDF/products/A-PSYCYCLE.1.pdf (accessed 7/22/12).

3. "Violence and Impact Forum," TKF Web site, at http://tkf.org/vif.html (accessed 5/23/06).

4. *Ibid.*

5. "From Murder to Forgiveness." The Faith and Politics Institute, at http://www.faithandpolitics.org/murder_forgiveness (accessed 7/12/12).

Exercise 14

Work with Words

Use context clues, word-part clues, and, if necessary, the dictionary to write definitions of the italicized words in the following sentences from Reading 3.

1. After their initial recruitment into a gang, they "earn" their membership and respect from their "homies." This "*rite of passage*" is usually violent. Sometimes it *entails* committing a crime; usually it means committing a violent crime against an innocent victim or against a member of another gang. (par. 2)

   rite of passage _____

   _____

2. *entails* _____

3. He sought the *solace* of his friends—gang members. He planned to replace his broken family for a community of friends—the gang. (par. 3)

   solace _____

4. With that split-second decision, the *course* of Tony's life was changed forever; Tariq's life was lost. (par. 5)

   course _____

5. Tony was also a victim of gangs and a culture of violence that is so *prevalent* in some communities. (par. 6)

   prevalent _____

6. Tony learned about his grandfather and Tariq's father becoming friends, and he referred to them in his emotional and *remorseful* speech at his trial, when he was sentenced. (par. 7)

   remorseful _____

7. They have tried to explain to me the *compassion* the Khamisa family has for me. (par. 8)

   compassion _____

© 2014 Wadsworth, Cengage Learning

8. Their violence prevention programs started in San Diego, but have now been *replicated* in Atlanta and Chicago. (par. 11)

replicated _____

Exercise 15

Check Your Understanding

Choose the best answers to the following multiple-choice questions based on Reading 3.

1. Which of the following is the best main idea statement for paragraph 1?
   a. Gangs are an example of negative connections.
   b. Our social connections can be positive or negative.
   c. The Mafia is an example of a negative connection.

2. According to the author, young people join gangs to find
   a. positive social connections.
   b. a rite of passage.
   c. a community support structure and a sense of self-esteem.

3. Tony's life as a young boy was
   a. not stable.
   b. just as comfortable as the lives of his friends.
   c. sheltered from gang violence.

4. Which of the following is the best main idea statement for paragraphs 4 and 5?
   a. The sequence of events on the night of January 21, 1995, forever changed Tony Hicks's life and led to the death of Tariq Khamisa.
   b. Tariq Khamisa was a San Diego State student who was in the wrong place at the wrong time.
   c. Tony was the first 15-year-old to be tried and convicted as an adult under a newly-passed California law.

5. What is the pattern of organization for paragraphs 4 and 5?
   a. definition
   b. comparison and contrast
   c. chronological order

Exercise 16

Distinguish Between Facts and Opinions

Choose the best answers to the following multiple-choice questions based on Reading 3. (There may be more than one answer for each question.) Then, follow the directions for question 3.

1. Which of the following sentences are statements of fact?
   a. Tony Hicks murdered Tariq Khamisa.
   b. Tony received a 25-year-to-life sentence after pleading guilty to first-degree murder.
   c. Tony got into trouble because his mother didn't know how to take care of him.

© 2014 Wadsworth, Cengage Learning

d. No one should have to suffer the death of a child.

e. Tony said he was sorry for what he did.

f. Azim Khamisa and Ples Felix founded the Tariq Khamisa Foundation to help prevent further violence among teenagers in the community.

2. Which of the following sentences are statements of opinion?

a. It is wrong to sentence a 15-year-old child as an adult.

b. It's a good thing that Tony delivered an emotional and remorseful speech at his trial.

c. The Tariq Khamisa Foundation sponsors the Violence Impact Forum.

d. The Violence Impact Forum is the best antiviolence program in the nation.

e. Through their work, Khamisa and Felix have reached 350,000 children.

f. The violence prevention program has been duplicated in Atlanta and Chicago.

3. Write an opinion about Reading 3 supported by a fact.

_____

_____

_____

Exercise 17

Recognize Author's Purpose

Choose the best answer to the following questions about the author's purpose in Reading 3.

1. What is the author's purpose for telling Tony's story in paragraphs 3 and 4?

a. To inform the reader about how the murder took place and about Tony's background

b. To persuade the reader that Tony was too young for the problem she had to deal with in life

c. To directly state the central idea of the reading

2. Why did the author include Tony's letter in the reading?

a. To make sure the reader is aware of Tony's confession of guilt

b. To demonstrate that Tony was literate enough to write a letter

c. To help the reader see Tony as an individual and a young person who was sorry for what he had done

3. Why did the author include information from the TKF Web site?

a. To encourage readers to donate money

b. So that readers will have a better idea of the violence prevention work the Tariq Khamisa Foundation does

c. So that readers can more easily find the central idea of the reading

© 2014 Wadsworth, Cengage Learning

4. The author's purpose for the entire reading is to
   a. inform the reader about Tony's involvement in gangs.
   b. persuade the reader that we need to teach young people to find nonviolent solutions to their problems.
   c. entertain the reader with Tony's interesting but sad story.

Exercise 18

Make Connections and Write

Write short answers to the following questions about Reading 3 based on your reading, your observations, and your point of view. Then, discuss your answers with your class group. Working together, prepare a report for your class as a whole or a written summary for your instructor.

1. What conclusions does Roberts draw about the two types of communities in the reading—the gang community and the community of the Tariq Khamisa Foundation?

   _____

   _____

   _____

   _____

2. What conclusions can you draw from Tony's experience about the choices that we make? Explain your answer.

   _____

   _____

   _____

   _____

   _____

   _____

3. What is your point of view on trying and sentencing people as young as 14 and 15 as adults? Explain your answer.

   _____

   _____

   _____

© 2014 Wadsworth, Cengage Learning

4. Do you know anyone who's been in a gang or been affected by gang activities? Explain how that person was affected.

_____

_____

_____

5. What is your point of view about gangs; and what can be done to reduce their influence over young people?

_____

_____

_____

Chapter Review

To aid your review of the reading skills in Chapter 9, study the Put It Together chart.

Put It Together: Critical Reading	
Skills and Concepts	Explanation
Fact (see pages 420–421)	A fact is a piece of information that can be checked or proven.
Opinion (see pages 420–421)	An opinion is a belief or feeling about something that reflects how we interpret facts.
Recognizing Opinions (see pages 427–429)	Word clues can indicate the expression of an opinion.
Worldview (see page 424)	A worldview reflects our belief system and is the basis for the way we understand the world.
Point of View (see page 424)	A point of view is an attitude or position about a subject, issue, or event.
Author's Purpose (see pages 424–425)	The author's purpose is the author's reason for writing. The most common general purposes are to inform, persuade, and entertain.
Conclusions (see pages 429–430)	A conclusion is a judgment or decision that you reach after careful thought.

To reinforce your thinking before taking the Mastery Tests, complete as many of the following activities as your instructor assigns.

© 2014 Wadsworth, Cengage Learning

REVIEW SKILLS

Answer the following skills-review questions individually or in a group.

1. Why is it important to be able to distinguish between facts and opinions? Give some examples of when you need this skill.

_____

_____

_____

_____

2. What are some important factors that influence our worldview?

_____

_____

_____

_____

3. What are the three primary purposes for published writing?

_____

_____

_____

_____

4. What process do you use to draw a conclusion about a reading?

_____

_____

_____

_____

_____

_____

© 2014 Wadsworth, Cengage Learning

Write

Find a newspaper or magazine article or editorial that *expresses an opinion* about something you are interested in. Then follow these steps.

1. Write a brief summary of the article (include facts and opinions).

2. Include a sentence or two about the author's purpose for writing.

3. Write your conclusions about the author's opinion. Consider:

   a. Do the author's facts convincingly support his or her opinion?

   b. Do you agree with the author's opinion? Explain your answer based on your worldview as well as your reading, your observations, and your experience.

COLLABORATE

In your groups, brainstorm some problems or concerns in your school community. Pick one problem or concern. (1) Explain the problem. (2) Make a list of the facts that you know about the problem. (3) Make a list of additional information you need to know to reach a conclusion about the problem. (4) After careful thought, come to a conclusion.

Your conclusion may be ways to solve the problem, the need to learn more about the problem or about resources to solve it, or even the recognition that there is no good solution. Be sure to explain your conclusion. As a group, prepare an oral presentation or written report on your work.

EXTEND YOUR THINKING

Identify a problem in your campus community about which you would like to learn more. Make a list of the questions you would like answered about the problem that you have identified, and who on your campus is the best person to answer your questions (a secretary, an instructor, an administrator, a counselor, a student). Set up a time to meet with that person. Ask your questions, and prepare to report back to the class the results of your interview. Has getting more facts on the problem changed your opinion about it?

 ## WORK THE WEB

Use a search engine such as *Google* to go to the AmeriCorps Web site. Then browse the site to answer the following questions.

1. What is AmeriCorps?

_____

_____

_____

© 2014 Wadsworth, Cengage Learning

2. What are some of the things AmeriCorps members can do?

_____

_____

_____

3. What are some of the benefits of being in AmeriCorps?

_____

_____

_____

4. Find a volunteer activity in which you would consider participating. Describe that activity and why you find it interesting.

_____

_____

_____

© 2014 Wadsworth, Cengage Learning

Name _____ Date _____

The Montgomery Bus Boycott: An African-American Community Challenges Segregation

— [ADAPTED FROM] JOHN MACK FARAGHER, MARY JO BUHLE, DANIEL CZITROM, AND SUSAN H. ARMITRAGE

TEXT BOOK The following reading from an American history textbook summarizes the struggle of African American people (1955–1956) to overturn the segregation they experienced on the Montgomery, Alabama, buses. You will recognize some famous people such as Rosa Parks and Martin Luther King, but you should keep in mind that ordinary citizens made the bus boycott work. As you read, think about: (1) the problem, (2) the decisions the community made about how to solve the problem, and (3) how the community followed up on its decisions. What conclusions can you draw about ordinary people's ability to make a difference? Under what circumstances are they able to do so?

1   A steady stream of cars and people jammed the streets around the Holt Street Baptist Church in Montgomery, Alabama. By early evening a patient, orderly, and determined crowd of more than 5,000 African Americans had packed the church and spilled over onto the sidewalks. Loudspeakers had to be set up for the thousands who could not squeeze inside. After a brief prayer and a reading from Scripture, all attention focused on the twenty-six-year-old minister—Martin Luther King Jr.— who was chosen to speak. "We are here this evening," he began slowly, "for serious business. We are here in a general sense because first and foremost we are American citizens, and we are determined to apply our citizenship to the fullness of its means."

2   Then the minister got down to specifics. Rosa Parks, a seamstress and well-known activist in Montgomery's African American community, had been taken from a bus, arrested, and put in jail for refusing to give up her seat to a white passenger on December 1, 1955. Montgomery's black community of 50,000 people had long suffered the humiliation of a strictly segregated bus system. Black people had to ride in the back of the bus. Drivers could order a whole row of black passengers to <u>vacate</u> their seats for one white person. Black people had to pay their fares at the front of the bus, and then step back outside and reenter through the rear door. The day of the mass meeting, more than 30,000 African Americans had answered a quickly organized call to <u>boycott</u> the city's buses in protest of Mrs. Parks's arrest. They walked or carpooled, but they did not take the bus. As the minister spoke faster and drew shouts of encouragement, he seemed to gather strength and confidence from the crowd. "You know, my friends, there comes a time when people get tired of being trampled over by the iron feet of oppression."

3   Even before he finished his speech, it was clear that the bus boycott would continue for more than just a day. The minister laid out the key <u>principles</u> that would guide the boycott—nonviolence, Christian love, unity. In his brief but moving address, the minister created a powerful sense of unity. "If we are wrong, justice is a lie," he told the clapping and shouting crowd. "And we are determined here in Montgomery to work and fight until justice runs down like water and righteousness like a mighty

Faragher, John Mack; Buhle, Mari Jo; Czitrom, Daniel H.; Armitage, Susan H., *Out of Many*, 6e, ©2009.
Printed and Electronically Reproduced by Permission of Pearson Education, Inc., Upper Saddle River, New Jersey.

© 2014 Wadsworth, Cengage Learning

stream. . . . Historians would look back at Montgomery," he noted, "and have to say: 'There lived a race of people, black people, of people who had the moral courage to stand up for their rights.'"

4   The Reverend Martin Luther King Jr. made his way out of the church to waves of applause and rows of hands reaching out to touch him. His powerful speech placed him into leadership of the Montgomery bus boycott—but he had not started the movement. When Rosa Parks was arrested, local activists with deep roots in the black protest tradition unified the community with the idea of a boycott. Mrs. Parks herself had served for twelve years as secretary of the local NAACP (National Association for the Advancement of Colored People) chapter. She was a <u>committed</u> opponent of segregation and was thoroughly respected in the city's African American community. E. D. Nixon, president of the Alabama NAACP, saw Mrs. Parks's arrest as the right case on which to make a stand. Nixon brought Montgomery's black ministers together on December 5 to coordinate an extended boycott of city buses. They formed the Montgomery Improvement Association (MIA) and chose Dr. King as their leader. Significantly, Mrs. Parks's lawyer was Clifford Durr, a white man with a history of representing black clients. His politically active wife Virginia, for whom Mrs. Parks worked as a seamstress, had fought for many years against the poll tax that prevented many blacks from voting.

poll tax
a payment that had to be made in order to vote, which made it difficult for poor African American and poor white people to vote

5   While Nixon organized black ministers, Jo Ann Robinson, an English teacher at Alabama State College, spread the word to the larger black community. Robinson led the Women's Political Council (WPC), an organization of black professional women founded in 1949. With women from her organization, Robinson wrote and distributed 50,000 copies of a leaflet telling the story of Mrs. Parks's arrest and urging all African-Americans to stay off city buses on December 5. They did. Now the MIA faced the more difficult task of keeping the boycott going. Success depended on providing <u>alternate</u> transportation for the 30,000 to 40,000 maids, cooks, janitors, and other black working people who needed to get to work.

6   The MIA coordinated a complicated system of car pools, using hundreds of private cars and volunteer drivers to provide as many as 20,000 rides each day. Many people walked. Local authorities, although shocked by the discipline and sense of purpose shown by Montgomery's African American community, refused to negotiate seriously. With the aid of the NAACP, the MIA brought the issue of bus segregation in Montgomery to federal court. Police harassed boycotters with traffic tickets and arrests. White racists exploded bombs in the homes of Dr. King and E. D. Nixon. The days turned into weeks, then months, but still the boycott continued. All along, mass meetings in Montgomery's African American churches helped boost <u>morale</u> with singing, praying, and stories of individual sacrifice. One elderly woman, refusing all suggestions that she drop out of the boycott on account of her age, made a remark that many in the movement repeated often: "My feets is tired, but my soul is rested."

7   The boycott reduced the bus company's <u>revenues</u> by two-thirds. In February 1956, city officials obtained <u>indictments</u> against King, Nixon, and 113 other boycotters under an old law forbidding interfering with business without "just cause or legal excuse." A month later King went on trial. Newspaper reporters and TV crews from around the country watched as the judge found King guilty, fined him $1,000, and released him on bond. But on June 4, a panel of three federal judges struck down Montgomery's bus segregation laws as <u>unconstitutional</u>. On November 13 the Supreme Court supported the district court ruling. After eleven hard months and against all odds, the boycotters had won.

© 2014 Wadsworth, Cengage Learning

8   The struggle to end legal segregation spread to several southern cities and towns. African American communities led these fights. With white supporters, they participated in protests such as boycotts, sit-ins, and nonviolent civil disobedience as well as important legal battles in state and federal courts.

civil disobedience
a form of protest that involves breaking a law that is considered unjust to get the law changed

Use context clues, word-part clues, and, if necessary, the dictionary to write definitions of the italicized words in the following sentences from the reading.

1. Drivers could order a whole row of black passengers to *vacate* their seats for one white person. (par. 2)

   vacate _____

2. The day of the mass meeting, more than 30,000 African Americans had answered a quickly organized call to *boycott* the city's buses in protest of Mrs. Parks's arrest. They walked or carpooled, but they did not take the bus. (par. 2)

   boycott _____

   _____

3. The minister laid out the key *principles* that would guide the boycott—nonviolence, Christian love, unity. (par. 3)

   principles _____

4. Mrs. Parks herself had served for twelve years as secretary of the local NAACP (National Association for the Advancement of Colored People) chapter. She was a *committed* opponent of segregation and was thoroughly respected in the city's African American community. (par. 4)

   committed _____

5. Success depended on providing *alternate* transportation for the 30,000 to 40,000 maids, cooks, janitors, and other black working people who needed to get to work. (par. 5)

   alternate _____

6. All along, mass meetings in Montgomery's African American churches helped boost *morale* with singing, praying, and stories of individual sacrifice. (par. 6)

   morale _____

7. The boycott reduced the bus company's *revenues* by two-thirds. In February 1956, city officials obtained *indictments* against King, Nixon, and 113 other boycotters under an old law forbidding interfering with business without "just cause or legal excuse." (par. 7)

   revenues _____

8. *indictments* _____

   _____

© 2014 Wadsworth, Cengage Learning

9. But on June 4, a panel of three federal judges struck down Montgomery's bus segregation laws as *unconstitutional*. (par. 7)

unconstitutional _____

Read the following sentences from or about the reading, and write "F" before statements of fact and "O" before statements of opinion.

_____ 10. Rosa Parks was arrested on December 1, 1955, in Montgomery, Alabama, for refusing to give up her seat on a bus to a white passenger.

_____ 11. Everybody living in Montgomery, Alabama, at the time should have agreed with what she did.

_____ 12. The leaders of the Montgomery bus boycott organized car pools so people could get to work.

_____ 13. A panel of federal judges struck down Montgomery's bus segregation laws as unconstitutional.

_____ 14. Without Rosa Parks's brave act and the boycott that followed, African Americans would never have been able to change the laws.

Choose the best answer to the following questions.

15. Which of the following best describes the author's purpose for writing this textbook selection?
    a. To persuade students to become activists in their communities about the issues facing them today
    b. To inform students about the Montgomery bus boycott, its causes, and the struggle of the African American community to overcome discrimination
    c. To point out the impossibility of changing old practices

16. Martin Luther King Jr. said in his Holt Street Baptist Church speech, "You know, my friends, there comes a time when people get tired of being trampled over by the iron feet of oppression." When he said this, his purpose was to
    a. make his speech more difficult to understand.
    b. give listeners a visual image so that "oppression" would have a greater impression.
    c. make his speech sound more important.

17. Which of the following factors do you think most likely influenced Martin Luther King's worldview about the civil rights struggle?
    a. his age, his children, his country
    b. his religion, his race, his experiences in the South
    c. his gender, his relationship to white ministers

© 2014 Wadsworth, Cengage Learning

Write short answers to the following questions based on your reading, your experience, and your observations.

18. What are some of the most important factors that formed the worldview of most of the boycotters? (What did most of them have in common?)

_____

_____

_____

_____

19. What conclusions can you draw from this reading about a community's ability to change things for the better?

_____

_____

_____

_____

20. Is there an issue in your community around which you think people could organize themselves and make a difference? Explain the issue and explain what you think people could do to solve the problem.

_____

_____

_____

_____

© 2014 Wadsworth, Cengage Learning

Name _____ Date _____

The Singer Solution to World Poverty

— [ADAPTED FROM] PETER SINGER

The following reading discusses world poverty and our responsibility to help solve the problem of children in other countries dying prematurely from malnutrition or preventable diseases. The author, Peter Singer, judges whether actions are right or wrong based on their consequences. As you read, consider the facts, the presentation of the problem, and the thinking process that leads the author to draw his conclusions.

1   In the Brazilian film *Central Station*, Dora is a retired school teacher who makes ends meet by sitting at the station writing letters for <u>illiterate</u> people. Suddenly she has an opportunity to pocket a thousand dollars. All she has to do is persuade a homeless nine-year-old boy to follow her to an address she has been given. (She is told he will be adopted by wealthy foreigners.) She delivers the boy, gets the money, spends some of it on a television set, and settles down to enjoy her new <u>acquisition</u>. Her neighbor spoils the fun, however, by telling her that the boy was too old to be adopted—he will be killed and his organs sold for transplantation. Perhaps Dora knew this all along, but after listening to her neighbor, she spends a troubled night. In the morning, Dora decides to take the boy back.

2   Suppose Dora had told her neighbor that it is a tough world, other people have nice new TVs too, and if selling the kid is the only way she can get one, well, he was only a street kid. She would then have become, in the eyes of the audience, a monster. She <u>redeems</u> herself only by taking considerable risks to save the boy.

3   At the end of the movie, in cinemas in the <u>affluent</u> nations of the world, people who would have been quick to condemn Dora if she had not rescued the boy go home to places far more comfortable than her apartment. In fact, the average family in the United States spends almost one-third of its income on things that are no more necessary to them than Dora's new TV was to her. Going out to nice restaurants, buying new clothes because the old ones are no longer stylish, vacationing at beach resorts—so much of our income is spent on things we don't really need. If we donated this income to one of a number of charities, that money could mean the difference between life and death for children in need.

4   All of this raises a question: In the end, what is the <u>ethical</u> difference between a Brazilian who sells a homeless child to organ <u>vendors</u> and an American who already has a TV and upgrades to a better one? We know, after all, that the money we spend on a fancier TV could be donated to an organization that would use it to save the lives of kids in need.

5   Of course, there are several differences between the two situations that could support different moral judgments about them. For one thing, to be able to send a child to death when he is standing right in front of you takes a chilling kind of heartlessness. It is much easier to ignore a request for money to help children you will never meet. As a <u>utilitarian philosopher</u>, I judge whether acts are right or wrong by their consequences. If the result of the American's failure to donate the money is that one more kid dies on the streets of a Brazilian city, then it is in some way just as bad as selling the kid to the organ vendors. There is a troubling problem if we can <u>condemn</u> Dora for taking the child to the organ vendors and not think about the American consumer's behavior as raising a serious moral issue.

moral
able to choose right over wrong

Peter Singer, "The Singer Solution to World Poverty" *New York Times* Magazine, Sunday, 9/5/99., Section 6, P. 60 Ny Edition. © 1999 Peter Singer. Used With Permission.

© 2014 Wadsworth, Cengage Learning

6   In his book *Living High and Letting Die*, the New York University philosopher Peter Unger presented a series of examples designed to make us think about our choices. He believes it is wrong to live well without giving money to help people who are hungry, <u>malnourished</u>, or dying from easily treatable illnesses like diarrhea. Unger reminds us that we, too, have opportunities to save the lives of children. We can give to organizations like UNICEF or Oxfam America. How much would we have to give one of these organizations to save the life of a child threatened by easily preventable diseases? (I do not believe that children are more worth saving than adults, but no one can argue that children have brought their poverty on themselves.) Unger called up some experts to make some realistic estimates that include the cost of raising money, administrative expenses, and the cost of delivering aid where it is most needed. By his calculation $200 in donations would help a sickly two-year-old transform into a healthy six-year-old—offering safe passage through childhood's most dangerous years. Unger even tells his readers that they can easily donate funds by using their credit card and calling one of these toll-free numbers: (800) 367-5437 for UNICEF; (800) 693-2687 for Oxfam America.

7   In the world as it is now, I have to conclude that each one of us who has money left over after meeting our basic needs should be giving most of it to help children suffering from life-threatening poverty. That's right. I'm saying that you shouldn't buy that new car, take that cruise, redecorate the house, or get that pricey new suit. After all, a thousand-dollar suit could save five children's lives.

8   So how does my philosophy break down in dollars and cents? An American household with an income of $50,000 spends around $30,000 annually on necessities, according to the Conference Board, a nonprofit economic research organization. Therefore, for a household bringing in $50,000 a year, donations to help the world's poor should be as close as possible to $20,000. The $30,000 required for necessities holds for higher incomes as well. So a household making $100,000 could <u>cut</u> a yearly check for $70,000. Again, the formula is simple: Whatever money you're spending on luxuries, not necessities, should be given away.

9   Psychologists tell us that people are not generous enough to sacrifice so much for strangers. They might be right, but they would be wrong to draw a moral conclusion from those facts. If we value the life of a child more than going to fancy restaurants, the next time we dine out we will know that we could have done something better with our money. If that makes living a morally decent life extremely difficult, well, then, that is the way things are. If we don't give that money to save the life of a child, then we should at least know that we are failing to live a morally decent life. It's not good to feel guilty, but knowing where we should be going is the first step toward heading in that direction.

Use context clues, word-part clues, and, if necessary, the dictionary to write definitions of the italicized words in the following sentences from the reading.

1. In the Brazilian film *Central Station*, Dora is a retired school teacher who makes ends meet by sitting at the station writing letters for *illiterate* people. (par. 1)

   illiterate _____

2. She delivers the boy, gets the money, spends some of it on a television set, and settles down to enjoy her new *acquisition*. (par. 1)

   acquisition _____

3. She *redeems* herself only by taking considerable risks to save the boy. (par. 2)

   redeems _____

© 2014 Wadsworth, Cengage Learning

4. At the end of the movie, in cinemas in the *affluent* nations of the world, people who would have been quick to condemn Dora if she had not rescued the boy go home to places far more comfortable than her apartment. (par. 3)

   affluent _____

5. All of this raises a question: In the end, what is the *ethical* difference between a Brazilian who sells a homeless child to organ *vendors* and an American who already has a TV and upgrades to a better one? We know, after all, that the money we spend on a fancier TV could be donated to an organization that would use it to save the lives of kids in need. (par. 4)

   ethical _____

6. vendors _____

7. As a *utilitarian philosopher,* I judge whether acts are right or wrong by their consequences. (par. 5)

   utilitarian philosopher _____

   _____

8. There is a troubling problem if we can *condemn* Dora for taking the child to the organ vendors and not think about the American consumer's behavior as raising a serious moral issue. (par. 5)

   condemn _____

9. He believes it is wrong to live well without giving money to help people who are hungry, *malnourished,* or dying from easily treatable illnesses like diarrhea. (par. 6)

   malnourished _____

   _____

10. So a household making $100,000 could *cut* a yearly check for $70,000. (par. 8)

    cut _____

Read the following sentences from or about the reading, and write "F" before statements of fact and "O" before statements of opinion.

_____ 11. According to Singer, the average family in the United States spends almost one-third of its income on things that are no more necessary to them than Dora's new TV was to her.

_____ 12. Dora should have known that exchanging the boy for $1,000 was wrong.

_____ 13. No one should enjoy luxuries while children are starving.

_____ 14. In his book *Living High and Letting Die,* the New York University philosopher Peter Unger presented a series of examples designed to make us think about our choices. He believes it is wrong to live well without giving money to help people who are hungry, malnourished, or dying from easily treatable illnesses like diarrhea.

© 2014 Wadsworth, Cengage Learning

Choose the best answer for the following questions.

15. What influences Singer's point of view in this reading?
    a. Being an author of two important books
    b. Being a professor at Princeton University
    c. Being a philosopher who judges whether acts are right or wrong by their consequences

16. What is the author's purpose for including the story about Dora at the beginning of this reading?
    a. To show right from wrong in a general sense
    b. To entertain the reader by making an argument more convincing
    c. To present a situation in which it's easy to know right from wrong so the reader will be able to apply the same judgment to his or her own actions

Write short answers to the following questions based on your reading, your experience, and your observations.

17. What is "the Singer Solution to World Poverty"?

    _____

    _____

18. List the reasons that Singer gives for his conclusions.

    _____

    _____

    _____

    _____

19. Do you think the author's conclusions apply to you? Explain why or why not.

    _____

    _____

    _____

20. Do you think the reading "The Singer Solution to World Poverty" will change the way people act? Explain your answer.

    _____

    _____

    _____

© 2014 Wadsworth, Cengage Learning

Additional Readings and Exercises

The following thought-provoking readings amplify the book's themes and provide additional skills practice.

© 2014 Wadsworth, Cengage Learning

Reading 1   Some Day My Prince Will Come

— KELLY MAYHEW AND ELENA MARIE PEIFER

In the following reading, Kelly Mayhew and Elena Peifer take a look at fairy tales, why we enjoy them, and the lessons we learn from them. As you read, pay close attention to the main ideas they present and their supporting details. Also, consider whether you agree with their analysis.

1   Fairy tales have captivated people's imaginations for centuries. Stories of princes saving princesses, fairy godmothers, wolves, goblins, evil queens, stepmothers, and stepsisters have been written, told, and acted out in various versions in most parts of the world. In the United States in the 1930s, Walt Disney began to bring fairy tales alive in the form of animation, starting with *Snow White and the Seven Dwarfs* in 1935. The children of today still watch these films, along with other classics such as *Sleeping Beauty, Cinderella, The Little Mermaid*, and *Beauty and the Beast*, thanks to streaming videos and the DVD player. Although the films take place in different locations and the stories are different, they have many similarities. They are all about the plight of a young woman of noble birth who has problems, frequently caused by the presence of an evil character who wants to keep her from fulfilling her dreams. These problems are later swept away by her Prince Charming, who comes to save her in some way. Since this formula has been told and retold for centuries, fairy tales continue to attract our attention because they are predictable and comforting, and we tend to believe that if we live by the formula, our dreams will come true.

2   Let's take a look at the basic formula of romantic fairy tales. First, there is the romantic ideal they depict, which is that there is a Prince Charming who will sweep the princess off her feet. Cinderella dances all night with her prince, who can't keep his eyes or hands off her. Snow White's prince can't help but kiss her when he sees her lying in her glass coffin. And Sleeping Beauty's prince comes running to her rescue just at the mere mention of her name and her predicament. These are powerful ideas and dreams that meet a deep need in people to feel loved and needed. And when people—in particular women—grow up, they may hold onto this unfulfillable and unrealistic dream and believe that there is a real Prince Charming out there who will save them, marry them, and live happily ever after with them. We know from these tales how romances should end; unfortunately, though, fairy tales never continue on to show the complexities, both the joys and sorrows, of marriage.

3   Next is the concept of a "damsel in distress" whom Prince Charming must save. This is important because it represents the image of the weak woman, the one who can't care for herself and who needs a man to save her. In his eyes she is worth saving only because he has an idea of her beauty and of how she will follow and obey him, which is a powerful image, for men in particular. Sleeping Beauty, lying beautifully asleep for 100 years, is a good example of the "damsel in distress." The prince's kiss is *so* powerful that it actually reanimates her; it wakes her up and makes her able to move again. This type of story reinforces the idea that women are whole only through the help and support of a man, that somehow a woman is helpless, not capable, and even not alive unless she has a man at her side. This idea of the helpless woman is not good for women to believe in because it renders them helpless and unwilling to live their lives on their own terms.

fulfilling
accomplishing, reaching (a goal)

ideal
something that is perfect but is unlikely to really happen

Kelly Mayhew and Elena Marie Peifer, "Someday My Prince Will Come"

© 2014 Wadsworth, Cengage Learning

And for men it enforces the notion that a woman cannot survive without a man, which gives men a lot of power in their relationships.

4   The power of the man-hero is made very clear in fairy tales if we look at who the prince rescues the princess from. He has to save her from some truly evil characters. Often this character is connected in some way to one of the other main characters. For instance, in Cinderella, there are Cinderella's evil stepmother and stepsisters, and in Snow White, there is the queen, who is also Snow White's stepmother. The evil character is frequently a woman who is deeply jealous of the young, beautiful heroine and who will stop at nothing to see her brought down, or even killed. Symbolically, we have a war going on here between youth and age and between weakness and power. As Susan Douglas argues in her book *Where the Girls Are: Growing Up Female with the Mass Media,* powerlessness is rewarded in fairy tales, and activity is punished. What does this mean? It means that women—usually the wicked witches—who have power or who want it are evil, nasty creatures who must be stopped. These fairy tales tell us that power in women is wrong. This is why it is almost always a man—the prince, for example—who thwarts the wicked plans of the evil stepmother/queen by rescuing the princess and rewarding her powerlessness. Although the fairy godmothers have some power, in Disney movies they are usually portly and comical figures. The most important women with power are the evil women, who fail over and over again.

5   The versions of fairy tales that we have available to us send extremely strong messages. The repetition of the fairy-tale formula has a great deal to do with how girls and boys grow up viewing each other and imagining their eventual relationships. The damsel in distress, Prince Charming, and evil queen/stepmother characters tell us a lot about how we view women, men, and romance. People often like to dismiss (or not recognize) the importance of these stories and movies. Some say that they are just "entertainment," but any story that we hear over and over again influences us. Haven't most girls dreamed of finding their Prince Charming? Haven't most boys thought that they could come to the aid of a (helpless) girl?

Exercise 1

Work with Words

Use context clues, word-part clues, and, if necessary, the dictionary, to choose the best definitions of the italicized words.

1. They are all about the *plight* of a young woman of noble birth who has problems, frequently caused by the presence of an evil character who wants to keep her from fulfilling her dreams. (par. 1)

   plight
   a. character
   b. health
   c. difficult situation

2. First, there is the romantic ideal they *depict,* which is that there is a Prince Charming who will sweep the princess off her feet. (par. 2)

   depict
   a. show
   b. reinforce
   c. invent

© 2014 Wadsworth, Cengage Learning

3. And when people—in particular women—grow up, they may hold onto this *unfulfillable* and unrealistic dream and believe that there is a real Prince Charming out there who will save them, marry them, and live happily ever after with them. (par. 2)

unfulfillable
a. possible to carry out
b. impossible to carry out
c. difficult to carry out

4. The prince's kiss is so powerful that it actually *reanimates her;* it wakes her up and it makes her able to move again. (par. 3)

reanimates her
a. thrills her
b. brings her back to life
c. turns her into an animal

5. This idea of the helpless woman is not good for women to believe in because it *renders* them helpless and unwilling to live their lives on their own terms. (par. 3)

renders
a. tears apart
b. makes
c. calls

Exercise 2

Check Your Understanding

Choose the best answer for each of the following multiple-choice questions based on Reading 1.

1. Which sentence expresses the main idea of the following four sentences?
   a. Cinderella dances all night with her prince.
   b. Snow White's prince can't help but kiss her.
   c. Sleeping Beauty's prince comes running to her rescue.
   d. The romantic ideal in fairy tales claims that there is a Prince Charming.

2. Which sentence expresses the main idea of the following four sentences?
   a. "Damsel in distress" is the way we refer to these weak women.
   b. Sleeping Beauty, lying beautifully asleep for 100 years, is a good example of the "damsel in distress."
   c. Frequently fairy tales portray the image of the weak woman who can't care for herself and needs a man to save her.
   d. The prince's kiss is *so* powerful that it wakes her up and makes her able to move again.

3. What is the thesis of "Some Day My Prince Will Come"?
   a. People have always loved fairy tales.
   b. Fairy tales teach us to have dreams that are unrealistic and to think of women as weak.

© 2014 Wadsworth, Cengage Learning

c. People all over the world love to watch Disney animated fairy tales.

d. The bad woman in the fairy tales is usually a stepmother or witch.

4. Which of the following is *not* true about fairy tales?
   a. There is usually a "damsel in distress."
   b. There is usually a Prince Charming.
   c. All of the good characters are thin.
   d. The evil women lose in the end.

5. Which of the following is *not* a reason the authors give for why people love fairy tales?
   a. They captivate our imaginations and give us dreams.
   b. The originally unfortunate heroine wins in the end.
   c. We know the formula, and we are comfortable with it.
   d. We love to sit around and hear a good story at night.

6. What idea do we get about men from fairy tales?
   a. Men are expected to save women, who are weaker.
   b. Men will also get help when they need it.
   c. Men may have problems also.
   d. Men fall in love with women once they know them well.

7. What idea do we get about women from fairy tales?
   a. Women can lead independent lives.
   b. Women can go to sleep and wake up 100 years later.
   c. Women should be active in creating their own lives.
   d. Women are weak and need a man.

Exercise 3

Make Connections and Write

Write short answers to the following questions about fairy tales and dreams based on your reading, your experience, and your observations.

1. What are your two favorite fairy tales or favorite stories? Why do you like them?

   _____

   _____

   _____

   _____

   _____

   _____

© 2014 Wadsworth, Cengage Learning

2. We all have dreams about how our lives will be. Where do you think those dreams come from?

_____

_____

_____

_____

_____

_____

3. What dreams do you have about your future? What has influenced your dreams?

_____

_____

_____

_____

_____

_____

_____

Reading 2

Survival of the Fittest? The Survivor Story

— KELLY MAYHEW

Several million Americans tuned in to watch the TV show *Survivor* in the summer of 2000, and in 2001, it was followed by *Survivor: The Australian Outback*. Since then, dozens of "reality TV" programs have followed. What is it about these programs that gets people so involved? As you read the following essay, consider how people think about themselves. Do you agree with Mayhew's thesis?

1   CBS launched its first *Survivor* series several years ago in the summer of 2000. Billed as "reality TV," *Survivor* took audiences by storm, inspiring *Survivor* parties and endless

© 2014 Wadsworth, Cengage Learning

conversations. There were also spin-offs, attempting to achieve the same kind of popularity as *Survivor* had. Along with *Big Brother*, there have been and would be a bunch of other shows of this type coming our way, not to mention more *Survivor* episodes in different locales and with new groups of people. Why was this show so popular? What kept people glued to their television screens week after week, wondering, with a weird kind of pleasure, who would be kicked off next? The answer is that *Survivor* and the similar shows go to the very heart of the ways Americans view individuals and their role in communities and how we define winners and losers in our society. *Survivor* was unique because it chose to explore these issues in a seemingly "natural" setting, thus making its audience buy into the illusion, or dream, that the contestants were reduced to their most basic states. We were led to think that the "best" and strongest *individual* would win the million-dollar prize. That we would want to see such a picture says a lot about us as Americans.

2   *Survivor* began as a mid-summer fill-in by a network hungry for ratings in the rerun-dominated summer viewing period. The creators of the show put fourteen "castaways" onto a supposedly deserted island in the middle of Micronesia, deprived them of outside contact, gave them very little food, and made them form two teams to compete against each other. As the show progressed night after night (for a total of 39), people were judged incompetent by their team members in a phony "Tribal Council" and kicked off the island. The last one left—the "survivor"—won a million dollars. Many people saw the exotic location as a way to experience—if not directly, at least vicariously through the contestants' actions every night—what it would be like to live "savagely," close to nature and the elements, like our prehistoric forebears. The winner, we were led to believe, would really prove himself or herself to be the strongest, the smartest, and the most "outdoorsy." So, night after night, we watched as people tried to fish, dealt with the unpredictable weather by staying warm or cool, fought off biting insects, and so on—all demonstrating what humans have to deal with when they are stripped of social niceties and conveniences. "Ah ha," we were supposed to think, "so this is what 'survival of the fittest' looks like!"

3   Yet there was nothing natural about the show at all. From the ridiculous *Gilligan's Island*–inspired decor of the "Tribal Council" to the fake Polynesian team names (like "Pagong"), *Survivor* was mere illusion, a television simulation, or imitation, of the "natural world." B.B., Sue, Rudy, Jervase, Ramona, Kelly, Colleen, Rich, Sean, and the rest had their lives engineered for however long they lasted in the game. The show's creators designed all sorts of humiliating "challenges" to keep things spicy: the contestants had to spend hours standing on boards in the water; or they had to keep their hand on a giant "immunity idol" (a cross between a totem pole and a tiki torch); or they had to eat insects; or they had to remember personal details about each other; or they had to recite lists of all the things that were dangerous about "their" island. In truth, if the contestants really had had to "survive," most of them would have starved to death, drowned, or caught some bacterial infection—slow, but more importantly, boring deaths indeed. It's no fun to watch someone suffer over a long period of time. It's much more fun to watch them possibly embarrass themselves, then lose their chance to wear the "immunity idol" that would prevent them from being eliminated from the competition during the next "Tribal Council" meeting.

4   *Survivor* played on people's desire to believe that the most capable individual would win the game. We all like to believe that we are winners, that we can "do it alone," not

© 2014 Wadsworth, Cengage Learning

Kelly Mayhew, "Survival of the Fittest? The Survivor Story."
Copyright © 2003 Kelly Mayhew. Used with permission.

take anyone's help, and make it big. And to do all of this in nature, where one's true character and abilities could emerge, was a stroke of genius on the part of the creators of *Survivor*. Yet the creators didn't stop there. They kept reminding the audience that they were pulling all the strings—like "a law of nature" or "a law of God," which added an even more unpredictable element to the show. Supposedly anyone who could make it through the obstacle course of the unfriendly environment and the ridiculous games would be chosen the "fittest" contestant of them all. While it seemed like many of the contestants came on the show because they were adventure or nature enthusiasts who thought it would be fun and profitable to test their abilities in such a setting, the person who won the million-dollar prize, Rich, was not an outdoorsman at all. He was a gay, pudgy (before his post-show tummy-tuck) corporate trainer. The folks who thought their rock-climbing or tree-loving attributes would help them to win were eliminated left and right. The people who could psychologically manipulate others or stay aloof from their colleagues by not getting personally involved with anyone were the last ones on the show. "Natural" ability, therefore, had nothing to do with who was "fittest."

underhandedness 5
cheating

Underhandedness, scheming, emotional distance, and dishonesty, however, had a lot to do with who would win. All of these behaviors are learned behaviors, products of an individualistic society such as exists in the United States. In a *real* natural landscape, back-stabbing your fellow travelers would lead to failure and perhaps death. If there were no hosts running around in luxury yachts monitoring your every move, if there were no cameras, no microphones, and no 35-million-person audience tuning in to see what you do next—you would need the help of your human companions. If only one of you knew how to find water, or make a fire, or fish, then you would have to work cooperatively. To survive, you would need each other—as every subsistence-level human society has known. While individual skills might gain special respect in such a community, people would have to work together so that everyone could eat, have shelter, and be protected from the ravages of nature. Individual attributes alone would get you nowhere. In a *real* survival experience, the winner would be plural, not singular. It would be the community, not the individual.

6   Thus, we can learn a great deal from watching *Survivor*. The show lets us see how the concepts of winning and losing and individualism function in our society. The individual winner, the so-called "fittest" person, is the one who can see that it is all "just a game." It is an illustrative game, however, because it reminds us that our beliefs about each other, about what it takes to get ahead in this world, are just that—beliefs. What would have happened if the show had valued cooperation instead of competition? Would people still have tuned in every night to watch people get along with each other? If not, perhaps we need to change the rules of *our* games to make room for such a possibility.

| Exercise 1 |

Work with Words

Use context clues, word-part clues, and, if necessary, the dictionary to define the italicized words.

1. There were also *spin-offs*, attempting to achieve the same kind of popularity as *Survivor* had. Along with *Big Brother*, there have been and will be a bunch of other shows of this type coming our way. (par. 1)

   spin-offs _____

© 2014 Wadsworth, Cengage Learning

2. Many people saw the exotic location as a way to experience—if not directly, but at least *vicariously* through the contestants' actions every night—what it would be like to live "savagely," close to nature and the elements, like our prehistoric *forebears* . (par. 2)

   vicariously _____

3. *forebears* _____

4. The people who could psychologically manipulate others or stay *aloof* from their colleagues by not getting personally involved with anyone were the last ones on the show. (par. 4)

   aloof _____

5. While individual skills might gain special respect in such a community, people would have to work together so that everyone could eat, have shelter, and be protected from the ravages of nature. Individual *attributes* alone would get you nowhere. (par. 5)

   attributes _____

Exercise 2

Check Your Understanding

Choose the best way to complete the following statements about Reading 2.

1. According to the author, *Survivor* was appealing to audiences because
   a. it showed naked men and women.
   b. it explored issues related to individuals and communities.
   c. it explored issues related to nature.

2. *Survivor* was billed as
   a. "reality TV."
   b. a documentary.
   c. a major TV movie.

3. The contestants had to form teams and live
   a. on tough city streets.
   b. on a boat in the middle of the ocean.
   c. on a seemingly deserted island.

4. The prize that went to the winner of the show was
   a. a hundred dollars.
   b. a hundred thousand dollars.
   c. a million dollars.

5. The "Tribal Council" was where
   a. contestants judged each other to see who would be eliminated from the show.
   b. contestants handed out jobs for the day.
   c. contestants got together to talk about their problems with each other.

© 2014 Wadsworth, Cengage Learning

6. According to the author, being a nature enthusiast
   a. determined the winner of the show.
   b. had nothing to do with winning because scheming and underhandedness won the day.
   c. saved people's lives on the show because it was essential to understand nature to be successful on the island.

7. In the author's opinion, surviving in a harsh environment
   a. depends on cooperation and not individualism.
   b. depends on individualism and not cooperation.
   c. depends on neither individualism nor cooperation, but on realism.

8. The thesis of the reading was that
   a. we can learn a lot from *Survivor* because it shows us how to win a lot of money.
   b. we can learn a lot from *Survivor* because it shows us how our beliefs about individualism and community, and "winners" or "losers," can be damaging to our society.
   c. we can learn a lot from *Survivor* because it gives us a realistic picture of how to live in a natural environment, but is also relevant to our daily lives.

Exercise 3

Make Connections and Write

Write short answers to the following questions based on your reading, your experience, and your observations.

1. Do you watch reality TV programs? Which ones? Why do you watch them? Explain your answer.

   _____

   _____

   _____

   _____

2. What do you think is more important: acting as an individual or acting for the benefit of the community? Why?

   _____

   _____

   _____

   _____

© 2014 Wadsworth, Cengage Learning

Reading 3 | # Families and Diversity

— William E. Thompson and Joseph V. Hickey

TEXT BOOK | The following reading from the textbook *Society in Focus* considers diverse families in America today. It examines the challenges they face and the results of their efforts. As you read, notice how the different patterns of organization are used to present the authors' ideas.

MINORITY FAMILIES

abound
exist in large numbers

1   Minority families—some by choice and others in response to discrimination and out of economic necessity—contribute to family diversity . . . While myths abound that all minority families are extended families with strong social support networks, ethnicity, race, class, and gender contribute to considerable diversity among minority families.

2   Certainly, severe poverty influences minority families. For example, nearly one-third of all African-Americans and Latinos live in poverty, and female-headed families represent almost three-quarters of all poor African-American families. And more than 60 percent of African-American children, in female-headed families, are currently classified by the government as poor.

3   Sharp declines in inner-city employment and cuts in government assistance to struggling families have taken an especially heavy toll on African-American and Latino families and have contributed to declining marriage rates, rising divorce rates, and a much greater number of female-headed households. Some of these trends have reinforced long-term pragmatic attitudes about the family among some minority groups. For example, instead of the traditional middle-class emphasis on the nuclear family and husband-wife relationships, many African-American families cope with scarcity and discrimination by seeking the assistance of extended families and fictive kin (close friends), as well as through flexible social networks.

scarcity
not enough resources

kin
relatives

4   Increasingly, African-American and some Latino families place more emphasis on child-rearing than on marriage. As a consequence, more than 50 percent of all African-American women who head families have never married, and African-American mothers tend to be younger than their white counterparts.

5   At first glance, two-parent African-American families, whose median adjusted incomes have grown relative to those of white families from 44 percent in 1949 to over 70 percent by the early 1990s, may appear to be like white middle-class families. But these families, accounting for almost half of all African-American families, provide much more progressive and flexible models of family life than the white majority. Of all families, they are the most egalitarian, with complementary and flexible family roles that allow for much greater participation of husbands in domestic and child care responsibilities than is characteristic of most white families.

6   Many African-American families also have stronger kin support systems—with many three-generation extended family households. Likewise, grandparents also may play greater roles in child care than they do in most white middle-class families. Because of economic marginalization and discrimination as well as cultural traditions, many Latino

Thompson, William E.; Hickey, Joseph V., *Society in Focus: An Introduction to Sociology,* 3e, ©1999. Printed and Electronically reproduced by permission of Pearson Education, Inc., Upper Saddle River, New Jersey.

© 2014 Wadsworth, Cengage Learning

anchored
attached,
connected

and Asian-American groups also emphasize extended families. During the past few decades, many groups from around the world have used extended family networks and "circular migrations" to relocate from developing to developed countries, as well as to shift from rural to urban areas. But many remain anchored to kin in their home countries.

7   The strong emphasis on family is called *familism*, or a strong attachment and commitment to family and kin, which characterizes the attitudes of many Latino groups toward family life. This is especially true of recent immigrants from Central and South America who make great efforts to keep in touch with kin, including sending much of their pay to support relatives in their home communities.

8   Despite powerful stereotypes of close-knit, "multigenerational" Asian-American families, there is considerable variation among Asian-American groups. Many recent immigrants from war-torn Southeast Asia do indeed stress extended family networks, and some groups are strongly patriarchal. Many other Asian-American families who have been in the United States for generations, however, live in nuclear families and maintain kin ties that differ little from those of white middle-class Americans. On the surface, this is also true of many wealthy transplants and professionals from Hong Kong, Singapore, and other parts of Asia. Most of these families, however, maintain strong ties to widely dispersed kin throughout the Pacific, which may include regular family visitations and gifts, loans, and joint business ventures with relatives that most middle-class Americans would consider to be "distant kin."

dispersed
spread out over a
wide area

GAY AND LESBIAN FAMILIES

9   One family type that has received little recognition until recently is the gay and lesbian family. By the mid-1990s, more than 1.5 million homosexual and lesbian couples lived together in stable and committed relationships, which a growing number of people recognize as "families." Philip Blumstein and Pepper Schwartz's (1983) research on American couples found that same-sex couples faced domestic concerns quite similar to those of their heterosexual counterparts—and they solved them in much the same ways.

Exercise 1

Work with Words

Use context clues, word-part clues, and, if necessary, the dictionary to choose the best definitions of the italicized words.

1. Some of these trends have reinforced long-term *pragmatic* attitudes about the family among some minority groups. (par. 3)

   pragmatic
   a. disinterested
   b. idealistic
   c. practical

2. For example, instead of the traditional middle-class emphasis on the *nuclear family* and husband-wife relationships, many African-American families cope with scarcity and discrimination by seeking the assistance of extended families and *fictive kin* (close friends), as well as through flexible social networks. (par. 3).

   nuclear family
   a. husband, wife, and children only
   b. husband, wife, and grandparents only
   c. husband and wife only

© 2014 Wadsworth, Cengage Learning

3. *fictive kin*
   a. made-up family members
   b. close friends
   c. African-American families

4. Many recent immigrants from war-torn Southeast Asia do indeed stress extended family networks, and some groups are strongly *patriarchal*. (par. 8)

   patriarchal
   a. dedicated to their country
   b. dominated by the father
   c. interested in networks

Exercise 2

Check Your Understanding

Answer the following questions about Reading 3.

1. In your own words, write the central idea of this reading.

   _____

   _____

   _____

2. What are three challenges that diverse families encounter?

   a. _____

   b. _____

   c. _____

3. What are two ways diverse families respond to the challenges they face?

   a. _____

   b. _____

Choose the best way to complete the following statements about Reading 3.

4. Paragraph 2 is organized primarily by
   a. definition.
   b. examples.
   c. cause and effect.

5. Paragraph 4 is organized primarily by
   a. cause and effect.
   b. comparison.
   c. definition.

© 2014 Wadsworth, Cengage Learning

6. Paragraph 5 is organized primarily by
   a. cause and effect.
   b. comparison and contrast.
   c. examples.

7. Paragraph 7 is organized primarily by
   a. cause and effect.
   b. definition.
   c. comparison and contrast.

8. Paragraph 8 is organized primarily by
   a. definition.
   b. cause and effect.
   c. comparison and contrast.

Exercise 3

Make Connections and Write

1. Would you describe your family as having *familism* as defined in this reading? Explain your answer.

_____

_____

_____

2. What strengths in your family have helped it to meet challenges?

_____

_____

_____

3. Are gay and lesbian families accepted in your community? Do you think that they will be soon, if they aren't already? Explain your answer.

_____

_____

_____

© 2014 Wadsworth, Cengage Learning

Reading 4

Disaster: Are You Ready?

—Vicki Chang

The following reading was written especially for *Joining a Community of Readers*. In it, the author discusses a series of natural disasters that took place in 2004 and 2005. She then proposes steps that you can take in your community to be prepared should a disaster strike where you live. As you read, consider what kind of natural disaster your area is vulnerable to, and what you and your neighbors could do to help one another in the event of a crisis.

submerging
forcing under water

1   Have you ever watched disaster coverage on the television news? If you have, you are familiar with the images that disasters bring. When the tsunami caused by an Indonesian earthquake hit parts of Asia in December 2004, we saw, repeatedly, scenes of a seemingly endless wave that just kept moving, drowning everyone in its path and submerging everything that got in its way—first beach chairs, then beachfront hotels, then houses farther inland. When Hurricane Katrina hit the Gulf Coast and New Orleans in August 2005, we saw aerial shots of New Orleans showing most of the city covered with water. There were repeated scenes of residents who didn't evacuate soon enough and were stranded on attics and rooftops and people fleeing to escape the water that was rushing into their homes. We also saw people who had taken refuge in the Convention Center, where there was not enough food or drink. When a devastating earthquake hit Pakistan later the same year, television viewers seemed to have become hardened to human tragedy, but once again we saw images of disaster. This time we saw buildings—schools especially—crumbling and killing thousands of people instantly.

2   All of these disasters happened in the span of one year, and the aftermath of each had something in common with the others: Rescue teams and supplies did not arrive fast enough. Television announcers told us over and over about the obstacles that slowed rescue and aid efforts. Local, national, and international governments were not prepared for the magnitude of these disasters. In some cases, the roads or airports were flooded; in other cases, the roads had collapsed or were nonexistent or insufficient. Recovering the bodies of those who had died was difficult and sometimes impossible. There were not enough medical personnel or supplies to help the injured. People didn't have enough food. People didn't have enough water. People didn't have shelter. We learned by watching the news that victims of disasters cannot expect help from outside sources for 72 hours or more.

3   These images of disaster should make you think about your own safety. Emergencies, after all, can happen anywhere. First responders—firefighters, police officers, and paramedics—might not be able to handle all of the calls for assistance during a large emergency or disaster.

4   To prepare for such an eventuality—a flood, an earthquake, a hurricane, a tornado, a fire—you can take two crucial steps: First, you can make an individual and family plan. To begin to do that, you can get a copy or read the online version of the booklet *Are You Ready?* published by FEMA (Federal Emergency Management Agency). [1]

Vicki Chang, "Are You Ready?" Copyright © 2006. Used with permission.

© 2014 Wadsworth, Cengage Learning

This publication will help you consider the possible risks to your community, the gathering and storage of emergency supplies, and an emergency plan.

COMMUNITY PLANNING

5   The next component of being prepared for an emergency is to organize your community or neighborhood group. Experience has shown that individuals and neighborhood groups might be on their own for 24 to 72 hours after the emergency; and in areas that are isolated people may be without services for even longer than that.

6   The saying, "there is strength in numbers," definitely applies when a neighborhood experiences major upheaval and devastation from a disaster. One person working alone will not be able to handle all of the problems that can arise. The feeling of self-reliance and knowledge that comes with disaster preparedness training can make a significant difference in how we respond and work more easily together to:

- find shelter, food, and water
- free people who are trapped
- protect each other's property
- offer first aid

7   By organizing your neighborhood for a disaster response, you will be able to identify human and material resources that can be shared. Which neighbors have construction skills and equipment? Who has first aid training and supplies? It is important to know *before* you need them. One lasting, very positive benefit of establishing a neighborhood disaster preparedness group is cohesiveness—your neighborhood can become a better place in which to live.[2]

FIRST STEPS TOWARD ORGANIZING

8   There are many examples of communities getting organized around the country. You can look on the Internet to find examples of how to go about it, but generally, these guidelines can get you started.

   a. Organize an initial meeting with 10 or 12 neighbors. Get to know one another, and put together important information about each household: Does a handicapped person live there who will need help in an emergency? Are there pets? How can neighbors contact one another if someone needs help?
   b. Compile a list of who in the group has skills: Who can help others turn off the gas and electricity? Who has first aid skills? Learning these skills yourself is also a good idea.
   c. Compile a list of where you can find emergency tools, equipment, and supplies.
   d. Make an out-of-state emergency contact list that includes friends or relatives who live at least 200 miles away through whom members of the family can contact one another. Local phones may not be working, or the circuits may be overloaded.

9   You can be the person to pull your community together. Talk to a neighbor to see if you can find someone who will work with you. Contact your local fire, police, or public health department to get further assistance with your plans. Search the Internet or go to the library for more information on how to be prepared. But, above all, do something, even if it's a small first step like having a neighborhood potluck dinner to get to know one another.

© 2014 Wadsworth, Cengage Learning

Notes

1. Federal Emergency Management Agency, *Are You Ready?* available at http://www. fema.gov/areyouready/ (accessed July 9, 2006).

2. *Neighborhood Preparedness and Response Manual: City of Oakland Core Program* (Oakland, Calif.: Citizens of Oakland Respond to Emergencies, 2000).

Exercise 1

Work with Words

Use context clues, word-part clues, and, if necessary, the dictionary to write the definitions of the italicized words.

1. When the *tsunami* caused by an Indonesian earthquake hit parts of Asia in December 2004, we saw, repeatedly, scenes of a seemingly endless wave that just kept moving, drowning everyone in its path and submerging everything that got in its way—first beach chairs, then beachfront hotels, then houses farther inland. (par. 1)

   tsunami _____

2. When Hurricane Katrina hit the Gulf Coast and New Orleans in August 2005, we saw *aerial* shots of New Orleans showing most of the city covered with water. (par. 1)

   aerial _____

3. All of these disasters happened in the *span* of one year, and the *aftermath* of each had something in common with the others: Rescue teams and supplies did not arrive fast enough. (par. 2)

   span _____

4. *aftermath* _____

5. Local, national, and international governments were not prepared for the *magnitude* of these disasters. (par. 2)

   magnitude _____

6. *First responders*—firefighters, police officers, and paramedics—might not be able to handle all of the calls for assistance during a large emergency or disaster. (par. 3)

   first responders _____

   _____

7. The next *component* of being prepared for an emergency is to organize your community or neighborhood group. (par. 5)

   component _____

© 2014 Wadsworth, Cengage Learning

Exercise 2

Check Your Understanding

Read the following sentences from or based on Reading 4, and write "F" before statements of fact and "O" before statements of opinion.

_____   1. A massive tsunami hit Asia in December 2004.

_____   2. There should have been a warning system in place to alert the residents to evacuate before the tsunami hit.

_____   3. Thousands of residents were stranded in New Orleans after Hurricane Katrina hit.

_____   4. Government at all levels didn't do as much as it could to help the Hurricane Katrina victims.

_____   5. It can take 72 hours or more for first responders to help victims of a natural disaster.

Exercise 3

Make Connections and Write

Write short answers to the following questions based on your reading, your experience, and your observations.

1. What conclusions can you draw for your own safety from recent experiences of natural disasters?

_____

_____

_____

_____

2. The author of Reading 4 states that when you organize a disaster preparedness group "your neighborhood can become a better place in which to live." What do you think she means by this statement? Explain your answer.

_____

_____

_____

_____

© 2014 Wadsworth, Cengage Learning

3. How many of your neighbors do you know? (1) Explain your relationships with your neighbors. (2) What can you do to help your neighbors form a disaster preparedness group?

_____

_____

_____

_____

_____

_____

© 2014 Wadsworth, Cengage Learning

Cumulative
Mastery Tests

 CUMULATIVE MASTERY TEST A

Loneliness

adapted from Wayne Weiten and Margaret Lloyd

 CUMULATIVE MASTERY TEST B

One Country, Two Worlds

adapted from Margaret L. Andersen and Howard F. Taylor

© 2014 Wadsworth, Cengage Learning

Name _____   Date _____

Loneliness

— [ADAPTED FROM] WAYNE WEITEN AND MARGARET LLOYD

TEXT BOOK **The following reading from a college psychology textbook discusses loneliness in our society today. It also suggests reasons that loneliness seems to be increasing. As you read, consider whether the descriptions of those who are affected by loneliness corresponds to your observations or experience. Also, consider whether the author's suggestions for solving the problem are realistic and helpful.**

---

anecdotal
based on stories, not formal studies

1   How many people are tormented by loneliness? Although we don't have a precise answer to this question, anecdotal evidence suggests that the number of people troubled by loneliness is substantial. Telephone hotlines for troubled people report that complaints of loneliness are the majority of their calls. No doubt some of the popularity of instant messaging and chat rooms can be traced to loneliness.

2   The information available on loneliness in specific age groups <u>contradicts</u> stereotypes. For example, although many assume that the loneliest age group is the elderly, this "distinction" actually belongs to adolescents and young adults. Gay and lesbian adolescents are particularly likely to be lonely. Another <u>vulnerable</u> group is beginning college students when they first leave home to live on campus. It is likely that frequent changes of schools, jobs, and relationships during adolescence and young adulthood all contribute to the high rates of loneliness for this age group. A second unexpected finding is that loneliness decreases with age, at least until the much later years of adulthood when one's friends begin to die.

THE ROOTS OF LONELINESS

3   Because any event that disturbs the patterns of a person's life may lead to loneliness, no one is <u>immune</u>. We'll consider the role of early experiences and social trends.

EARLY EXPERIENCES

chronic
reoccurring, continual

4   The seeds for chronic loneliness are likely sown early in life. A key problem seems to be early negative social behavior that leads to rejection by peers and teachers. Children who are aggressive or withdrawn are likely to suffer peer rejection even in preschool.

SOCIAL TRENDS

5   Some social commentators and psychologists are concerned about recent trends that seem to be <u>undermining</u> social connections in our culture. Single working mothers and fathers may be so pressed for time that they have little time to keep up with adult relationships. Because of busy schedules, face-to-face interactions at home are reduced as family members eat on the run, on their own, or in front of the TV. The fact that people watch television so much tends to <u>diminish</u> meaningful family conversation. While technology makes life easier in some respects and does provide opportunities for meaningful relationships, it has its downside. For example, superficial social

From Weiten. *Psychology, 7e.* © 2008 Wadsworth, a part of Cengage Learning, Inc. Reproduced by permission. www.cengage.com/permissions.

© 2014 Wadsworth, Cengage Learning

interactions become more common as people order their meals at drive-up windows, do their banking at drive-through facilities, and so forth. Finally, people are spending more time alone at computers in their offices and homes, reducing opportunities for face-to-face interactions.

CONQUERING LONELINESS

6   The personal consequences associated with habitual loneliness can be painful and sometimes overwhelming: low self-esteem, hostility, depression, alcoholism, <u>psychosomatic</u> illness, and, possibly, suicide. Although there are no simple solutions to loneliness, there are some effective ones.

boon
blessing, advantage

7   One option is to use the Internet to overcome loneliness, although this approach can be a two-edged sword. On the plus side, the Internet is an obvious boon to busy people and those with physical disabilities. Moreover, shy people can interact without the anxiety involved in face-to-face communication. But if lonely people spend a lot of time online, do they have less time to devote to face-to-face relationships? Do shy individuals develop the self-confidence to pursue relationships offline? Research will provide the answers to these important questions.

8   A second suggestion is to avoid the temptation to withdraw from social situations. A study that asked people what they did when they felt lonely found the top responses to be "read" and "listen to music." If used occasionally, reading and listening to music can be constructive ways of dealing with loneliness. However, as long-term strategies, they do nothing to help a lonely person acquire "real-world" friends. The importance of staying active socially cannot be overemphasized. Recall that <u>proximity</u> is a powerful factor in the development of close relationships. To make friends, you have to be around people.

thwart
prevent

cultivate
develop

nonverbal
not using words

9   Finally, to thwart loneliness, you need to cultivate your social skills. Lonely people, especially, should focus on reading others' nonverbal signals, deepening the level of their self-disclosure, engaging in active listening, improving their conversational skills, and developing an assertive communication style.

Use context clues, word-part clues, and, if necessary, the dictionary to choose the best definition for the meaning of each of the italicized words in the following sentences from the reading.

1. The information available on loneliness in specific age groups *contradicts* stereotypes. For example, although many assume that the loneliest age group is the elderly, this "distinction" actually belongs to adolescents and young adults. (par. 2)

   contradicts
   a. supports
   b. proves
   c. goes against

2. Gay and lesbian adolescents are particularly likely to be lonely. Another *vulnerable* group is beginning college students. (par. 2)

   vulnerable
   a. likely to be hurt
   b. evidently strong
   c. resistant

© 2014 Wadsworth, Cengage Learning

3. Because any event that disturbs the patterns of a person's life may lead to loneliness, no one is *immune*. (par. 3)

   immune
   a. eventually at risk
   b. completely protected
   c. overly exposed

4. Some social commentators and psychologists are concerned about recent trends that seem to be *undermining* social connections in our culture. Single working mothers and fathers may be so pressed for time that they have little time to keep up with adult relationships. (par. 5)

   undermining
   a. strengthening
   b. reinforcing
   c. weakening

5. The fact that people watch television so much tends to *diminish* meaningful family conversation. (par. 5)

   diminish
   a. reduce
   b. drown out
   c. eliminate

6. The personal consequences associated with habitual loneliness can be painful and sometimes overwhelming: low self-esteem, hostility, depression, alcoholism, *psychosomatic* illness, and, possibly, suicide. (par. 6)

   psychosomatic
   a. physiological and sociological
   b. psychological and scientific
   c. involving both mind and body

7. Recall *that proximity* is a powerful factor in the development of close relationships. To make friends, you have to be around people. (par. 8)

   Proximity
   a. nearness
   b. approximation
   c. intimacy

Choose the best answer to the following questions from or about the reading.

8. What is the best topic for paragraph 2?
   a. loneliness and whom it affects
   b. age groups and lifestyles
   c. gays and loneliness

9. What is the best statement of the main idea for paragraph 2?
   a. Elderly people are most likely to be lonely.
   b. The rate of loneliness by age group does not follow stereotypes.
   c. Gay and lesbian adolescents are particularly likely to be lonely.

© 2014 Wadsworth, Cengage Learning

10. Which of the following is a reasonable inference about paragraph 2?
    a. Gay and lesbian adolescents don't need friends.
    b. Loneliness decreases with age because old people don't need to have so many friends.
    c. Adolescents are among the loneliest groups because they are going through changes in their life and trying to figure out where they fit in.

11. What is the best statement of the main idea for paragraph 5?
    a. Because of busy schedules, face-to-face interactions at home are reduced as family members eat on the run, on their own, or in front of the TV.
    b. Recent trends seem to be undermining our social connections.
    c. People are spending more time alone at computers in their offices and homes, reducing opportunities for face-to-face interactions.

12. What is the dominant pattern of organization of paragraph 5?
    a. examples
    b. chronological order
    c. definition

13. Which of the following are supporting details for the idea that recent trends seem to be undermining meaningful social connections? (Circle all that apply.)
    a. watching television
    b. face-to-face interactions
    c. buying meals at drive-up windows

14. Which of the following is the best statement of the author's purpose for writing?
    a. to entertain the reader by giving examples of people who are lonely
    b. to inform the reader about how common loneliness is and suggest some possible ways of dealing with it
    c. to encourage the reader to study the problem of loneliness further

Read the following sentences from or about the reading, and write "F" before statements of fact and "O" before statements of opinion.

_____ 15. The best way to overcome loneliness is to make friends on the Internet.

_____ 16. Watching television is not good for lonely people.

_____ 17. Because of busy schedules, face-to-face interactions at home are reduced as family members eat on the run, on their own, or in front of the TV.

_____ 18. The author suggests various ways to avoid being lonely.

© 2014 Wadsworth, Cengage Learning

Write short answers to the following questions based on your reading, your experience, and your observations.

19. Have you or someone you know ever felt lonely? What were the circumstances that contributed to the loneliness? Explain.

_____

_____

_____

_____

_____

20. What conclusions does the author draw for some ways to solve the problem of loneliness? List them. Now, explain whether these suggestions would help you or someone you know who is lonely by considering the advantages and disadvantages of each solution.

_____

_____

_____

_____

_____

© 2014 Wadsworth, Cengage Learning

Name _____ Date _____

One Country, Two Worlds

— [ADAPTED FROM] MARGARET L. ANDERSEN AND HOWARD F. TAYLOR

TEXT BOOK The following reading, from a college sociology textbook provides statistics to demonstrate the inequality of wealth distribution in the United States. As you read, think about how the authors make the reader understand how living in poverty or wealth affects people's everyday lives and their futures.

1   One afternoon in a major U.S. city, two women go shopping. They are friends—wealthy, suburban women who shop for leisure. They meet in a gourmet restaurant and eat imported foods while discussing their children's private schools. They also talk about the volunteer work they do in the local hospital, but they don't worry too much about their own health care, at least not financially, because both are fully covered through <u>ample</u> health insurance policies. After lunch, they spend the afternoon in exquisite stores— some of them large, elegant department stores; others, intimate boutiques where the staff knows them by name. When one of the women stops to use the bathroom in one store, she enters a beautifully furnished room with an upholstered chair, a marble sink with brass faucets, fresh flowers on a wooden pedestal, shining mirrors, plenty of hand towels, and jars of lotion and soaps. The toilet is in a private stall with solid doors. In the stall there is soft toilet paper and another small vase of flowers.

marginal
barely enough

2   The same day, in a different part of town, another woman goes shopping. She lives on a marginal income she earns as a stitcher in a clothing factory. Her daughter has outgrown last year's pair of shoes and badly needs a new pair. The woman goes to a nearby discount store where she hopes to find a pair of shoes for under $15, but she dreads the experience. She knows her daughter would like other new things—a bathing suit for the summer, a pair of jeans, and a blouse. But this summer her daughter will have to wear hand-me-downs because medical bills over the winter have <u>depleted</u> the little money the family has left after paying for food and rent. For the mother, shopping is not recreation. Instead, it is a bitter chore that reminds her of the things she is unable to get for her daughter.

3   While this woman is shopping, she, too, stops to use the bathroom. She enters a vast space with sinks and mirrors lined up on one side of the room and several stalls on the other. The tile floor is gritty and gray. The locks on the stall doors are missing or broken. Some of the overhead lights are burned out, so the room has dark shadows. In the stall, the toilet paper is coarse. When the woman washes her hands, she discovers there is no soap in the metal dispensers. The mirror before her is cracked. She exits quickly, feeling as though she is being watched.

class
position in society based on economic status

distinction
related to belonging to a certain group

4   Two scenarios, one society. The difference is the mark of a society built upon class inequality. The signs are all around you. Think about the clothing you wear. Are some labels worth more than others? Do others in your group [among your friends] see the same <u>marks</u> of distinction and status in clothing labels? Do some people you know never seem to wear the "right" labels? Whether it is clothing, bathrooms, schools, homes, or access to health care, the effect of class inequality is enormous, giving privileges and resources to some and leaving others struggling to get by.

From Andersen/Taylor, *Sociology*, 5e. © 2009 Cengage Learning.

© 2014 Wadsworth, Cengage Learning

5   Great inequality divides society. Nevertheless, most people think that in the United States equal opportunity exists for all. There is a tendency among some people to blame individuals for their own "failure," or to think their success is due to individual achievement. Many people think the poor are lazy and do not value work. At the same time, the rich are often admired for their supposed initiative, drive, and motivation. Neither is an accurate portrayal. There are many hard-working individuals who are poor, and most rich people have inherited their wealth rather than earned it themselves.

initiative
ability to take charge

6   Understanding inequality requires knowing some basic economic and sociological terms. Inequality is often presented as a matter of differences in income, which is one important measure of class standing. But, in addition to income inequality, there are vast inequalities in who owns what—that is, the wealth of different groups.

7   *Income* is the amount of money brought into a household from various sources (wages, investment income, dividends, and so on) during a given period. In recent years, income growth has been greatest for the richest segment of the population; for everyone else, income (controlling for the value of the dollar) has either been relatively flat or has grown at a far slower rate.[1] This has contributed to growing inequality in the United States. But inequality becomes even more apparent when you consider both wealth and income.

flat
unchanged

8   *Wealth* is the monetary value of everything a person actually owns. It is calculated by adding all financial <u>assets</u> (stocks, bonds, property, insurance, savings, investments, and so on) and subtracting debts. This gives a dollar amount that is one's <u>net worth</u>. Unlike income, wealth is <u>cumulative</u>—that is, its value tends to increase through investment. It can be passed on to the next generation, giving those who inherit wealth a considerable advantage in accumulating more resources.

9   To understand the significance of wealth compared to income in determining class status, imagine two college graduates graduating in the same year, from the same college, with the same major and the same grade point average. Imagine further that upon graduation both students get jobs with the same salary in the same organization. One of the student's parents paid all the student's college expenses and gave her a car upon graduation. The other student worked while in school and graduated with substantial debt from student loans. This student's family has no money with which to help support her. Who is better off? Same salary, same <u>credentials</u>, but wealth (even if modest) matters. It gives one person an advantage that will be played out many times over as the young worker buys a home, finances her own children's education, and possibly inherits additional assets.

modest
relatively small

10   Where is all the wealth in the United States? The wealthiest 1 percent own 34 percent of all net worth; the bottom 90 percent control only 29 percent. . . . Moreover, there has been an increase in the concentration of wealth since the 1980s, making the United States one of the most "unequal nations in the world."[2]

11   In contrast to the vast amount of wealth and income controlled by the richest people in the country, a very large proportion of Americans have hardly any financial assets once debt is subtracted. . . . The American Dream of owning a home, a new car, taking annual vacations, and sending one's children to good schools—not to mention saving for a comfortable retirement—is increasingly out of reach for many. When you see the amount of income and wealth controlled by a small segment of the population, a <u>sobering</u> picture of class inequality becomes clear.

1. U.S. Census Bureau. 2010. *Historical Income Tables Households, Table H-3*. www .census.gov

2. Mishel, Lawrence, Jared Bernsteing, and Heidi Shierholz. 2008. *State of Working America 2008/2009*. Washington, DC: Economic Policy Institute.

© 2014 Wadsworth, Cengage Learning

Use context clues, word-part clues, and, if necessary, the dictionary to choose the best definition for the meaning of each of the italicized words in the following sentences from the reading.

1. They also talk about the volunteer work they do in the local hospital, but they don't worry too much about their own health care, at least not financially, because both are fully covered through *ample* health insurance policies. (par. 1)

   ample
   a. fat
   b. inefficient
   c. generous

2. But this summer the daughter will have to wear hand-me-downs because medical bills over the winter have *depleted* the little money left after food and rent. (par. 2)

   depleted
   a. used up
   b. saved
   c. wasted

3. The difference is the mark of a society built upon class inequality. The signs are all around you. Think about the clothing you wear. Are some labels worth more than others? Do others in your group see the same *marks* of distinction and status in clothing labels? (par. 4)

   marks
   a. scars
   b. signs
   c. labels

4. Same salary, same *credentials*, but wealth (even if modest) matters. (par. 9)

   credentials
   a. college degrees
   b. appearances
   c. class backgrounds

5. When you see the amount of income and wealth controlled by a small segment of the population, a *sobering* picture of class inequality becomes clear. (par. 11)

   sobering
   a. not drunk
   b. broad
   c. serious

© 2014 Wadsworth, Cengage Learning

Use the context clues to write the definitions of the italicized words in the following sentences.

6. *Wealth* is the monetary value of everything one actually owns. It is calculated by adding all financial *assets* (stocks, bonds, property, insurance, savings, investments, and so on) and subtracting debts which gives a dollar amount that is one's *net worth*. (par. 8)

   assets _____

7. *net worth* _____

8. Wealth allows you to acquire more assets over generations, giving advantages to future generations that they might not have had on their own. Unlike income, wealth is *cumulative*—that is, its value tends to increase through investment; it can be passed on to the next generation, giving those who inherit wealth a considerable advantage in accumulating more resources. (par. 8)

   Cumulative _____

Choose the best answer to the following questions from or about the reading.

9. Which of the following best describes the combined patterns of organization of paragraphs 1-3?
   a. Examples and definition
   b. Examples and comparison/contrast
   c. Comparison contrast and chronological order

10. Which of the following is a reasonable inference from paragraph 1?
    a. The volunteer work the women do in the local hospital exposes them to people who don't have health insurance.
    b. They are probably overweight since they eat in such fancy restaurants.
    c. They don't really care that much about poor people in the hospitals because they are so well off.

11. Which of the following is a reasonable inference from paragraphs 2 and 3?
    a. Because she is poor, she thinks the security people are watching her because they suspect she might steal something.
    b. She has a lot of problems, but they are not going to get her down.
    c. The bathroom that is in bad condition will probably get fixed soon.

12. What is the best main idea statement of paragraph 5?
    a. In the United States equal opportunity exists for all; people just need to work hard to get ahead.
    b. Even though most people think that if you work hard you can be successful in this society, most rich people have inherited their money, and many very hard-working people remain poor.
    c. Poor people stay poor because they are lazy and do not value work.

© 2014 Wadsworth, Cengage Learning

13. What are the basic patterns of organization of paragraphs 6-8?
    a. process and comparison contrast
    b. definition and cause and effect
    c. chronological order and definition

14. What is the main idea of paragraph 8?
    a. It is much easier for the children and grandchildren of the wealthy to become even more rich.
    b. Wealth is the value in dollars of everything someone owns.
    c. Those who are extremely wealthy need to pay more money in taxes.

Read the following sentences from or about the reading, and write "F" before statements of fact and "O" before statements of opinion in or related to the reading.

_____ 15. The wealthiest 1 percent own 34 percent of all net worth.

_____ 16. It's not fair that two college graduates with the exact same credentials don't have the same chances in life.

_____ 17. Poor people don't even have a chance to get ahead.

_____ 18. A very large proportion of Americans have hardly any financial assets once debt is subtracted.

Write short answers to the following questions based on your reading, your experience, and your observations.

19. Why do you think the author included paragraph 9? How does the information in paragraph 9 relate to your life?

_____

_____

_____

_____

_____

20. Do you agree that the unequal distribution of wealth in the United States is unfair? Why or why not?

_____

_____

_____

_____

_____

© 2014 Wadsworth, Cengage Learning

Index

© 2014 Wadsworth, Cengage Learning

© 2014 Wadsworth, Cengage Learning

© 2014 Wadsworth, Cengage Learning